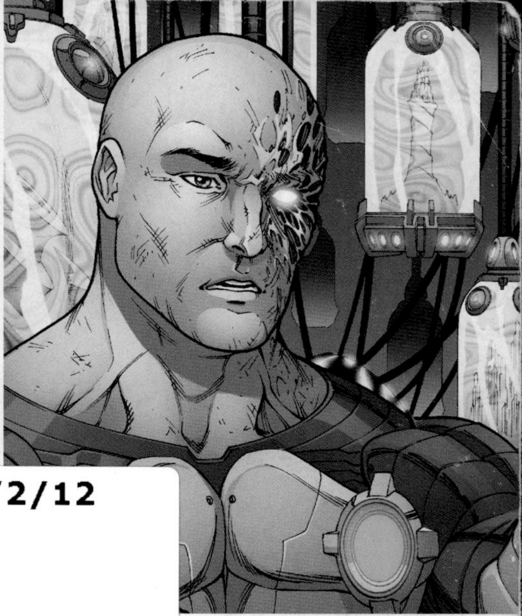

DC Universe Online Legends

VOLUME TWO

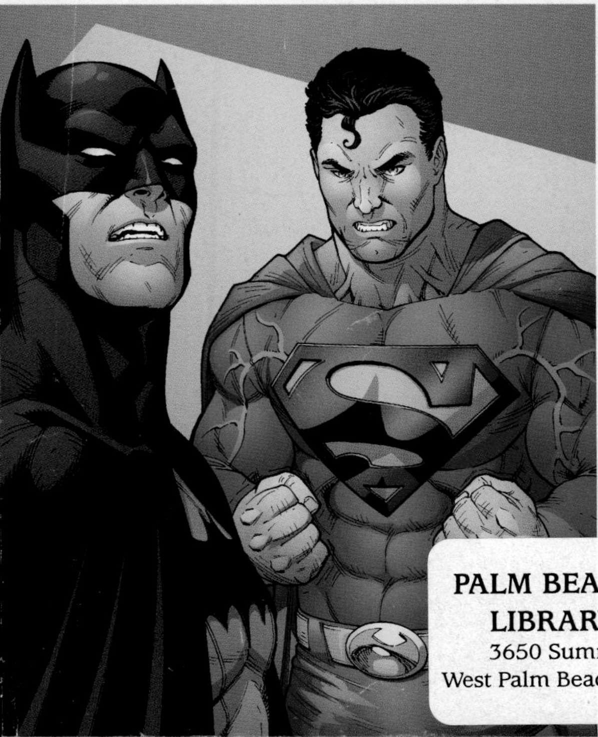

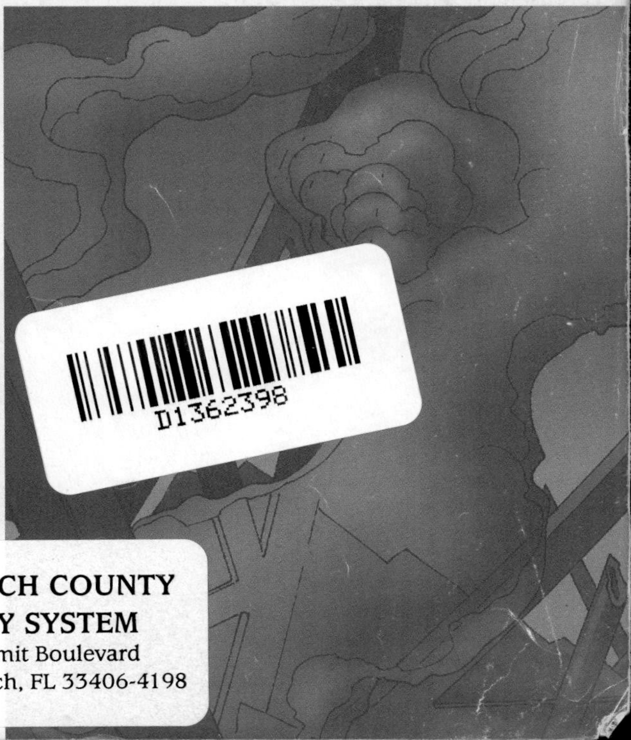

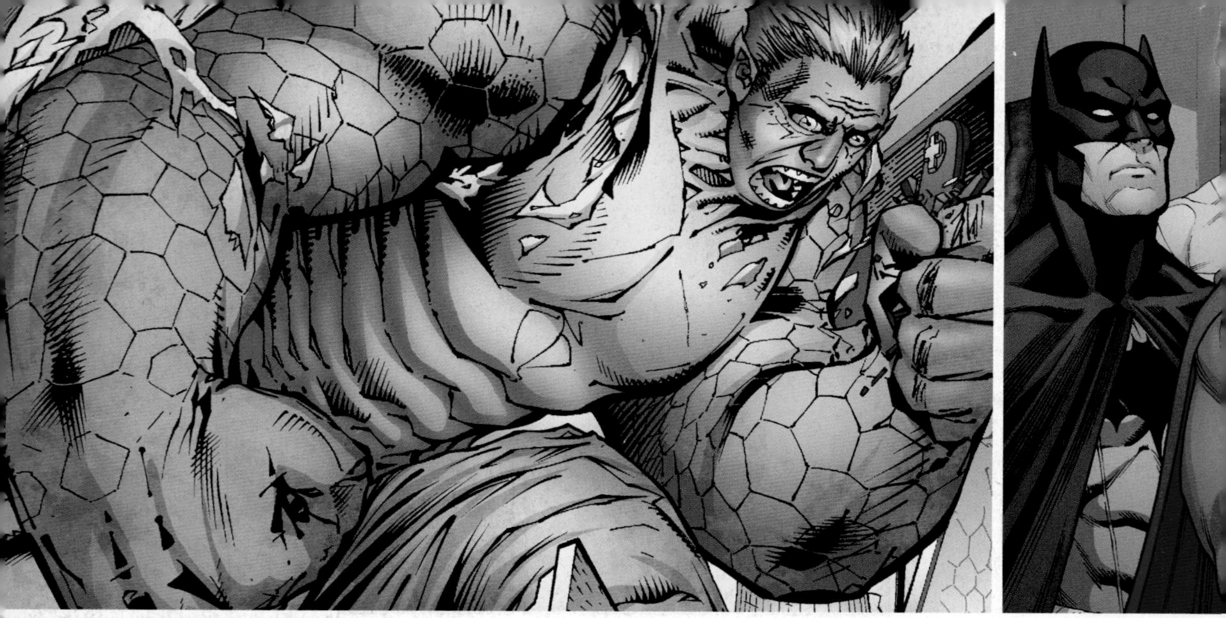

Marv Wolfman
Tony Bedard
Writers

Mike S. Miller
Howard Porter
John Livesay
Sergio Sandoval
Artists

Carrie Strachan
Randy Mayor
Jorge Gonzalez
Colorists

Wes Abbott
Letterer

Ed Benes
Jorge Gonzalez
Cover Artists

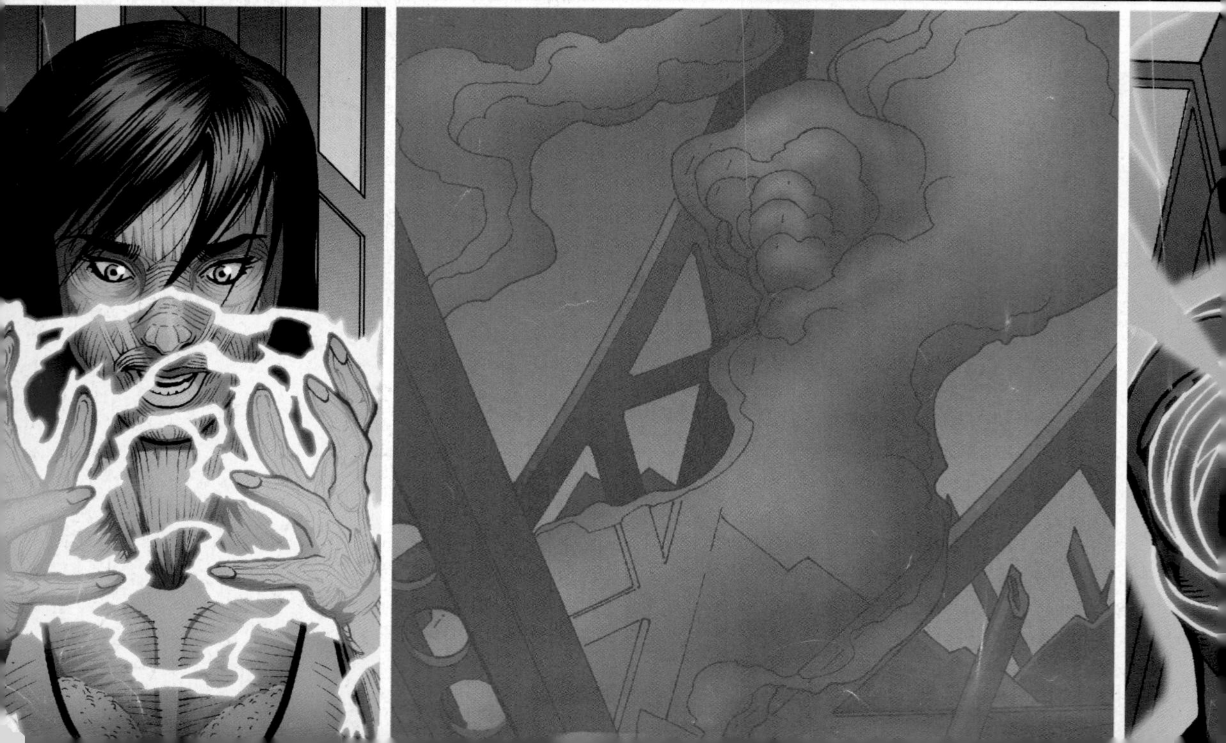

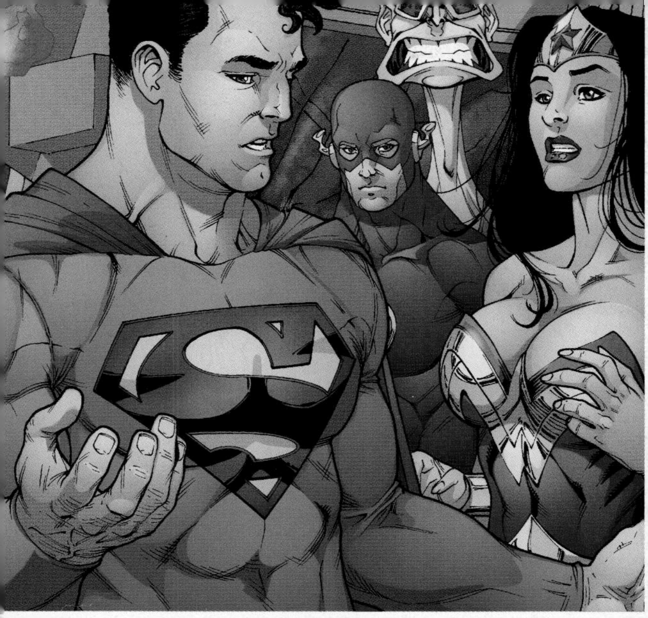

DC Universe Online Legends

VOLUME TWO

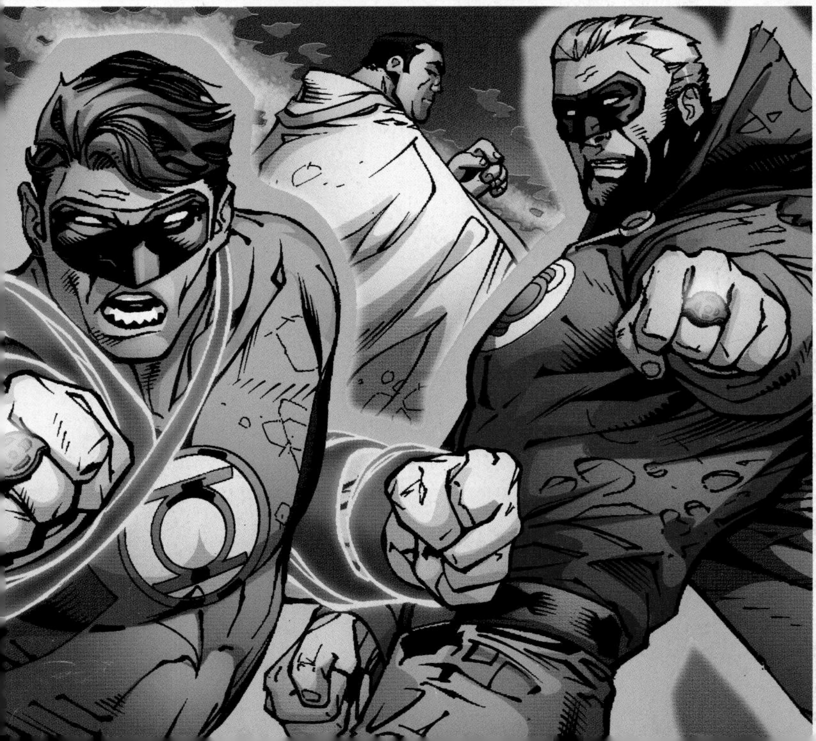

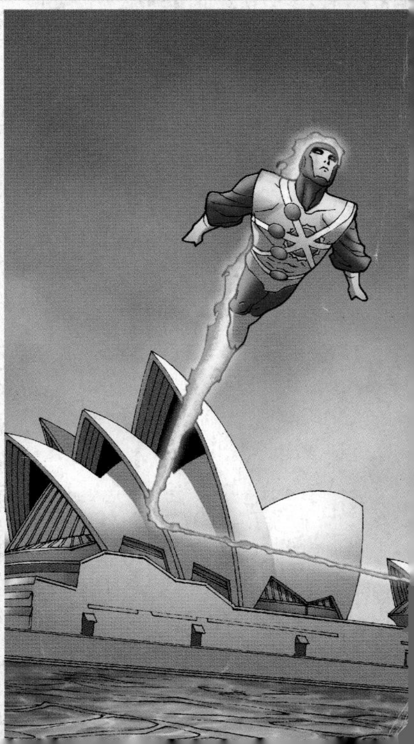

DC UNIVERSE ONLINE LEGENDS
VOLUME TWO

Published by DC Comics. Cover and compilation Copyright © 2012 DC Comics. All Rights Reserved.

Originally published in single magazine form in DC UNIVERSE ONLINE LEGENDS 8-15 Copyright © 2011 DC Comics.
All Rights Reserved. All characters, their distinctive likenesses and related elements featured in this publication are
trademarks of DC Comics. The stories, characters and incidents featured in this publication are entirely fictional.
DC Comics does not read or accept unsolicited ideas, stories or artwork.

DC Comics, 1700 Broadway, New York, NY 10019
A Warner Bros. Entertainment Company.
Printed by RR Donnelley, Salem, VA, USA. 2/10/12. First Printing.
ISBN: 978-1-4012-3386-0

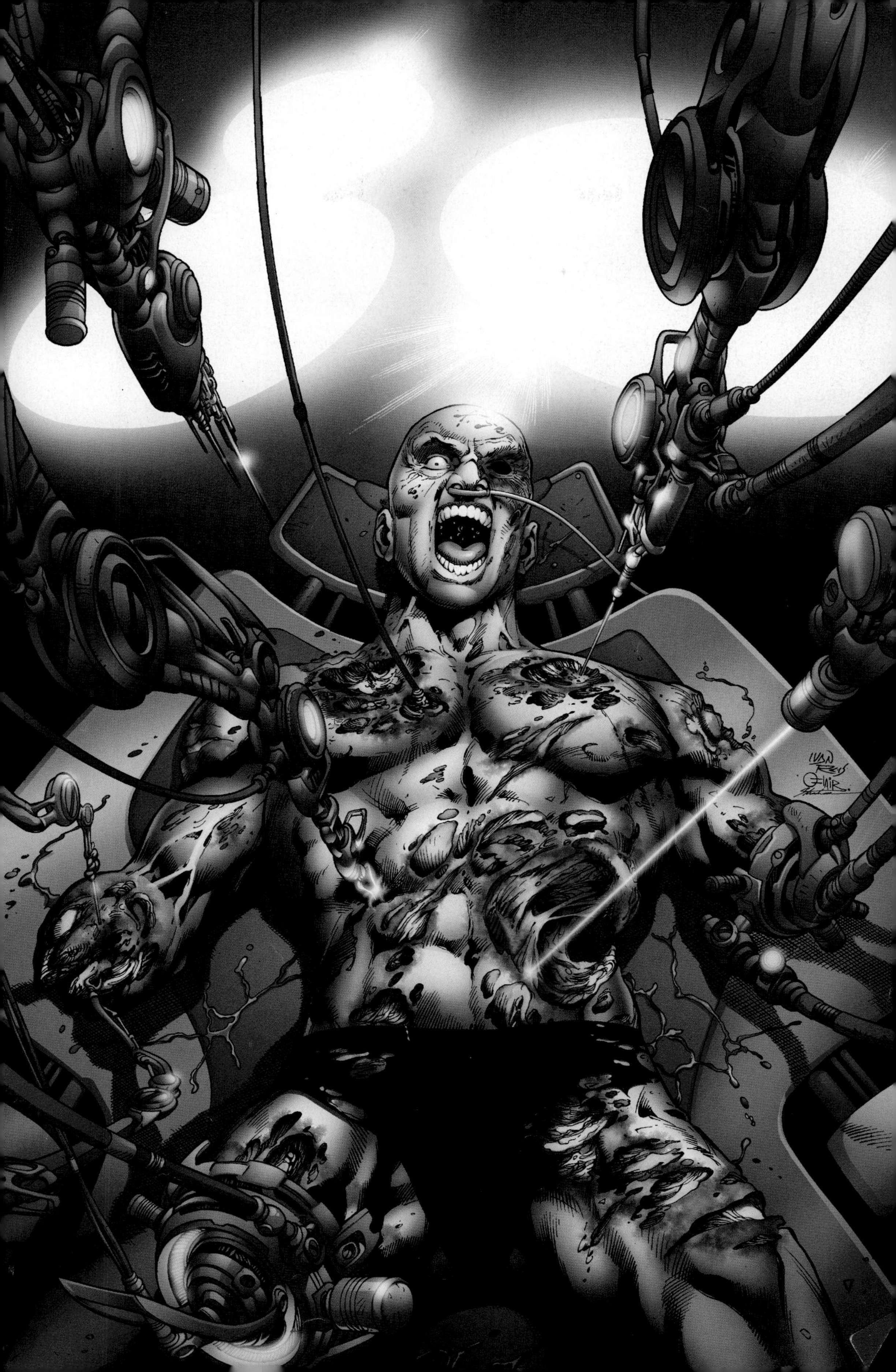

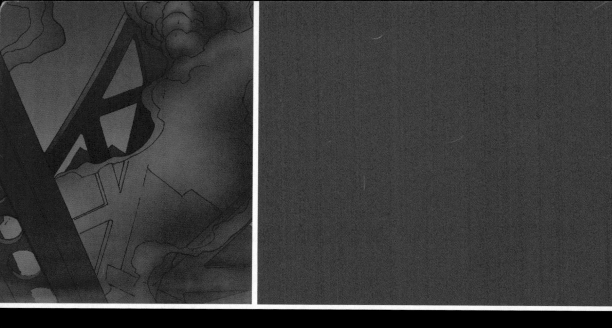

RECONSTRUCTION

Tony Bedard
Writer

Mike S. Miller
Artist

Cover by Ed Benes & Randy Mayor

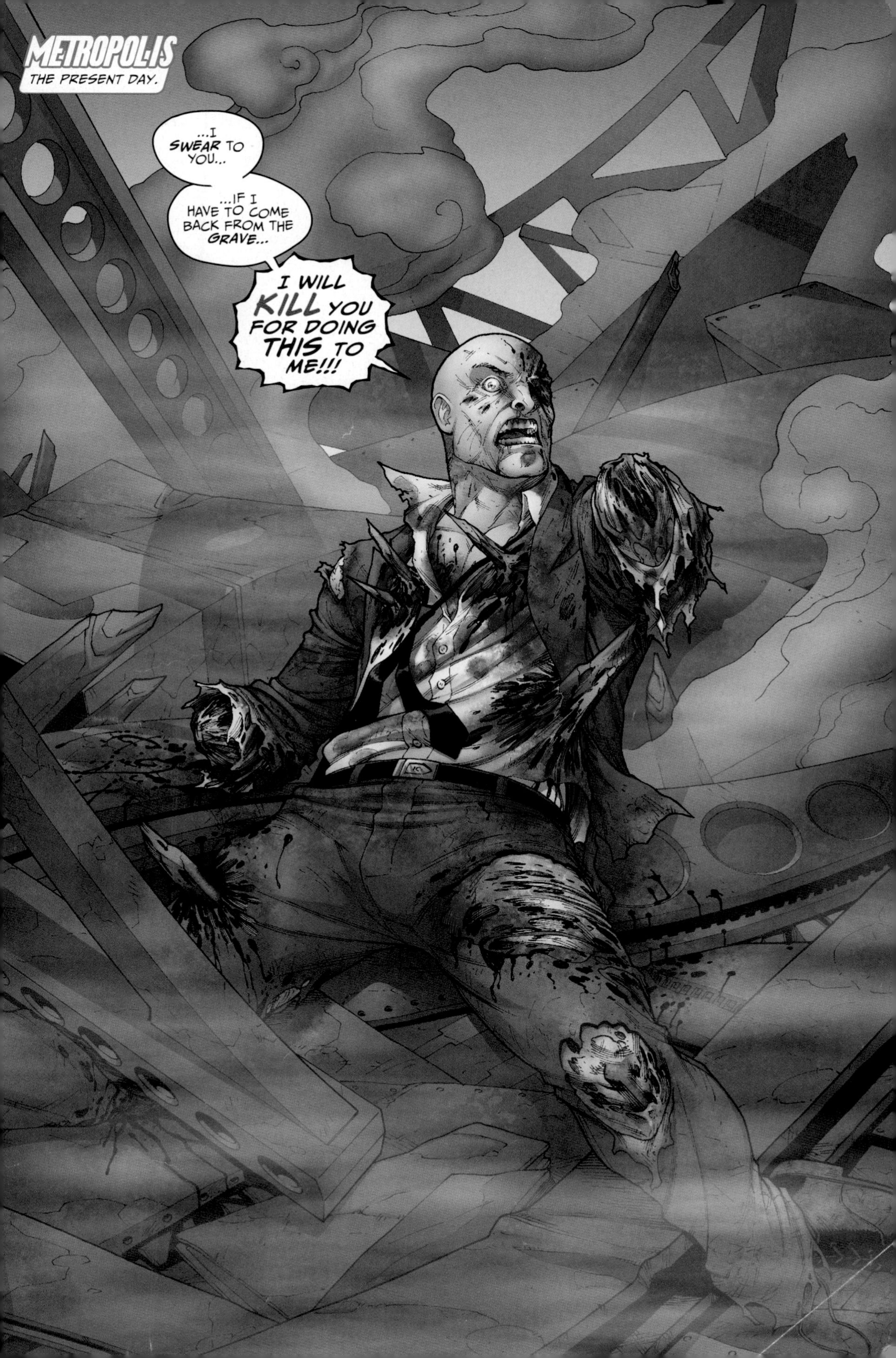
METROPOLIS
THE PRESENT DAY.
...I SWEAR TO YOU...
...IF I HAVE TO COME BACK FROM THE GRAVE...
I WILL KILL YOU FOR DOING THIS TO ME!!!

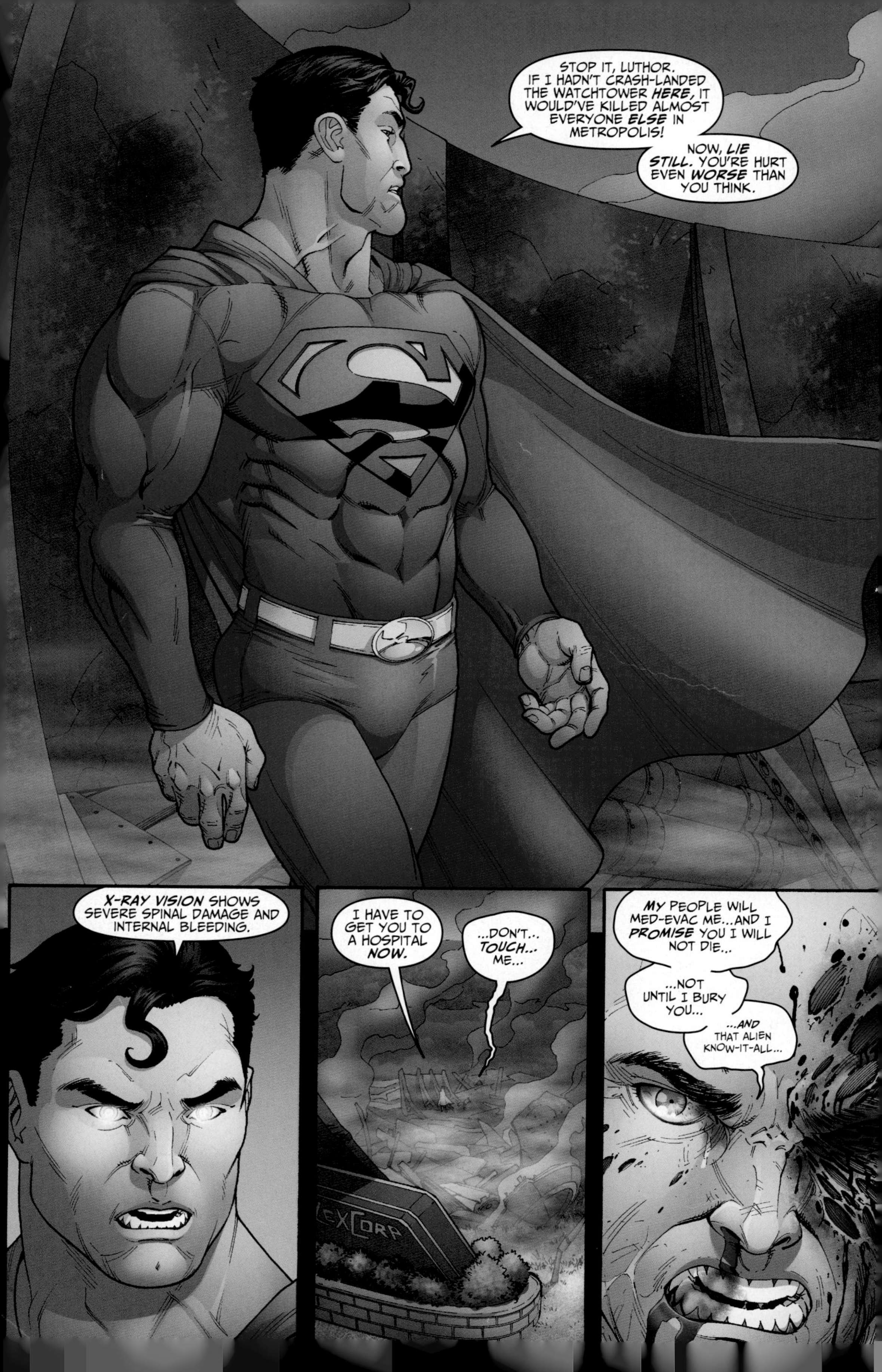
STOP IT, LUTHOR. IF I HADN'T CRASH-LANDED THE WATCHTOWER HERE, IT WOULD'VE KILLED ALMOST EVERYONE ELSE IN METROPOLIS!
NOW, LIE STILL. YOU'RE HURT EVEN WORSE THAN YOU THINK.
X-RAY VISION SHOWS SEVERE SPINAL DAMAGE AND INTERNAL BLEEDING.
I HAVE TO GET YOU TO A HOSPITAL NOW.
...DON'T... TOUCH... ME...
LEXCORP
MY PEOPLE WILL MED-EVAC ME...AND I PROMISE YOU I WILL NOT DIE...
...NOT UNTIL I BURY YOU...
...AND THAT ALIEN KNOW-IT-ALL...

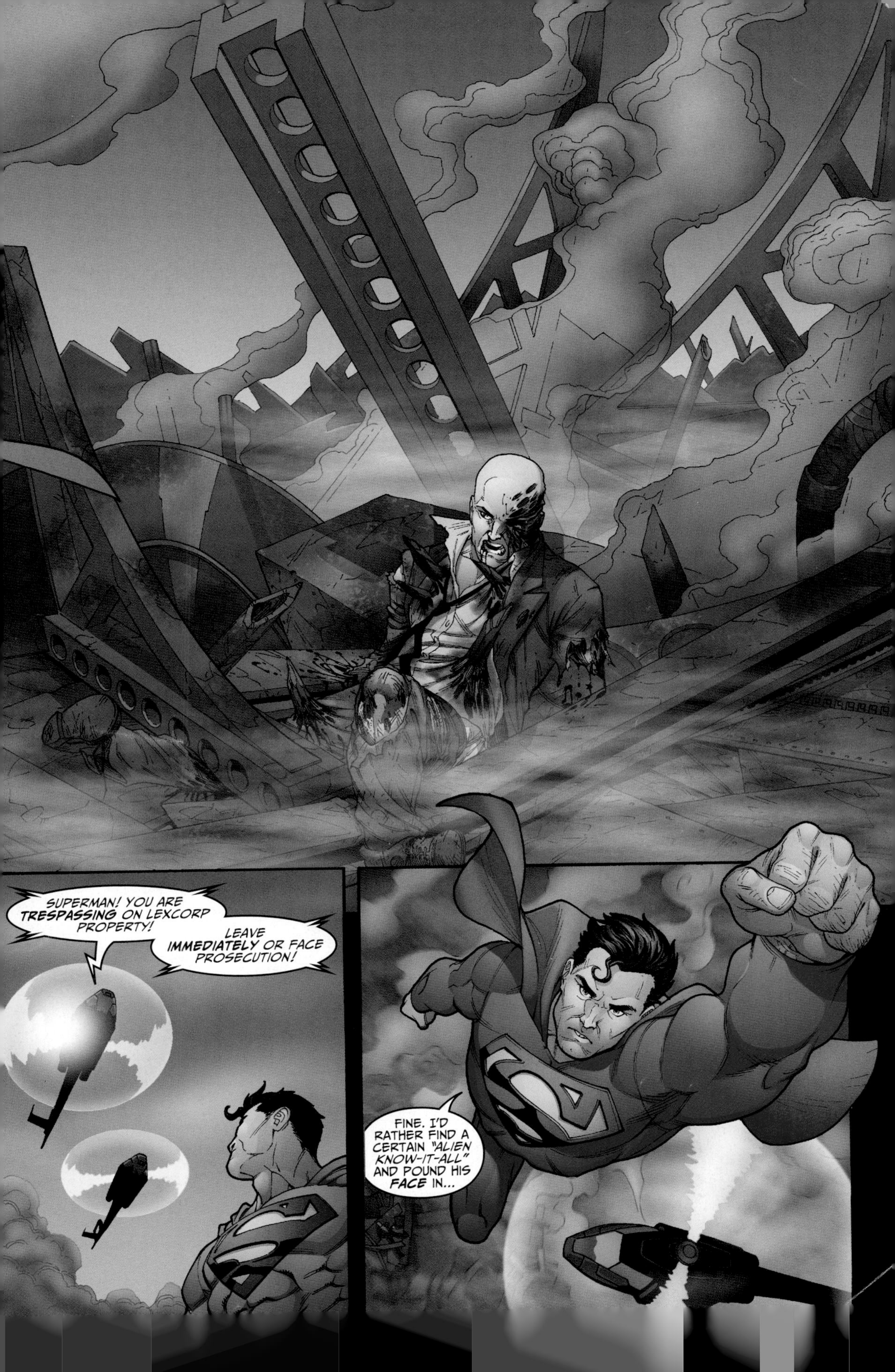
SUPERMAN! YOU ARE TRESPASSING ON LEXCORP PROPERTY!
LEAVE IMMEDIATELY OR FACE PROSECUTION!
FINE. I'D RATHER FIND A CERTAIN "ALIEN KNOW-IT-ALL" AND POUND HIS FACE IN...

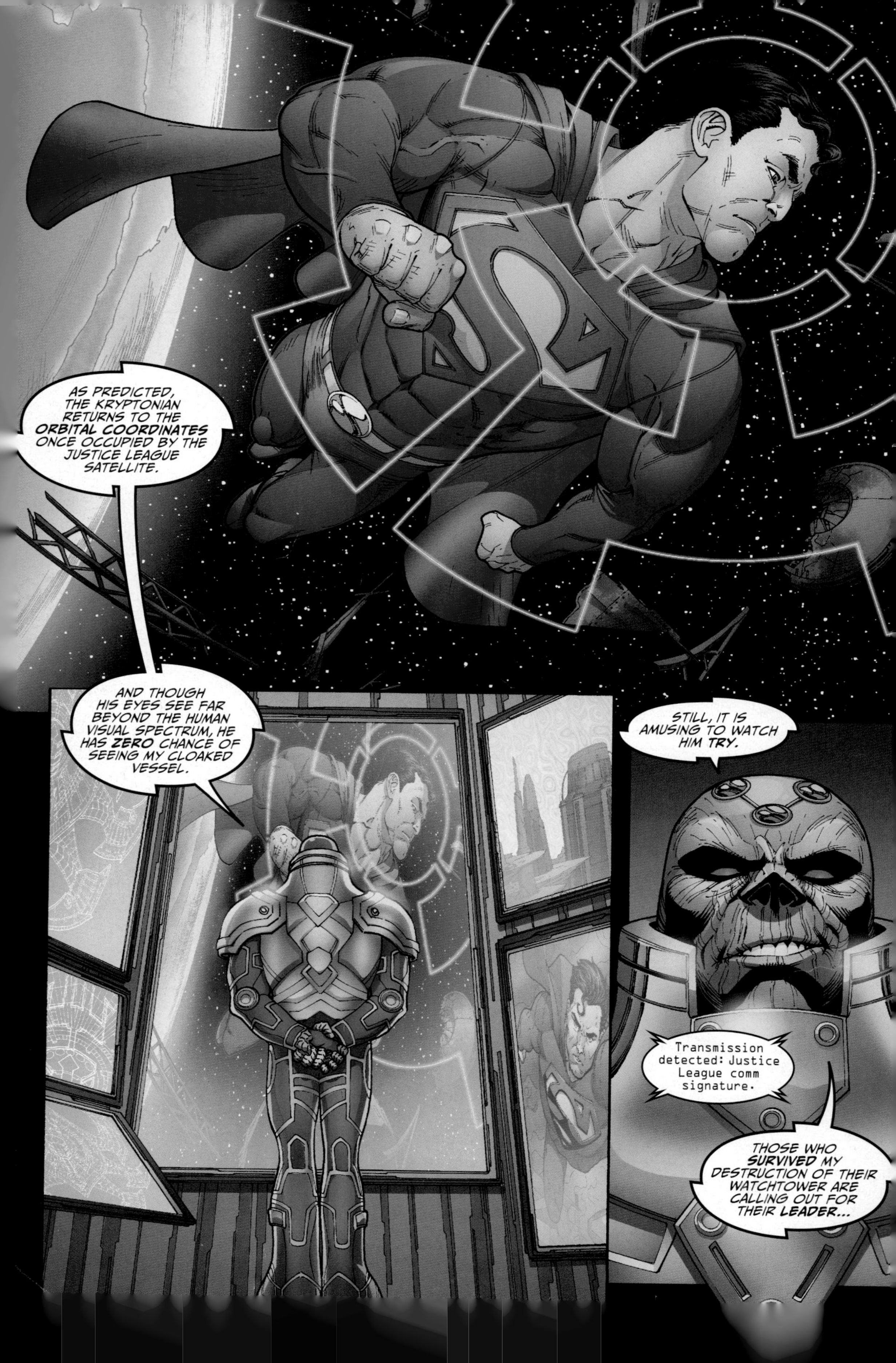
AS PREDICTED, THE KRYPTONIAN RETURNS TO THE ORBITAL COORDINATES ONCE OCCUPIED BY THE JUSTICE LEAGUE SATELLITE.
AND THOUGH HIS EYES SEE FAR BEYOND THE HUMAN VISUAL SPECTRUM, HE HAS ZERO CHANCE OF SEEING MY CLOAKED VESSEL.
STILL, IT IS AMUSING TO WATCH HIM TRY.
Transmission detected: Justice League comm signature.
THOSE WHO SURVIVED MY DESTRUCTION OF THEIR WATCHTOWER ARE CALLING OUT FOR THEIR LEADER...

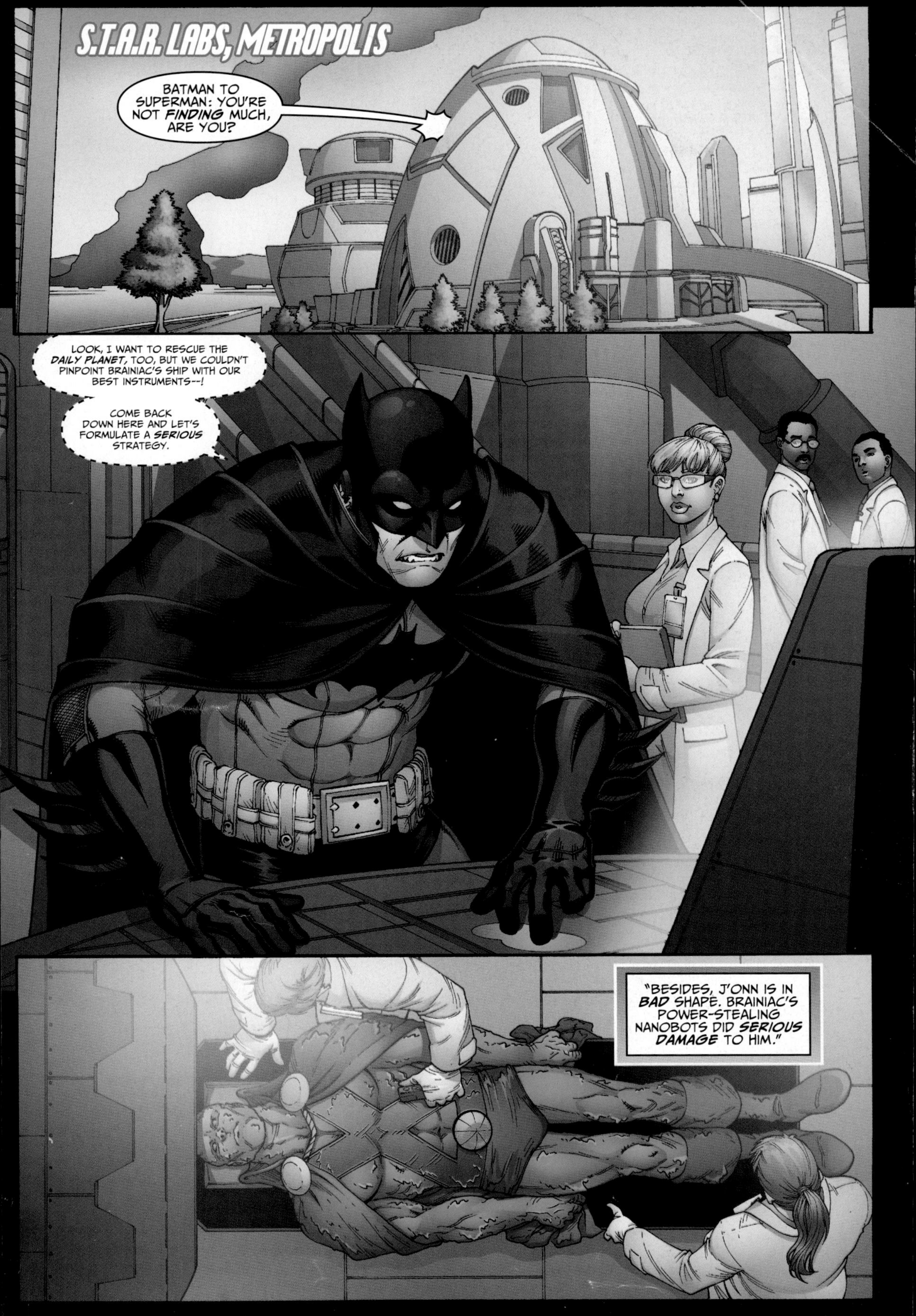
S.T.A.R. LABS, METROPOLIS
BATMAN TO SUPERMAN: YOU'RE NOT FINDING MUCH, ARE YOU?
LOOK, I WANT TO RESCUE THE DAILY PLANET, TOO, BUT WE COULDN'T PINPOINT BRAINIAC'S SHIP WITH OUR BEST INSTRUMENTS--!
COME BACK DOWN HERE AND LET'S FORMULATE A SERIOUS STRATEGY.
"BESIDES, J'ONN IS IN BAD SHAPE. BRAINIAC'S POWER-STEALING NANOBOTS DID SERIOUS DAMAGE TO HIM."

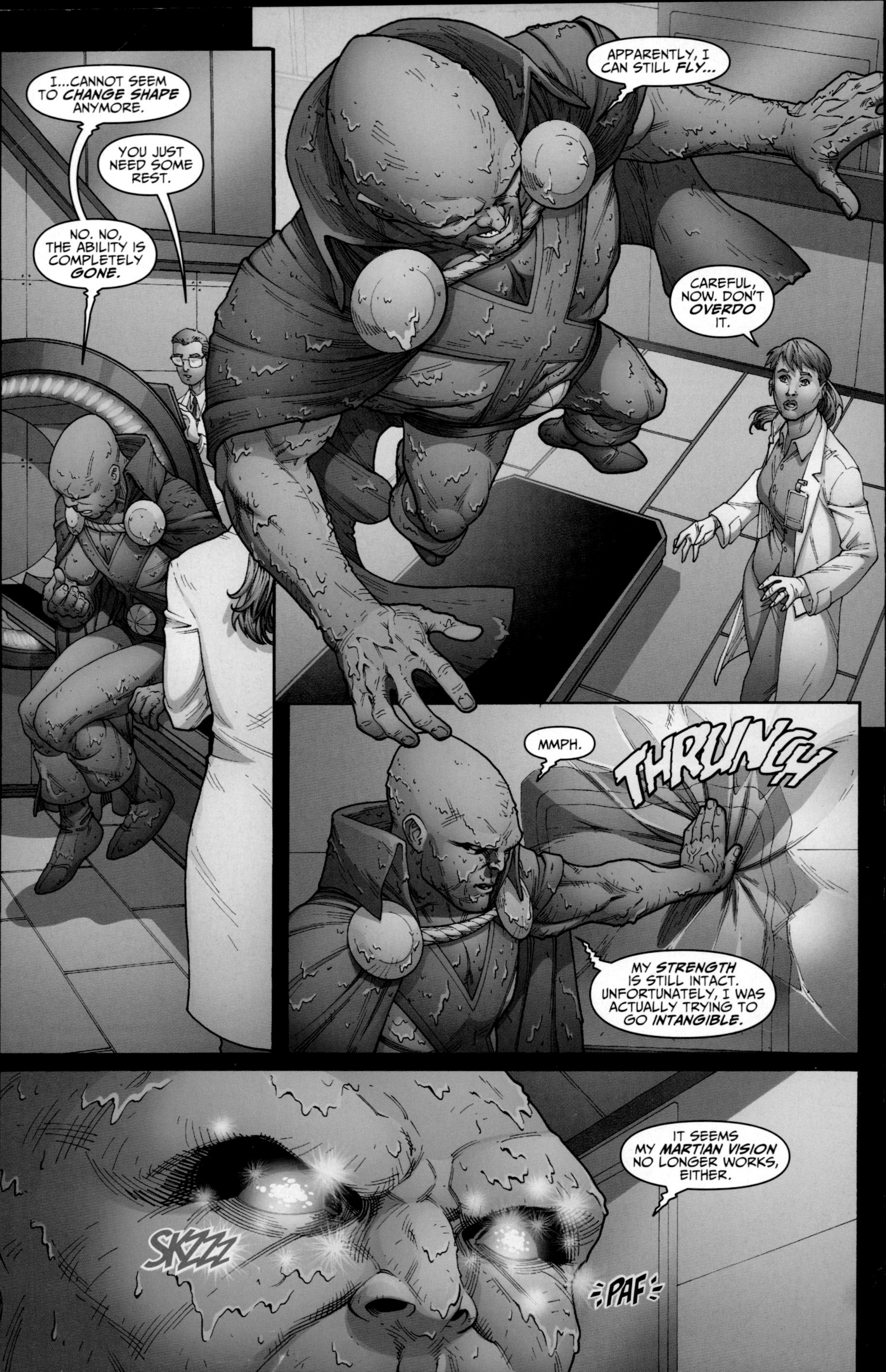
I...CANNOT SEEM TO CHANGE SHAPE ANYMORE.
YOU JUST NEED SOME REST.
NO. NO, THE ABILITY IS COMPLETELY GONE.
APPARENTLY, I CAN STILL FLY...
CAREFUL, NOW. DON'T OVERDO IT.
MMPH.
THRUNCH
MY STRENGTH IS STILL INTACT. UNFORTUNATELY, I WAS ACTUALLY TRYING TO GO INTANGIBLE.
IT SEEMS MY MARTIAN VISION NO LONGER WORKS, EITHER.
SKZZZ
PAF

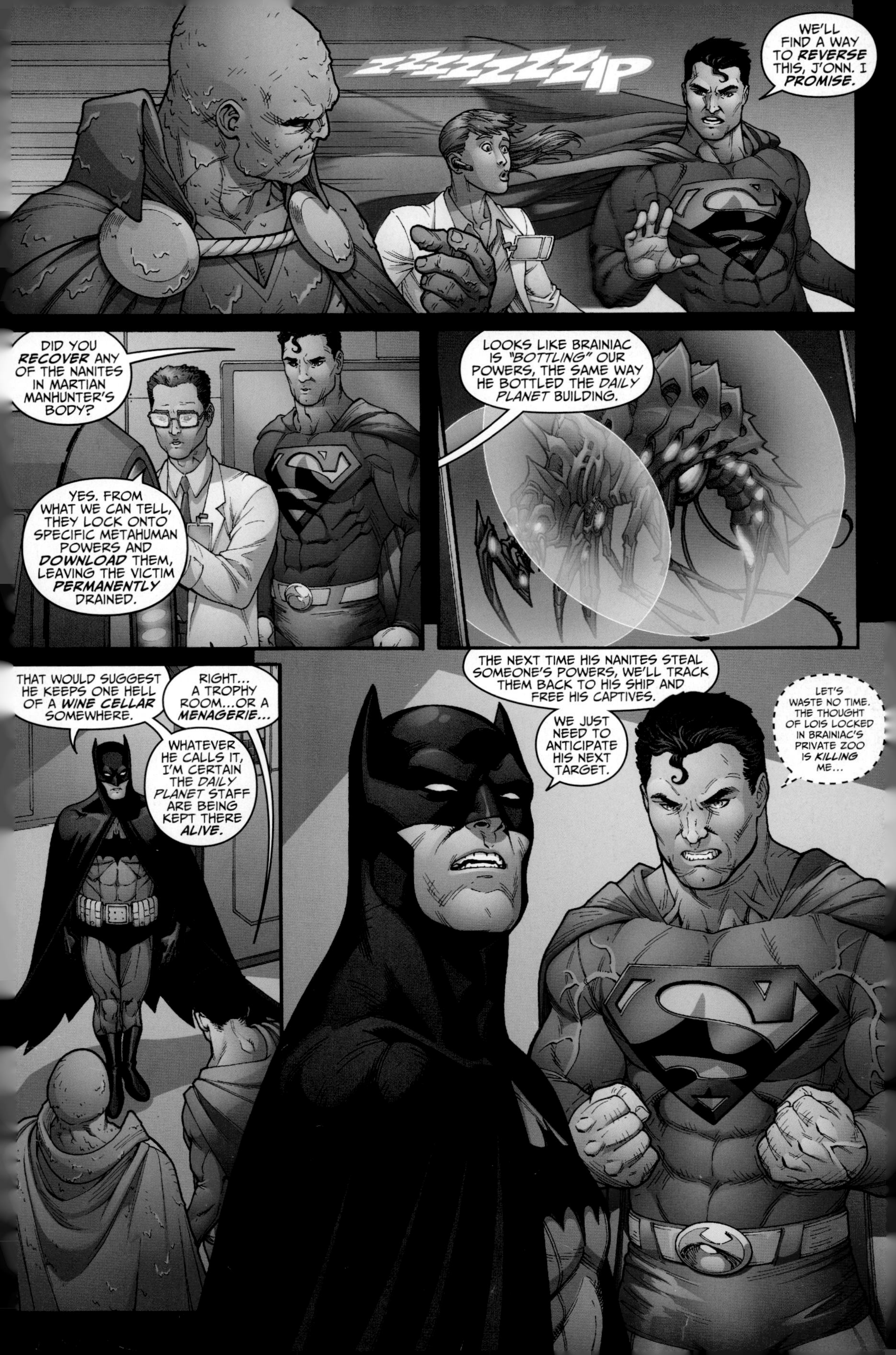
ZZZZZZZZIP
WE'LL FIND A WAY TO REVERSE THIS, J'ONN. I PROMISE.
DID YOU RECOVER ANY OF THE NANITES IN MARTIAN MANHUNTER'S BODY?
YES. FROM WHAT WE CAN TELL, THEY LOCK ONTO SPECIFIC METAHUMAN POWERS AND DOWNLOAD THEM, LEAVING THE VICTIM PERMANENTLY DRAINED.
LOOKS LIKE BRAINIAC IS "BOTTLING" OUR POWERS, THE SAME WAY HE BOTTLED THE DAILY PLANET BUILDING.
THAT WOULD SUGGEST HE KEEPS ONE HELL OF A WINE CELLAR SOMEWHERE.
RIGHT... A TROPHY ROOM...OR A MENAGERIE...
WHATEVER HE CALLS IT, I'M CERTAIN THE DAILY PLANET STAFF ARE BEING KEPT THERE ALIVE.
THE NEXT TIME HIS NANITES STEAL SOMEONE'S POWERS, WE'LL TRACK THEM BACK TO HIS SHIP AND FREE HIS CAPTIVES.
WE JUST NEED TO ANTICIPATE HIS NEXT TARGET.
LET'S WASTE NO TIME. THE THOUGHT OF LOIS LOCKED IN BRAINIAC'S PRIVATE ZOO IS KILLING ME...

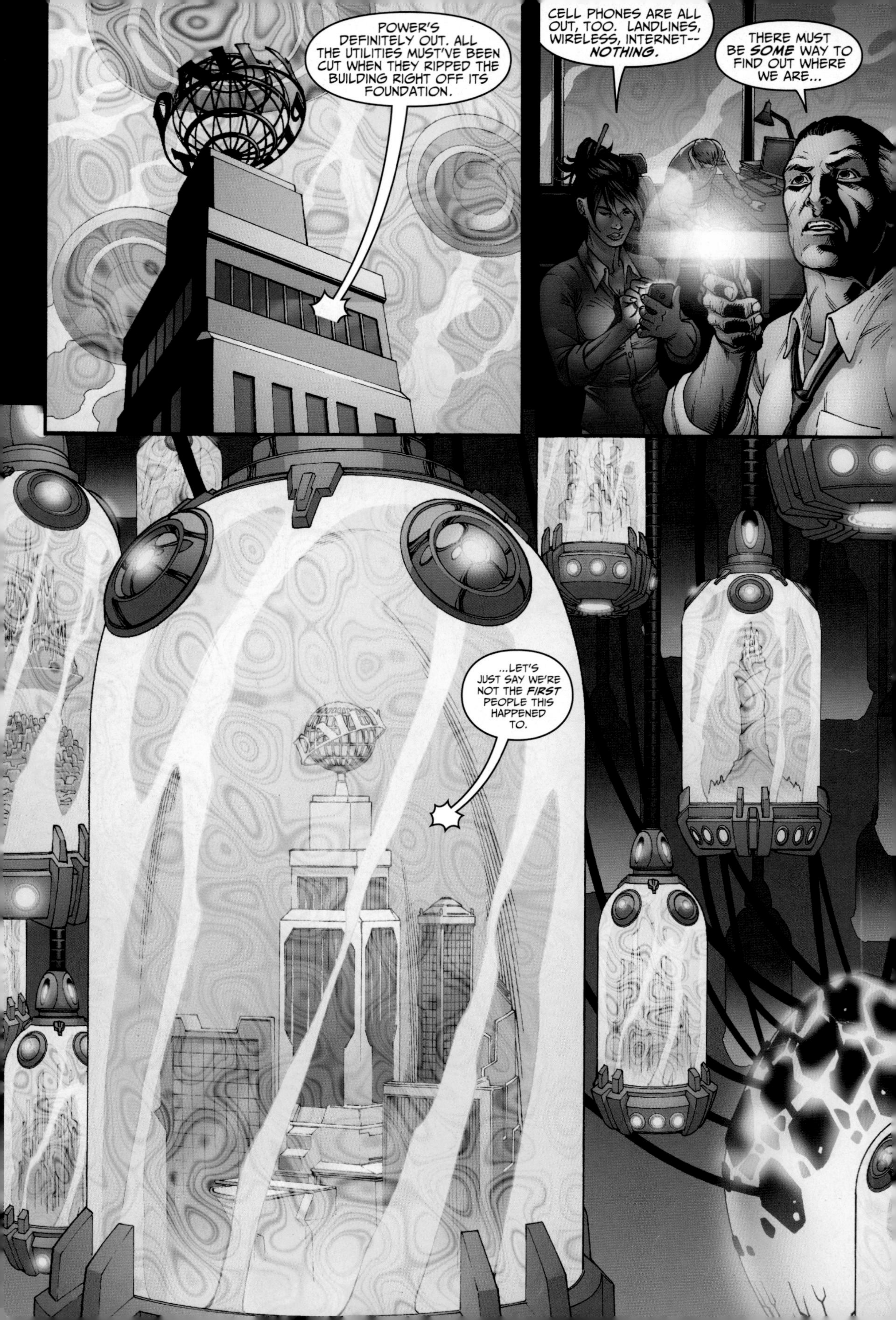
POWER'S DEFINITELY OUT. ALL THE UTILITIES MUST'VE BEEN CUT WHEN THEY RIPPED THE BUILDING RIGHT OFF ITS FOUNDATION.
CELL PHONES ARE ALL OUT, TOO. LANDLINES, WIRELESS, INTERNET-- NOTHING.
THERE MUST BE SOME WAY TO FIND OUT WHERE WE ARE...
...LET'S JUST SAY WE'RE NOT THE FIRST PEOPLE THIS HAPPENED TO.

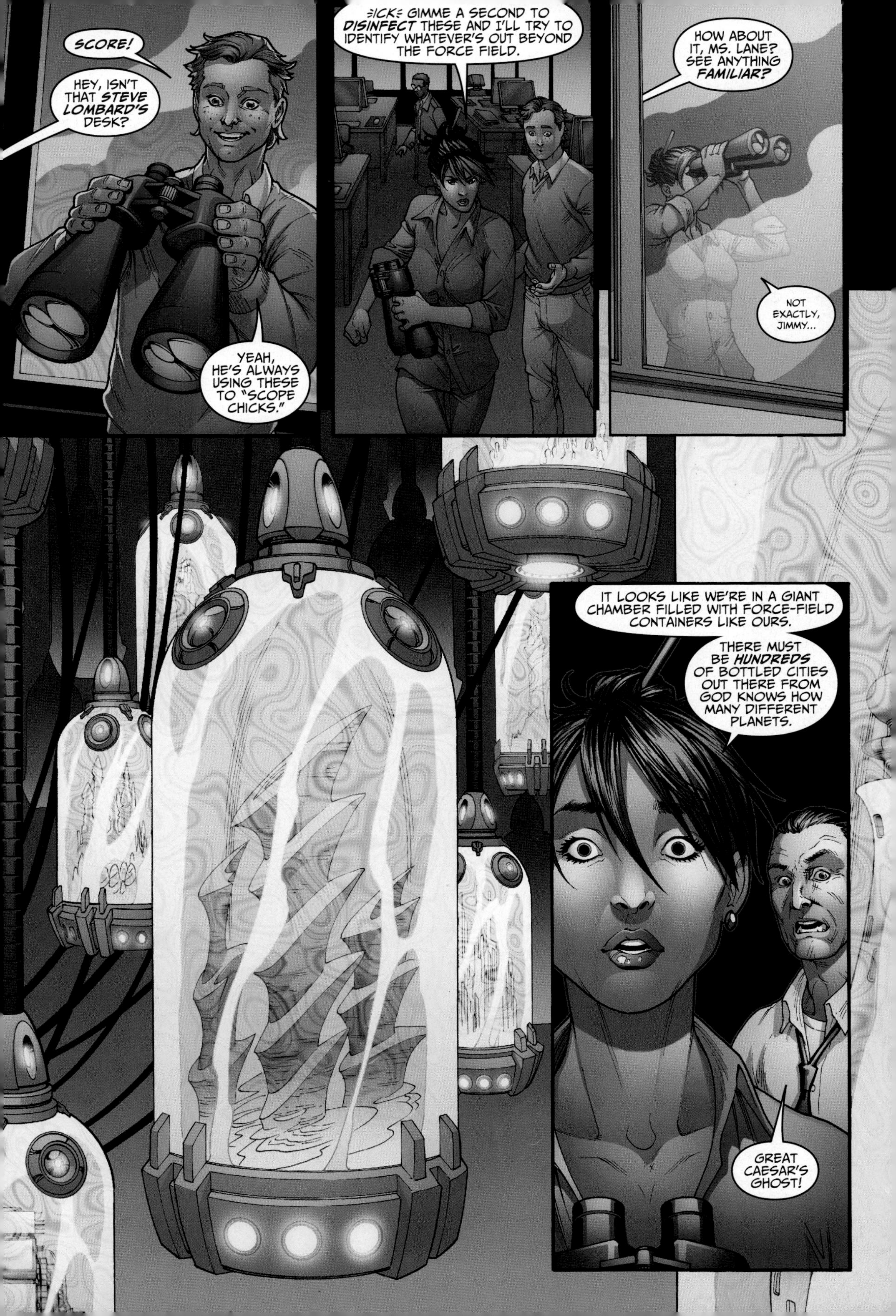
SCORE!
HEY, ISN'T THAT STEVE LOMBARD'S DESK?
YEAH, HE'S ALWAYS USING THESE TO "SCOPE CHICKS."
ICK GIMME A SECOND TO DISINFECT THESE AND I'LL TRY TO IDENTIFY WHATEVER'S OUT BEYOND THE FORCE FIELD.
HOW ABOUT IT, MS. LANE? SEE ANYTHING FAMILIAR?
NOT EXACTLY, JIMMY...
IT LOOKS LIKE WE'RE IN A GIANT CHAMBER FILLED WITH FORCE-FIELD CONTAINERS LIKE OURS.
THERE MUST BE HUNDREDS OF BOTTLED CITIES OUT THERE FROM GOD KNOWS HOW MANY DIFFERENT PLANETS.
GREAT CAESAR'S GHOST!

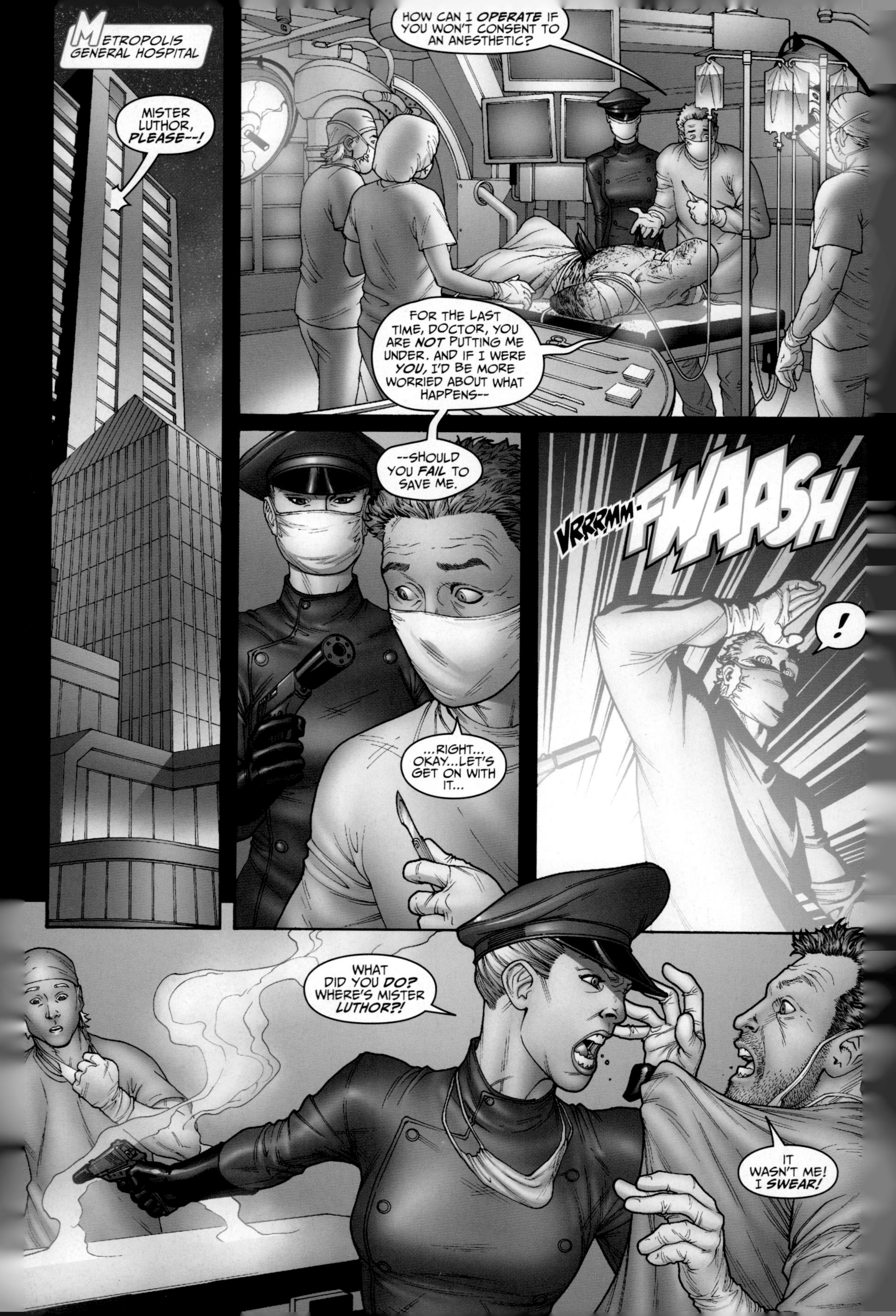
METROPOLIS GENERAL HOSPITAL
MISTER LUTHOR, PLEASE--!
HOW CAN I OPERATE IF YOU WON'T CONSENT TO AN ANESTHETIC?
FOR THE LAST TIME, DOCTOR, YOU ARE NOT PUTTING ME UNDER. AND IF I WERE YOU, I'D BE MORE WORRIED ABOUT WHAT HAPPENS--
--SHOULD YOU FAIL TO SAVE ME.
...RIGHT... OKAY...LET'S GET ON WITH IT...
VRRRMM-FWAASH
!
WHAT DID YOU DO? WHERE'S MISTER LUTHOR?!
IT WASN'T ME! I SWEAR!

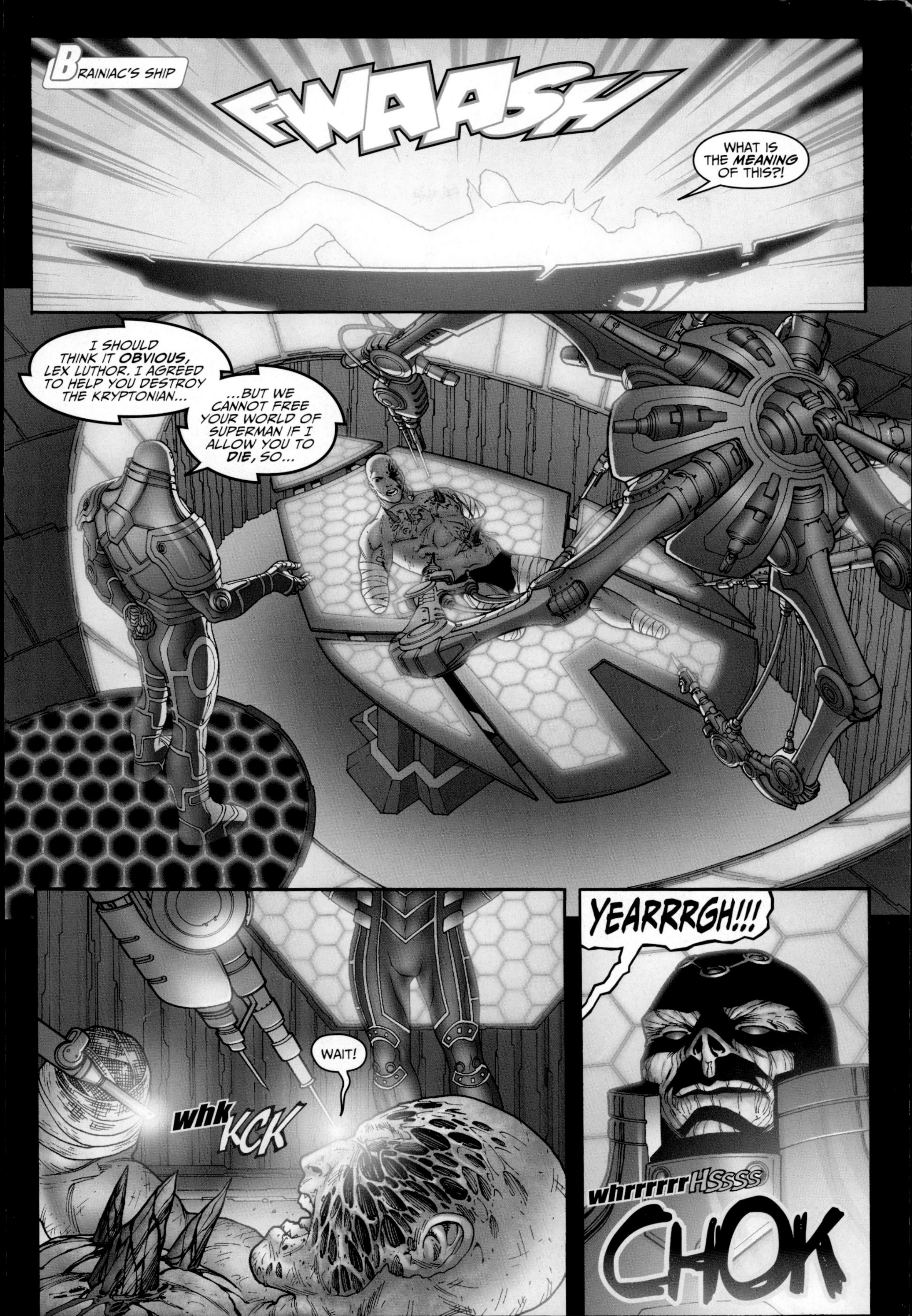
BRAINIAC'S SHIP
FWAASH
WHAT IS THE MEANING OF THIS?!
I SHOULD THINK IT OBVIOUS, LEX LUTHOR. I AGREED TO HELP YOU DESTROY THE KRYPTONIAN...
...BUT WE CANNOT FREE YOUR WORLD OF SUPERMAN IF I ALLOW YOU TO DIE, SO...
WAIT!
whk KCK
YEARRRGH!!!
whrrrrrrHSSSS
CHOK

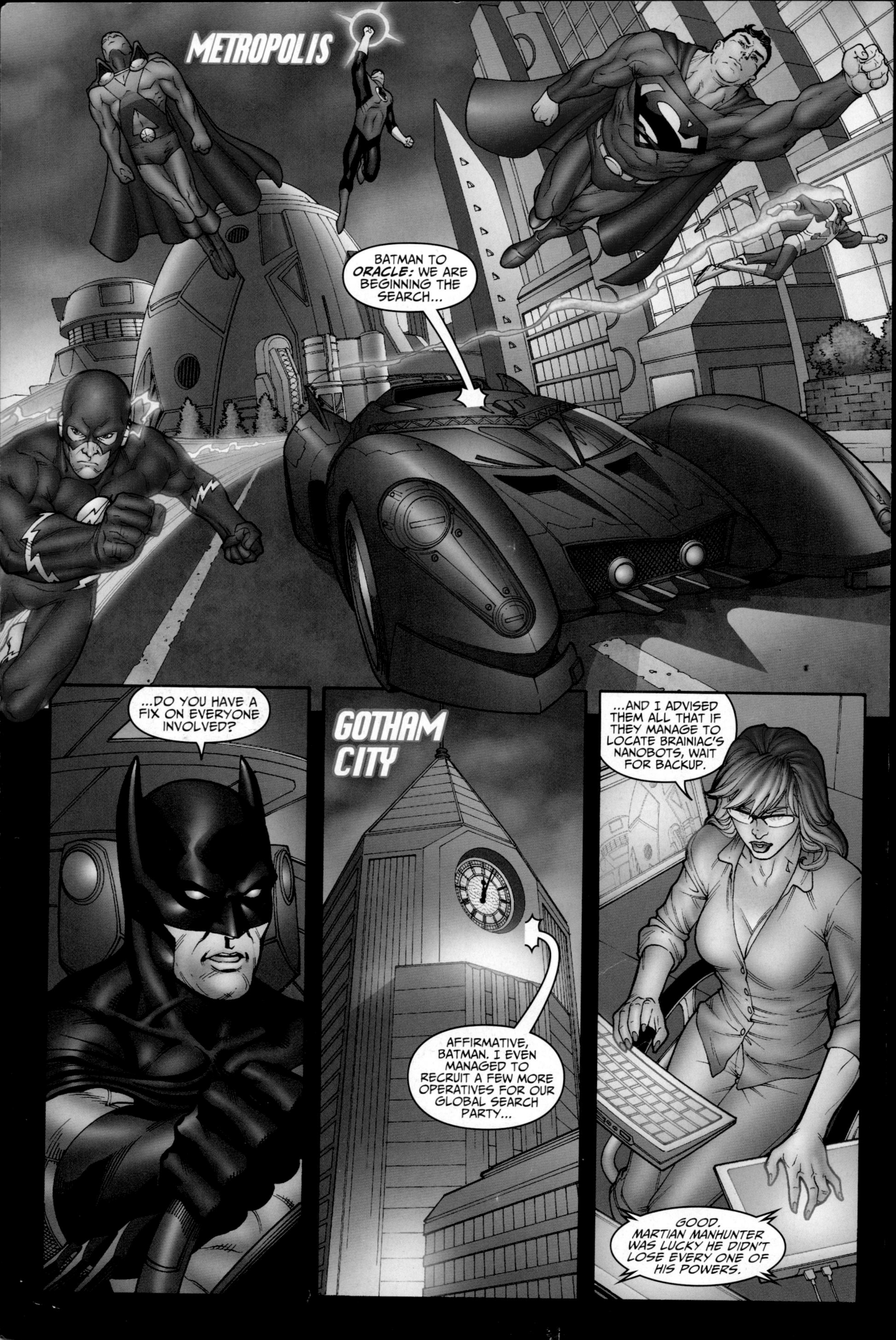
METROPOLIS
BATMAN TO ORACLE: WE ARE BEGINNING THE SEARCH...
...DO YOU HAVE A FIX ON EVERYONE INVOLVED?
GOTHAM CITY
AFFIRMATIVE, BATMAN. I EVEN MANAGED TO RECRUIT A FEW MORE OPERATIVES FOR OUR GLOBAL SEARCH PARTY...
...AND I ADVISED THEM ALL THAT IF THEY MANAGE TO LOCATE BRAINIAC'S NANOBOTS, WAIT FOR BACKUP.
GOOD. MARTIAN MANHUNTER WAS LUCKY HE DIDN'T LOSE EVERY ONE OF HIS POWERS.

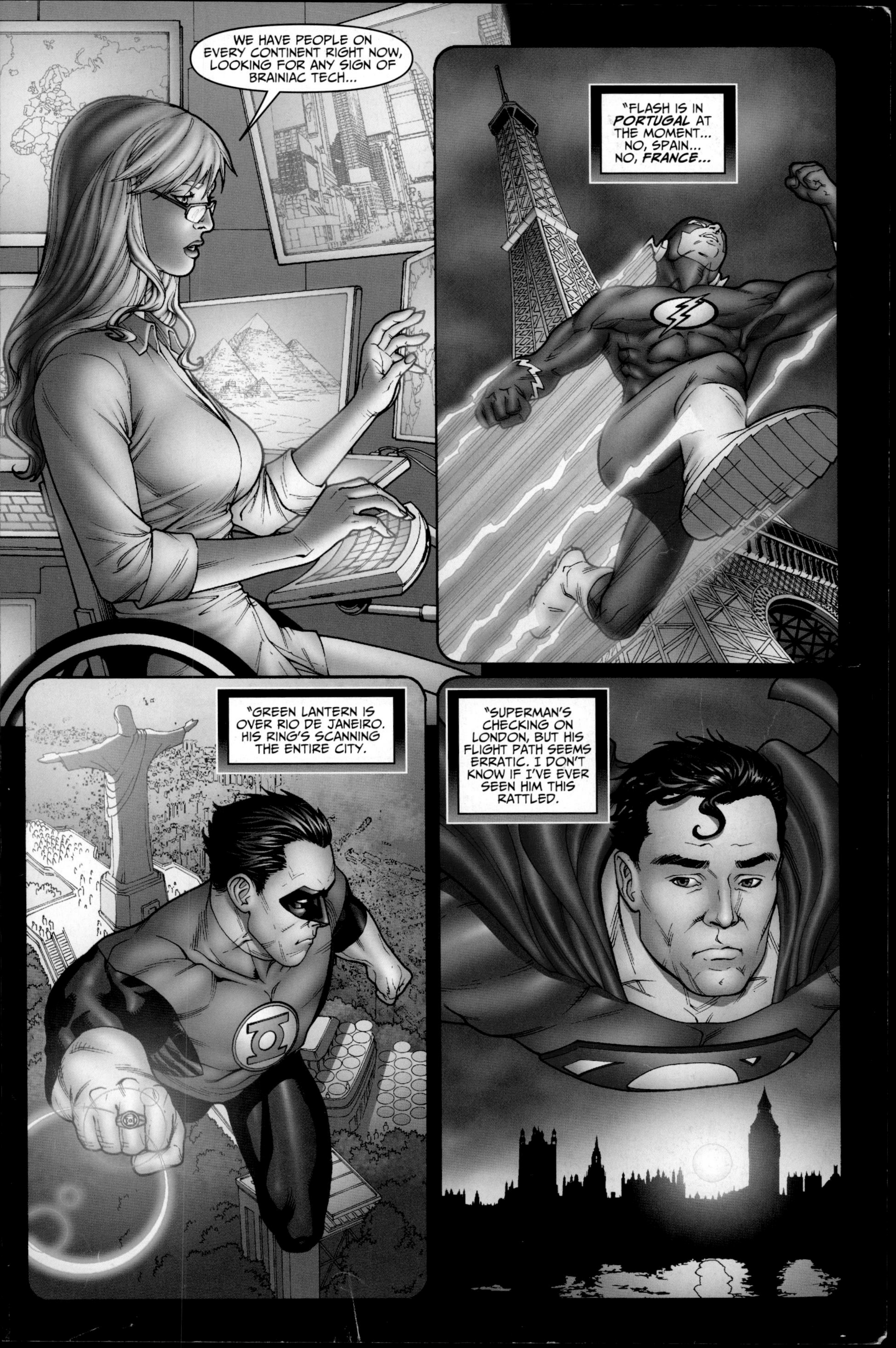
WE HAVE PEOPLE ON EVERY CONTINENT RIGHT NOW, LOOKING FOR ANY SIGN OF BRAINIAC TECH...
"FLASH IS IN PORTUGAL AT THE MOMENT... NO, SPAIN... NO, FRANCE...
"GREEN LANTERN IS OVER RIO DE JANEIRO. HIS RING'S SCANNING THE ENTIRE CITY.
"SUPERMAN'S CHECKING ON LONDON, BUT HIS FLIGHT PATH SEEMS ERRATIC. I DON'T KNOW IF I'VE EVER SEEN HIM THIS RATTLED.

"I'VE GOT PEOPLE CHECKING AUSTRALIA-- ESPECIALLY THE INTERIOR SECTIONS WHERE BRAINIAC COULD SET UP A BASE WITH NO ONE AROUND FOR MILES.

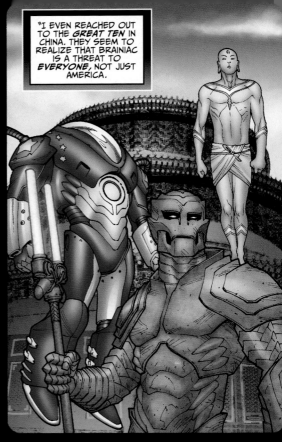

"I EVEN REACHED OUT TO THE *GREAT TEN* IN CHINA. THEY SEEM TO REALIZE THAT BRAINIAC IS A THREAT TO *EVERYONE,* NOT JUST AMERICA.

"AND OVER IN RUSSIA, THE ROCKET REDS ARE HELPING, TOO--

"--THOUGH IF THEY FIND BRAINIAC, IT'LL BE A MATTER OF HOURS BEFORE HIS TECHNOLOGY SHOWS UP ON THE BLACK MARKET.

"FINALLY, MARTIAN MANHUNTER *INSISTED* ON PITCHING IN, SO I GAVE HIM NORTHERN AFRICA.

"SO FAR, *NONE* OF THEM HAS FOUND ANY TRACE OF BRAINIAC."

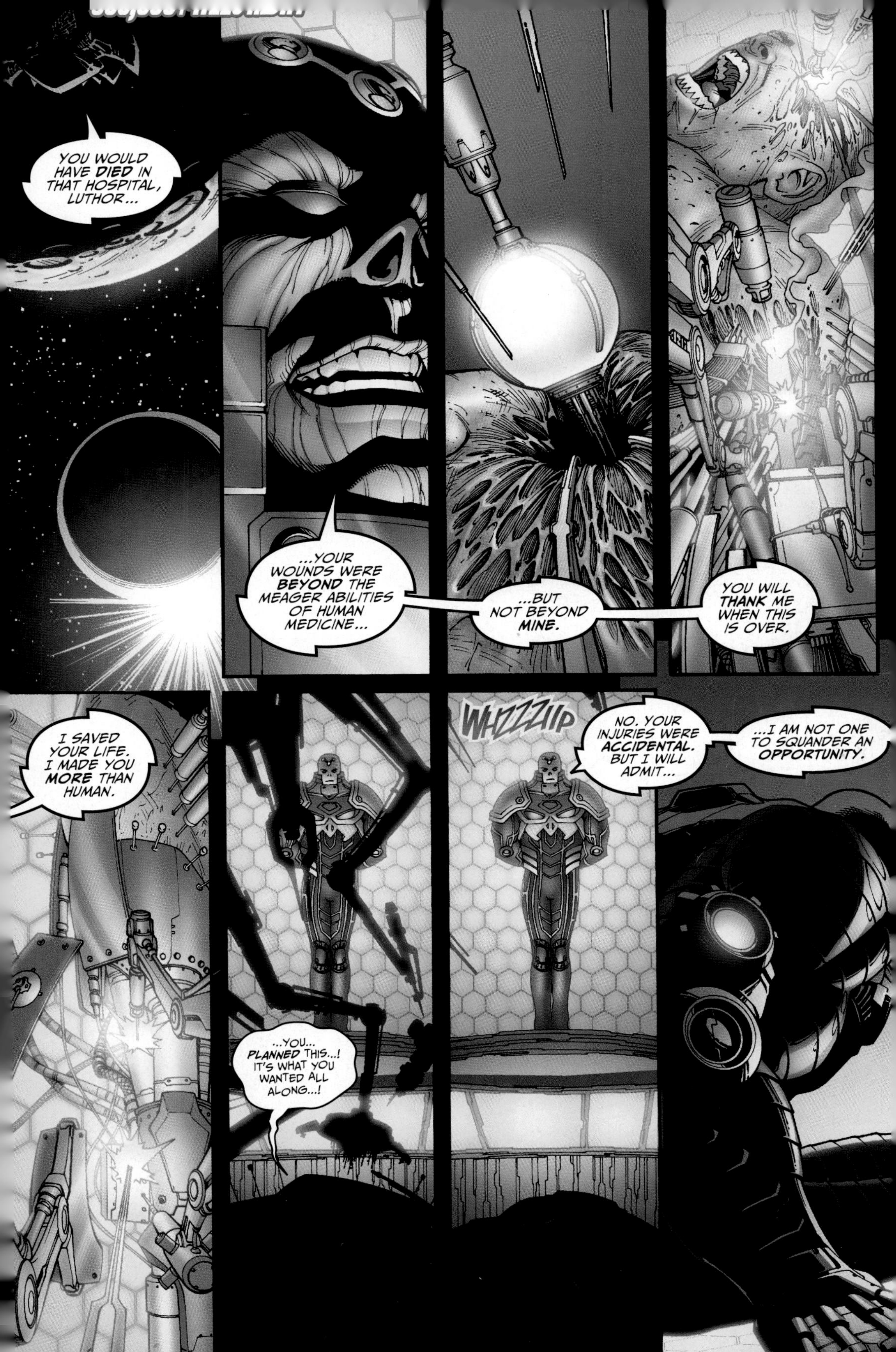
YOU WOULD HAVE DIED IN THAT HOSPITAL, LUTHOR...
...YOUR WOUNDS WERE BEYOND THE MEAGER ABILITIES OF HUMAN MEDICINE...
...BUT NOT BEYOND MINE.
YOU WILL THANK ME WHEN THIS IS OVER.
I SAVED YOUR LIFE. I MADE YOU MORE THAN HUMAN.
...YOU... PLANNED THIS...! IT'S WHAT YOU WANTED ALL ALONG...!
WHZZZIP
NO. YOUR INJURIES WERE ACCIDENTAL. BUT I WILL ADMIT...
...I AM NOT ONE TO SQUANDER AN OPPORTUNITY.

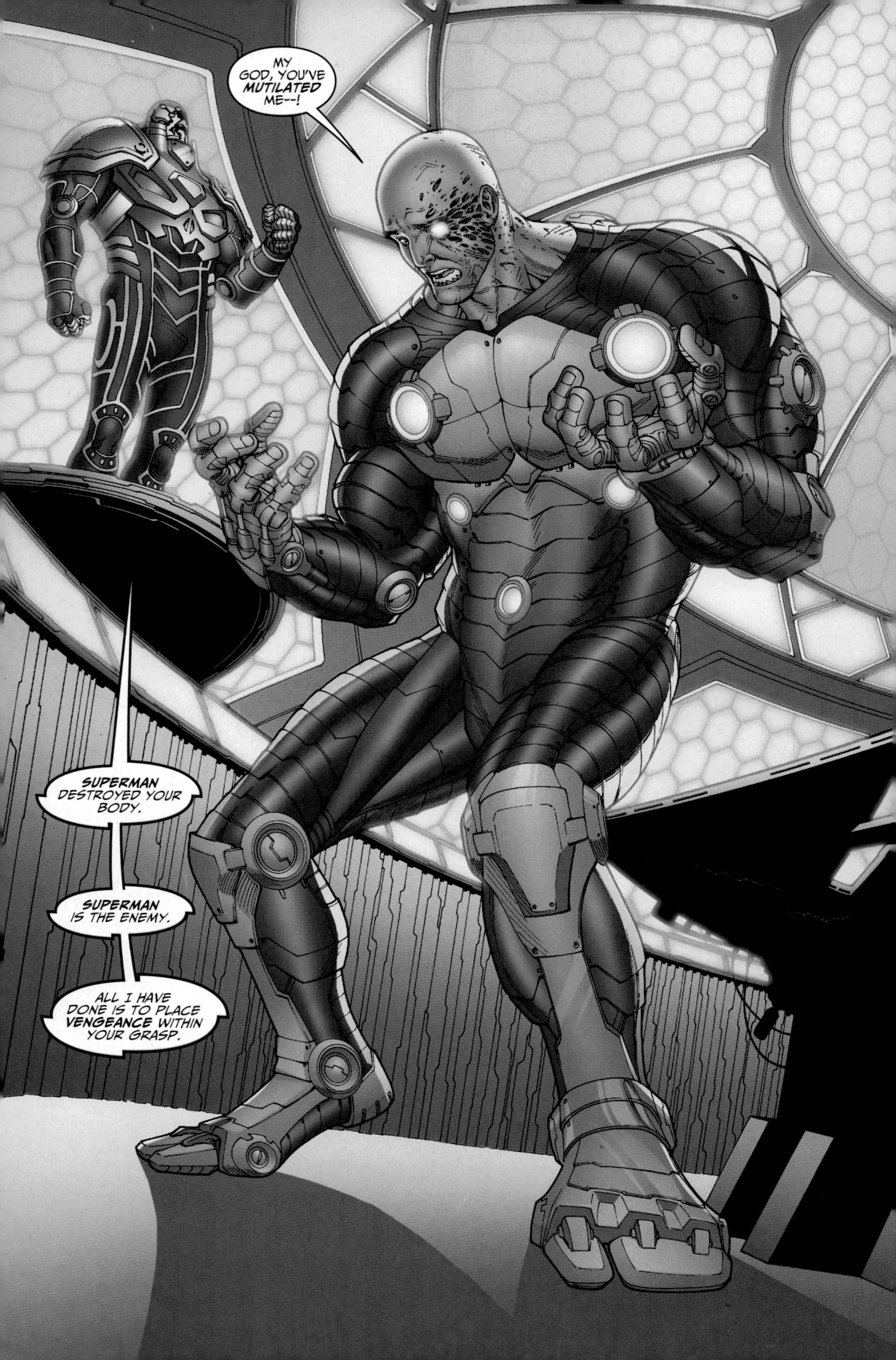
MY GOD, YOU'VE MUTILATED ME--!
SUPERMAN DESTROYED YOUR BODY.
SUPERMAN IS THE ENEMY.
ALL I HAVE DONE IS TO PLACE VENGEANCE WITHIN YOUR GRASP.

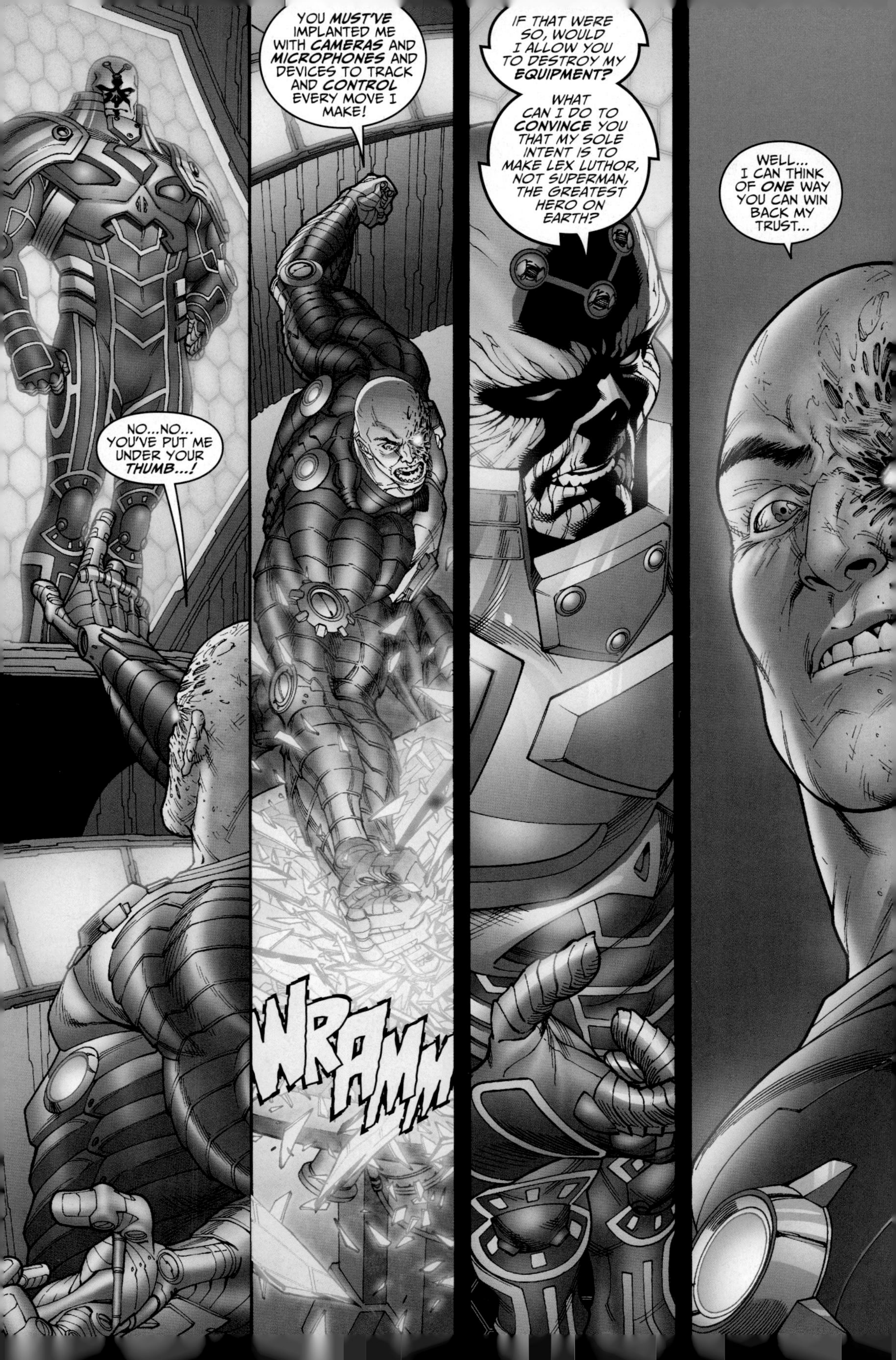
NO...NO... YOU'VE PUT ME UNDER YOUR THUMB...!
YOU MUST'VE IMPLANTED ME WITH CAMERAS AND MICROPHONES AND DEVICES TO TRACK AND CONTROL EVERY MOVE I MAKE!
WRAMM
IF THAT WERE SO, WOULD I ALLOW YOU TO DESTROY MY EQUIPMENT?
WHAT CAN I DO TO CONVINCE YOU THAT MY SOLE INTENT IS TO MAKE LEX LUTHOR, NOT SUPERMAN, THE GREATEST HERO ON EARTH?
WELL... I CAN THINK OF ONE WAY YOU CAN WIN BACK MY TRUST...

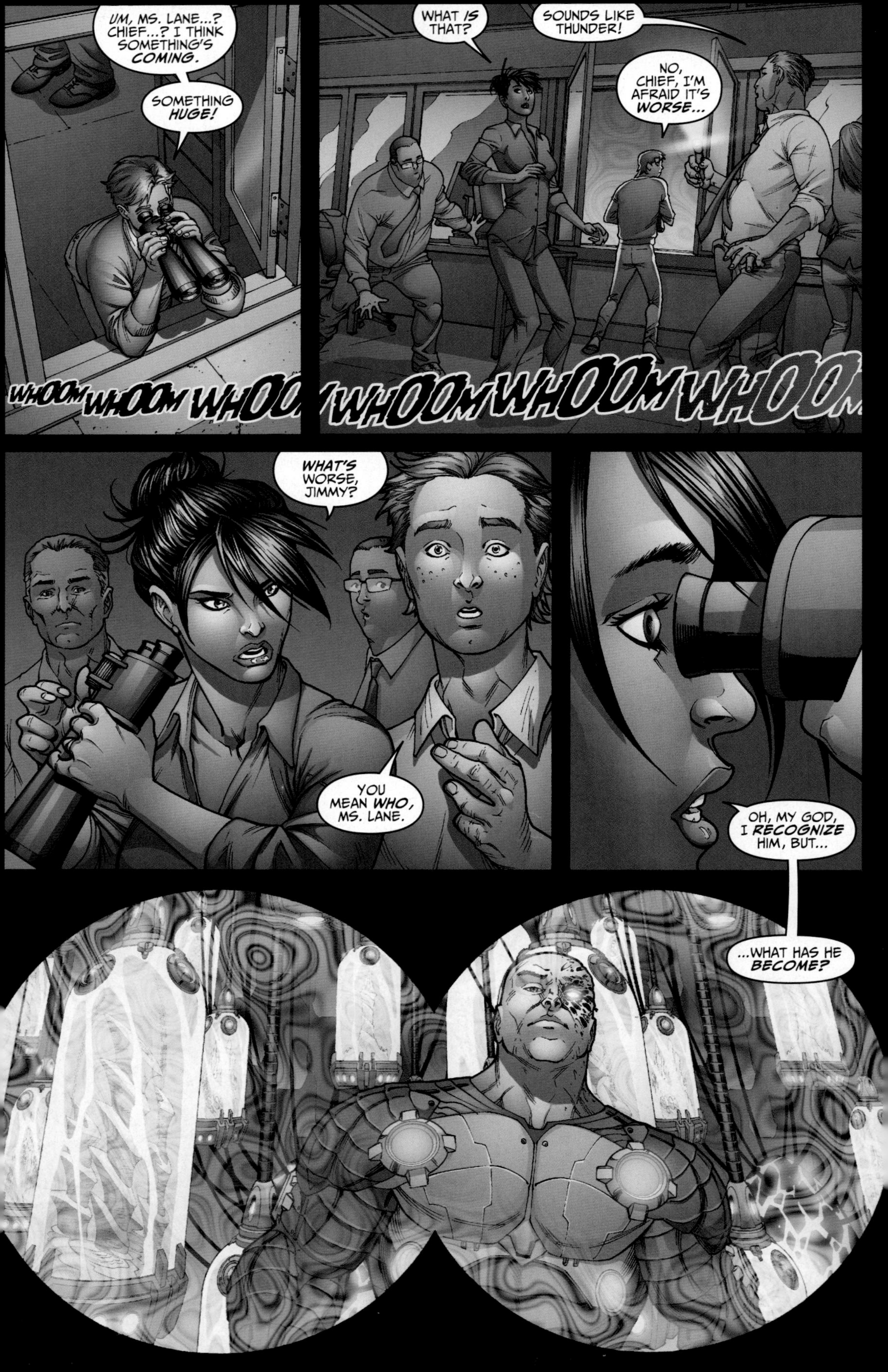
UM, MS. LANE...? CHIEF...? I THINK SOMETHING'S COMING.
SOMETHING HUGE!
WHOOM WHOOM WHOOM
WHAT IS THAT?
SOUNDS LIKE THUNDER!
NO, CHIEF, I'M AFRAID IT'S WORSE...
WHOOM WHOOM WHOOM
WHAT'S WORSE, JIMMY?
YOU MEAN WHO, MS. LANE.
OH, MY GOD, I RECOGNIZE HIM, BUT...
...WHAT HAS HE BECOME?

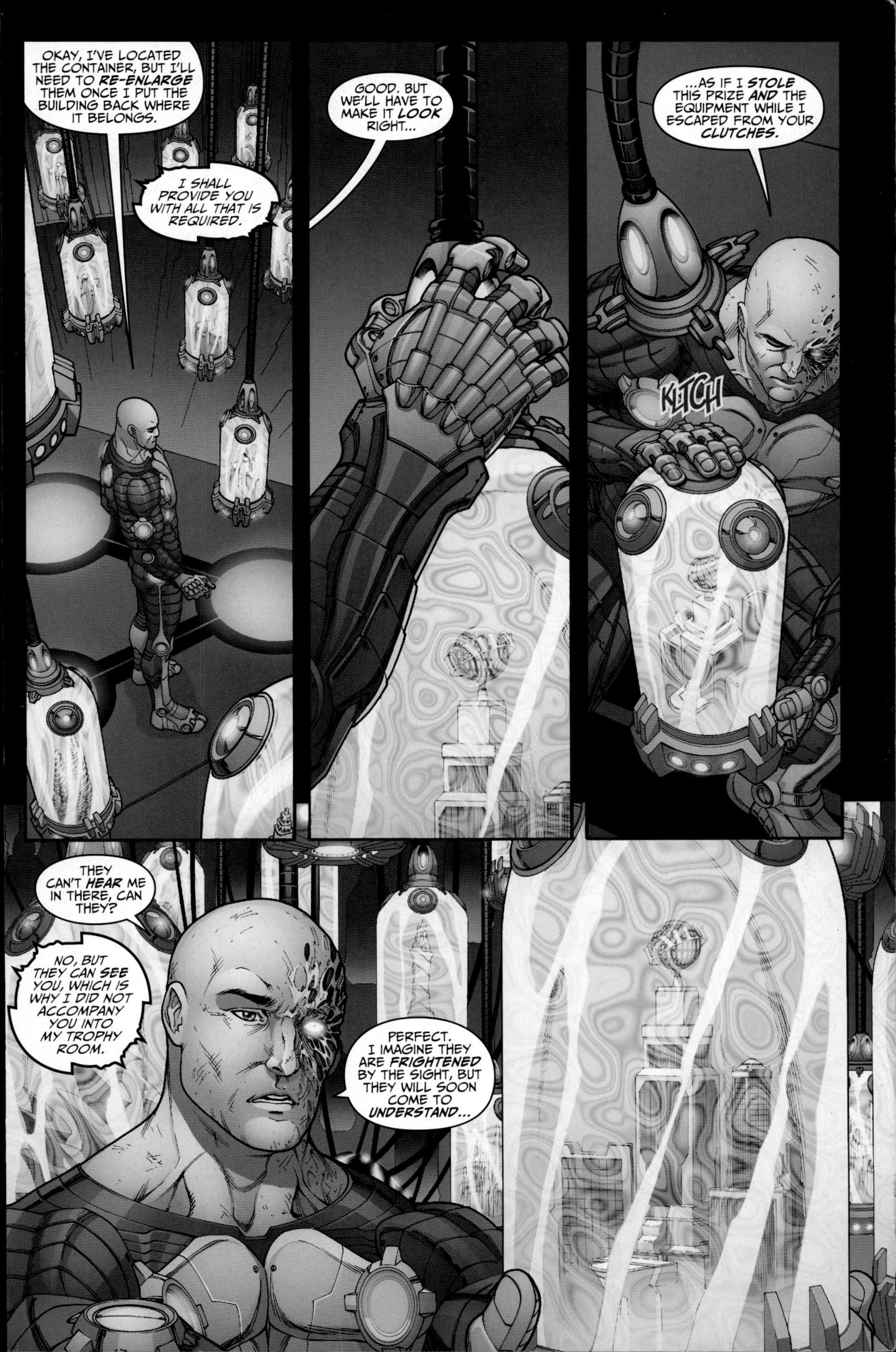
OKAY, I'VE LOCATED THE CONTAINER, BUT I'LL NEED TO RE-ENLARGE THEM ONCE I PUT THE BUILDING BACK WHERE IT BELONGS.
I SHALL PROVIDE YOU WITH ALL THAT IS REQUIRED.
GOOD. BUT WE'LL HAVE TO MAKE IT LOOK RIGHT...
...AS IF I STOLE THIS PRIZE AND THE EQUIPMENT WHILE I ESCAPED FROM YOUR CLUTCHES.
KLTCH
THEY CAN'T HEAR ME IN THERE, CAN THEY?
NO, BUT THEY CAN SEE YOU, WHICH IS WHY I DID NOT ACCOMPANY YOU INTO MY TROPHY ROOM.
PERFECT. I IMAGINE THEY ARE FRIGHTENED BY THE SIGHT, BUT THEY WILL SOON COME TO UNDERSTAND...

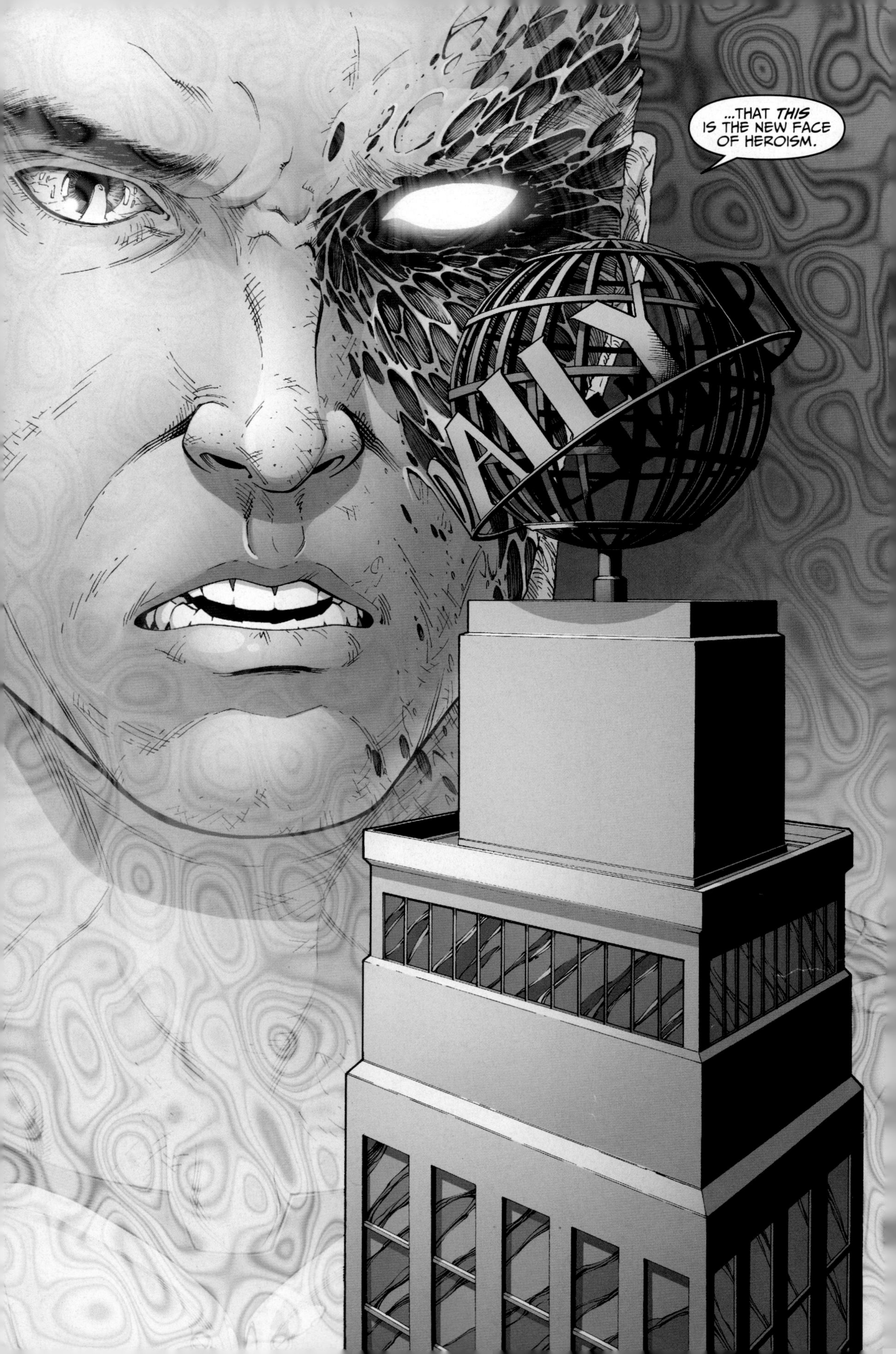
...THAT *THIS* IS THE NEW FACE OF HEROISM.

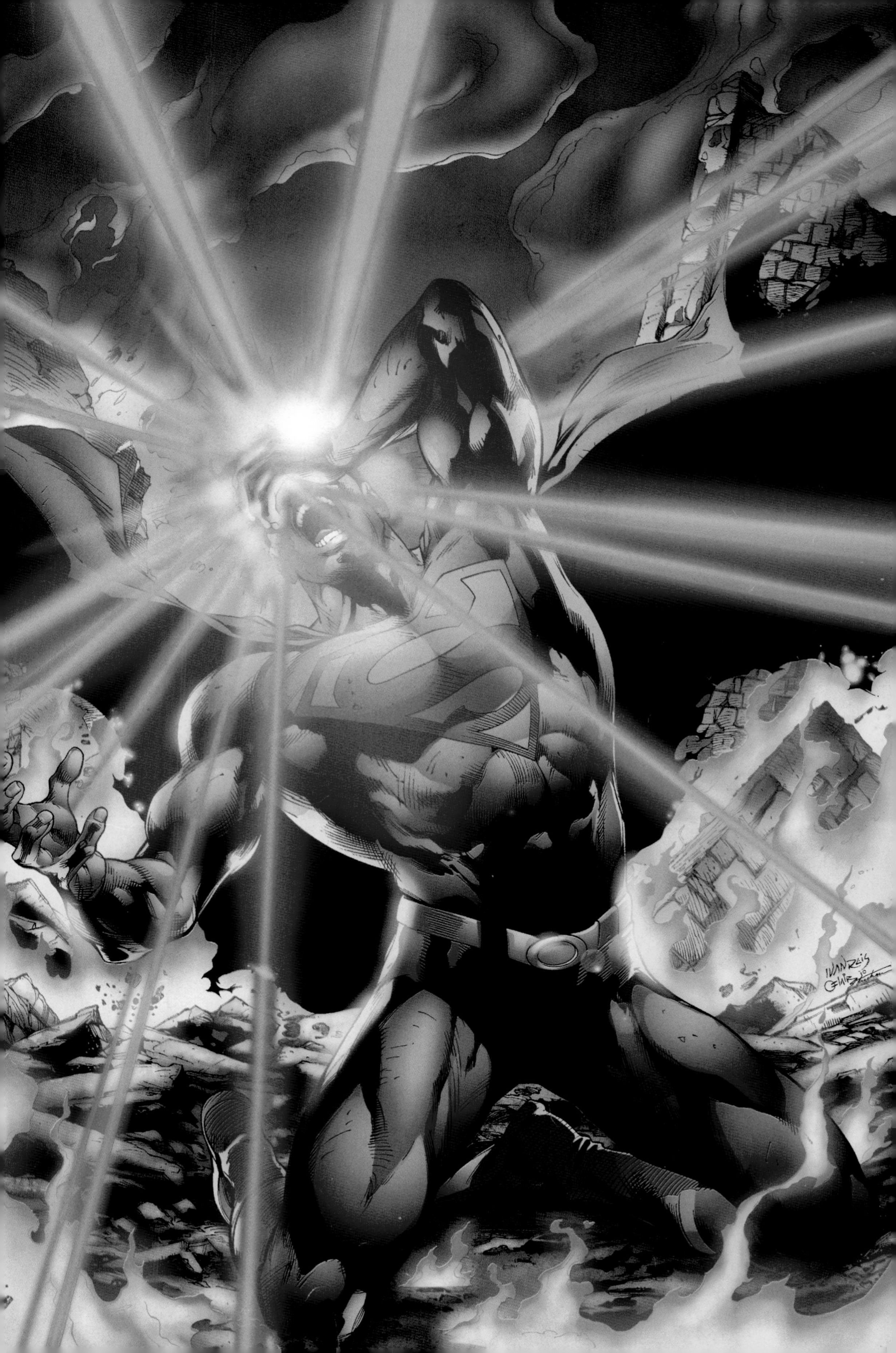

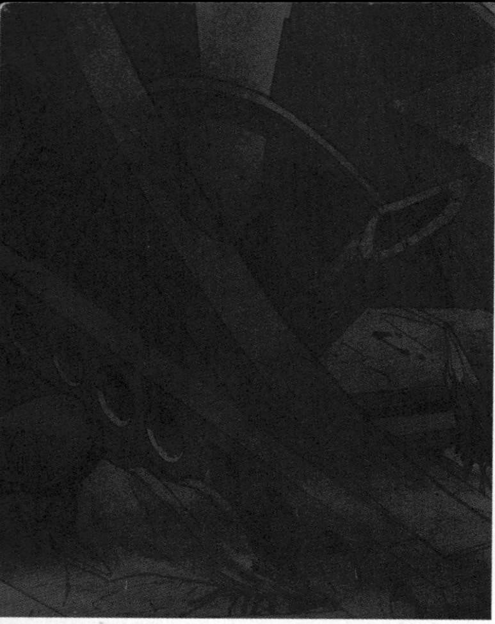
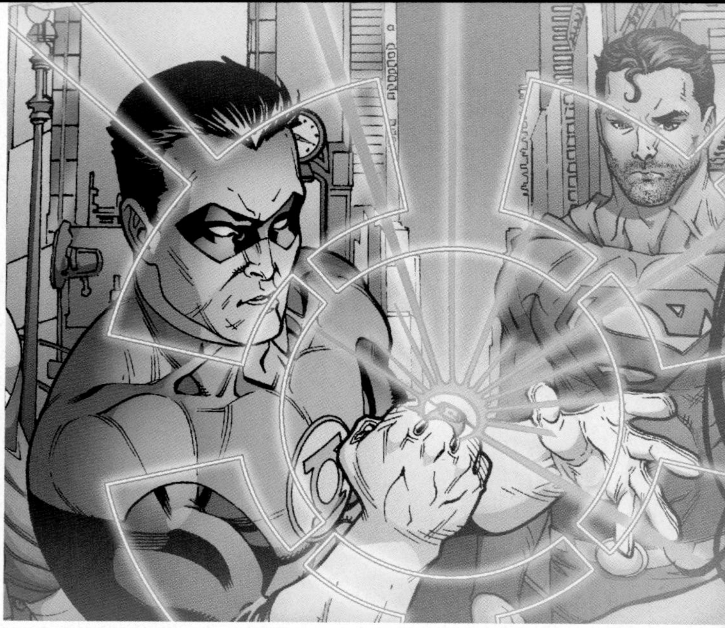

ANARCHY AT ARKHAM

Marv Wolfman
Writer

Mike S. Miller & Sergio Sandoval
Artists

Cover by Ivan Reis, Oclair Albert & Carrie Strachan

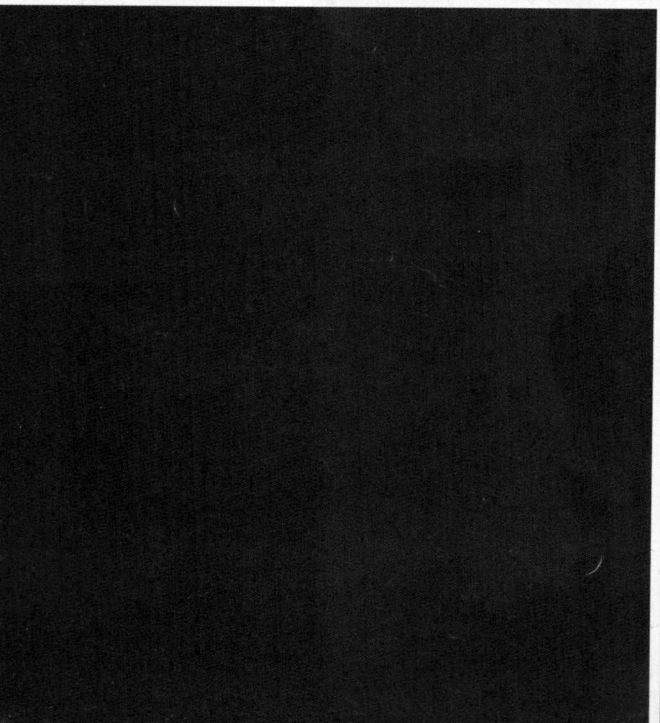
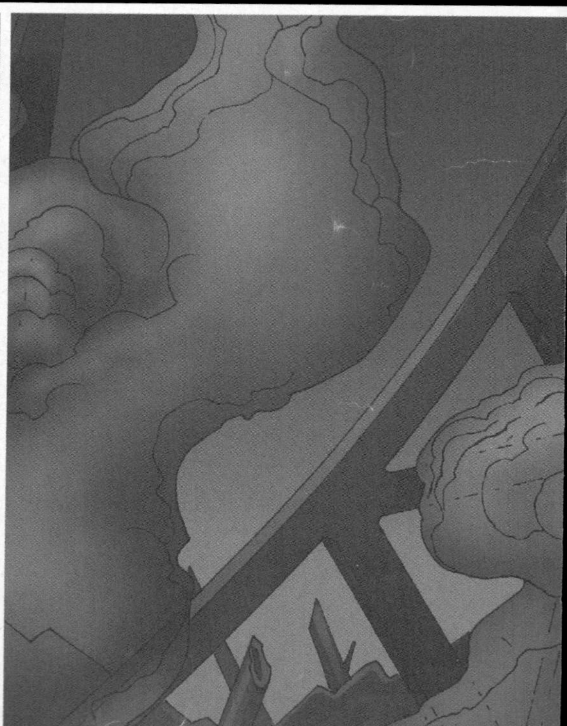

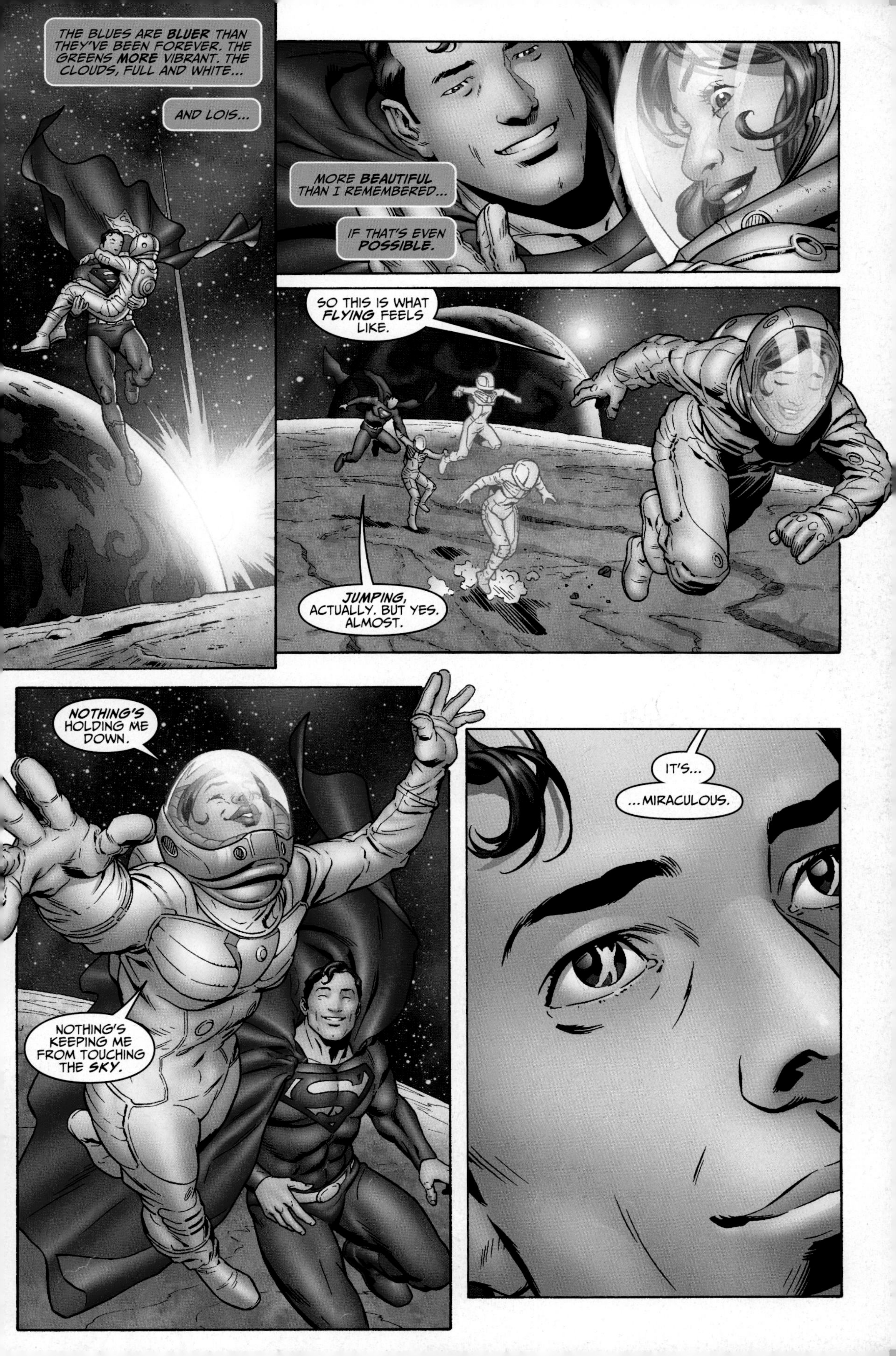
THE BLUES ARE BLUER THAN THEY'VE BEEN FOREVER. THE GREENS MORE VIBRANT. THE CLOUDS, FULL AND WHITE...
AND LOIS...
MORE BEAUTIFUL THAN I REMEMBERED...
IF THAT'S EVEN POSSIBLE.
SO THIS IS WHAT FLYING FEELS LIKE.
JUMPING, ACTUALLY. BUT YES. ALMOST.
NOTHING'S HOLDING ME DOWN.
NOTHING'S KEEPING ME FROM TOUCHING THE SKY.
IT'S...
...MIRACULOUS.

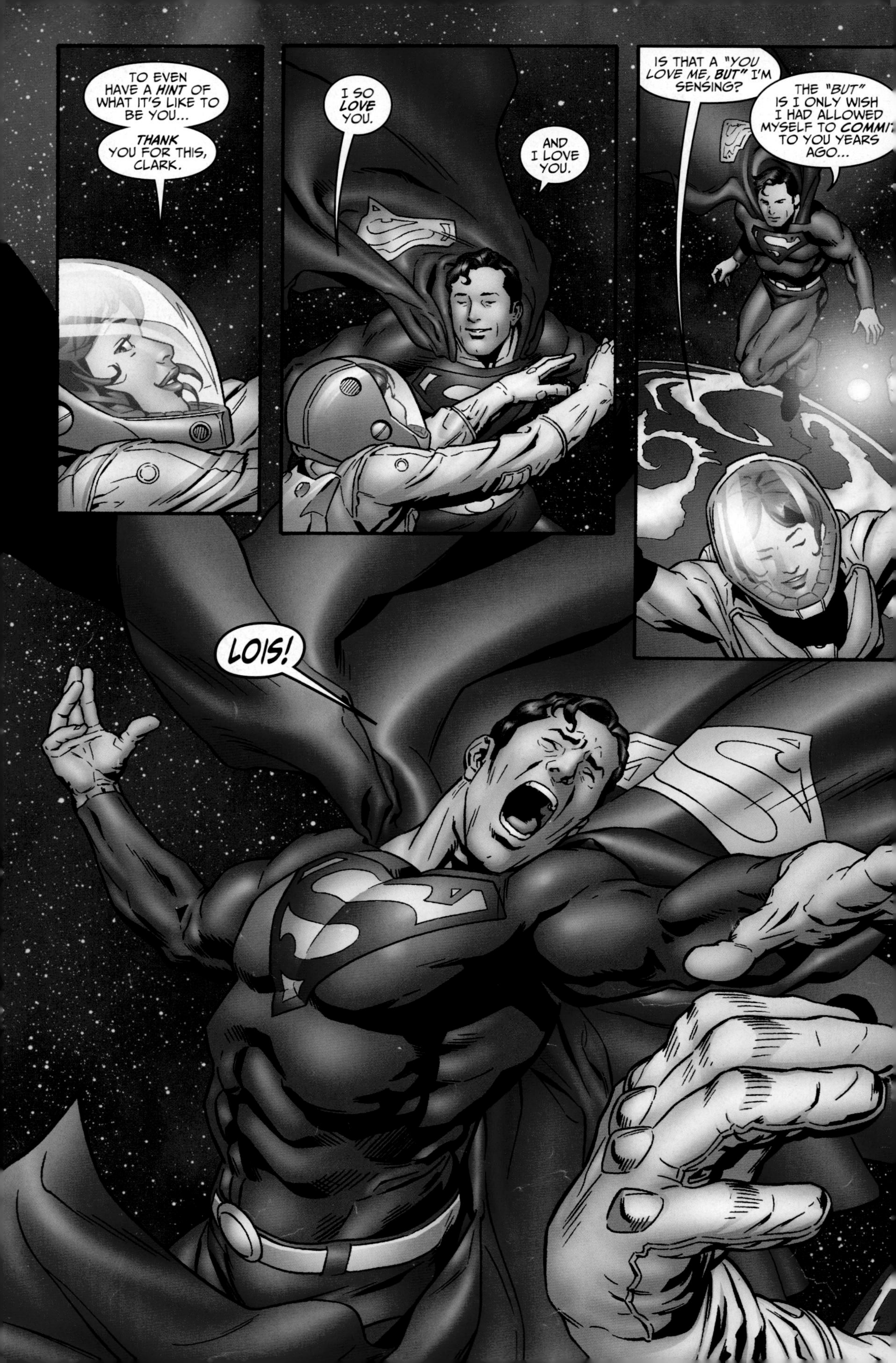
TO EVEN HAVE A HINT OF WHAT IT'S LIKE TO BE YOU...
THANK YOU FOR THIS, CLARK.
I SO LOVE YOU.
AND I LOVE YOU.
IS THAT A "YOU LOVE ME, BUT" I'M SENSING?
THE "BUT" IS I ONLY WISH I HAD ALLOWED MYSELF TO COMMIT TO YOU YEARS AGO...
LOIS!

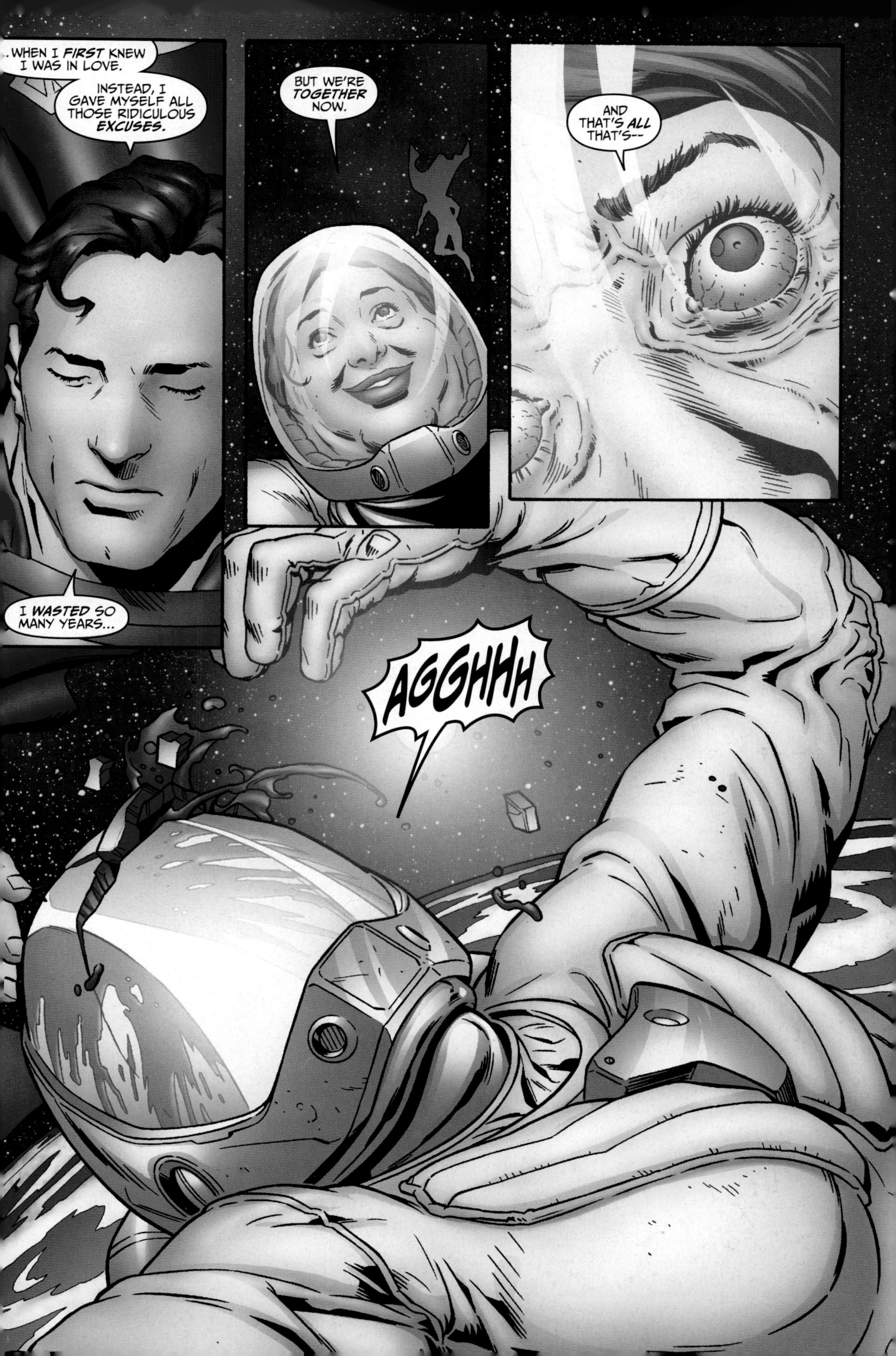

...WHEN I FIRST KNEW I WAS IN LOVE.
INSTEAD, I GAVE MYSELF ALL THOSE RIDICULOUS EXCUSES.
I WASTED SO MANY YEARS...
BUT WE'RE TOGETHER NOW.
AND THAT'S ALL THAT'S--
AGGHHH

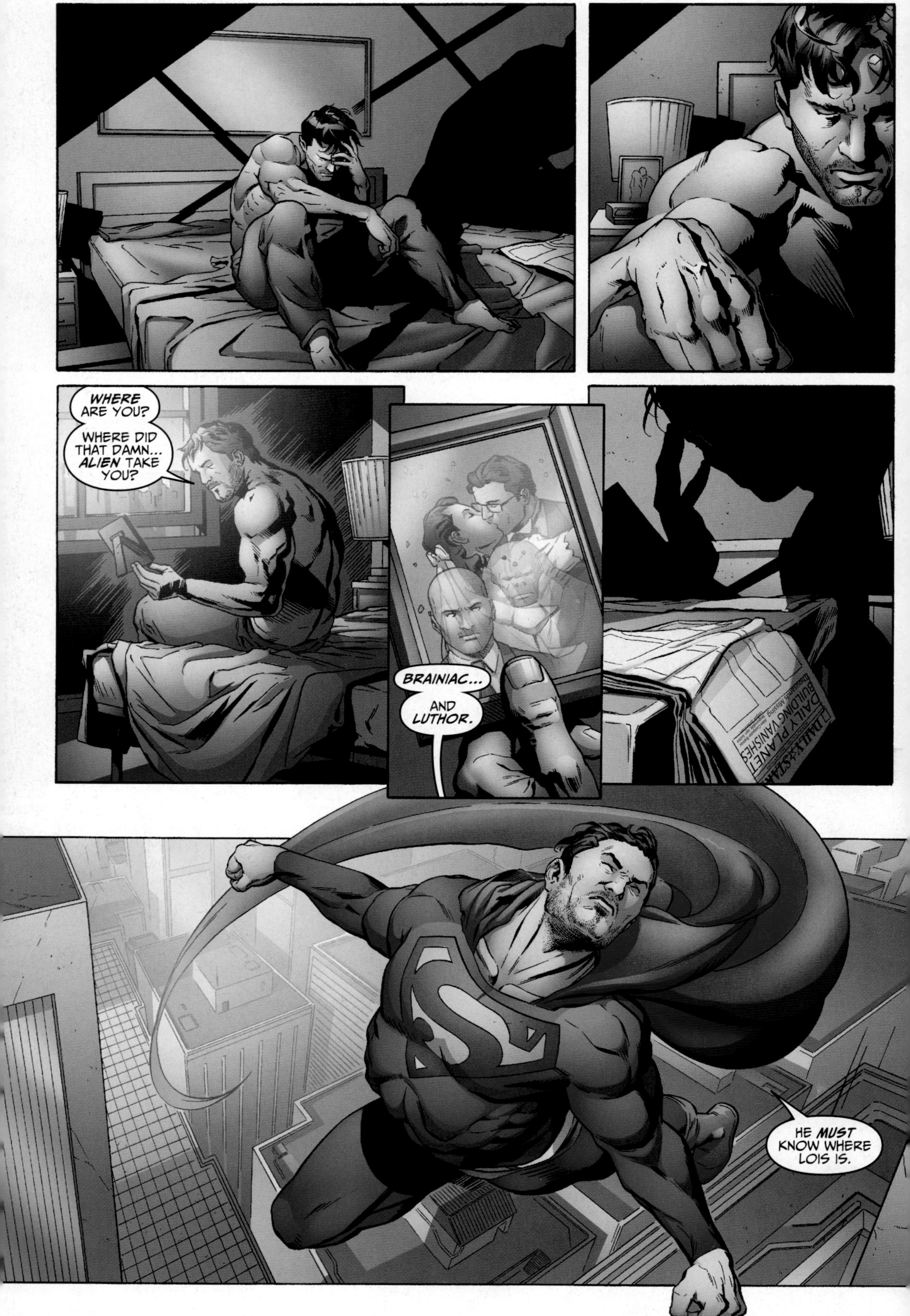
WHERE ARE YOU?
WHERE DID THAT DAMN... ALIEN TAKE YOU?
BRAINIAC...
AND LUTHOR.
DAILY PLANET
BUILDING VANISHES
HE MUST KNOW WHERE LOIS IS.

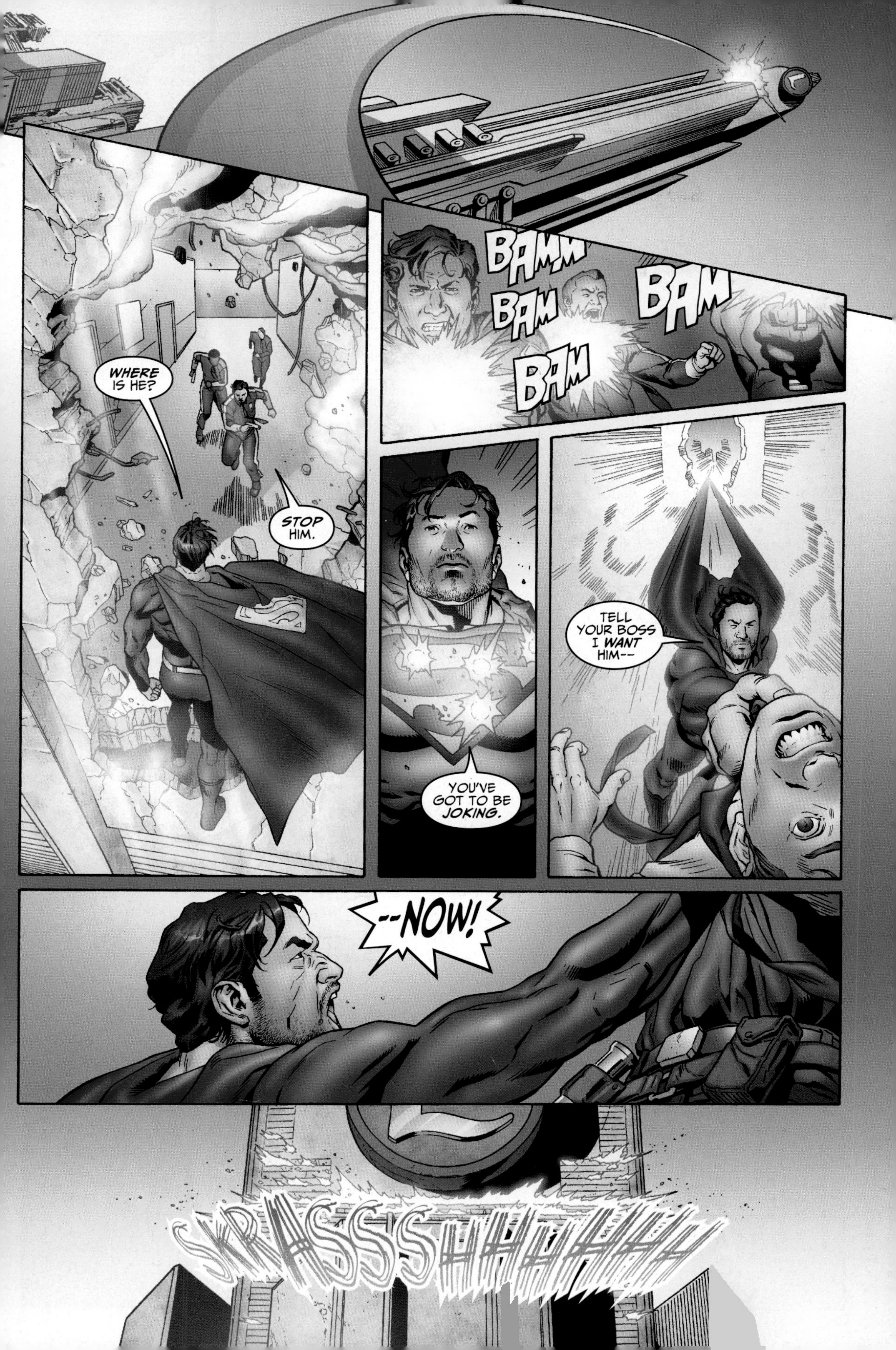

WHERE IS HE?
STOP HIM.
BAMM
BAM
BAM
BAM
YOU'VE GOT TO BE JOKING.
TELL YOUR BOSS I WANT HIM--
--NOW!
SKRASSSSHHHHHHH

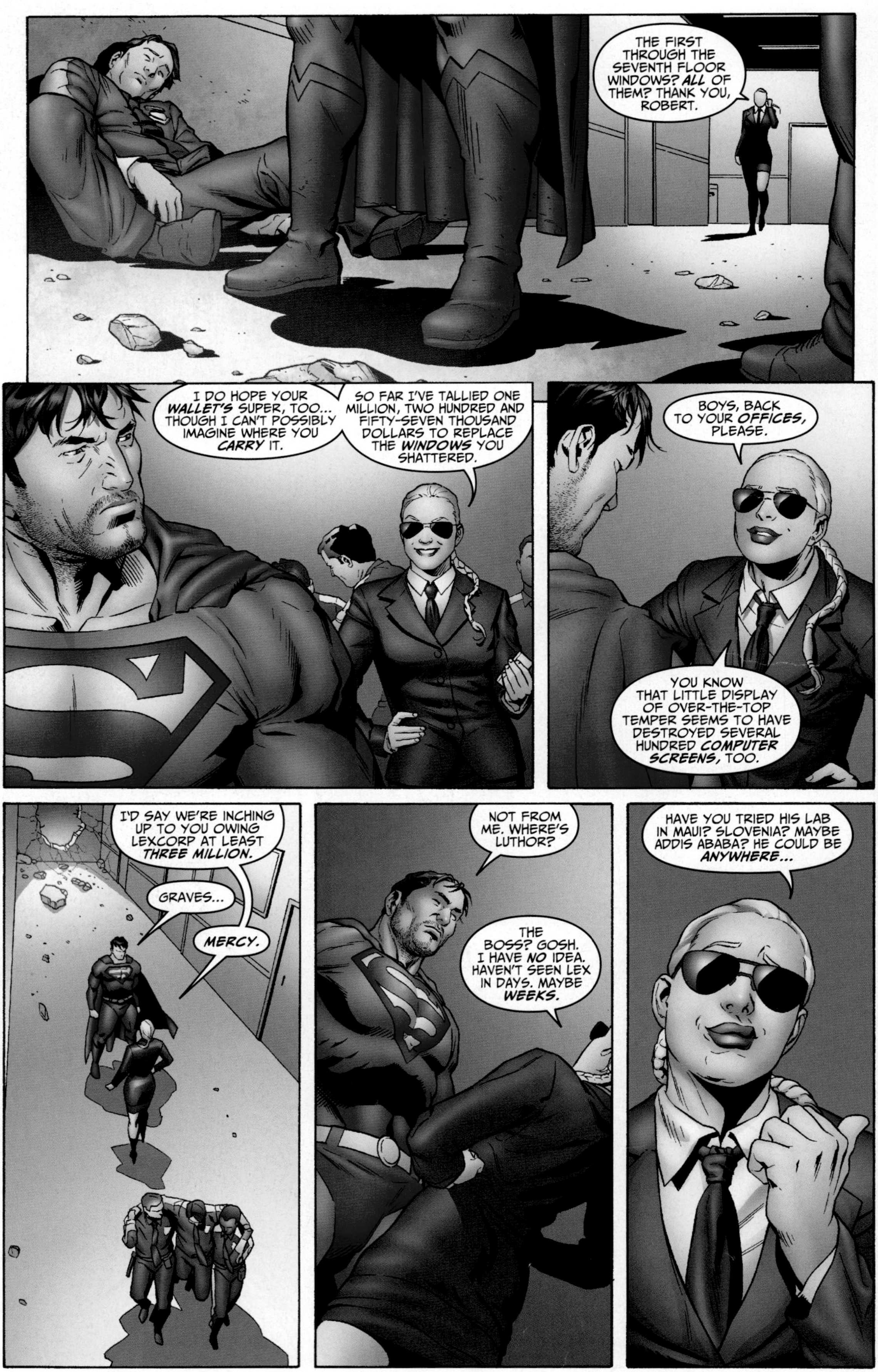
THE FIRST THROUGH THE SEVENTH FLOOR WINDOWS? ALL OF THEM? THANK YOU, ROBERT.
I DO HOPE YOUR WALLET'S SUPER, TOO... THOUGH I CAN'T POSSIBLY IMAGINE WHERE YOU CARRY IT.
SO FAR I'VE TALLIED ONE MILLION, TWO HUNDRED AND FIFTY-SEVEN THOUSAND DOLLARS TO REPLACE THE WINDOWS YOU SHATTERED.
BOYS, BACK TO YOUR OFFICES, PLEASE.
YOU KNOW THAT LITTLE DISPLAY OF OVER-THE-TOP TEMPER SEEMS TO HAVE DESTROYED SEVERAL HUNDRED COMPUTER SCREENS, TOO.
I'D SAY WE'RE INCHING UP TO YOU OWING LEXCORP AT LEAST THREE MILLION.
GRAVES...
MERCY.
NOT FROM ME. WHERE'S LUTHOR?
THE BOSS? GOSH. I HAVE NO IDEA. HAVEN'T SEEN LEX IN DAYS. MAYBE WEEKS.
HAVE YOU TRIED HIS LAB IN MAUI? SLOVENIA? MAYBE ADDIS ABABA? HE COULD BE ANYWHERE...

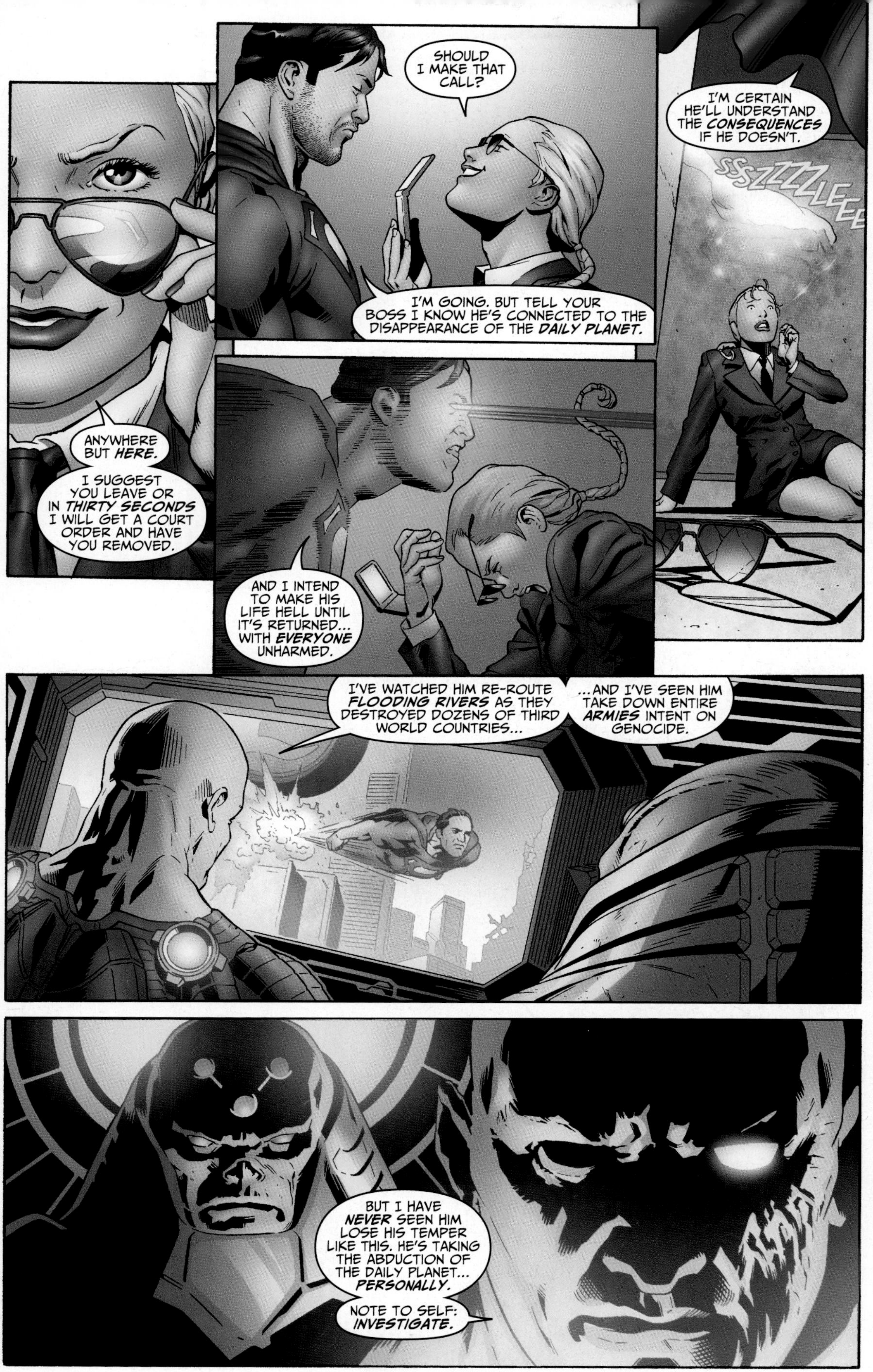

SHOULD I MAKE THAT CALL?
I'M CERTAIN HE'LL UNDERSTAND THE CONSEQUENCES IF HE DOESN'T.
ANYWHERE BUT HERE.
I SUGGEST YOU LEAVE OR IN THIRTY SECONDS I WILL GET A COURT ORDER AND HAVE YOU REMOVED.
I'M GOING. BUT TELL YOUR BOSS I KNOW HE'S CONNECTED TO THE DISAPPEARANCE OF THE DAILY PLANET.
AND I INTEND TO MAKE HIS LIFE HELL UNTIL IT'S RETURNED... WITH EVERYONE UNHARMED.
SSSZZZZLEEE
I'VE WATCHED HIM RE-ROUTE FLOODING RIVERS AS THEY DESTROYED DOZENS OF THIRD WORLD COUNTRIES...
...AND I'VE SEEN HIM TAKE DOWN ENTIRE ARMIES INTENT ON GENOCIDE.
BUT I HAVE NEVER SEEN HIM LOSE HIS TEMPER LIKE THIS. HE'S TAKING THE ABDUCTION OF THE DAILY PLANET... PERSONALLY.
NOTE TO SELF: INVESTIGATE.

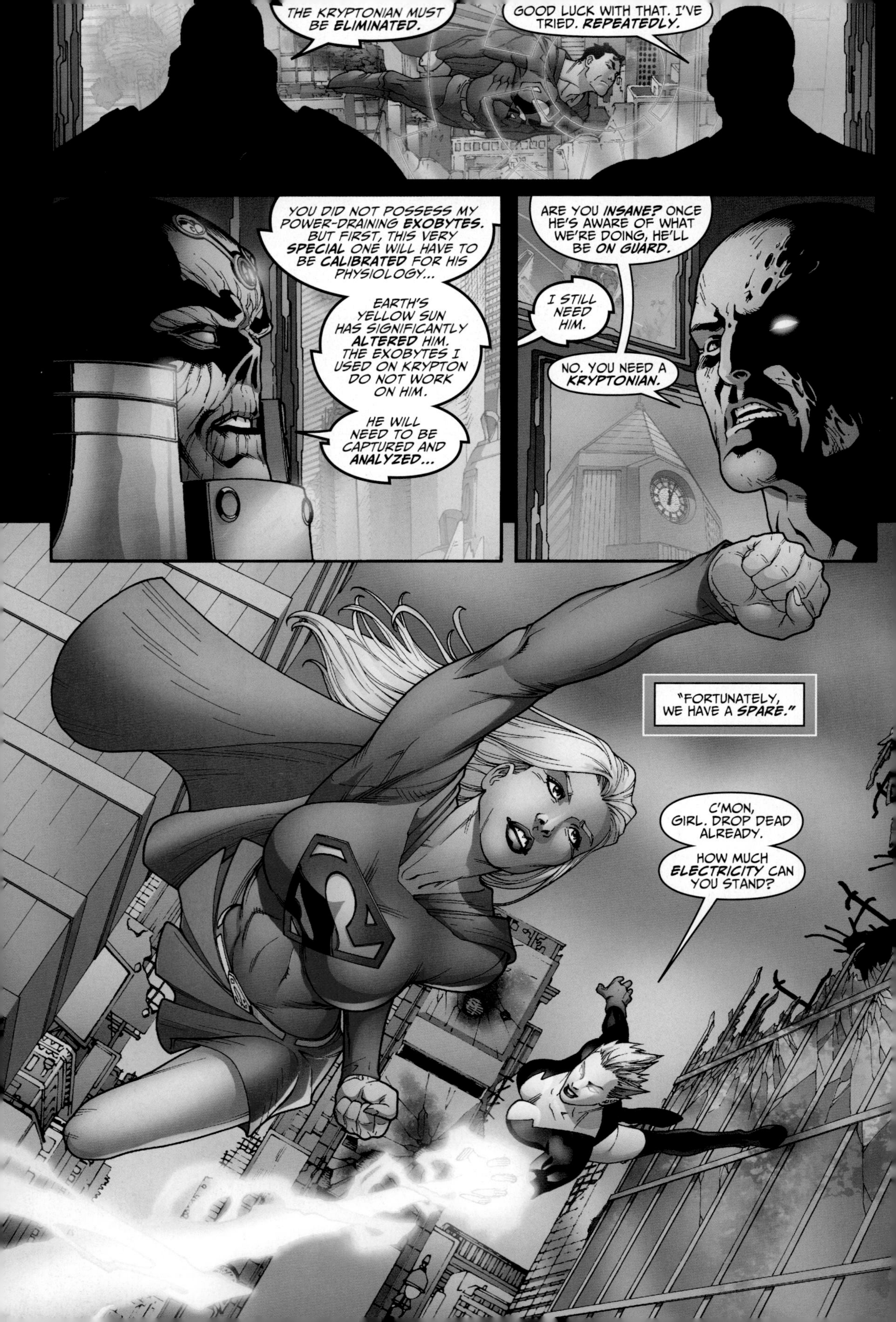
THE KRYPTONIAN MUST BE ELIMINATED.
GOOD LUCK WITH THAT. I'VE TRIED. REPEATEDLY.
YOU DID NOT POSSESS MY POWER-DRAINING EXOBYTES. BUT FIRST, THIS VERY SPECIAL ONE WILL HAVE TO BE CALIBRATED FOR HIS PHYSIOLOGY...
EARTH'S YELLOW SUN HAS SIGNIFICANTLY ALTERED HIM. THE EXOBYTES I USED ON KRYPTON DO NOT WORK ON HIM.
HE WILL NEED TO BE CAPTURED AND ANALYZED...
ARE YOU INSANE? ONCE HE'S AWARE OF WHAT WE'RE DOING, HE'LL BE ON GUARD.
I STILL NEED HIM.
NO. YOU NEED A KRYPTONIAN.
"FORTUNATELY, WE HAVE A SPARE."
C'MON, GIRL. DROP DEAD ALREADY.
HOW MUCH ELECTRICITY CAN YOU STAND?

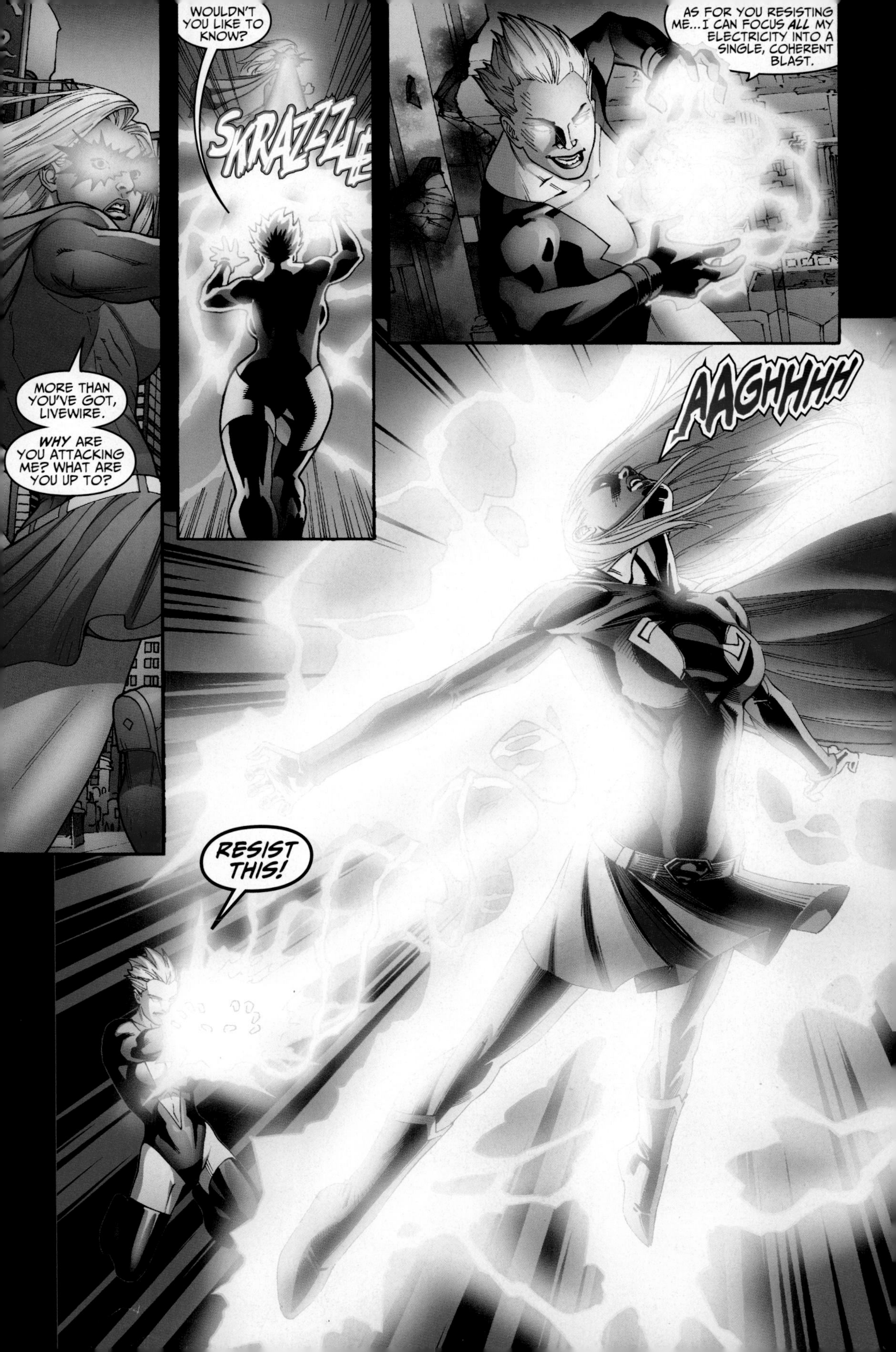
WOULDN'T YOU LIKE TO KNOW?
SKRAZZZZZZ
MORE THAN YOU'VE GOT, LIVEWIRE.
WHY ARE YOU ATTACKING ME? WHAT ARE YOU UP TO?
AS FOR YOU RESISTING ME... I CAN FOCUS ALL MY ELECTRICITY INTO A SINGLE, COHERENT BLAST.
AAGHHHH
RESIST THIS!

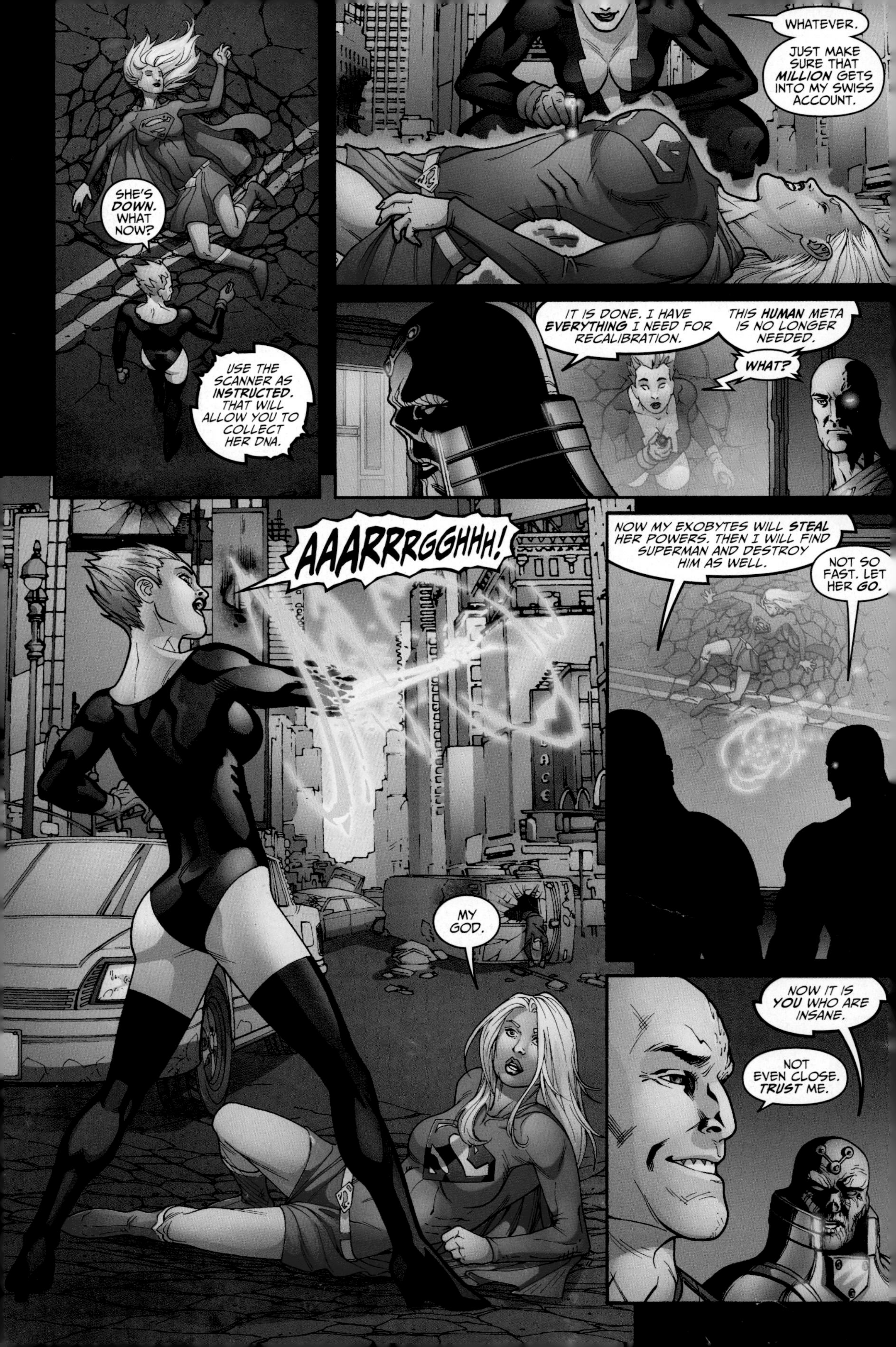
SHE'S DOWN. WHAT NOW?
USE THE SCANNER AS INSTRUCTED. THAT WILL ALLOW YOU TO COLLECT HER DNA.
WHATEVER.
JUST MAKE SURE THAT MILLION GETS INTO MY SWISS ACCOUNT.
IT IS DONE. I HAVE EVERYTHING I NEED FOR RECALIBRATION.
THIS HUMAN META IS NO LONGER NEEDED.
WHAT?
AAARRRGGHHH!
MY GOD.
NOW MY EXOBYTES WILL STEAL HER POWERS. THEN I WILL FIND SUPERMAN AND DESTROY HIM AS WELL.
NOT SO FAST. LET HER GO.
NOW IT IS YOU WHO ARE INSANE.
NOT EVEN CLOSE. TRUST ME.

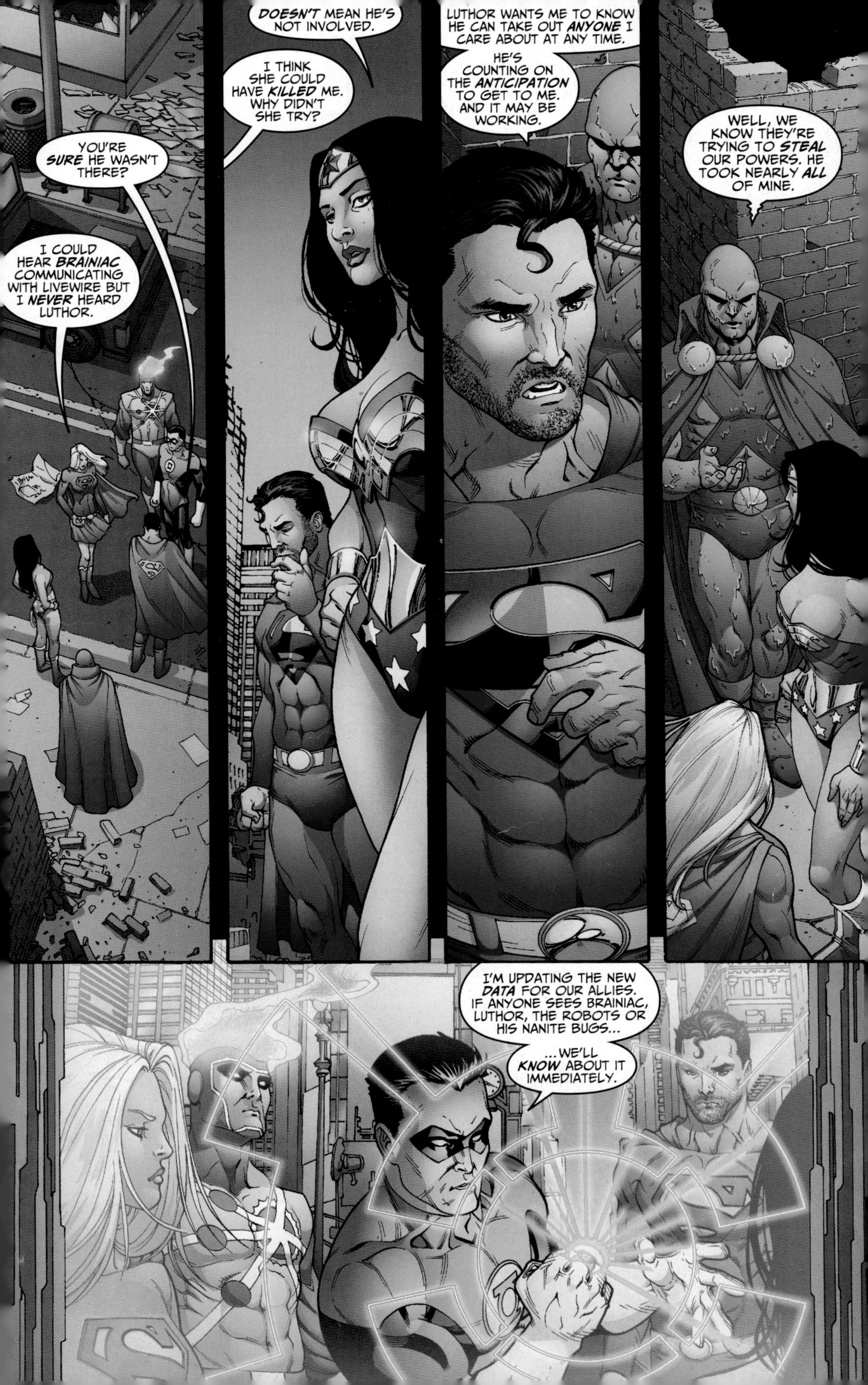
YOU'RE SURE HE WASN'T THERE?
I COULD HEAR BRAINIAC COMMUNICATING WITH LIVEWIRE BUT I NEVER HEARD LUTHOR.
DOESN'T MEAN HE'S NOT INVOLVED.
I THINK SHE COULD HAVE KILLED ME. WHY DIDN'T SHE TRY?
LUTHOR WANTS ME TO KNOW HE CAN TAKE OUT ANYONE I CARE ABOUT AT ANY TIME.
HE'S COUNTING ON THE ANTICIPATION TO GET TO ME. AND IT MAY BE WORKING.
WELL, WE KNOW THEY'RE TRYING TO STEAL OUR POWERS. HE TOOK NEARLY ALL OF MINE.
I'M UPDATING THE NEW DATA FOR OUR ALLIES. IF ANYONE SEES BRAINIAC, LUTHOR, THE ROBOTS OR HIS NANITE BUGS...
...WE'LL KNOW ABOUT IT IMMEDIATELY.

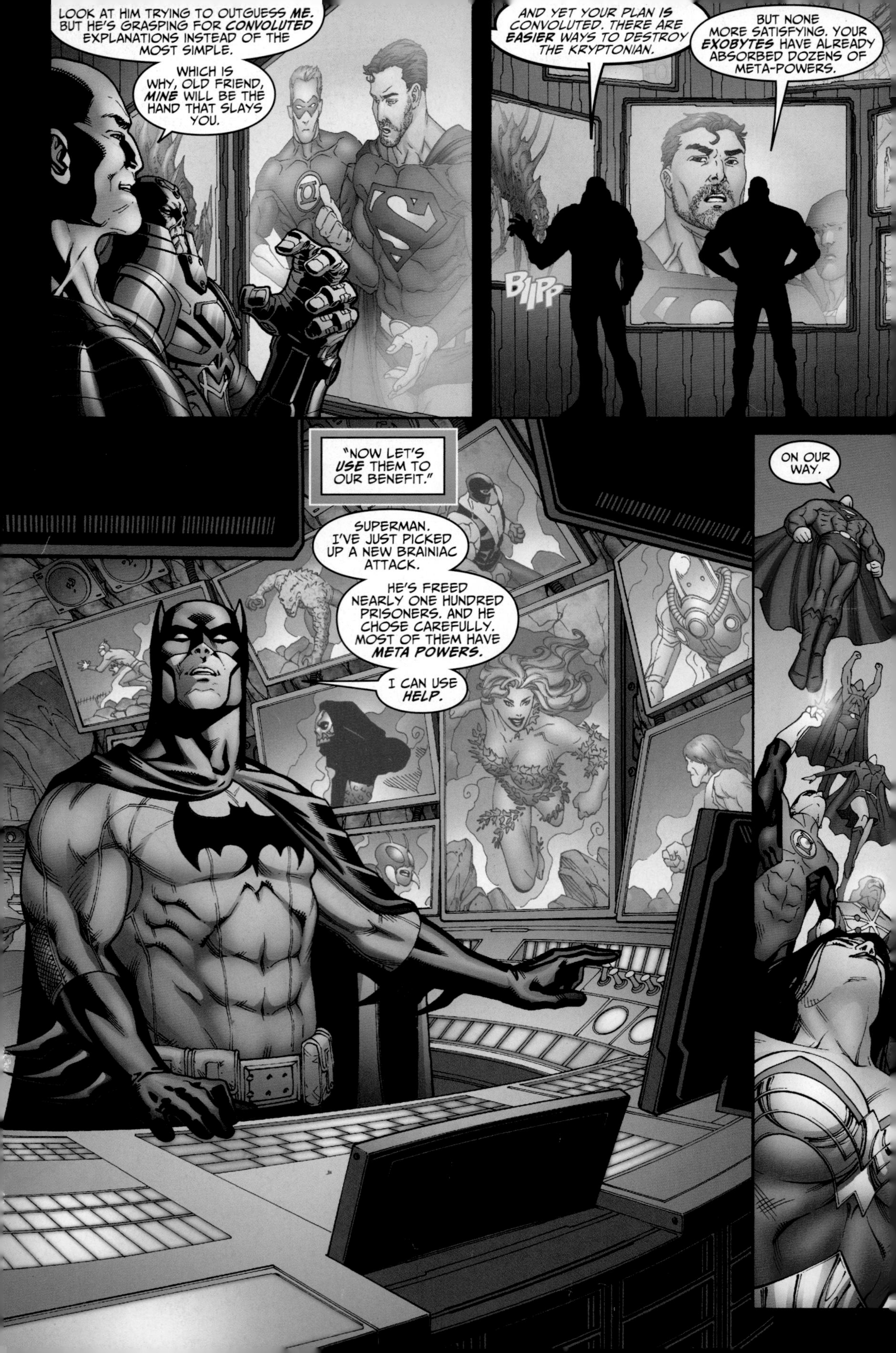

LOOK AT HIM TRYING TO OUTGUESS ME. BUT HE'S GRASPING FOR CONVOLUTED EXPLANATIONS INSTEAD OF THE MOST SIMPLE.
WHICH IS WHY, OLD FRIEND, MINE WILL BE THE HAND THAT SLAYS YOU.
AND YET YOUR PLAN IS CONVOLUTED. THERE ARE EASIER WAYS TO DESTROY THE KRYPTONIAN.
BUT NONE MORE SATISFYING. YOUR EXOBYTES HAVE ALREADY ABSORBED DOZENS OF META-POWERS.
BIIPP
"NOW LET'S USE THEM TO OUR BENEFIT."
SUPERMAN. I'VE JUST PICKED UP A NEW BRAINIAC ATTACK.
HE'S FREED NEARLY ONE HUNDRED PRISONERS. AND HE CHOSE CAREFULLY. MOST OF THEM HAVE META POWERS.
I CAN USE HELP.
ON OUR WAY.

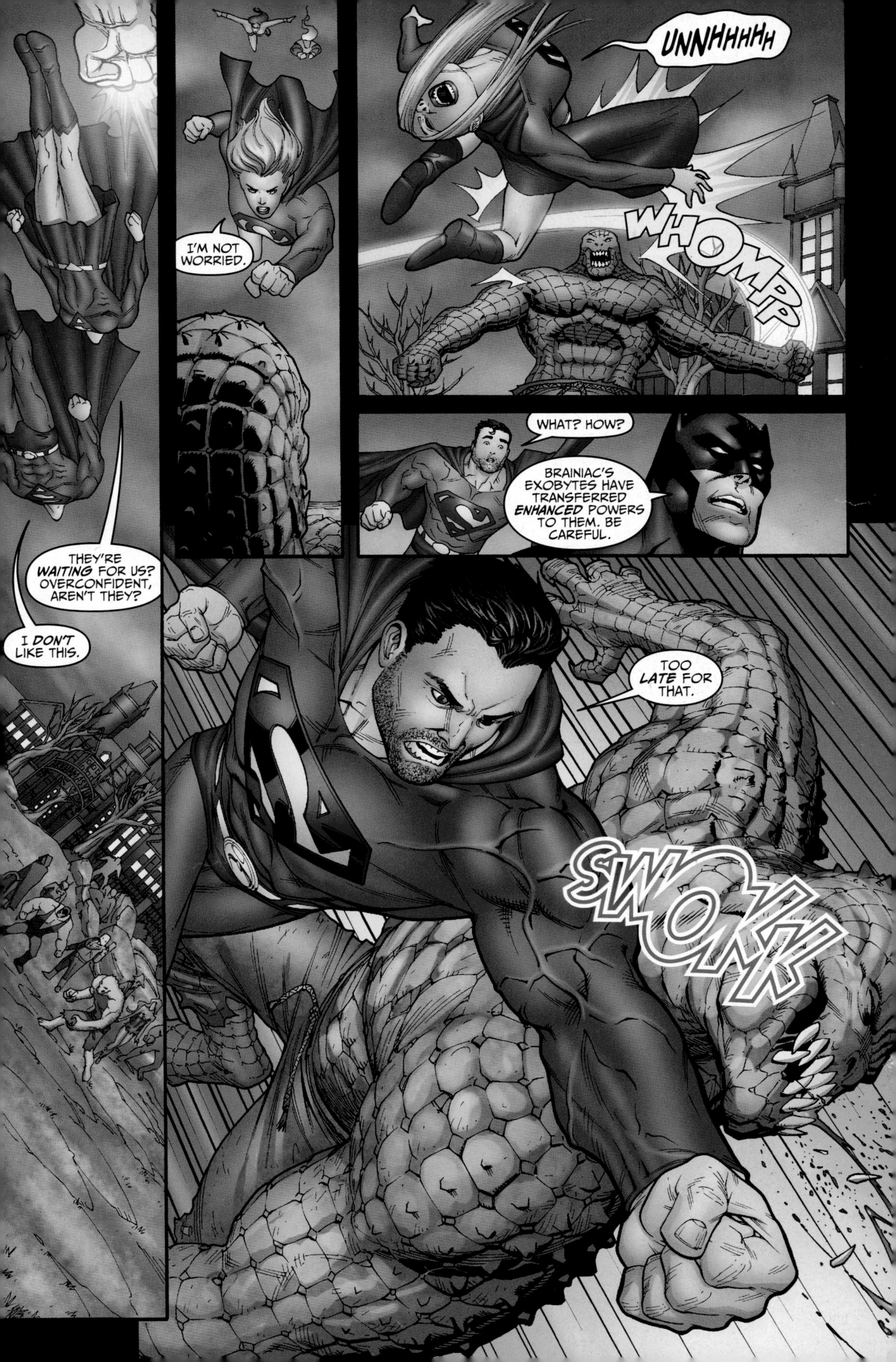
THEY'RE WAITING FOR US? OVERCONFIDENT, AREN'T THEY?
I DON'T LIKE THIS.
I'M NOT WORRIED.
UNNHHHHH
WHOMP
WHAT? HOW?
BRAINIAC'S EXOBYTES HAVE TRANSFERRED ENHANCED POWERS TO THEM. BE CAREFUL.
TOO LATE FOR THAT.
SWOK

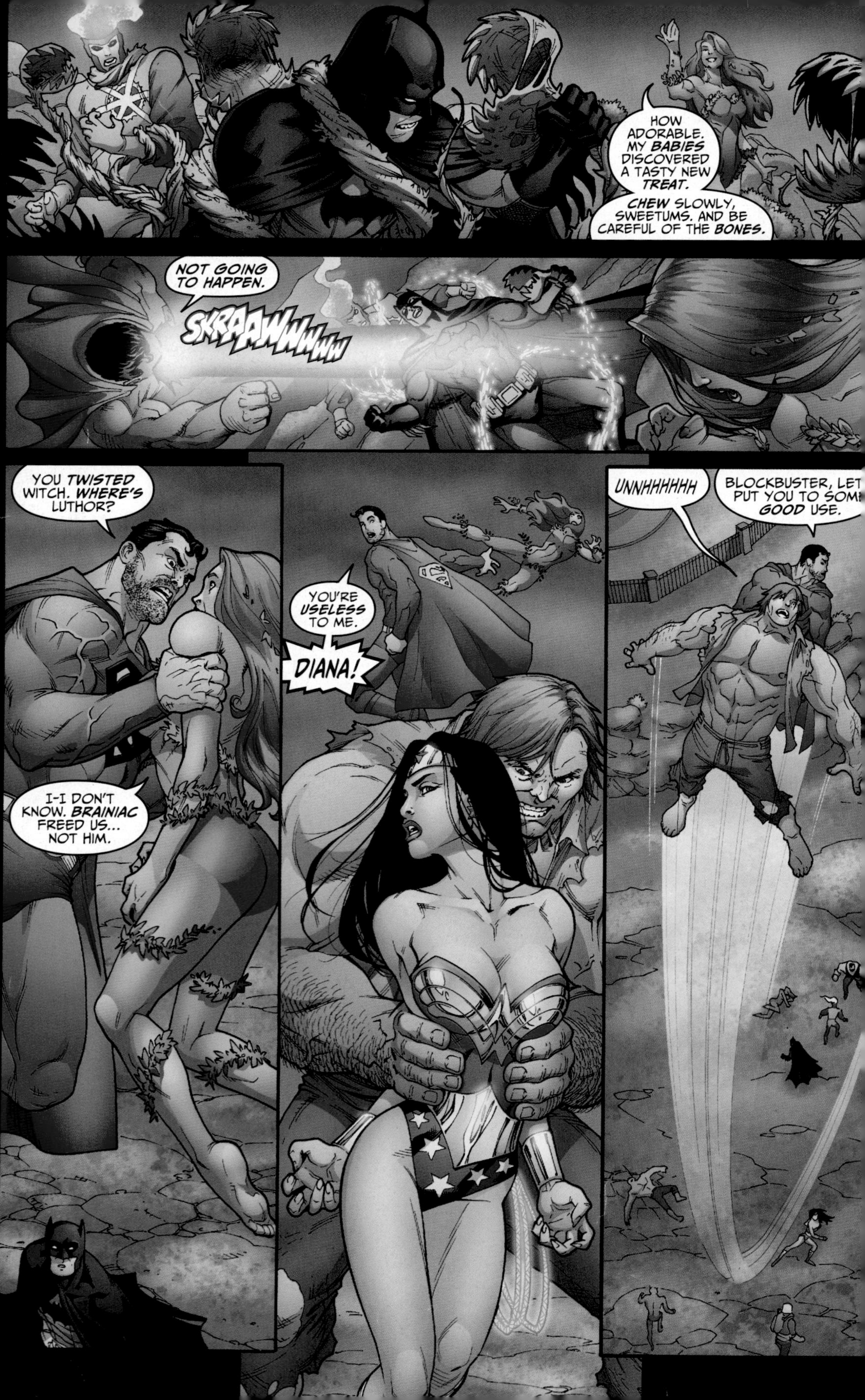
HOW ADORABLE. MY BABIES DISCOVERED A TASTY NEW TREAT.
CHEW SLOWLY, SWEETUMS. AND BE CAREFUL OF THE BONES.
NOT GOING TO HAPPEN.
SKRAAWWWWW
YOU TWISTED WITCH. WHERE'S LUTHOR?
I-I DON'T KNOW. BRAINIAC FREED US... NOT HIM.
YOU'RE USELESS TO ME.
DIANA!
UNNHHHHHH
BLOCKBUSTER, LET PUT YOU TO SOM GOOD USE.

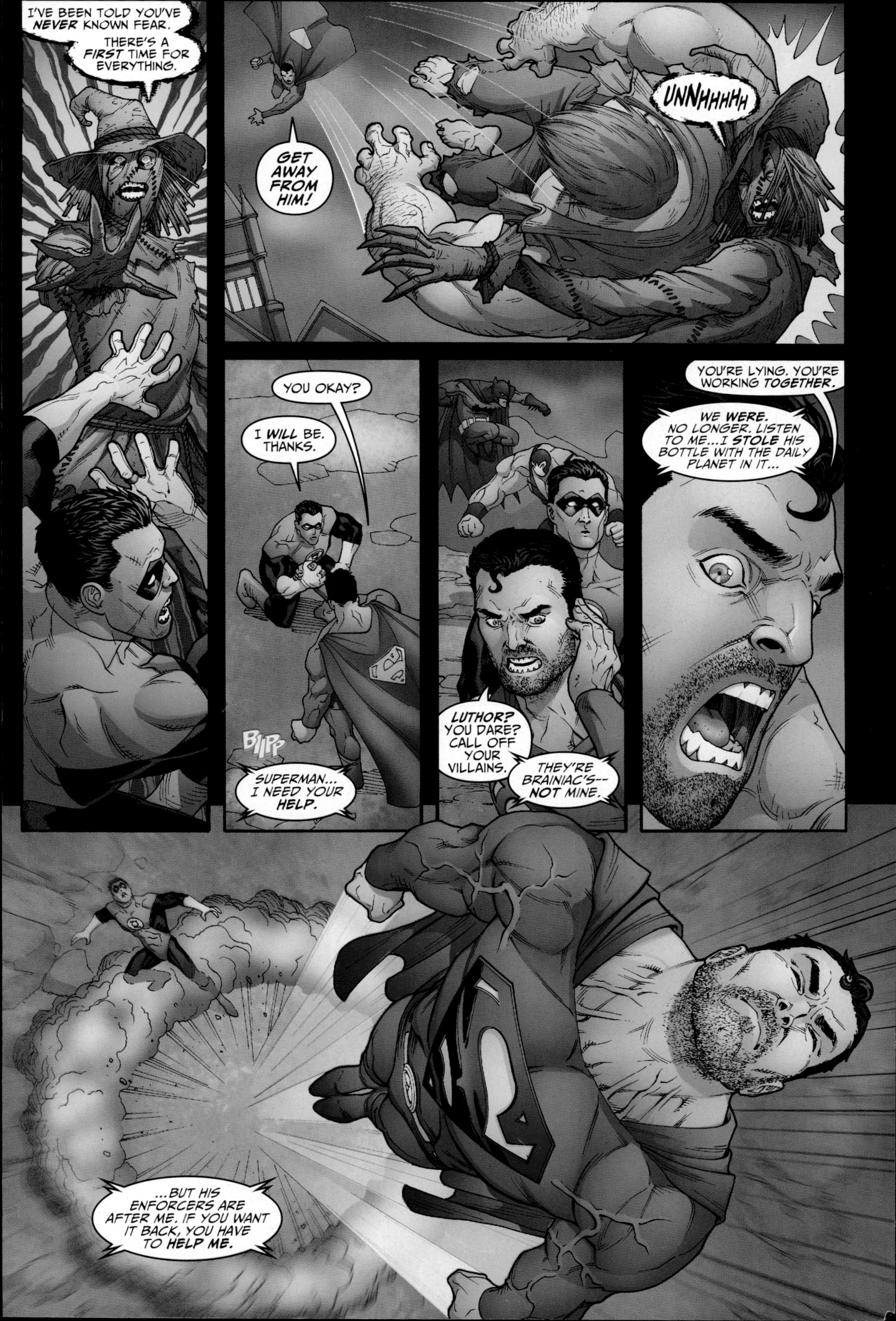

I'VE BEEN TOLD YOU'VE NEVER KNOWN FEAR.
THERE'S A FIRST TIME FOR EVERYTHING.
GET AWAY FROM HIM!
UNNHHHHH
YOU OKAY?
I WILL BE. THANKS.
BLIPP
SUPERMAN... I NEED YOUR HELP.
LUTHOR? YOU DARE? CALL OFF YOUR VILLAINS.
THEY'RE BRAINIAC'S-- NOT MINE.
YOU'RE LYING. YOU'RE WORKING TOGETHER.
WE WERE. NO LONGER. LISTEN TO ME...I STOLE HIS BOTTLE WITH THE DAILY PLANET IN IT...
...BUT HIS ENFORCERS ARE AFTER ME. IF YOU WANT IT BACK, YOU HAVE TO HELP ME.

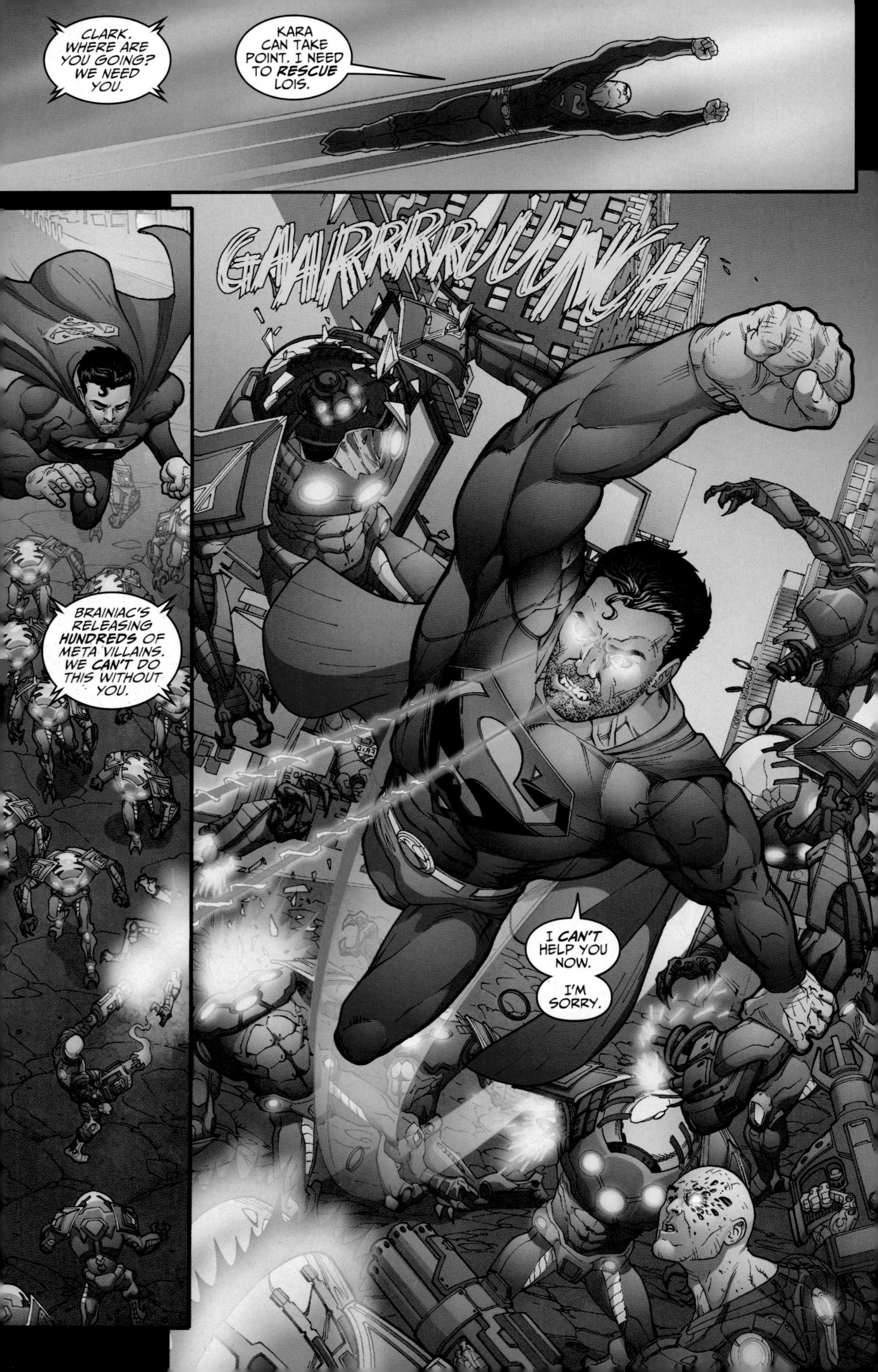
CLARK. WHERE ARE YOU GOING? WE NEED YOU.
KARA CAN TAKE POINT. I NEED TO RESCUE LOIS.
GAARRRUUNCH
BRAINIAC'S RELEASING HUNDREDS OF META VILLAINS. WE CAN'T DO THIS WITHOUT YOU.
I CAN'T HELP YOU NOW.
I'M SORRY.

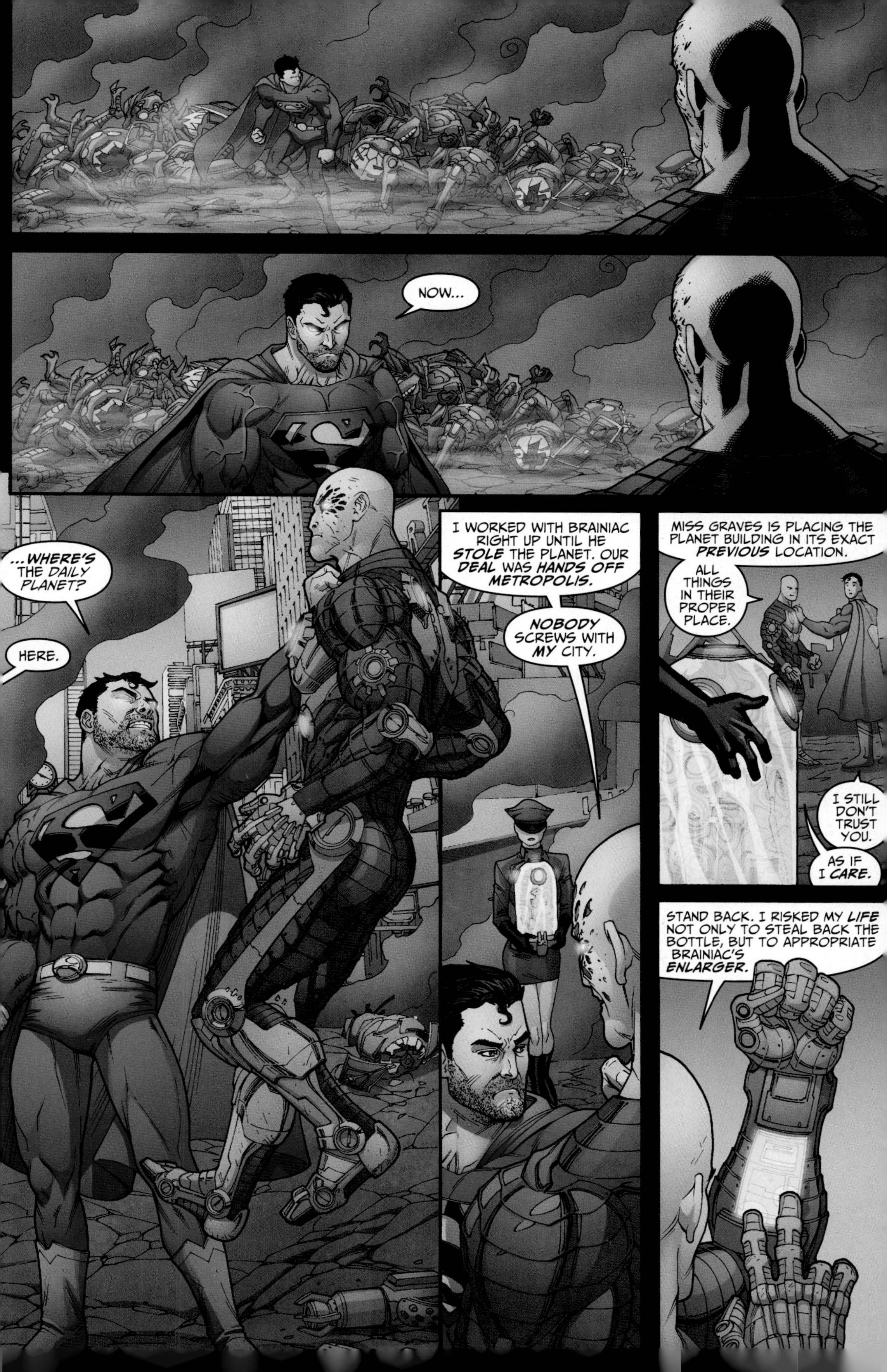
NOW...
...WHERE'S THE DAILY PLANET?
HERE.
I WORKED WITH BRAINIAC RIGHT UP UNTIL HE STOLE THE PLANET. OUR DEAL WAS HANDS OFF METROPOLIS.
NOBODY SCREWS WITH MY CITY.
MISS GRAVES IS PLACING THE PLANET BUILDING IN ITS EXACT PREVIOUS LOCATION.
ALL THINGS IN THEIR PROPER PLACE.
I STILL DON'T TRUST YOU.
AS IF I CARE.
STAND BACK. I RISKED MY LIFE NOT ONLY TO STEAL BACK THE BOTTLE, BUT TO APPROPRIATE BRAINIAC'S ENLARGER.

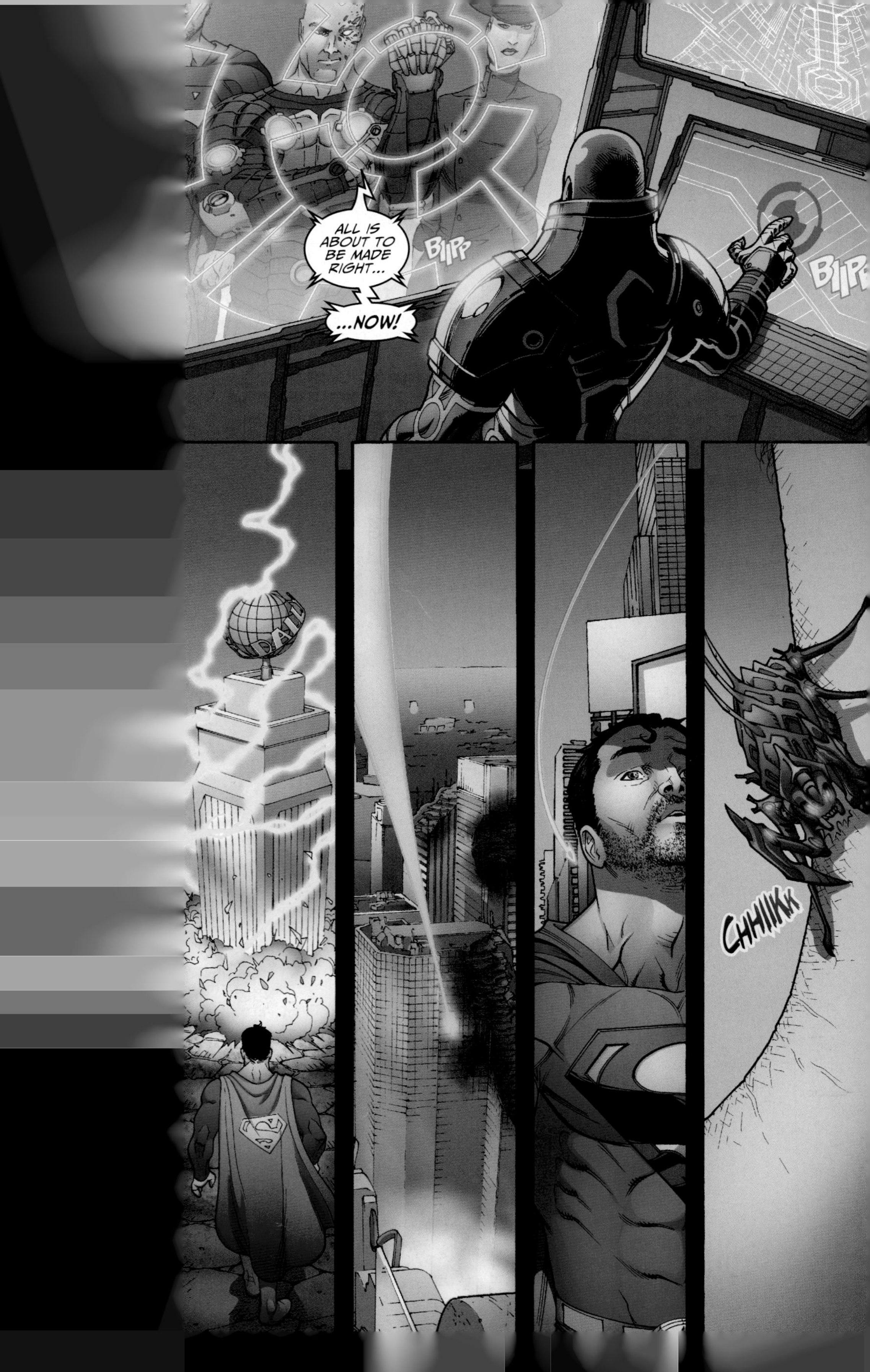
ALL IS ABOUT TO BE MADE RIGHT...
...NOW!
BIIPP
CHHIIKK

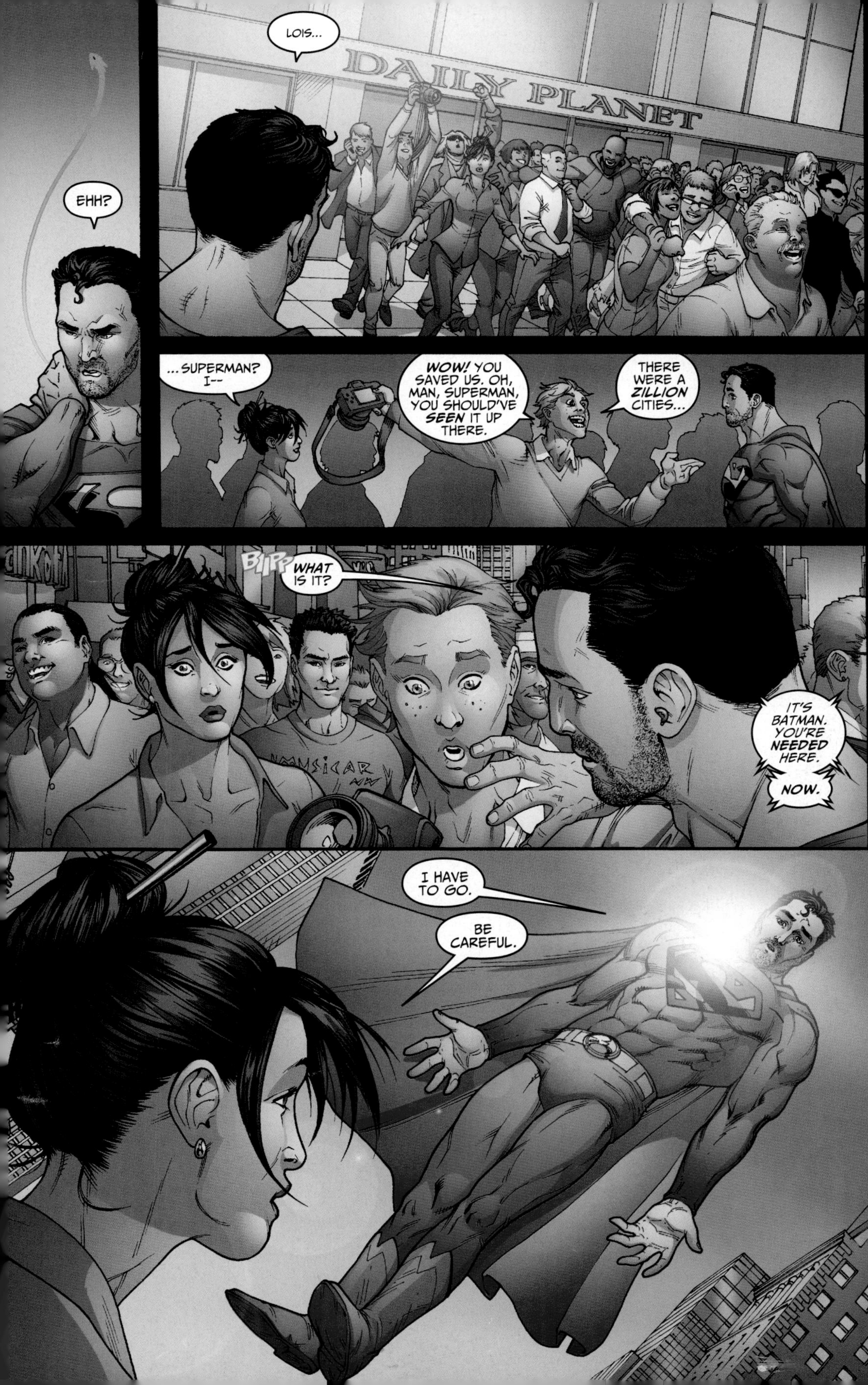
EHH?
LOIS...
...SUPERMAN? I--
WOW! YOU SAVED US. OH, MAN, SUPERMAN, YOU SHOULD'VE SEEN IT UP THERE.
THERE WERE A ZILLION CITIES...
DAILY PLANET
BLIPP
WHAT IS IT?
IT'S BATMAN. YOU'RE NEEDED HERE.
NOW.
I HAVE TO GO.
BE CAREFUL.

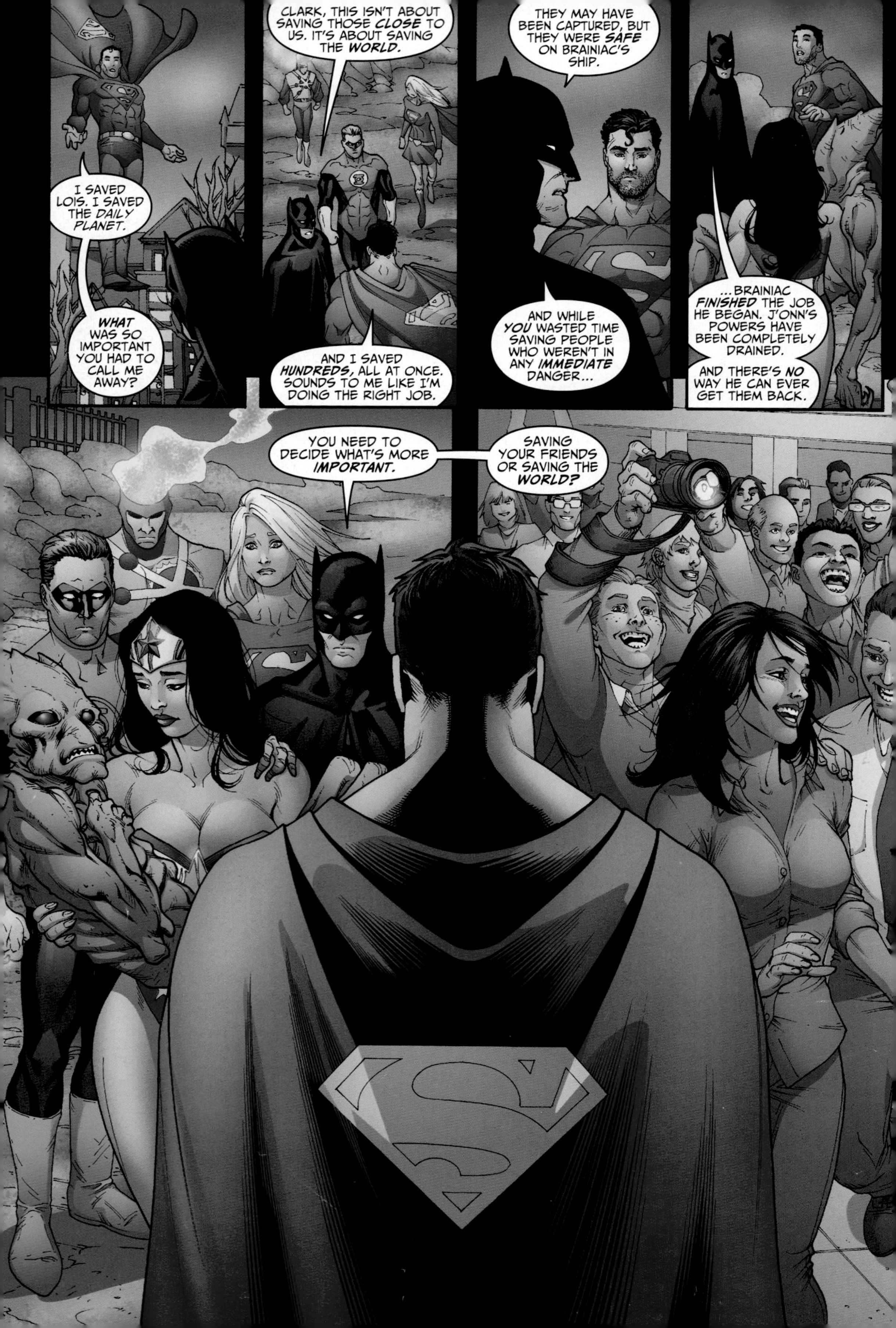

I SAVED LOIS. I SAVED THE DAILY PLANET.
WHAT WAS SO IMPORTANT YOU HAD TO CALL ME AWAY?
CLARK, THIS ISN'T ABOUT SAVING THOSE CLOSE TO US. IT'S ABOUT SAVING THE WORLD.
AND I SAVED HUNDREDS, ALL AT ONCE. SOUNDS TO ME LIKE I'M DOING THE RIGHT JOB.
THEY MAY HAVE BEEN CAPTURED, BUT THEY WERE SAFE ON BRAINIAC'S SHIP.
AND WHILE YOU WASTED TIME SAVING PEOPLE WHO WEREN'T IN ANY IMMEDIATE DANGER...
...BRAINIAC FINISHED THE JOB HE BEGAN. J'ONN'S POWERS HAVE BEEN COMPLETELY DRAINED.
AND THERE'S NO WAY HE CAN EVER GET THEM BACK.
YOU NEED TO DECIDE WHAT'S MORE IMPORTANT.
SAVING YOUR FRIENDS OR SAVING THE WORLD?

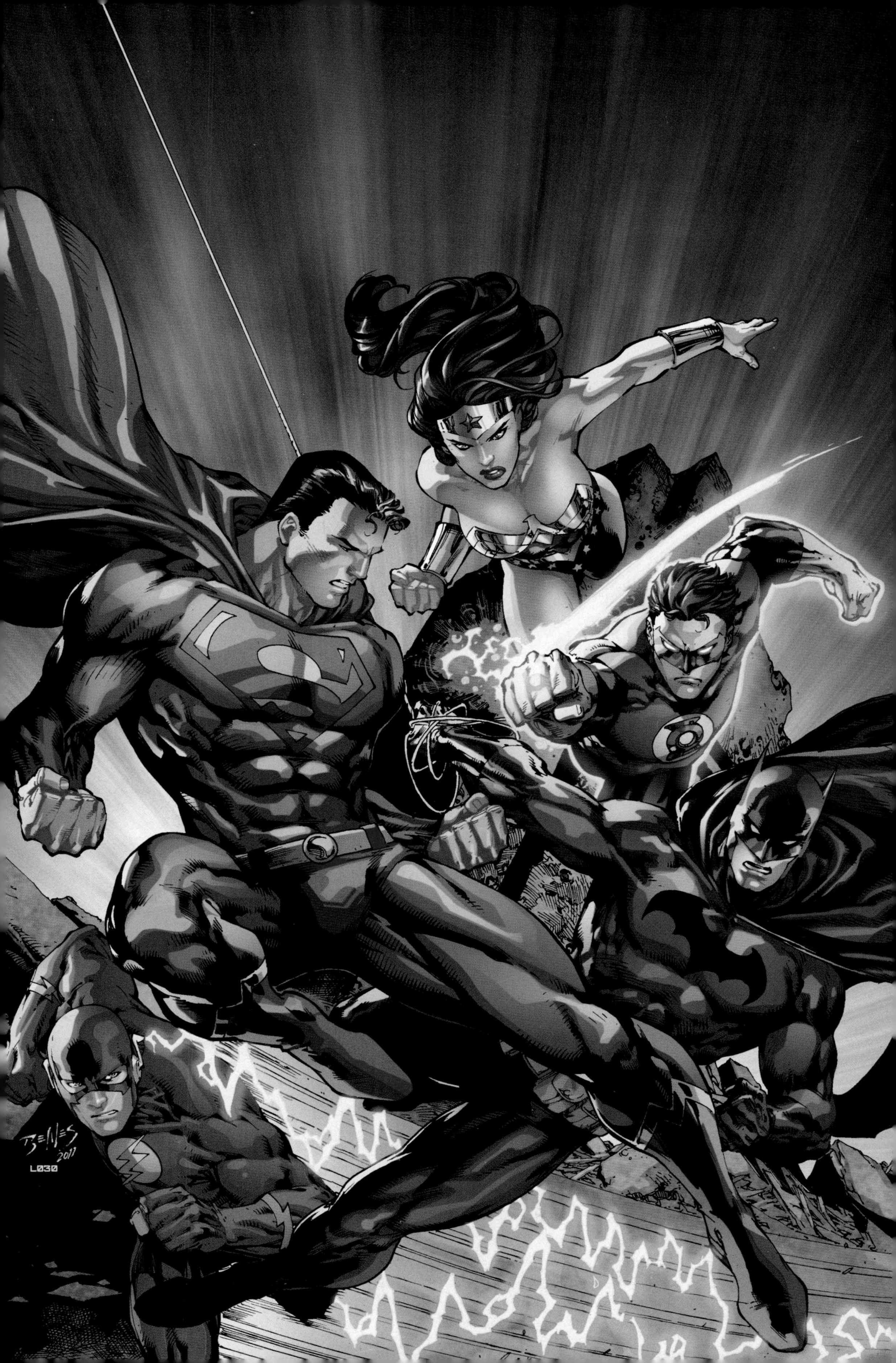

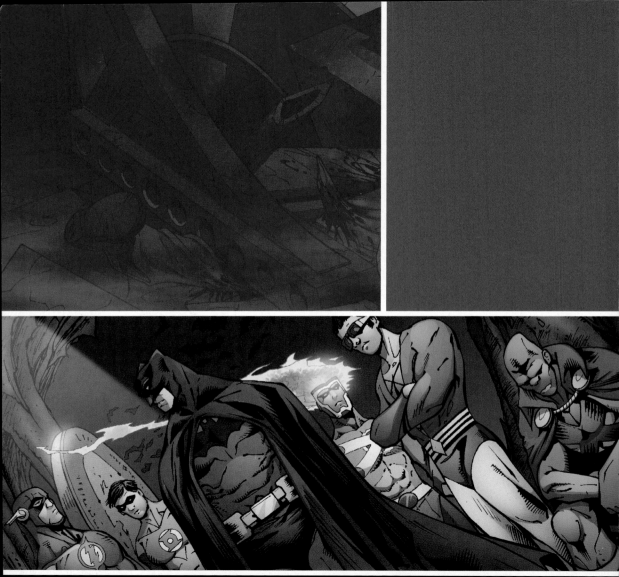

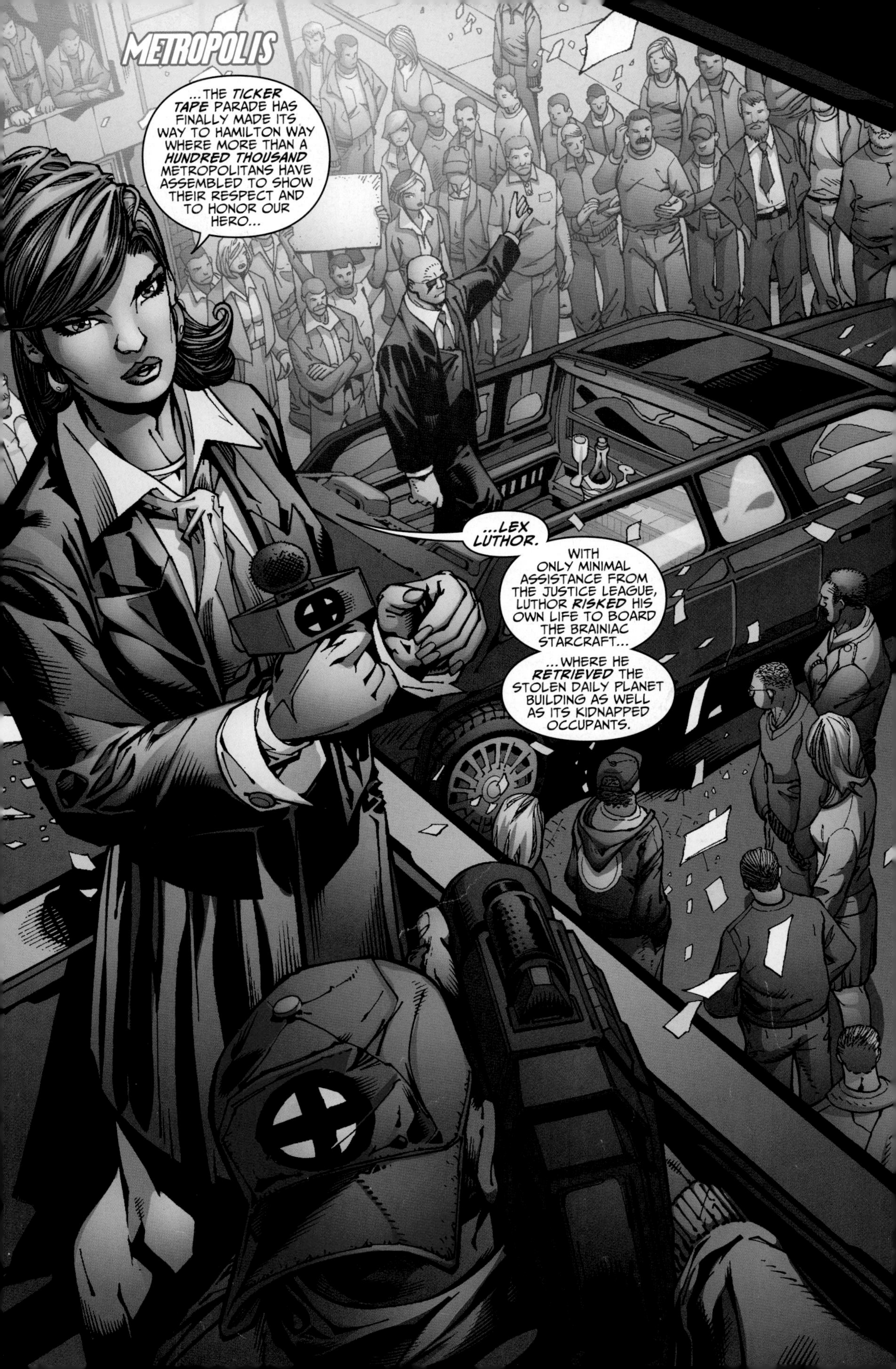
METROPOLIS
...THE TICKER TAPE PARADE HAS FINALLY MADE ITS WAY TO HAMILTON WAY WHERE MORE THAN A HUNDRED THOUSAND METROPOLITANS HAVE ASSEMBLED TO SHOW THEIR RESPECT AND TO HONOR OUR HERO...
...LEX LUTHOR.
WITH ONLY MINIMAL ASSISTANCE FROM THE JUSTICE LEAGUE, LUTHOR RISKED HIS OWN LIFE TO BOARD THE BRAINIAC STARCRAFT...
...WHERE HE RETRIEVED THE STOLEN DAILY PLANET BUILDING AS WELL AS ITS KIDNAPPED OCCUPANTS.

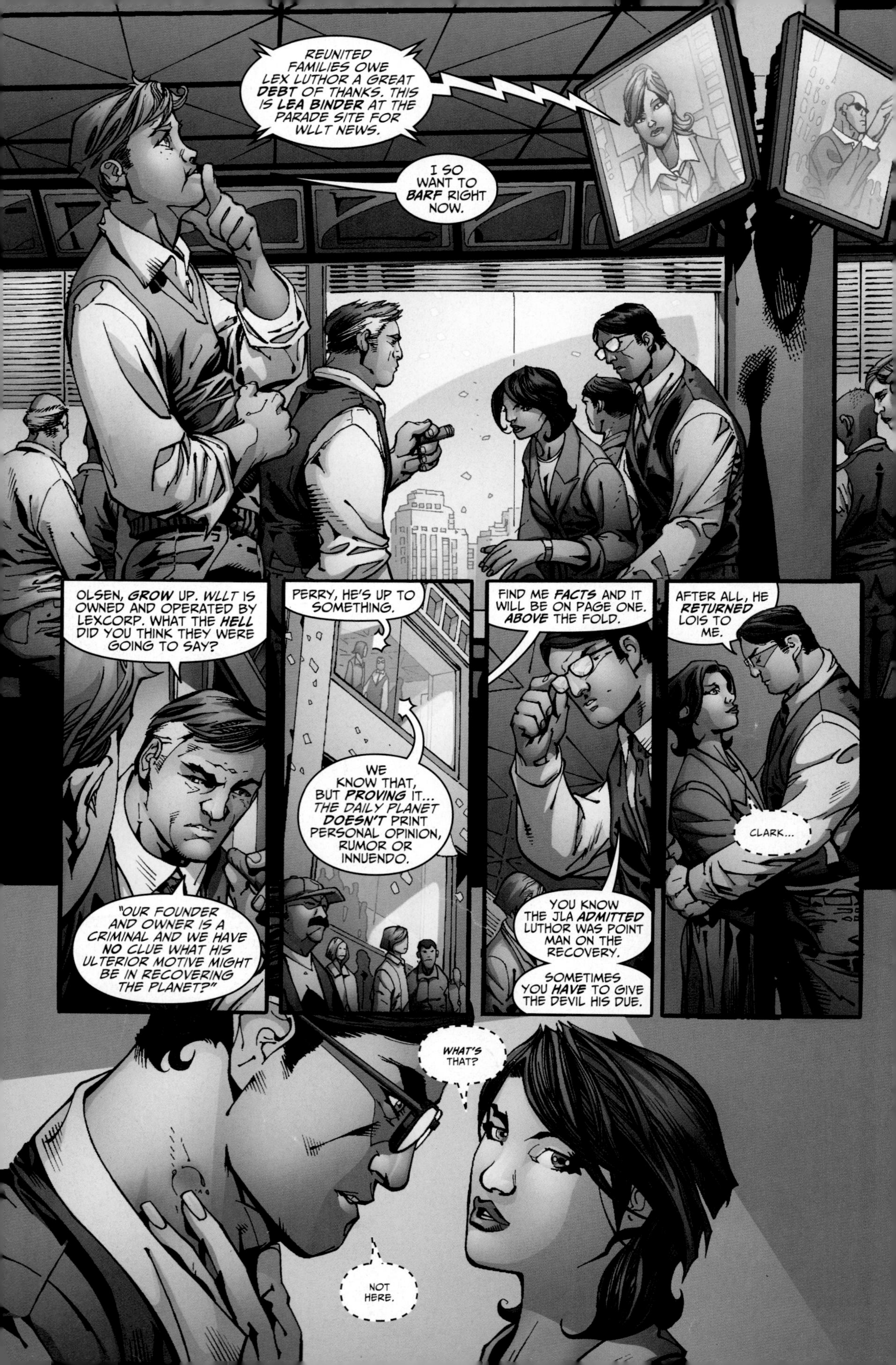
REUNITED FAMILIES OWE LEX LUTHOR A GREAT DEBT OF THANKS. THIS IS LEA BINDER AT THE PARADE SITE FOR WLLT NEWS.
I SO WANT TO BARF RIGHT NOW.
OLSEN, GROW UP. WLLT IS OWNED AND OPERATED BY LEXCORP. WHAT THE HELL DID YOU THINK THEY WERE GOING TO SAY?
"OUR FOUNDER AND OWNER IS A CRIMINAL AND WE HAVE NO CLUE WHAT HIS ULTERIOR MOTIVE MIGHT BE IN RECOVERING THE PLANET?"
PERRY, HE'S UP TO SOMETHING.
WE KNOW THAT, BUT PROVING IT... THE DAILY PLANET DOESN'T PRINT PERSONAL OPINION, RUMOR OR INNUENDO.
FIND ME FACTS AND IT WILL BE ON PAGE ONE. ABOVE THE FOLD.
YOU KNOW THE JLA ADMITTED LUTHOR WAS POINT MAN ON THE RECOVERY.
SOMETIMES YOU HAVE TO GIVE THE DEVIL HIS DUE.
AFTER ALL, HE RETURNED LOIS TO ME.
CLARK...
WHAT'S THAT?
NOT HERE.

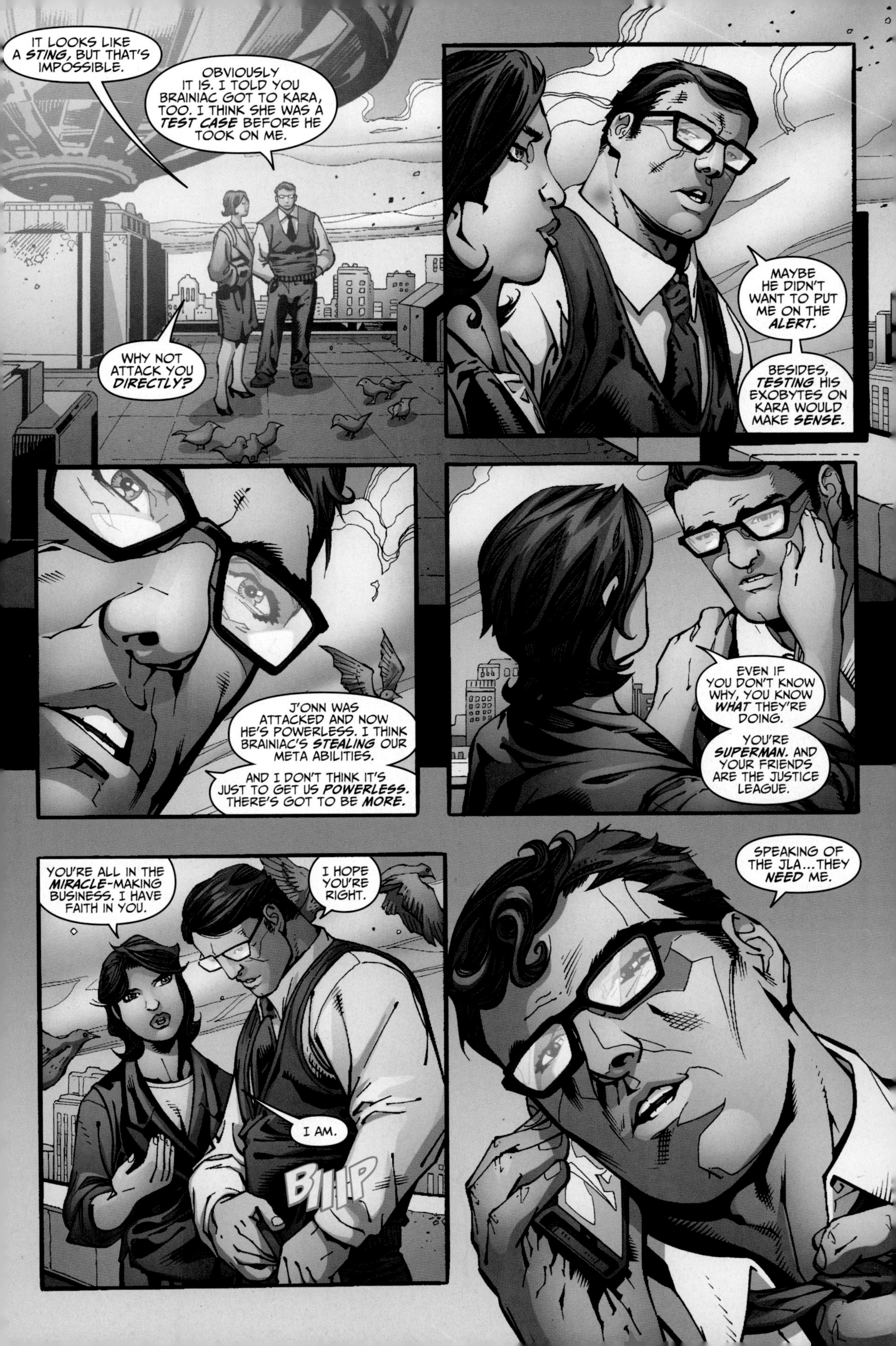
IT LOOKS LIKE A STING, BUT THAT'S IMPOSSIBLE.
OBVIOUSLY IT IS. I TOLD YOU BRAINIAC GOT TO KARA, TOO. I THINK SHE WAS A TEST CASE BEFORE HE TOOK ON ME.
WHY NOT ATTACK YOU DIRECTLY?
MAYBE HE DIDN'T WANT TO PUT ME ON THE ALERT.
BESIDES, TESTING HIS EXOBYTES ON KARA WOULD MAKE SENSE.
J'ONN WAS ATTACKED AND NOW HE'S POWERLESS. I THINK BRAINIAC'S STEALING OUR META ABILITIES.
AND I DON'T THINK IT'S JUST TO GET US POWERLESS. THERE'S GOT TO BE MORE.
EVEN IF YOU DON'T KNOW WHY, YOU KNOW WHAT THEY'RE DOING.
YOU'RE SUPERMAN. AND YOUR FRIENDS ARE THE JUSTICE LEAGUE.
YOU'RE ALL IN THE MIRACLE-MAKING BUSINESS. I HAVE FAITH IN YOU.
I HOPE YOU'RE RIGHT.
I AM.
BIIIP
SPEAKING OF THE JLA...THEY NEED ME.

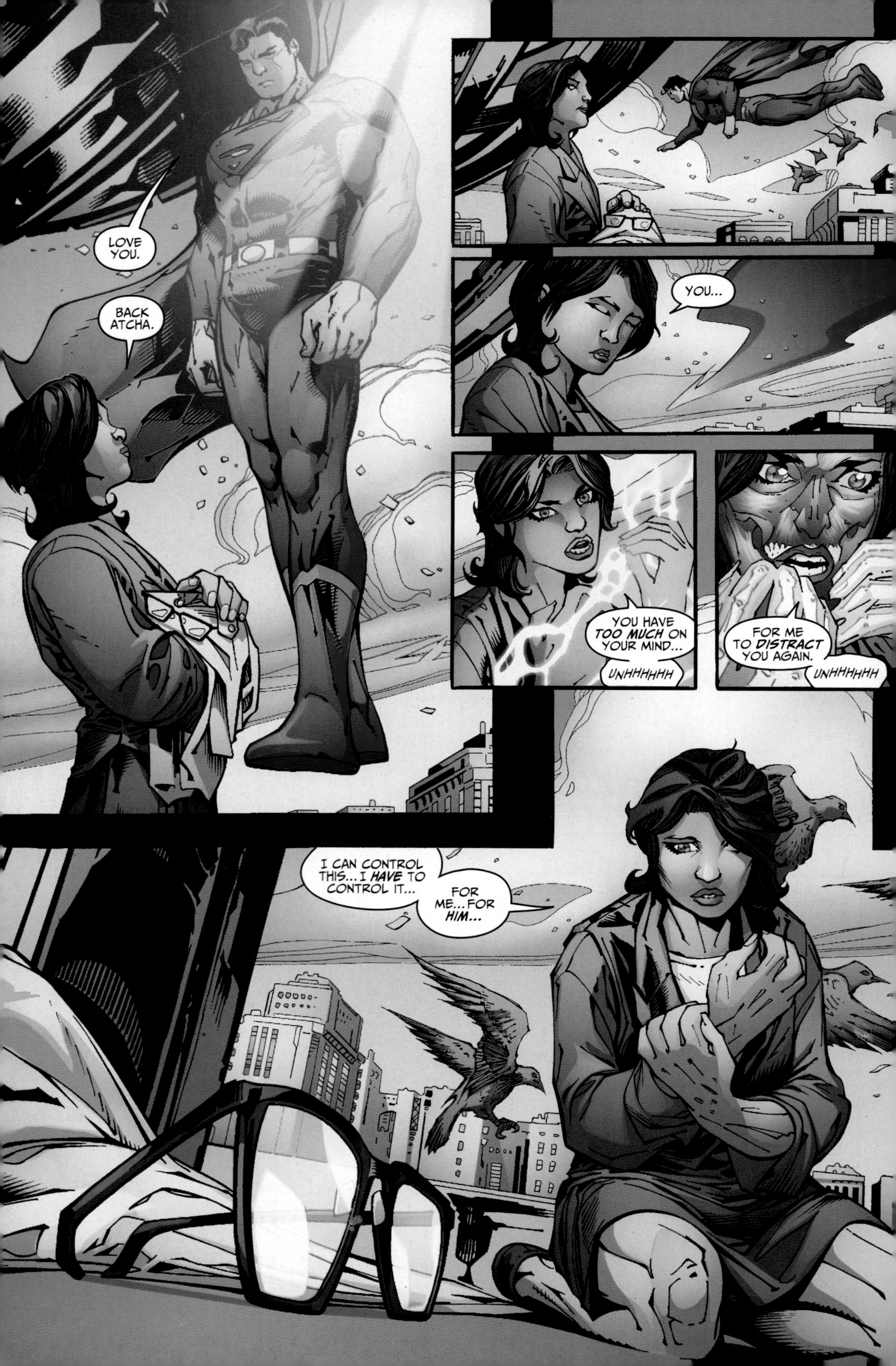
LOVE YOU.
BACK ATCHA.
YOU...
YOU HAVE TOO MUCH ON YOUR MIND...
UNHHHHHH
FOR ME TO DISTRACT YOU AGAIN.
UNHHHHHH
I CAN CONTROL THIS... I HAVE TO CONTROL IT...
FOR ME... FOR HIM...

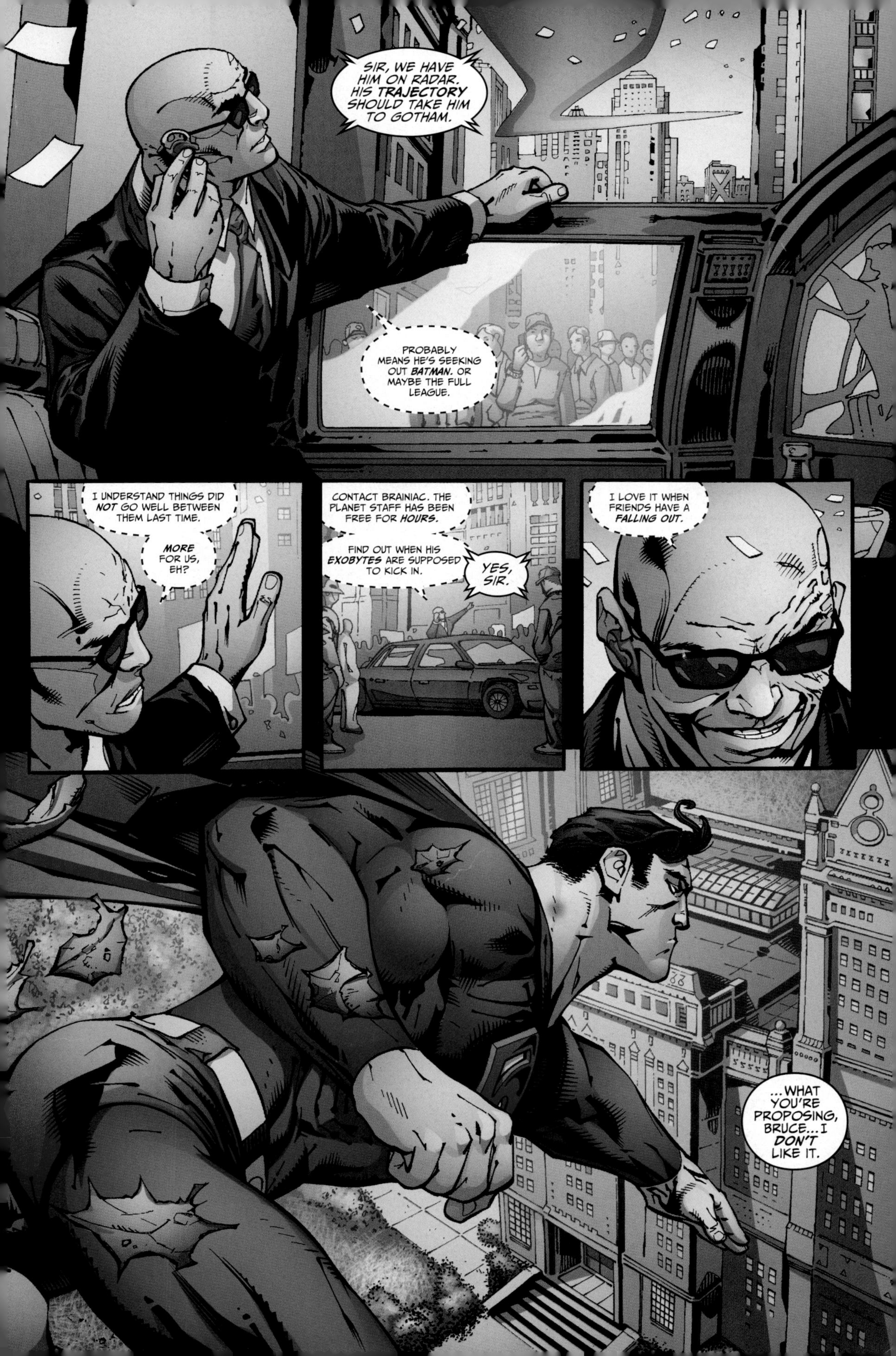
SIR, WE HAVE HIM ON RADAR. HIS TRAJECTORY SHOULD TAKE HIM TO GOTHAM.
PROBABLY MEANS HE'S SEEKING OUT BATMAN. OR MAYBE THE FULL LEAGUE.
I UNDERSTAND THINGS DID NOT GO WELL BETWEEN THEM LAST TIME.
MORE FOR US, EH?
CONTACT BRAINIAC. THE PLANET STAFF HAS BEEN FREE FOR HOURS.
FIND OUT WHEN HIS EXOBYTES ARE SUPPOSED TO KICK IN.
YES, SIR.
I LOVE IT WHEN FRIENDS HAVE A FALLING OUT.
...WHAT YOU'RE PROPOSING, BRUCE...I DON'T LIKE IT.

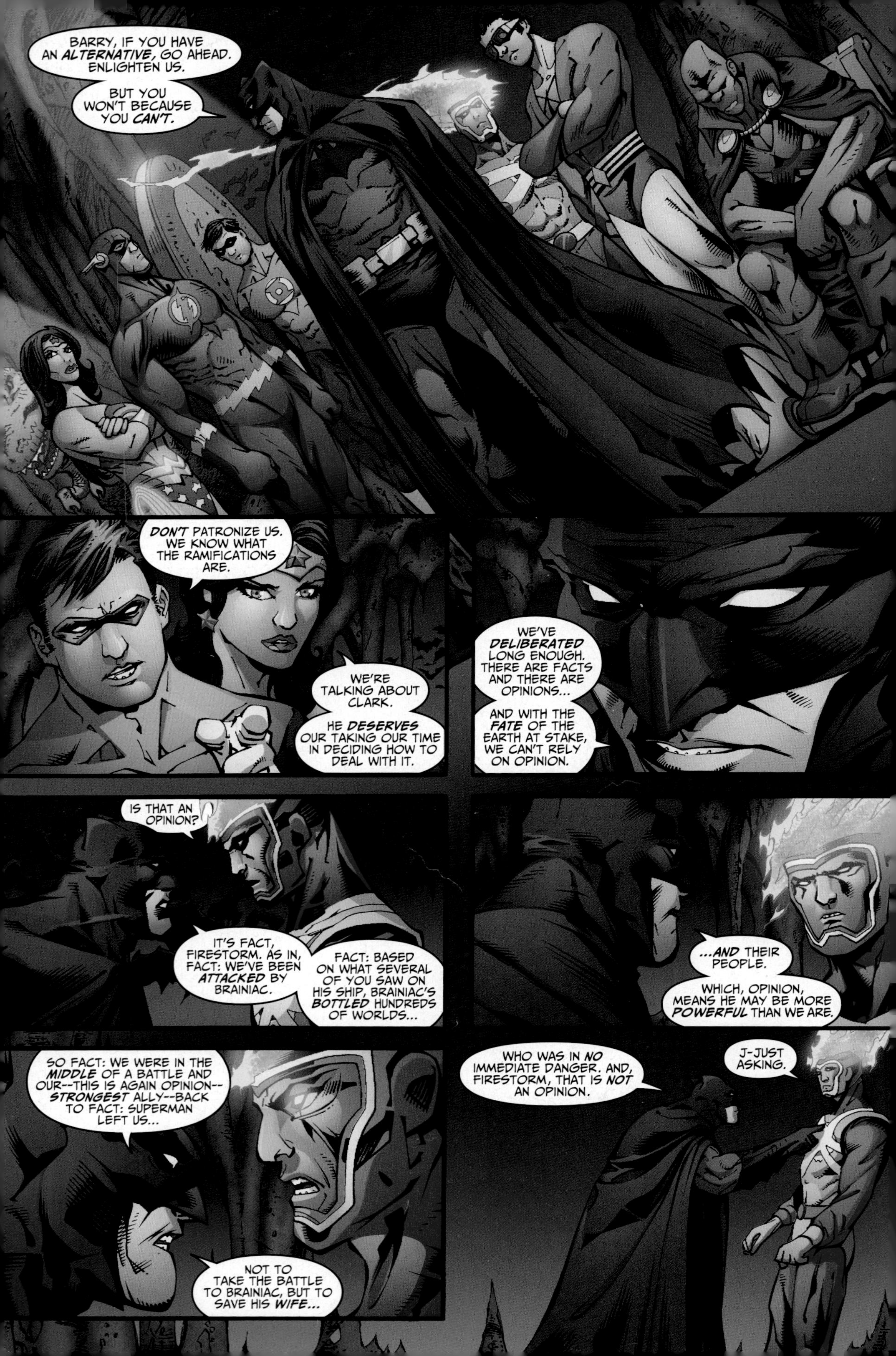
BARRY, IF YOU HAVE AN ALTERNATIVE, GO AHEAD. ENLIGHTEN US.
BUT YOU WON'T BECAUSE YOU CAN'T.
DON'T PATRONIZE US. WE KNOW WHAT THE RAMIFICATIONS ARE.
WE'RE TALKING ABOUT CLARK.
HE DESERVES OUR TAKING OUR TIME IN DECIDING HOW TO DEAL WITH IT.
WE'VE DELIBERATED LONG ENOUGH. THERE ARE FACTS AND THERE ARE OPINIONS...
AND WITH THE FATE OF THE EARTH AT STAKE, WE CAN'T RELY ON OPINION.
IS THAT AN OPINION?
IT'S FACT, FIRESTORM. AS IN, FACT: WE'VE BEEN ATTACKED BY BRAINIAC.
FACT: BASED ON WHAT SEVERAL OF YOU SAW ON HIS SHIP, BRAINIAC'S BOTTLED HUNDREDS OF WORLDS...
...AND THEIR PEOPLE.
WHICH, OPINION, MEANS HE MAY BE MORE POWERFUL THAN WE ARE.
SO FACT: WE WERE IN THE MIDDLE OF A BATTLE AND OUR--THIS IS AGAIN OPINION--STRONGEST ALLY--BACK TO FACT: SUPERMAN LEFT US...
NOT TO TAKE THE BATTLE TO BRAINIAC, BUT TO SAVE HIS WIFE...
WHO WAS IN NO IMMEDIATE DANGER. AND, FIRESTORM, THAT IS NOT AN OPINION.
J-JUST ASKING.

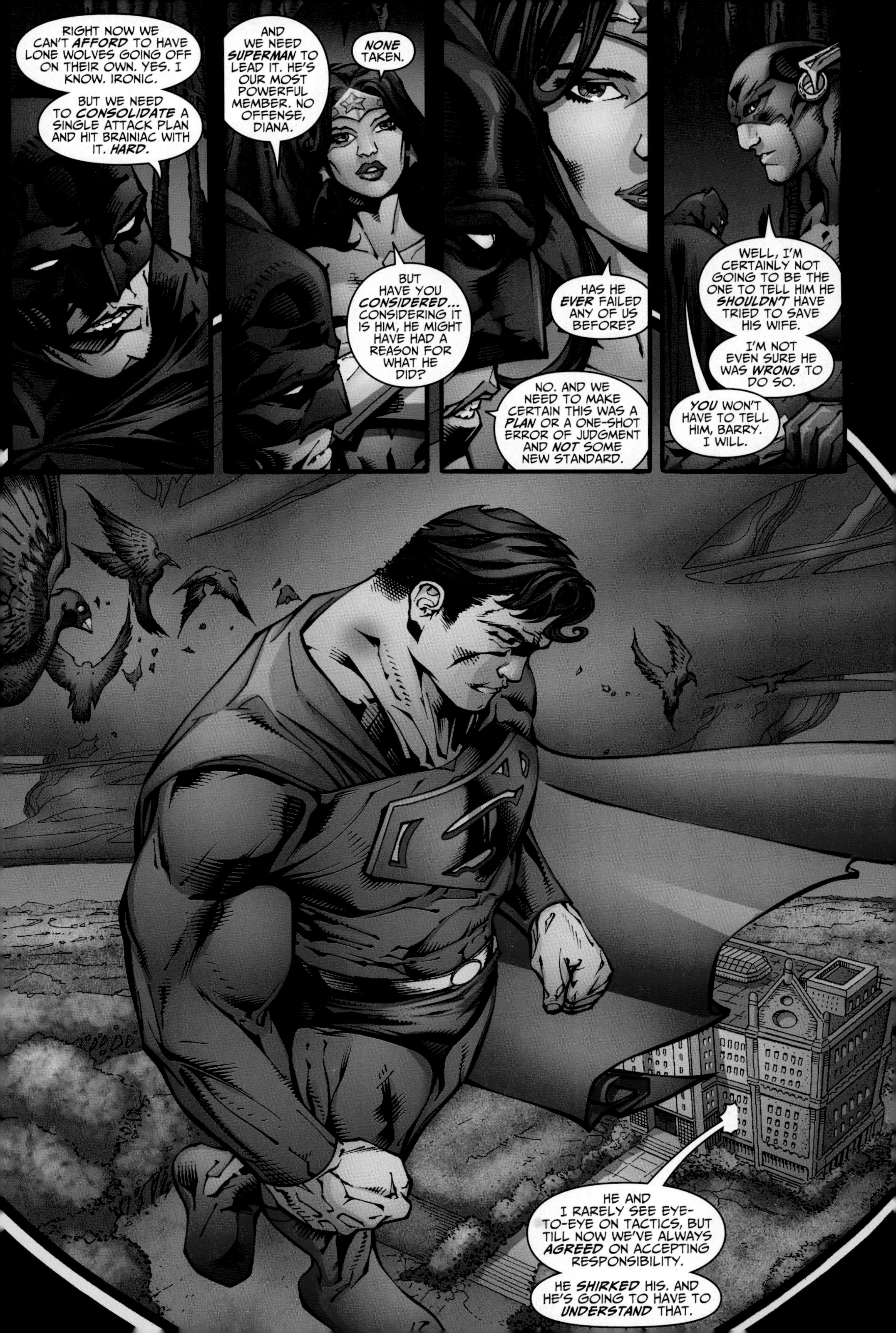
RIGHT NOW WE CAN'T AFFORD TO HAVE LONE WOLVES GOING OFF ON THEIR OWN. YES. I KNOW. IRONIC.
BUT WE NEED TO CONSOLIDATE A SINGLE ATTACK PLAN AND HIT BRAINIAC WITH IT. HARD.
AND WE NEED SUPERMAN TO LEAD IT. HE'S OUR MOST POWERFUL MEMBER. NO OFFENSE, DIANA.
NONE TAKEN.
BUT HAVE YOU CONSIDERED... CONSIDERING IT IS HIM, HE MIGHT HAVE HAD A REASON FOR WHAT HE DID?
HAS HE EVER FAILED ANY OF US BEFORE?
NO. AND WE NEED TO MAKE CERTAIN THIS WAS A PLAN OR A ONE-SHOT ERROR OF JUDGMENT AND NOT SOME NEW STANDARD.
WELL, I'M CERTAINLY NOT GOING TO BE THE ONE TO TELL HIM HE SHOULDN'T HAVE TRIED TO SAVE HIS WIFE.
I'M NOT EVEN SURE HE WAS WRONG TO DO SO.
YOU WON'T HAVE TO TELL HIM, BARRY. I WILL.
HE AND I RARELY SEE EYE-TO-EYE ON TACTICS, BUT TILL NOW WE'VE ALWAYS AGREED ON ACCEPTING RESPONSIBILITY.
HE SHIRKED HIS. AND HE'S GOING TO HAVE TO UNDERSTAND THAT.

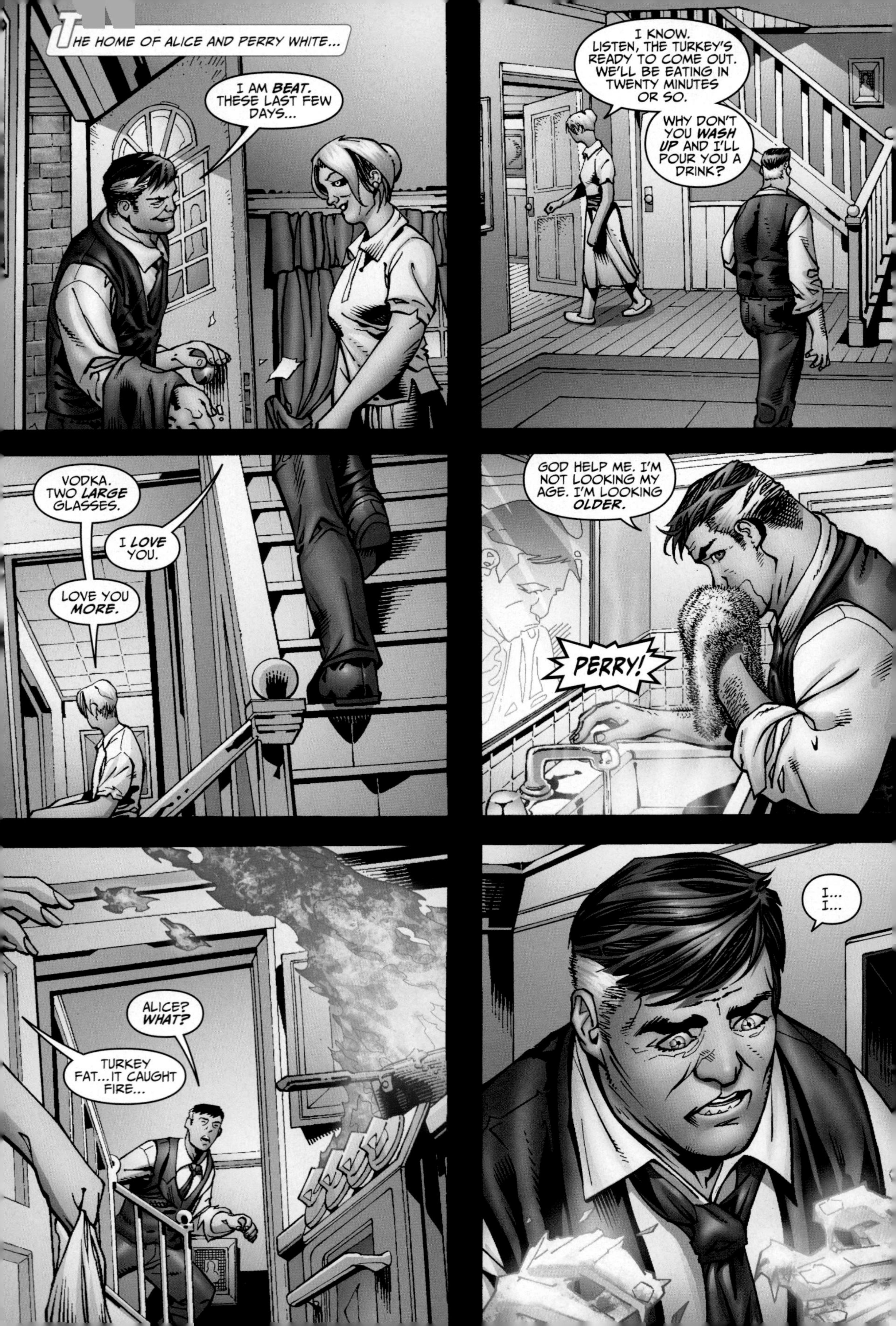
THE HOME OF ALICE AND PERRY WHITE...
I AM BEAT. THESE LAST FEW DAYS...
I KNOW. LISTEN, THE TURKEY'S READY TO COME OUT. WE'LL BE EATING IN TWENTY MINUTES OR SO.
WHY DON'T YOU WASH UP AND I'LL POUR YOU A DRINK?
VODKA. TWO LARGE GLASSES.
I LOVE YOU.
LOVE YOU MORE.
GOD HELP ME. I'M NOT LOOKING MY AGE. I'M LOOKING OLDER.
PERRY!
ALICE? WHAT?
TURKEY FAT...IT CAUGHT FIRE...
I... I...

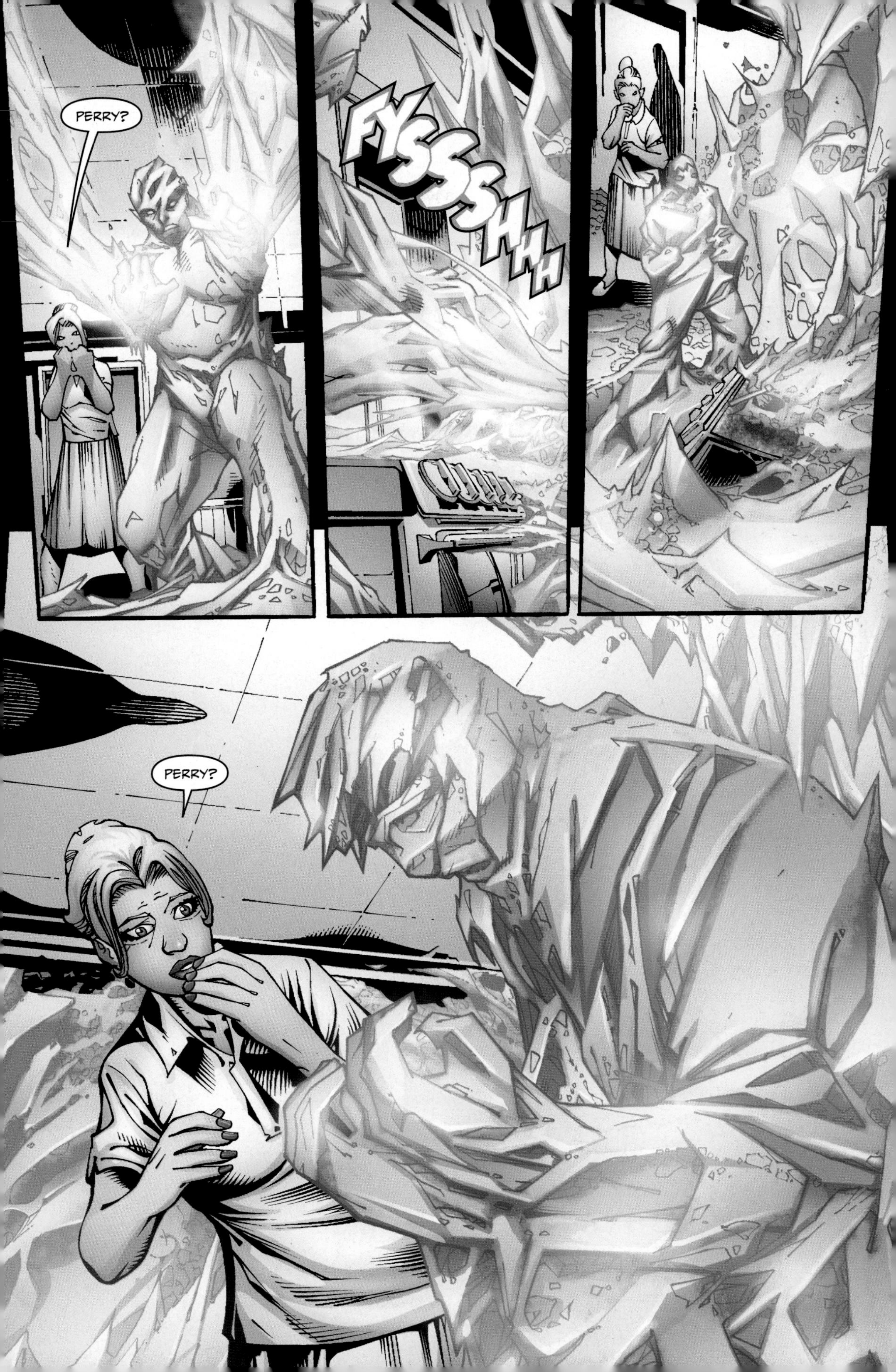
PERRY?
FYSSSHHH
PERRY?

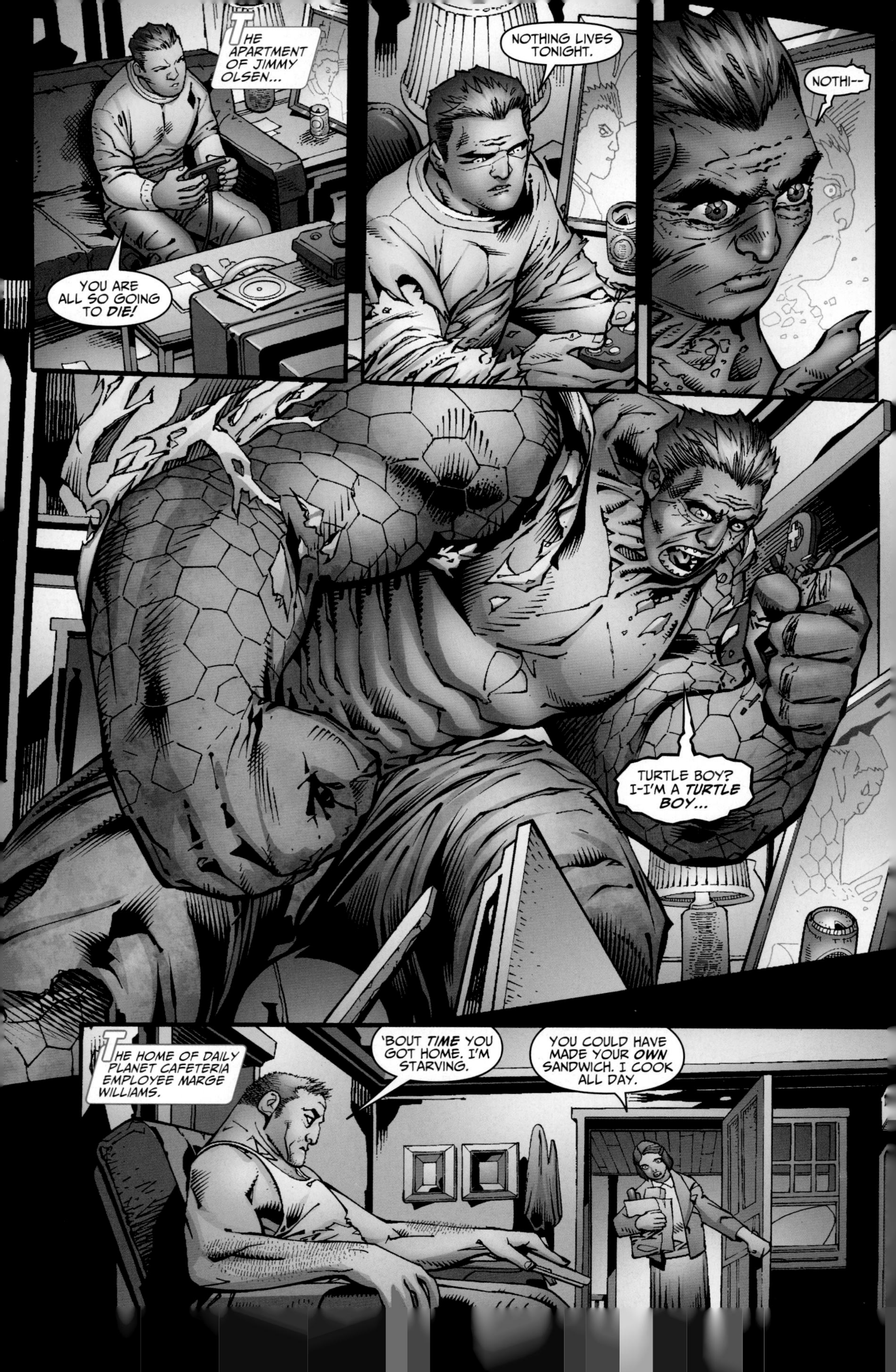
THE APARTMENT OF JIMMY OLSEN...
YOU ARE ALL SO GOING TO DIE!
NOTHING LIVES TONIGHT.
NOTHI--
TURTLE BOY? I-I'M A TURTLE BOY...
THE HOME OF DAILY PLANET CAFETERIA EMPLOYEE MARGE WILLIAMS.
'BOUT TIME YOU GOT HOME. I'M STARVING.
YOU COULD HAVE MADE YOUR OWN SANDWICH. I COOK ALL DAY.

I SHOULDA. THOSE *PLANET* PEOPLE EAT BETTER'N I EVER DO.

THE PLANET *TREATS* ME BETTER.

SHUT THE HELL UP AND MAKE ME *DINNER*.

DON'T YOU *DARE*...

...PUSH ME!

HUH?

SKRASS

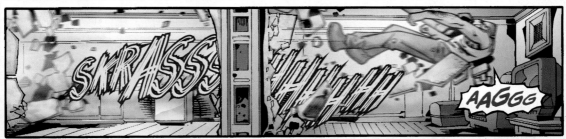

SKRASSS

AAGGG

HAROLD? HAROLD?

DEAD?

'BOUT TIME.

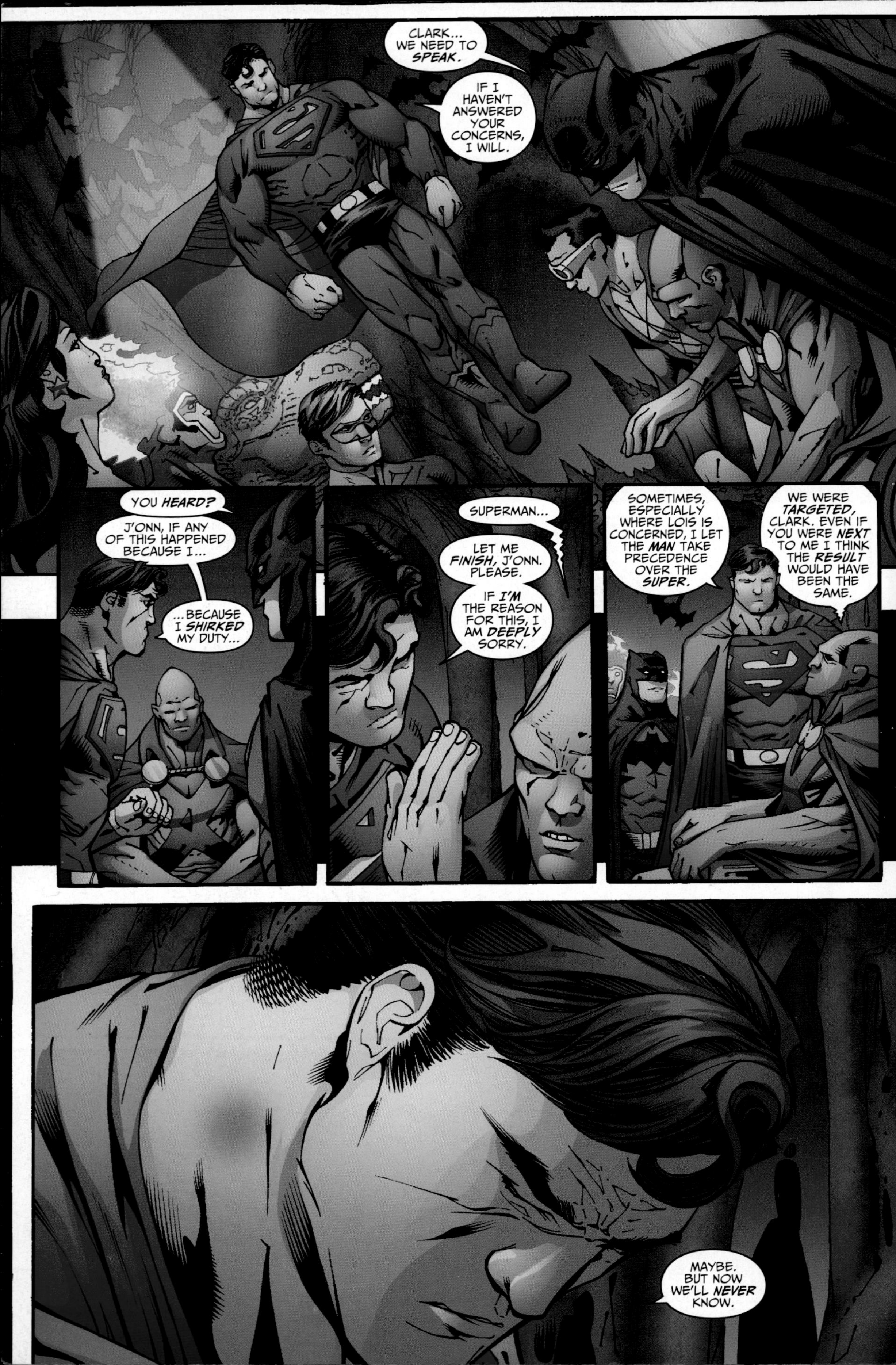
CLARK... WE NEED TO SPEAK.
IF I HAVEN'T ANSWERED YOUR CONCERNS, I WILL.
YOU HEARD?
J'ONN, IF ANY OF THIS HAPPENED BECAUSE I...
...BECAUSE I SHIRKED MY DUTY...
SUPERMAN...
LET ME FINISH, J'ONN. PLEASE.
IF I'M THE REASON FOR THIS, I AM DEEPLY SORRY.
SOMETIMES, ESPECIALLY WHERE LOIS IS CONCERNED, I LET THE MAN TAKE PRECEDENCE OVER THE SUPER.
WE WERE TARGETED, CLARK. EVEN IF YOU WERE NEXT TO ME I THINK THE RESULT WOULD HAVE BEEN THE SAME.
MAYBE. BUT NOW WE'LL NEVER KNOW.

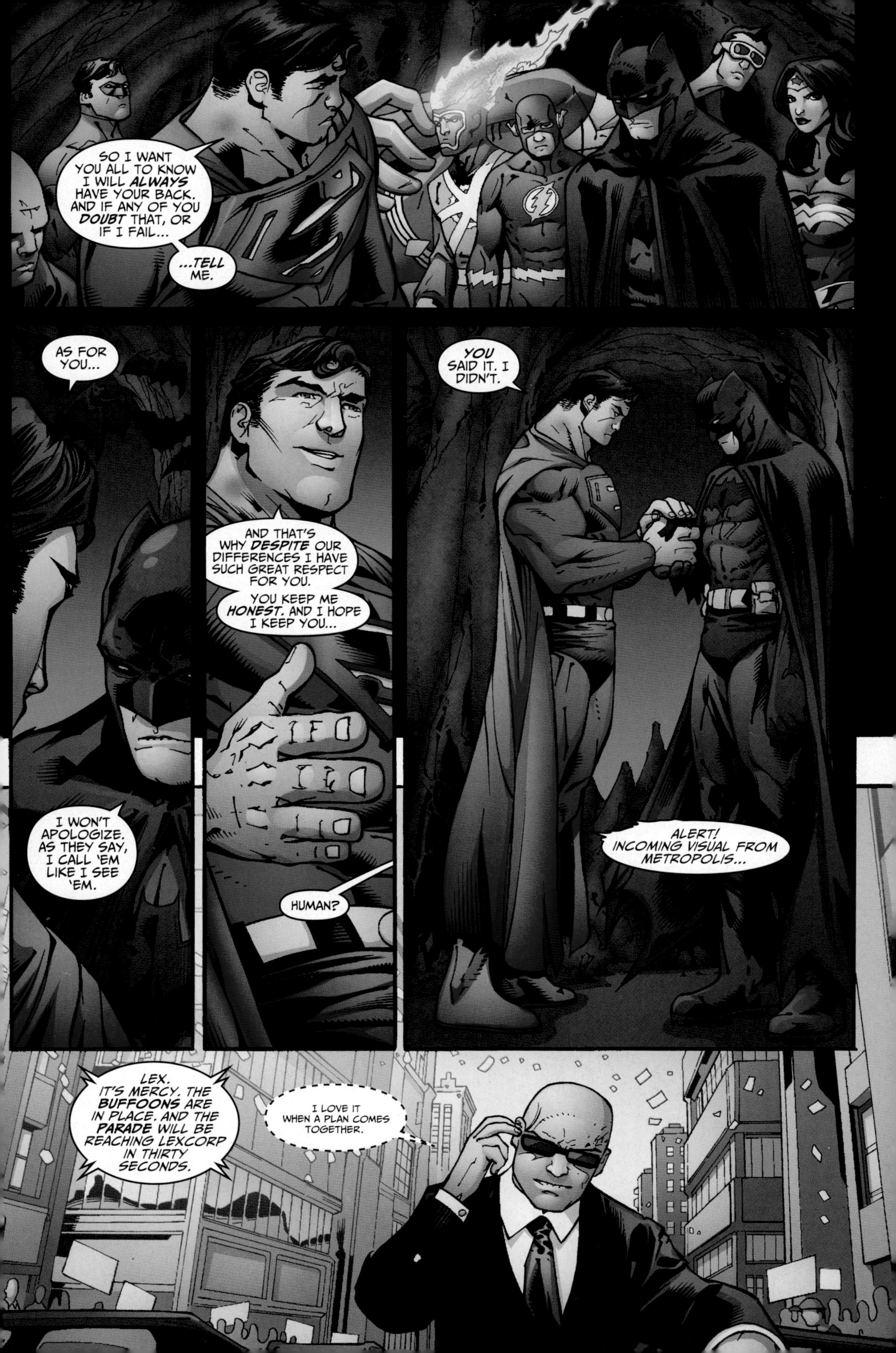
SO I WANT YOU ALL TO KNOW I WILL ALWAYS HAVE YOUR BACK. AND IF ANY OF YOU DOUBT THAT, OR IF I FAIL...
...TELL ME.
AS FOR YOU...
I WON'T APOLOGIZE. AS THEY SAY, I CALL 'EM LIKE I SEE 'EM.
AND THAT'S WHY DESPITE OUR DIFFERENCES I HAVE SUCH GREAT RESPECT FOR YOU.
YOU KEEP ME HONEST. AND I HOPE I KEEP YOU...
HUMAN?
YOU SAID IT. I DIDN'T.
ALERT! INCOMING VISUAL FROM METROPOLIS...
LEX. IT'S MERCY. THE BUFFOONS ARE IN PLACE. AND THE PARADE WILL BE REACHING LEXCORP IN THIRTY SECONDS.
I LOVE IT WHEN A PLAN COMES TOGETHER.

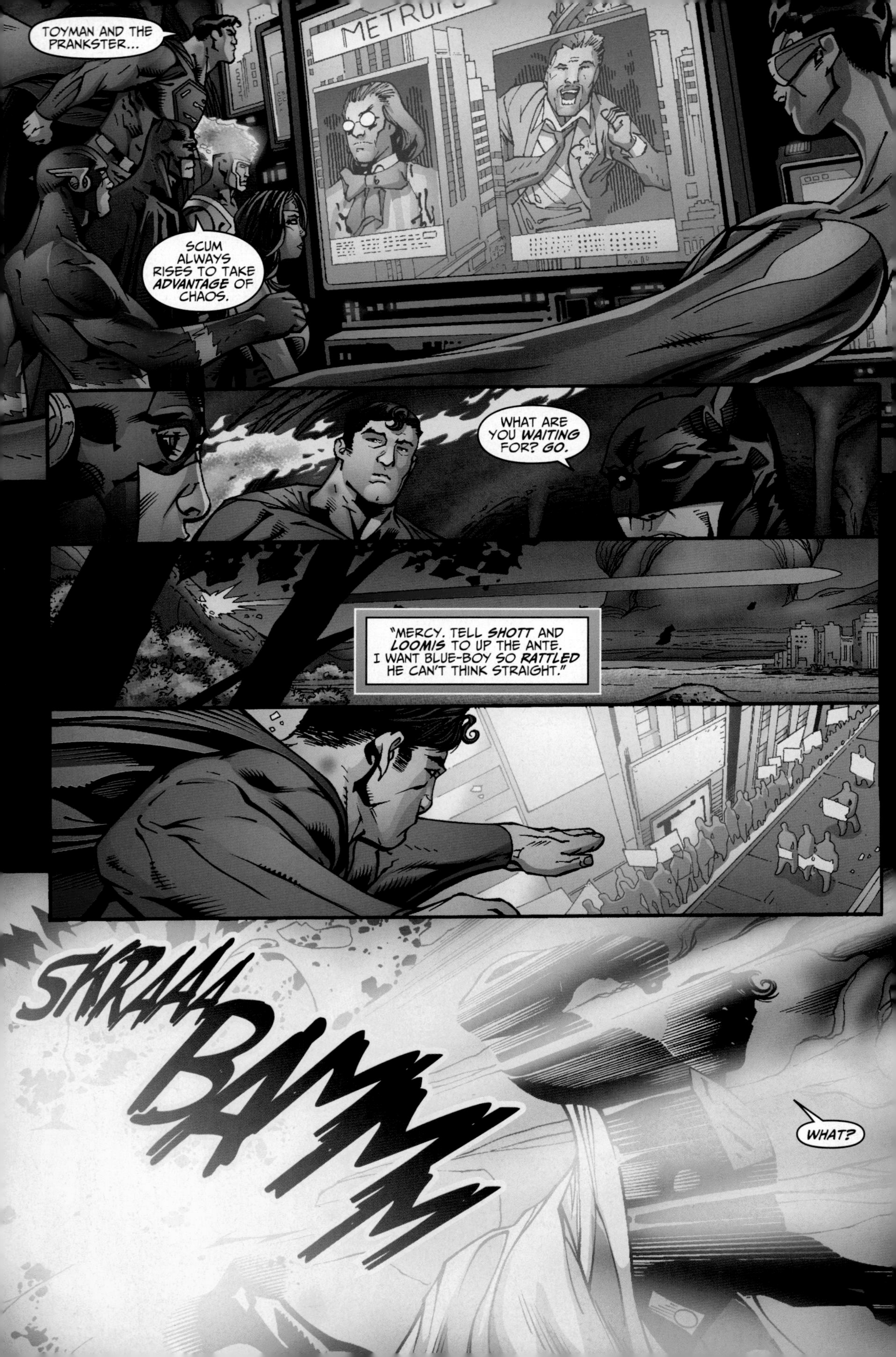
TOYMAN AND THE PRANKSTER...
METROPOLIS
SCUM ALWAYS RISES TO TAKE *ADVANTAGE* OF CHAOS.
WHAT ARE YOU *WAITING* FOR? *GO.*
"MERCY. TELL *SHOTT* AND *LOOMIS* TO UP THE ANTE. I WANT BLUE-BOY SO *RATTLED* HE CAN'T THINK STRAIGHT."
SKRAAA BAMM
WHAT?

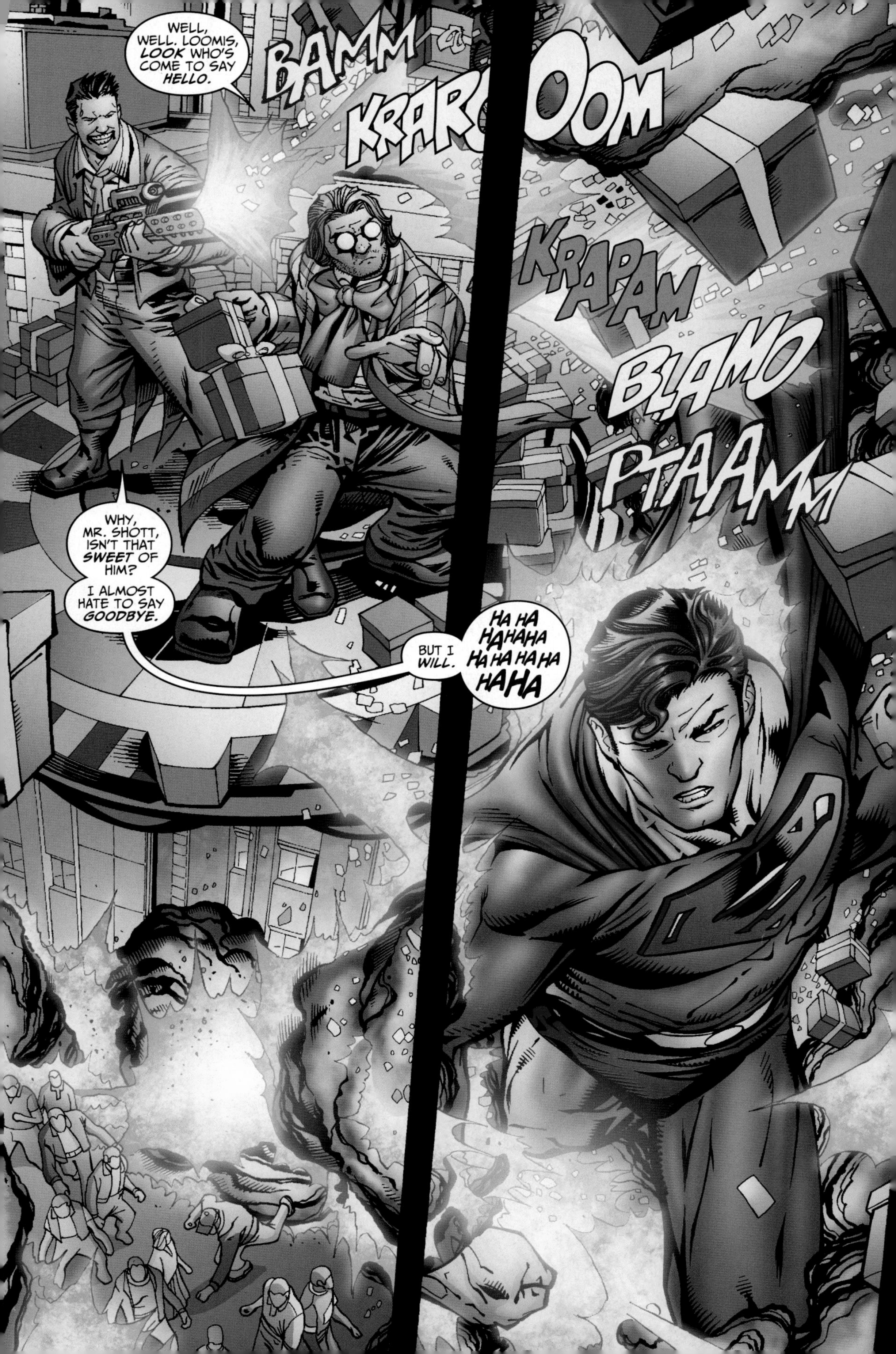
WELL, WELL. LOOMIS, LOOK WHO'S COME TO SAY HELLO.
BAMM
KRAROOOM
KRAPAM
BLAMO
PTAAMM
WHY, MR. SHOTT, ISN'T THAT SWEET OF HIM?
I ALMOST HATE TO SAY GOODBYE.
BUT I WILL.
HA HA HAHAHA HA HA HA HA HA HAHA

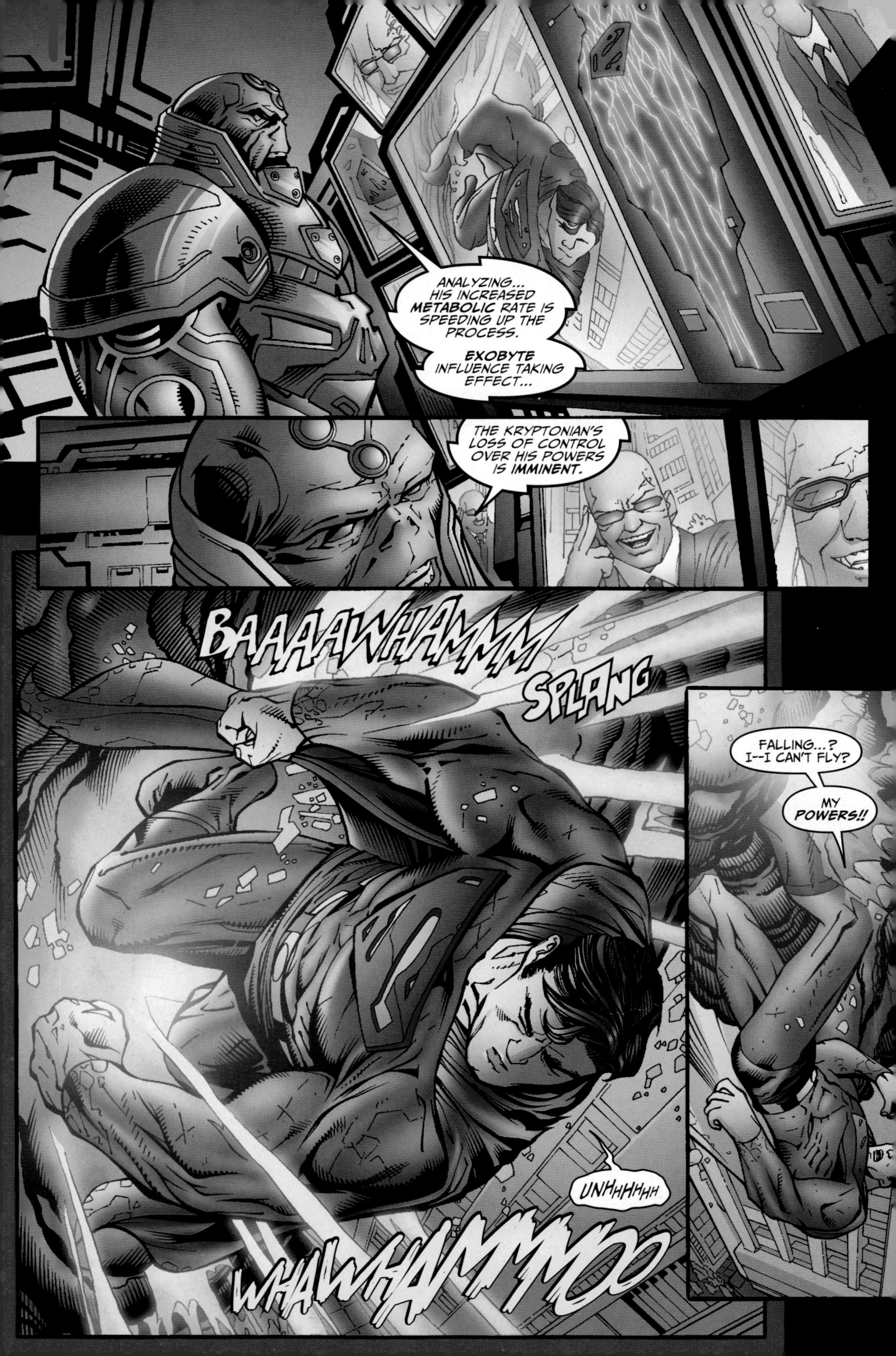

ANALYZING... HIS INCREASED METABOLIC RATE IS SPEEDING UP THE PROCESS.
EXOBYTE INFLUENCE TAKING EFFECT...
THE KRYPTONIAN'S LOSS OF CONTROL OVER HIS POWERS IS IMMINENT.
BAAAAWHAMMM
SPLANG
FALLING...? I--I CAN'T FLY?
MY POWERS!!
UNHHHHHH
WHAWHAMMMOO

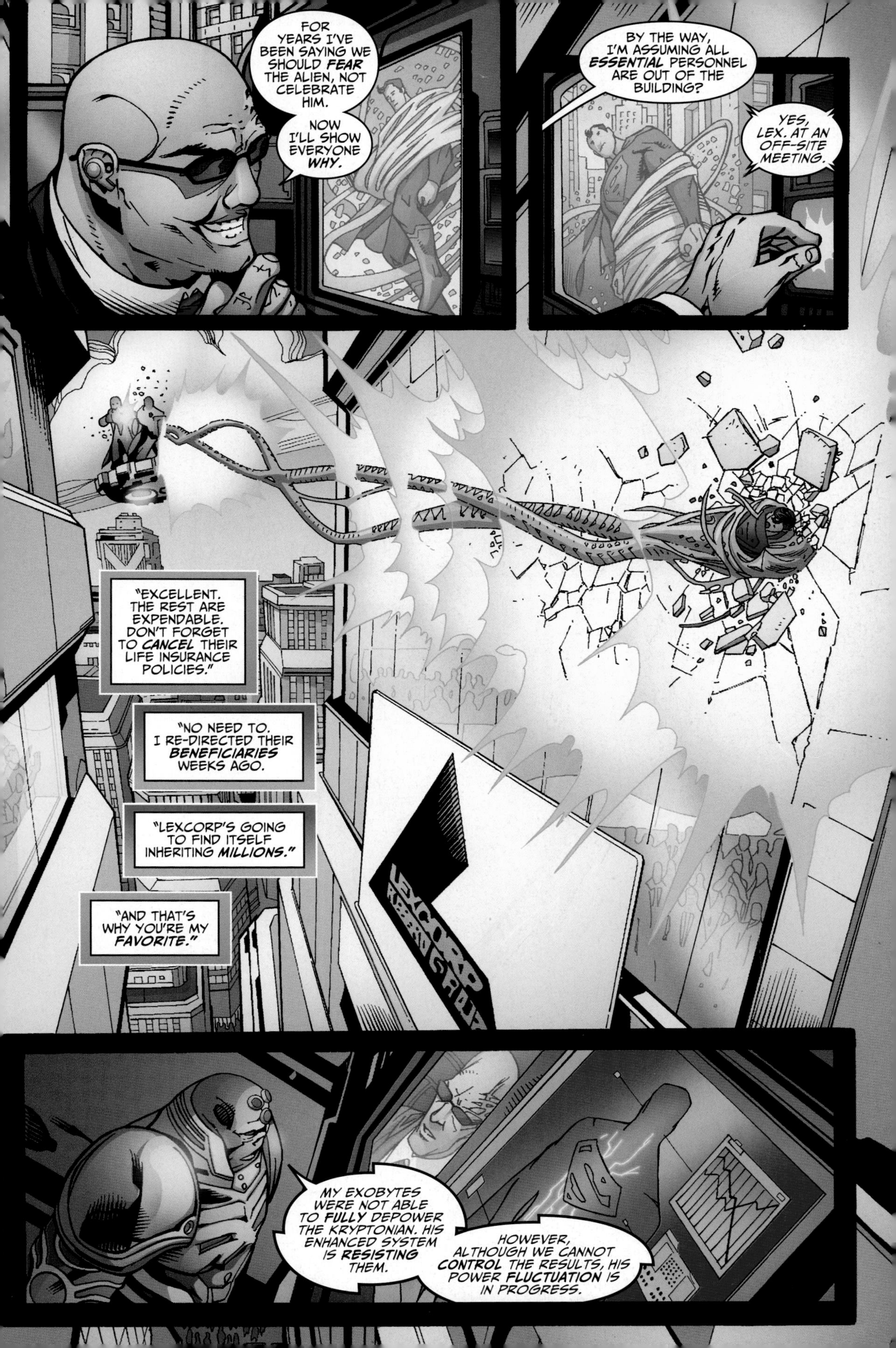
FOR YEARS I'VE BEEN SAYING WE SHOULD FEAR THE ALIEN, NOT CELEBRATE HIM.
NOW I'LL SHOW EVERYONE WHY.
BY THE WAY, I'M ASSUMING ALL ESSENTIAL PERSONNEL ARE OUT OF THE BUILDING?
YES, LEX. AT AN OFF-SITE MEETING.
"EXCELLENT. THE REST ARE EXPENDABLE. DON'T FORGET TO CANCEL THEIR LIFE INSURANCE POLICIES."
"NO NEED TO. I RE-DIRECTED THEIR BENEFICIARIES WEEKS AGO.
"LEXCORP'S GOING TO FIND ITSELF INHERITING MILLIONS."
"AND THAT'S WHY YOU'RE MY FAVORITE."
MY EXOBYTES WERE NOT ABLE TO FULLY DEPOWER THE KRYPTONIAN. HIS ENHANCED SYSTEM IS RESISTING THEM.
HOWEVER, ALTHOUGH WE CANNOT CONTROL THE RESULTS, HIS POWER FLUCTUATION IS IN PROGRESS.

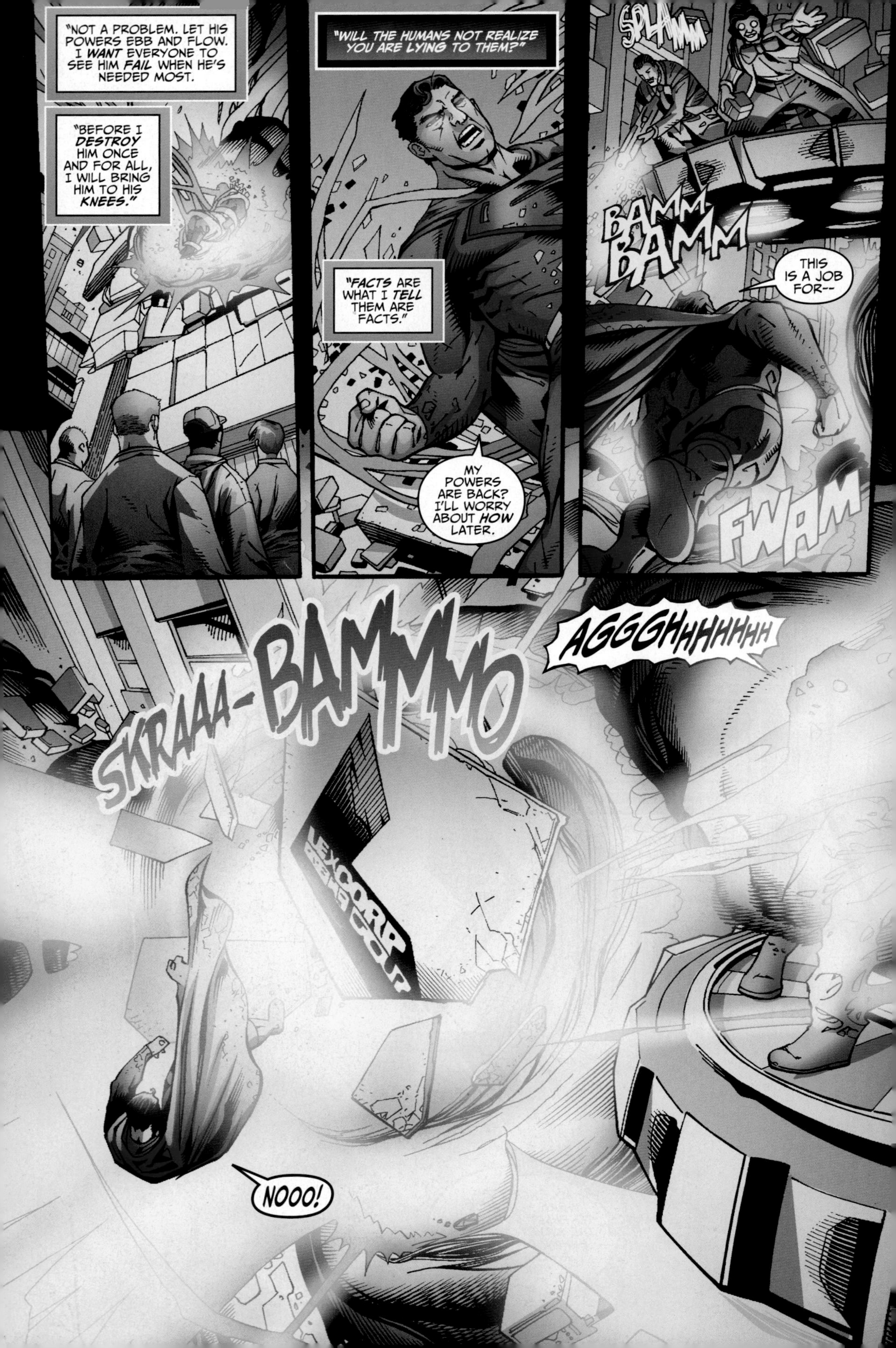
"NOT A PROBLEM. LET HIS POWERS EBB AND FLOW. I WANT EVERYONE TO SEE HIM FAIL WHEN HE'S NEEDED MOST.
"BEFORE I DESTROY HIM ONCE AND FOR ALL, I WILL BRING HIM TO HIS KNEES."
"WILL THE HUMANS NOT REALIZE YOU ARE LYING TO THEM?"
"FACTS ARE WHAT I TELL THEM ARE FACTS."
MY POWERS ARE BACK? I'LL WORRY ABOUT HOW LATER.
SPLAMMM
BAMM BAMM
THIS IS A JOB FOR--
FWAM
SKRAAA-BAMMMO
AGGGHHHHHH
LEXCORP
NOOO!

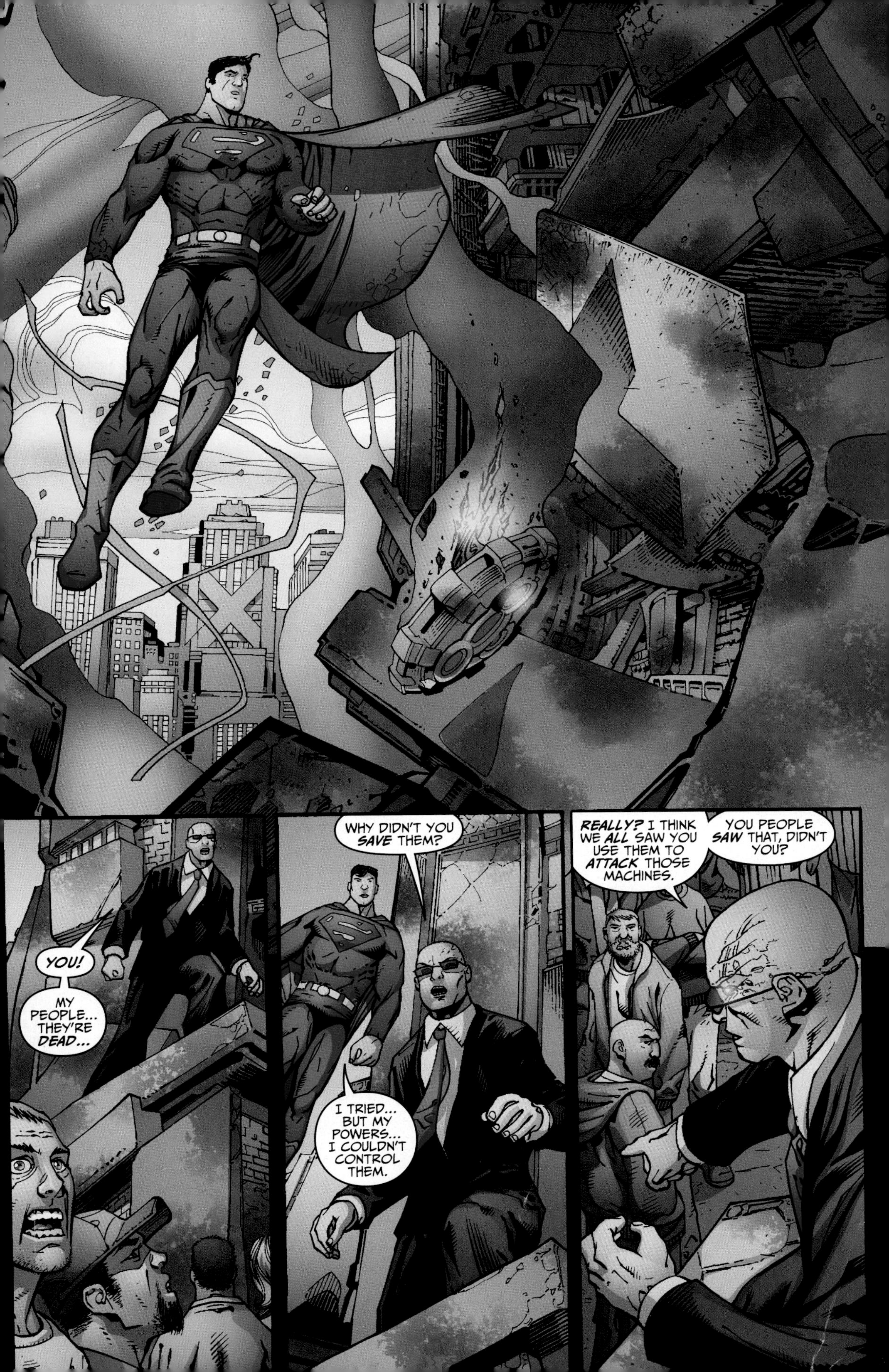
YOU!
MY PEOPLE... THEY'RE DEAD...
WHY DIDN'T YOU SAVE THEM?
I TRIED... BUT MY POWERS... I COULDN'T CONTROL THEM.
REALLY? I THINK WE ALL SAW YOU USE THEM TO ATTACK THOSE MACHINES.
YOU PEOPLE SAW THAT, DIDN'T YOU?

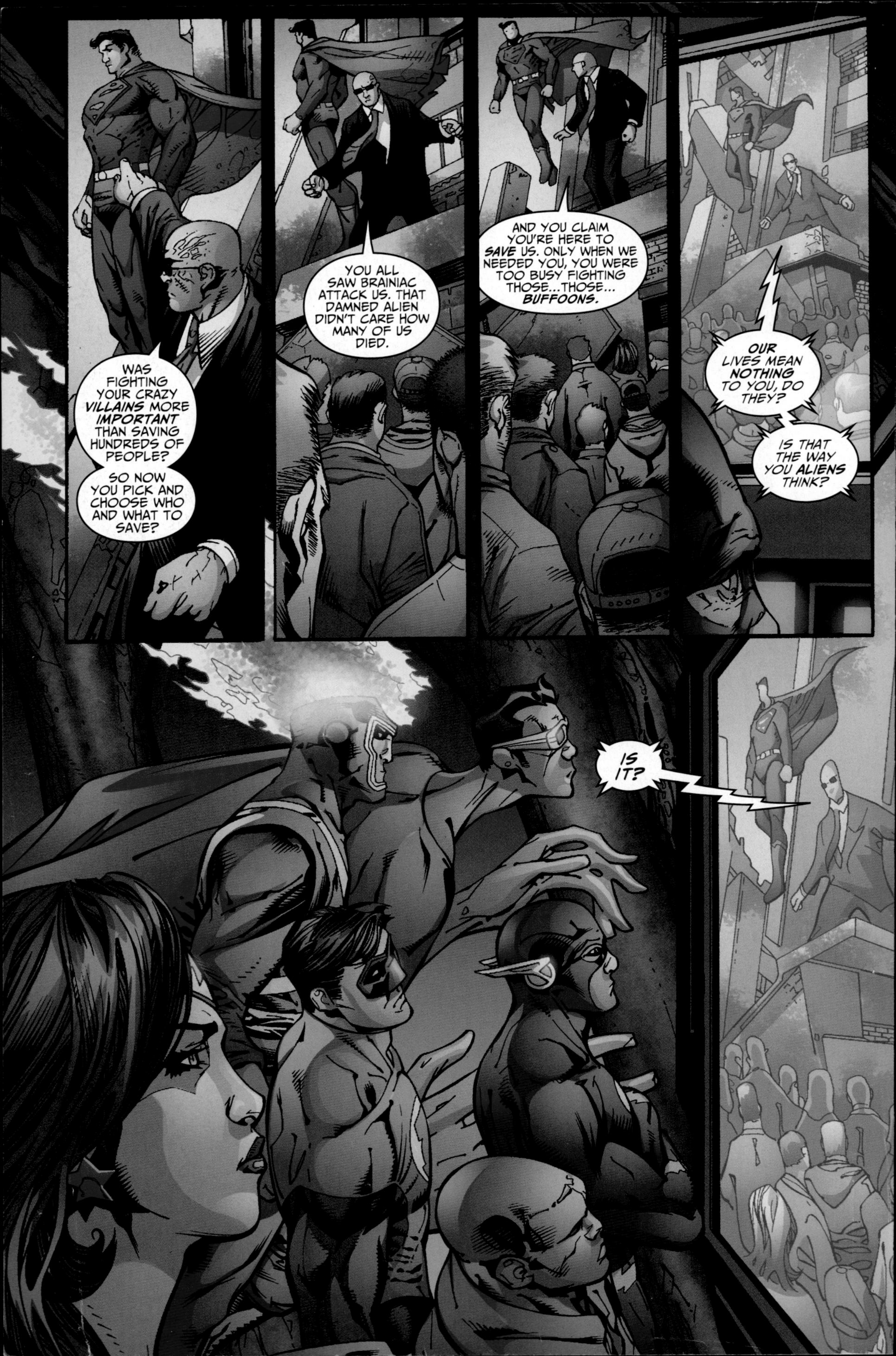

WAS FIGHTING YOUR CRAZY VILLAINS MORE IMPORTANT THAN SAVING HUNDREDS OF PEOPLE?
SO NOW YOU PICK AND CHOOSE WHO AND WHAT TO SAVE?
YOU ALL SAW BRAINIAC ATTACK US. THAT DAMNED ALIEN DIDN'T CARE HOW MANY OF US DIED.
AND YOU CLAIM YOU'RE HERE TO SAVE US. ONLY WHEN WE NEEDED YOU, YOU WERE TOO BUSY FIGHTING THOSE...THOSE... BUFFOONS.
OUR LIVES MEAN NOTHING TO YOU, DO THEY?
IS THAT THE WAY YOU ALIENS THINK?
IS IT?

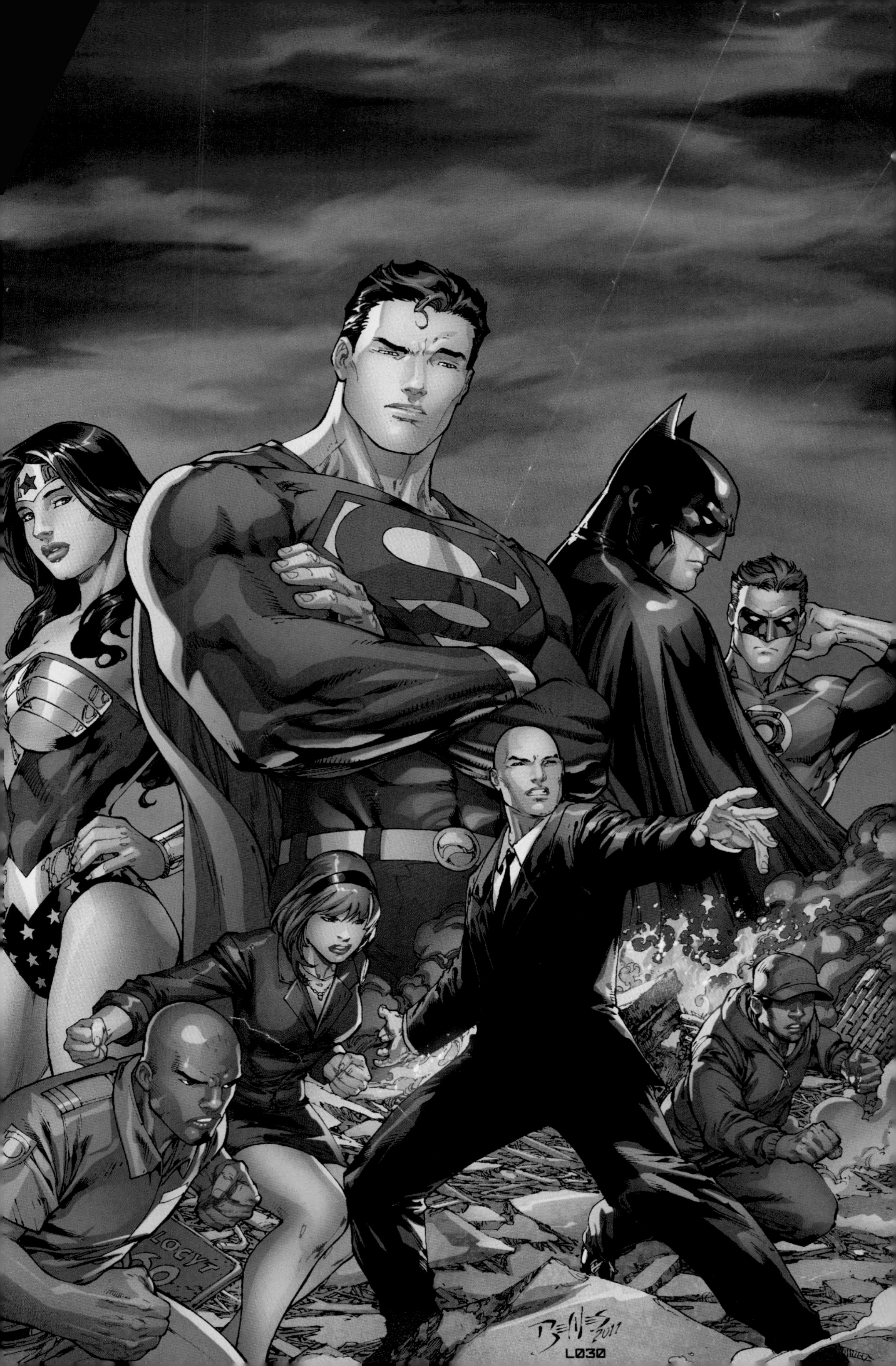
L030

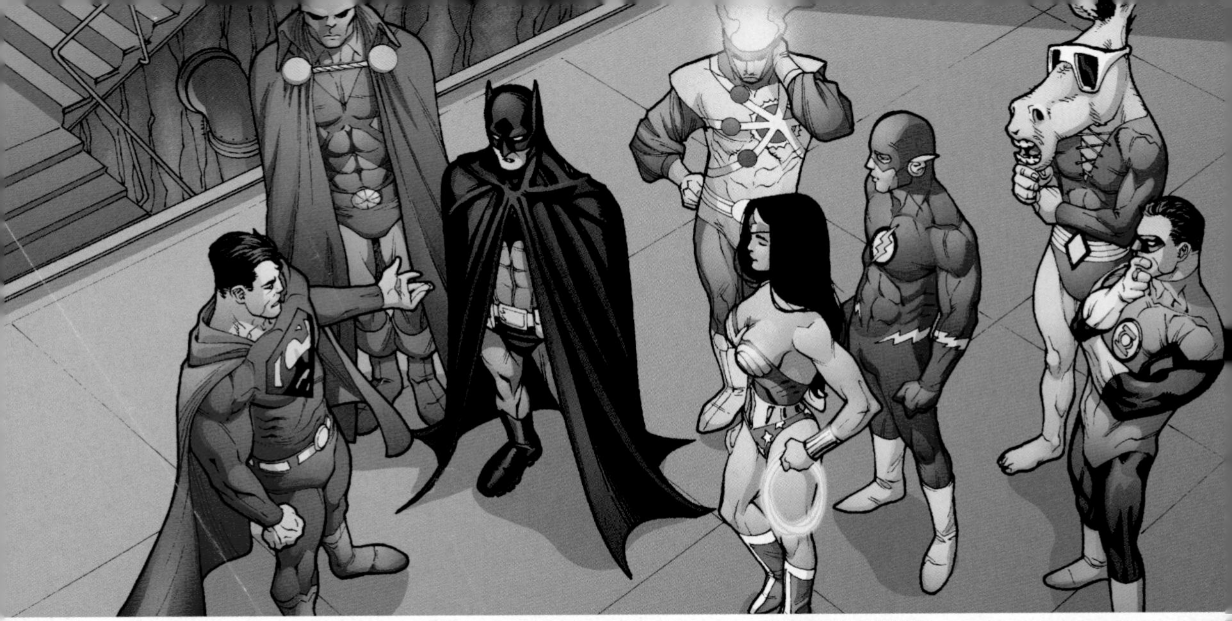

LOST

Marv Wolfman
Writer

Mike S. Miller
Artist

Cover by Ed Benes & Jorge Gonzalez

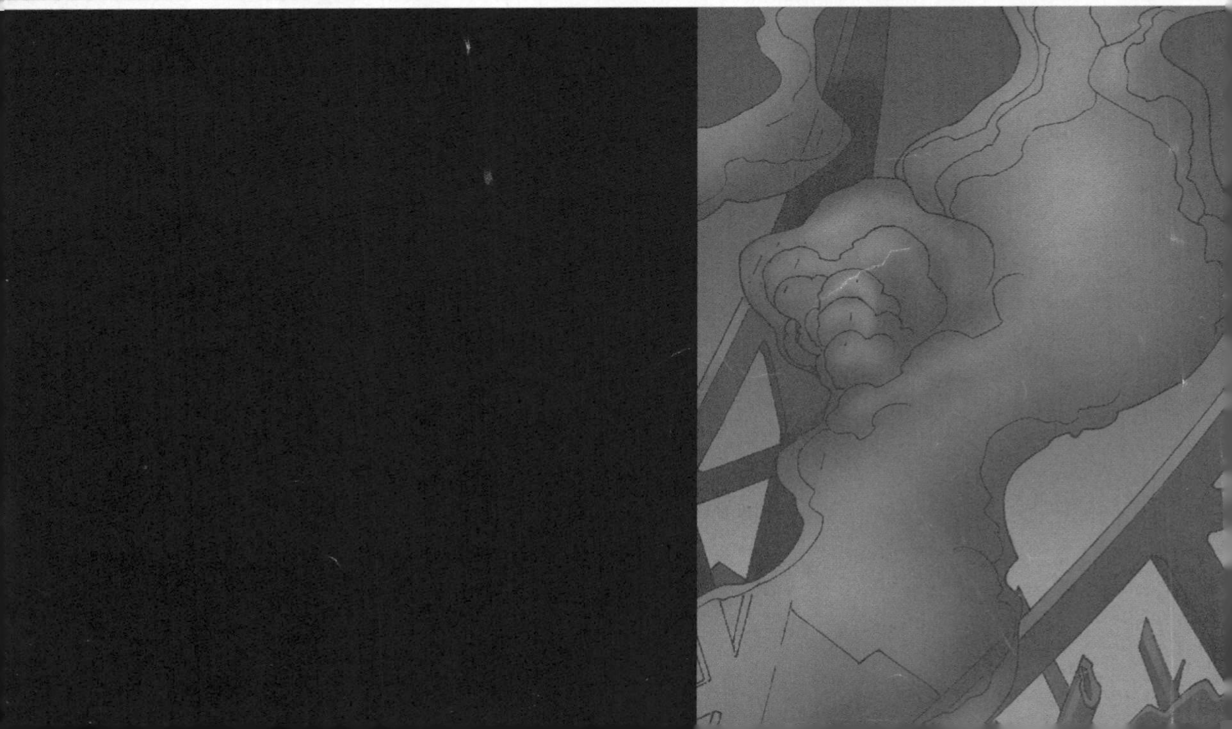

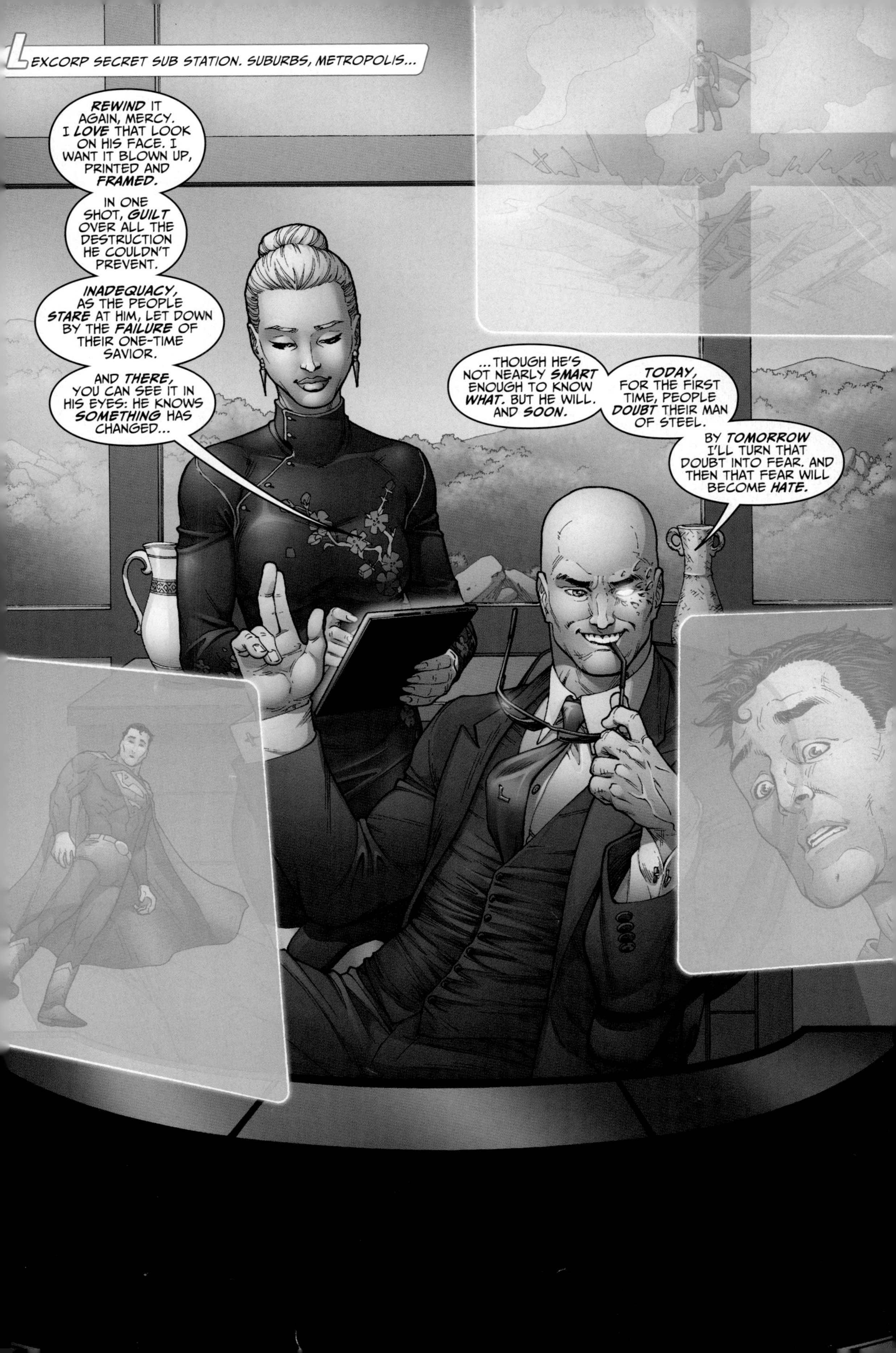
LEXCORP SECRET SUB STATION. SUBURBS, METROPOLIS...
REWIND IT AGAIN, MERCY. I LOVE THAT LOOK ON HIS FACE. I WANT IT BLOWN UP, PRINTED AND FRAMED.
IN ONE SHOT, GUILT OVER ALL THE DESTRUCTION HE COULDN'T PREVENT.
INADEQUACY, AS THE PEOPLE STARE AT HIM, LET DOWN BY THE FAILURE OF THEIR ONE-TIME SAVIOR.
AND THERE, YOU CAN SEE IT IN HIS EYES: HE KNOWS SOMETHING HAS CHANGED...
...THOUGH HE'S NOT NEARLY SMART ENOUGH TO KNOW WHAT. BUT HE WILL. AND SOON.
TODAY, FOR THE FIRST TIME, PEOPLE DOUBT THEIR MAN OF STEEL.
BY TOMORROW I'LL TURN THAT DOUBT INTO FEAR. AND THEN THAT FEAR WILL BECOME HATE.

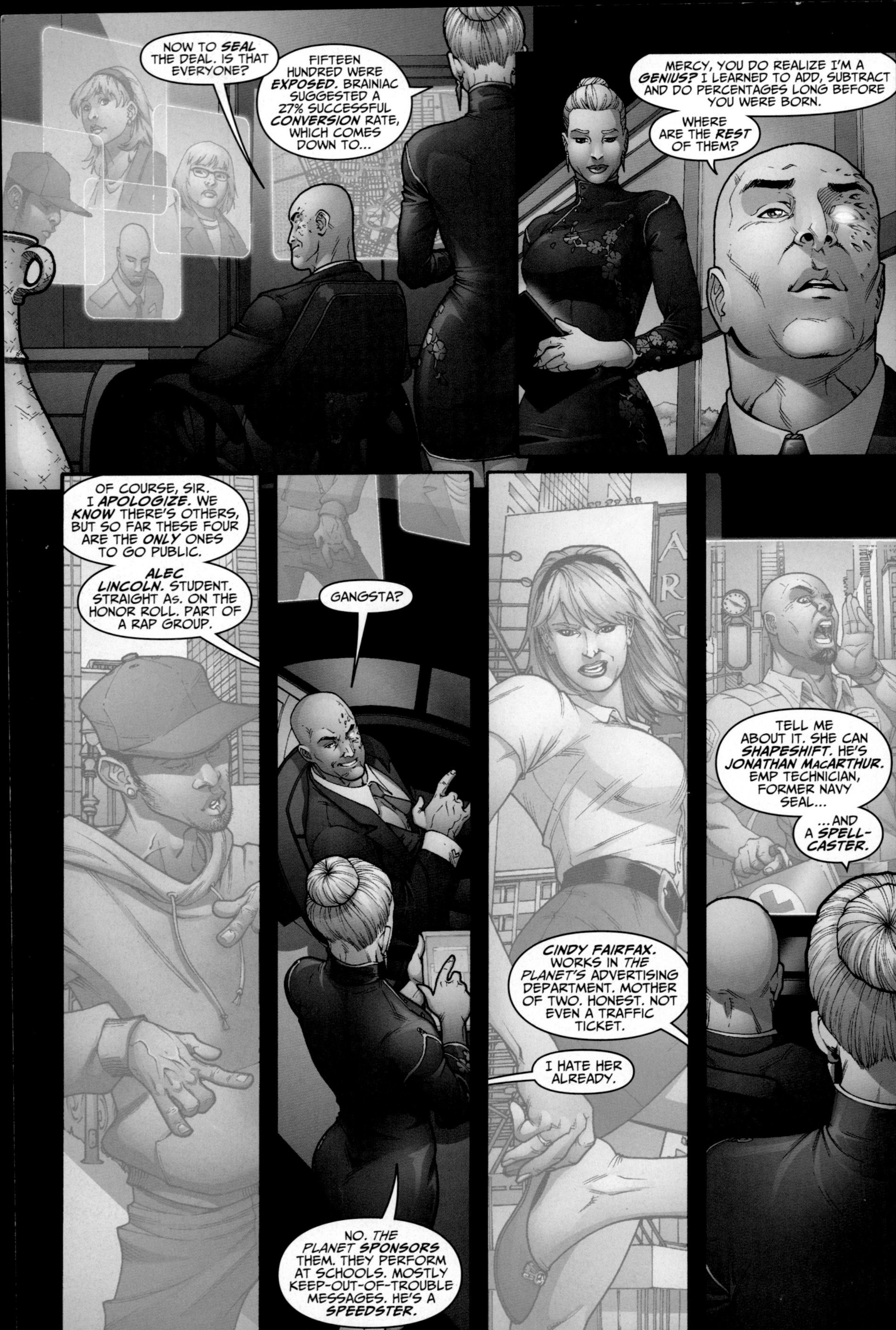
NOW TO SEAL THE DEAL. IS THAT EVERYONE?
FIFTEEN HUNDRED WERE EXPOSED. BRAINIAC SUGGESTED A 27% SUCCESSFUL CONVERSION RATE, WHICH COMES DOWN TO...
MERCY, YOU DO REALIZE I'M A GENIUS? I LEARNED TO ADD, SUBTRACT AND DO PERCENTAGES LONG BEFORE YOU WERE BORN.
WHERE ARE THE REST OF THEM?
OF COURSE, SIR. I APOLOGIZE. WE KNOW THERE'S OTHERS, BUT SO FAR THESE FOUR ARE THE ONLY ONES TO GO PUBLIC.
ALEC LINCOLN. STUDENT. STRAIGHT As. ON THE HONOR ROLL. PART OF A RAP GROUP.
GANGSTA?
NO. THE PLANET SPONSORS THEM. THEY PERFORM AT SCHOOLS. MOSTLY KEEP-OUT-OF-TROUBLE MESSAGES. HE'S A SPEEDSTER.
CINDY FAIRFAX. WORKS IN THE PLANET'S ADVERTISING DEPARTMENT. MOTHER OF TWO. HONEST. NOT EVEN A TRAFFIC TICKET.
I HATE HER ALREADY.
TELL ME ABOUT IT. SHE CAN SHAPESHIFT. HE'S JONATHAN MacARTHUR. EMP TECHNICIAN, FORMER NAVY SEAL...
...AND A SPELL-CASTER.

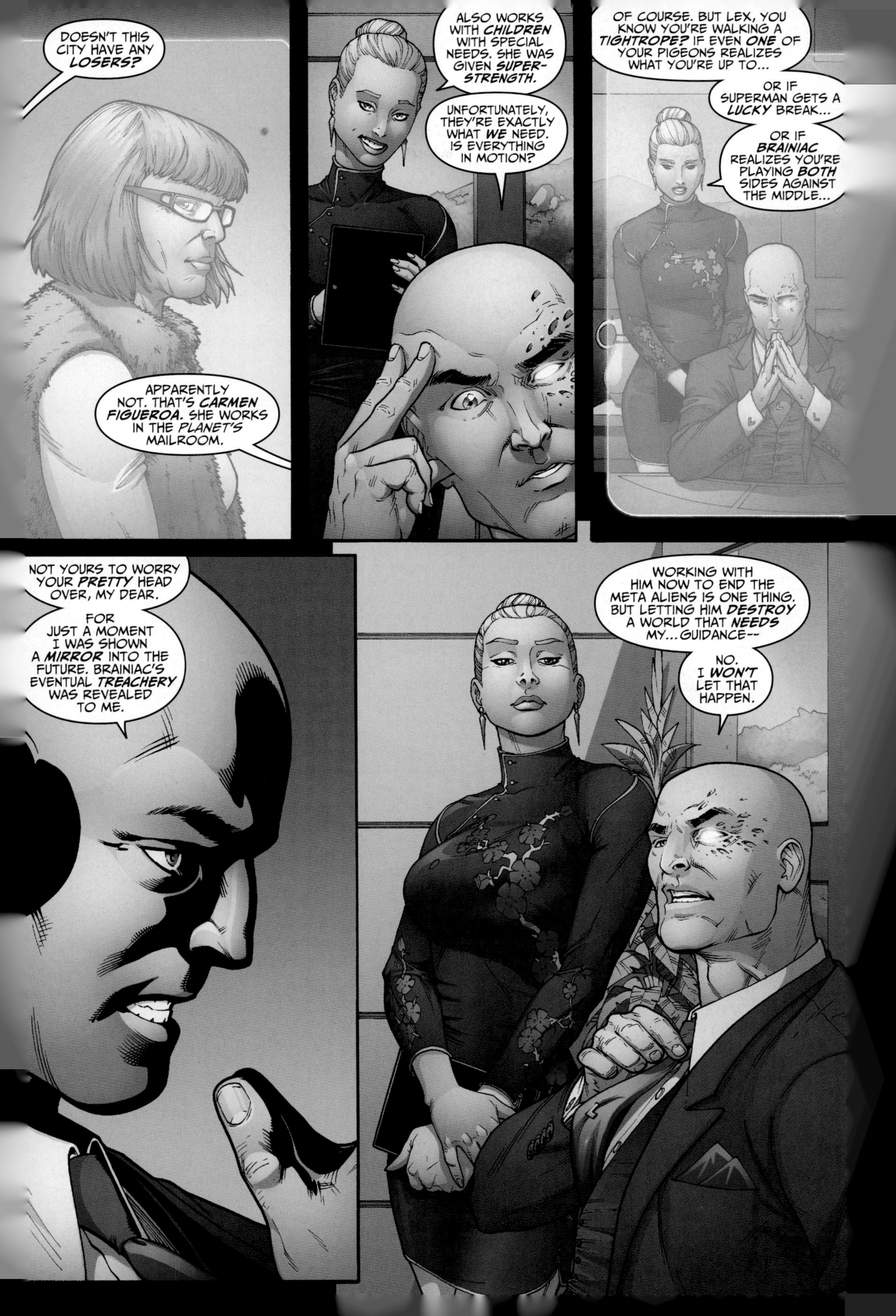
DOESN'T THIS CITY HAVE ANY LOSERS?
APPARENTLY NOT. THAT'S CARMEN FIGUEROA. SHE WORKS IN THE PLANET'S MAILROOM.
ALSO WORKS WITH CHILDREN WITH SPECIAL NEEDS. SHE WAS GIVEN SUPER-STRENGTH.
UNFORTUNATELY, THEY'RE EXACTLY WHAT WE NEED. IS EVERYTHING IN MOTION?
OF COURSE. BUT LEX, YOU KNOW YOU'RE WALKING A TIGHTROPE? IF EVEN ONE OF YOUR PIGEONS REALIZES WHAT YOU'RE UP TO...
OR IF SUPERMAN GETS A LUCKY BREAK...
OR IF BRAINIAC REALIZES YOU'RE PLAYING BOTH SIDES AGAINST THE MIDDLE...
NOT YOURS TO WORRY YOUR PRETTY HEAD OVER, MY DEAR.
FOR JUST A MOMENT I WAS SHOWN A MIRROR INTO THE FUTURE. BRAINIAC'S EVENTUAL TREACHERY WAS REVEALED TO ME.
WORKING WITH HIM NOW TO END THE META ALIENS IS ONE THING. BUT LETTING HIM DESTROY A WORLD THAT NEEDS MY...GUIDANCE--
NO. I WON'T LET THAT HAPPEN.

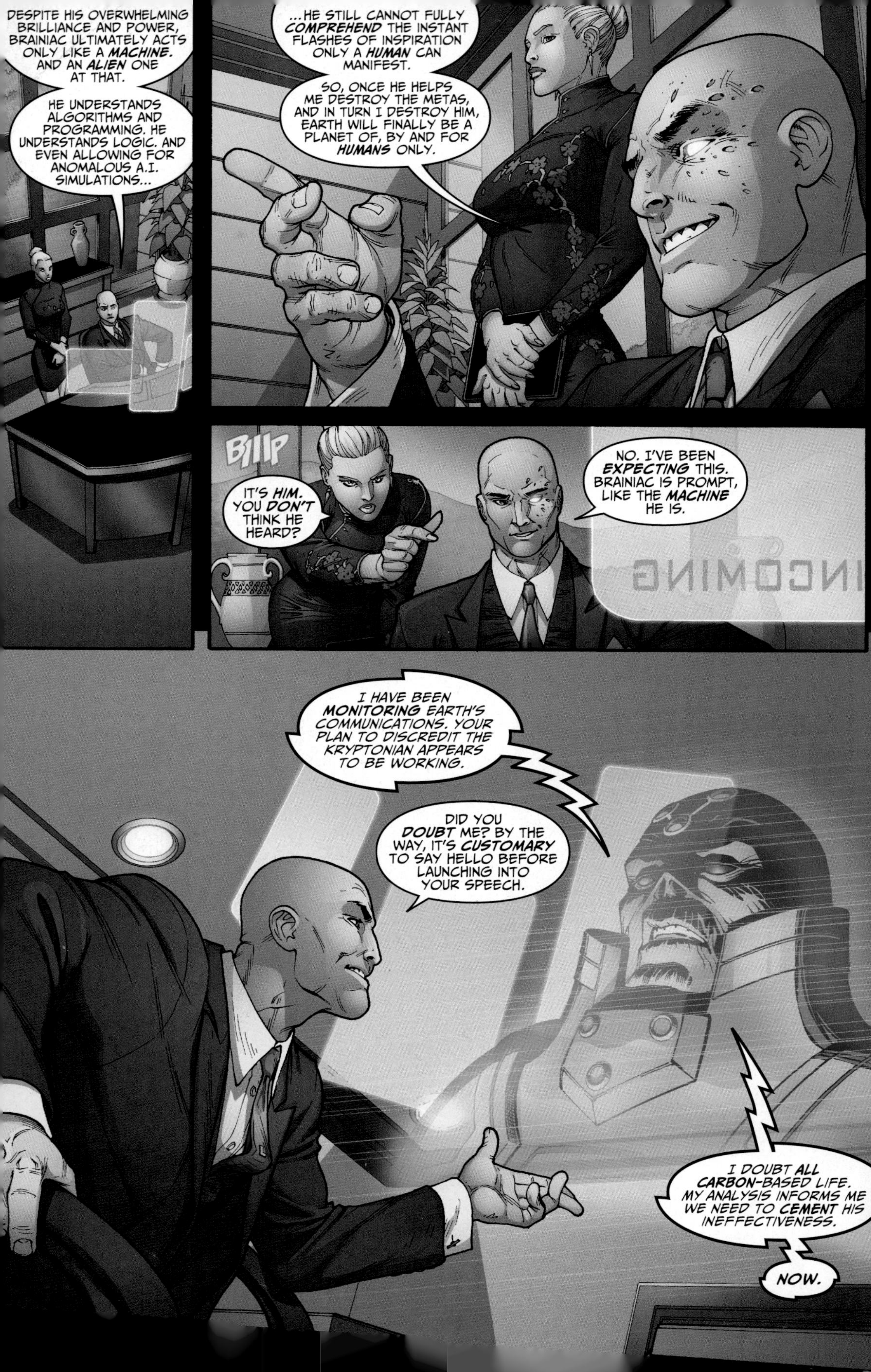
DESPITE HIS OVERWHELMING BRILLIANCE AND POWER, BRAINIAC ULTIMATELY ACTS ONLY LIKE A MACHINE. AND AN ALIEN ONE AT THAT.
HE UNDERSTANDS ALGORITHMS AND PROGRAMMING. HE UNDERSTANDS LOGIC. AND EVEN ALLOWING FOR ANOMALOUS A.I. SIMULATIONS...
...HE STILL CANNOT FULLY COMPREHEND THE INSTANT FLASHES OF INSPIRATION ONLY A HUMAN CAN MANIFEST.
SO, ONCE HE HELPS ME DESTROY THE METAS, AND IN TURN I DESTROY HIM, EARTH WILL FINALLY BE A PLANET OF, BY AND FOR HUMANS ONLY.
BIIIP
IT'S HIM. YOU DON'T THINK HE HEARD?
NO. I'VE BEEN EXPECTING THIS. BRAINIAC IS PROMPT, LIKE THE MACHINE HE IS.
INCOMING
I HAVE BEEN MONITORING EARTH'S COMMUNICATIONS. YOUR PLAN TO DISCREDIT THE KRYPTONIAN APPEARS TO BE WORKING.
DID YOU DOUBT ME? BY THE WAY, IT'S CUSTOMARY TO SAY HELLO BEFORE LAUNCHING INTO YOUR SPEECH.
I DOUBT ALL CARBON-BASED LIFE. MY ANALYSIS INFORMS ME WE NEED TO CEMENT HIS INEFFECTIVENESS.
NOW.

"ALREADY IN MOTION. WE HAVE OUR *INITIAL* CAST OF DELIGHTFUL CHARACTERS."

HI. I'M CINDY. HOLD ON WHILE I *REACH* YOU.

BUT, BUT...YOU'RE A *SNAKE*?!

AND ONCE YOU'RE FREE I'LL JUST BE A *MOM* AGAIN. YOU OKAY?

YEAH. WOW.

MS. FAIRFAX?

AREN'T YOU *LEX LUTHOR*?

GOOD TO BE *RECOGNIZED.* IT'LL MAKE THINGS GO FASTER.

I APPRECIATE HOW YOU'RE USING YOUR NEWFOUND *POWERS* TO HELP OTHERS. BUT IF YOU COME WITH ME...

...YOU CAN BE SAVING *THOUSANDS* INSTEAD OF JUST THE *COMMON STRAY.* WHAT DO YOU SAY?

LET'S DO IT, THEN.

I *LIKE* IT.

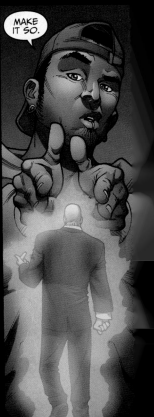

MAKE IT SO.

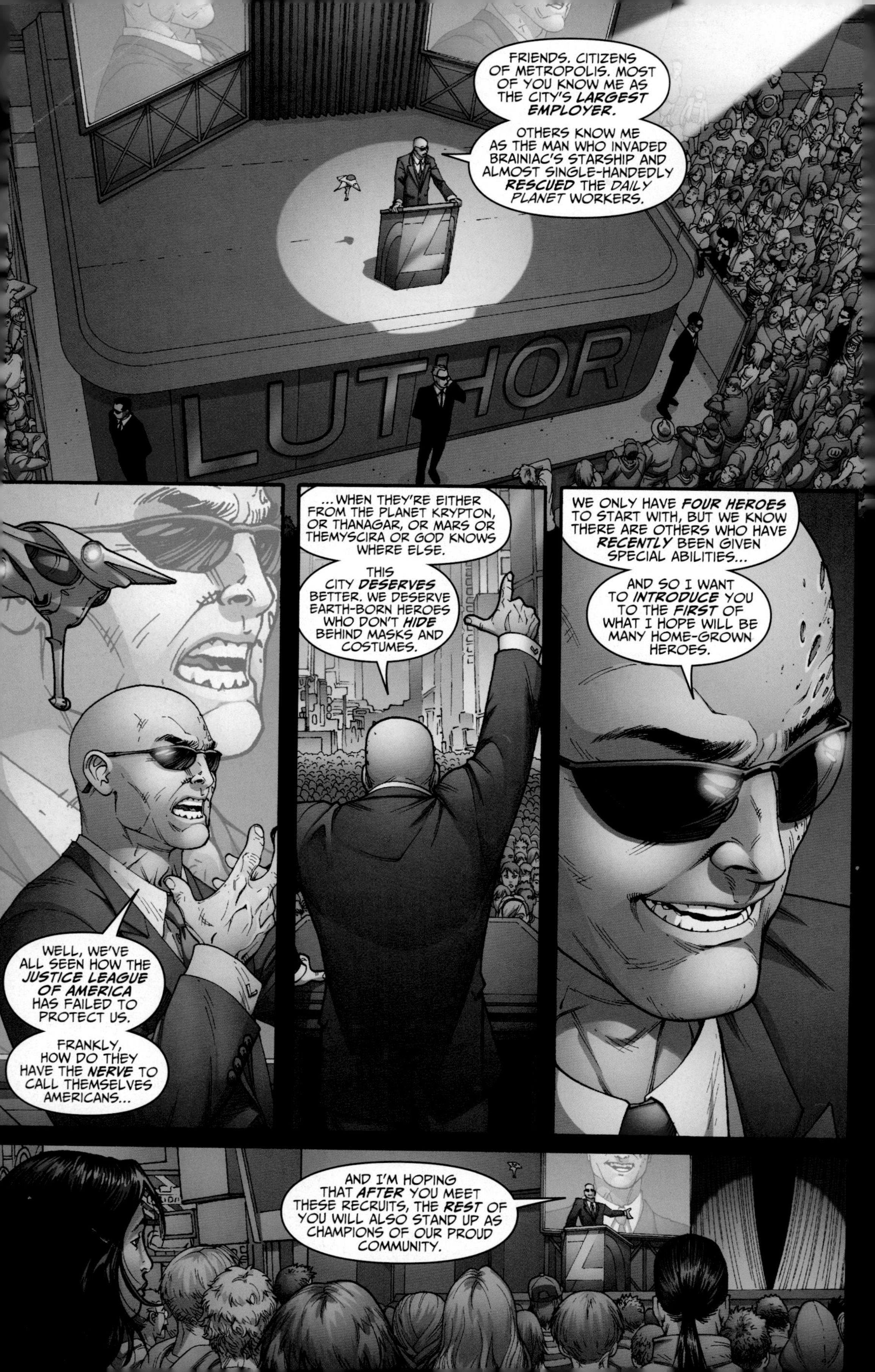
FRIENDS. CITIZENS OF METROPOLIS. MOST OF YOU KNOW ME AS THE CITY'S *LARGEST EMPLOYER.*
OTHERS KNOW ME AS THE MAN WHO INVADED BRAINIAC'S STARSHIP AND ALMOST SINGLE-HANDEDLY *RESCUED* THE *DAILY PLANET* WORKERS.
LUTHOR
WELL, WE'VE ALL SEEN HOW THE *JUSTICE LEAGUE OF AMERICA* HAS FAILED TO PROTECT US.
FRANKLY, HOW DO THEY HAVE THE *NERVE* TO CALL THEMSELVES AMERICANS...
...WHEN THEY'RE EITHER FROM THE PLANET KRYPTON, OR THANAGAR, OR MARS OR THEMYSCIRA OR GOD KNOWS WHERE ELSE.
THIS CITY *DESERVES* BETTER. WE DESERVE EARTH-BORN HEROES WHO DON'T *HIDE* BEHIND MASKS AND COSTUMES.
WE ONLY HAVE *FOUR HEROES* TO START WITH, BUT WE KNOW THERE ARE OTHERS WHO HAVE *RECENTLY* BEEN GIVEN SPECIAL ABILITIES...
AND SO I WANT TO *INTRODUCE* YOU TO THE *FIRST* OF WHAT I HOPE WILL BE MANY HOME-GROWN HEROES.
AND I'M HOPING THAT *AFTER* YOU MEET THESE RECRUITS, THE *REST* OF YOU WILL ALSO STAND UP AS CHAMPIONS OF OUR PROUD COMMUNITY.

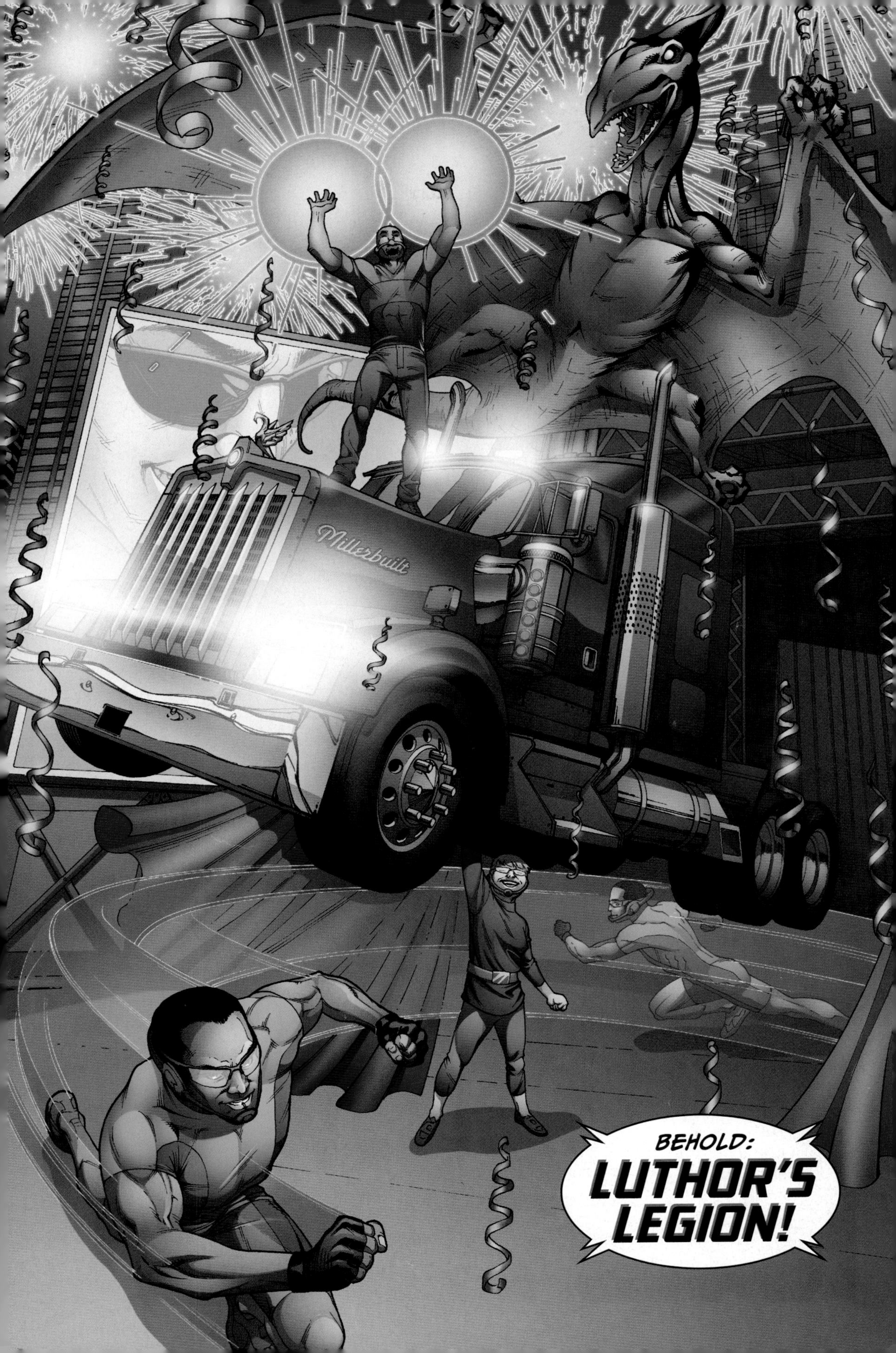
Millerbuilt
BEHOLD:
LUTHOR'S LEGION!

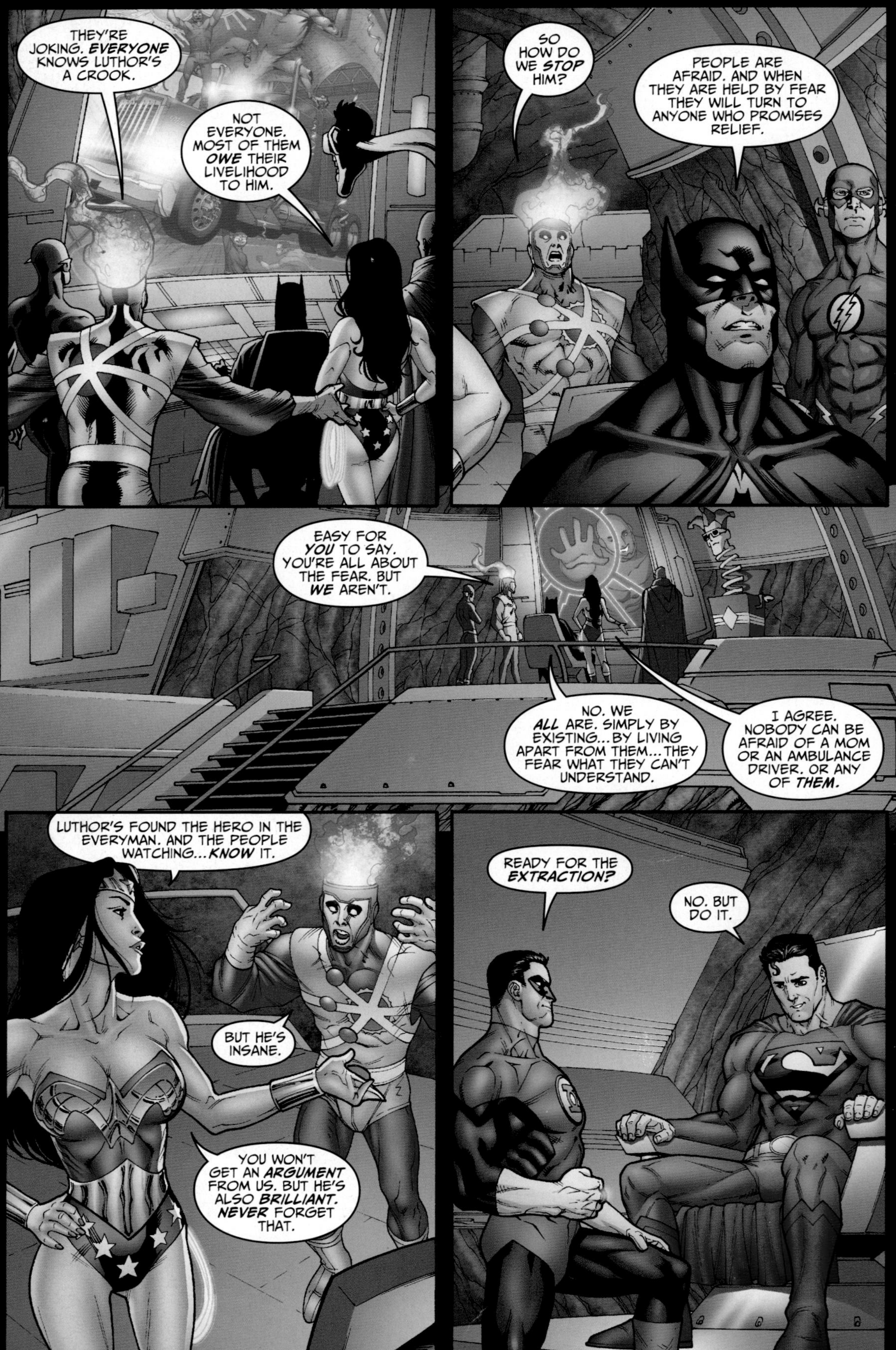
THEY'RE JOKING. EVERYONE KNOWS LUTHOR'S A CROOK.
NOT EVERYONE. MOST OF THEM OWE THEIR LIVELIHOOD TO HIM.
SO HOW DO WE STOP HIM?
PEOPLE ARE AFRAID. AND WHEN THEY ARE HELD BY FEAR THEY WILL TURN TO ANYONE WHO PROMISES RELIEF.
EASY FOR YOU TO SAY. YOU'RE ALL ABOUT THE FEAR. BUT WE AREN'T.
NO. WE ALL ARE. SIMPLY BY EXISTING... BY LIVING APART FROM THEM... THEY FEAR WHAT THEY CAN'T UNDERSTAND.
I AGREE. NOBODY CAN BE AFRAID OF A MOM OR AN AMBULANCE DRIVER. OR ANY OF THEM.
LUTHOR'S FOUND THE HERO IN THE EVERYMAN. AND THE PEOPLE WATCHING... KNOW IT.
BUT HE'S INSANE.
YOU WON'T GET AN ARGUMENT FROM US. BUT HE'S ALSO BRILLIANT. NEVER FORGET THAT.
READY FOR THE EXTRACTION?
NO. BUT DO IT.

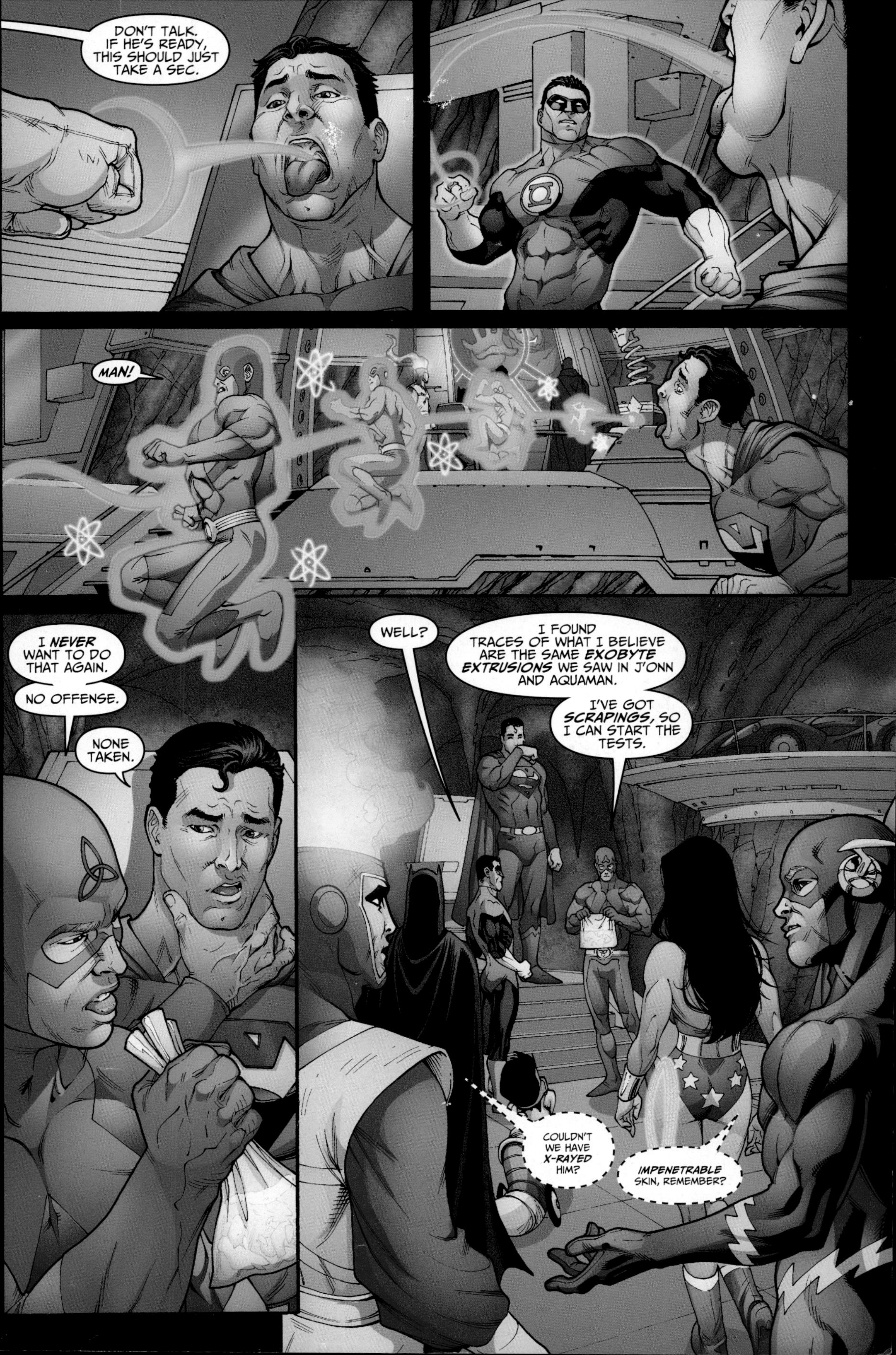
DON'T TALK. IF HE'S READY, THIS SHOULD JUST TAKE A SEC.
MAN!
I NEVER WANT TO DO THAT AGAIN.
NO OFFENSE.
NONE TAKEN.
WELL?
I FOUND TRACES OF WHAT I BELIEVE ARE THE SAME EXOBYTE EXTRUSIONS WE SAW IN J'ONN AND AQUAMAN.
I'VE GOT SCRAPINGS, SO I CAN START THE TESTS.
COULDN'T WE HAVE X-RAYED HIM?
IMPENETRABLE SKIN, REMEMBER?

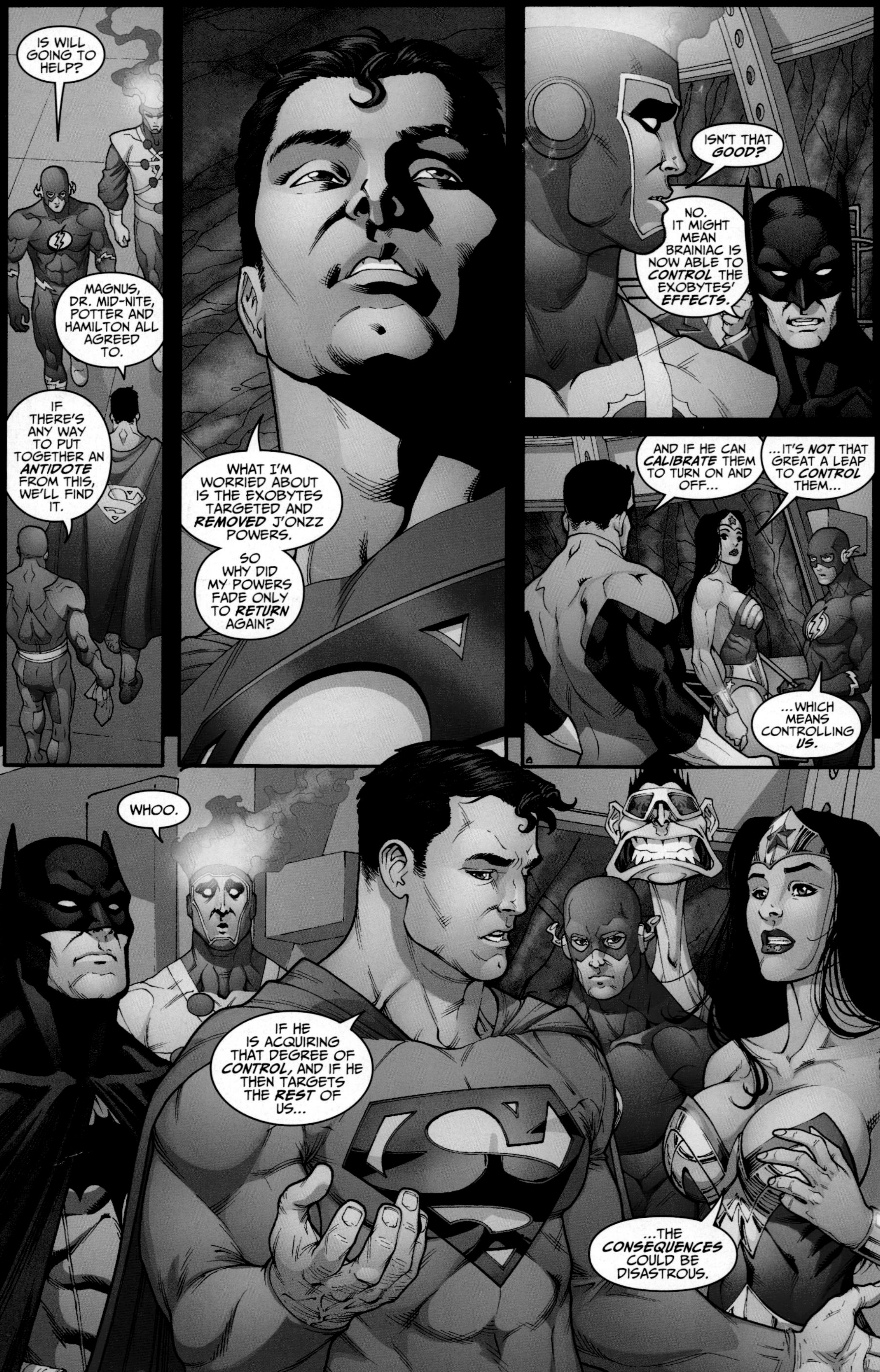
IS WILL GOING TO HELP?
MAGNUS, DR. MID-NITE, POTTER AND HAMILTON ALL AGREED TO.
IF THERE'S ANY WAY TO PUT TOGETHER AN ANTIDOTE FROM THIS, WE'LL FIND IT.
WHAT I'M WORRIED ABOUT IS THE EXOBYTES TARGETED AND REMOVED J'ONZZ POWERS.
SO WHY DID MY POWERS FADE ONLY TO RETURN AGAIN?
ISN'T THAT GOOD?
NO. IT MIGHT MEAN BRAINIAC IS NOW ABLE TO CONTROL THE EXOBYTES' EFFECTS.
AND IF HE CAN CALIBRATE THEM TO TURN ON AND OFF...
...IT'S NOT THAT GREAT A LEAP TO CONTROL THEM...
...WHICH MEANS CONTROLLING US.
WHOO.
IF HE IS ACQUIRING THAT DEGREE OF CONTROL, AND IF HE THEN TARGETS THE REST OF US...
...THE CONSEQUENCES COULD BE DISASTROUS.

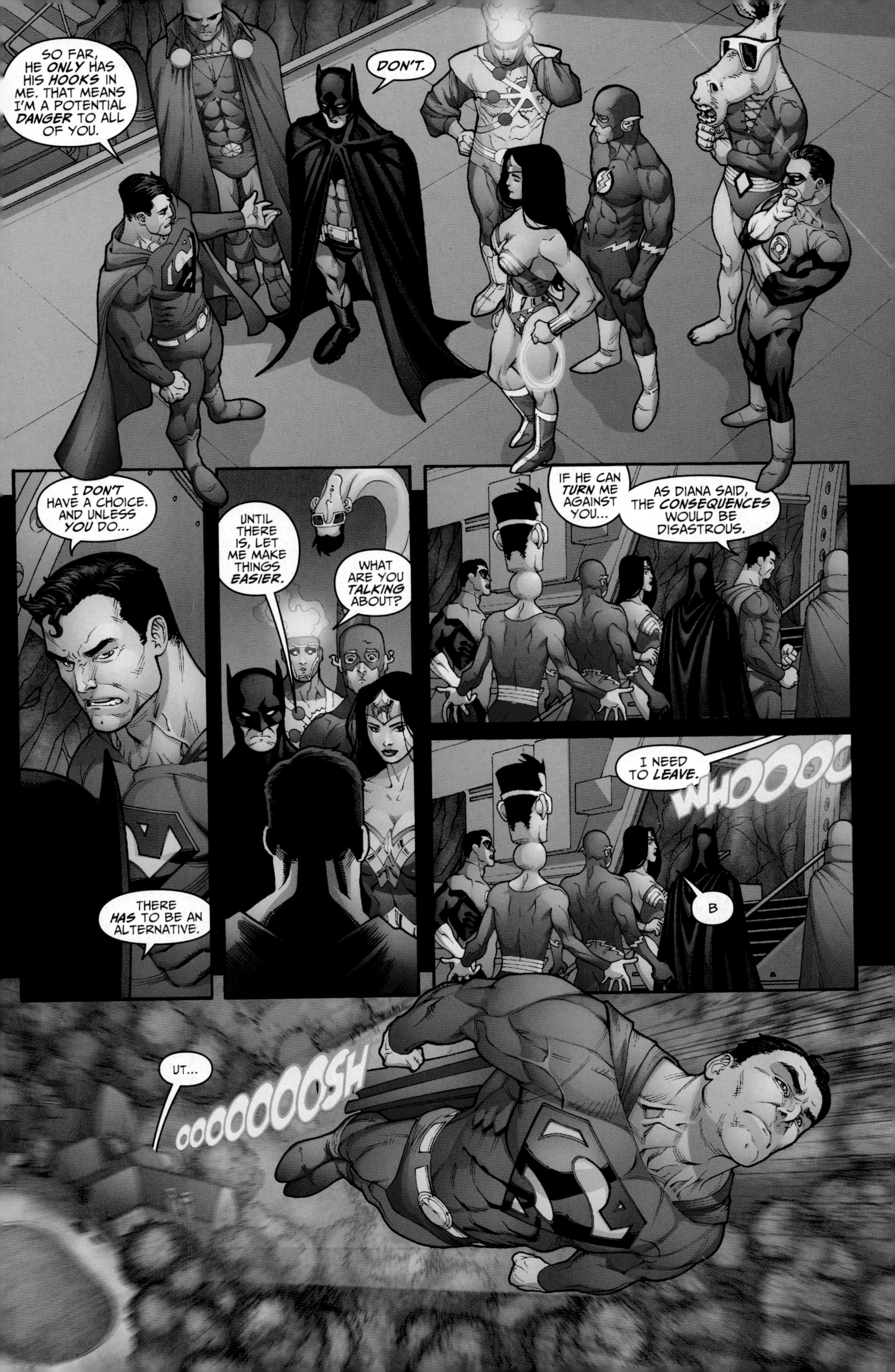
SO FAR, HE ONLY HAS HIS HOOKS IN ME. THAT MEANS I'M A POTENTIAL DANGER TO ALL OF YOU.
DON'T.
I DON'T HAVE A CHOICE. AND UNLESS YOU DO...
THERE HAS TO BE AN ALTERNATIVE.
UNTIL THERE IS, LET ME MAKE THINGS EASIER.
WHAT ARE YOU TALKING ABOUT?
IF HE CAN TURN ME AGAINST YOU...
AS DIANA SAID, THE CONSEQUENCES WOULD BE DISASTROUS.
I NEED TO LEAVE.
WHOOOOO
B
UT...
OOOOOOOOSH

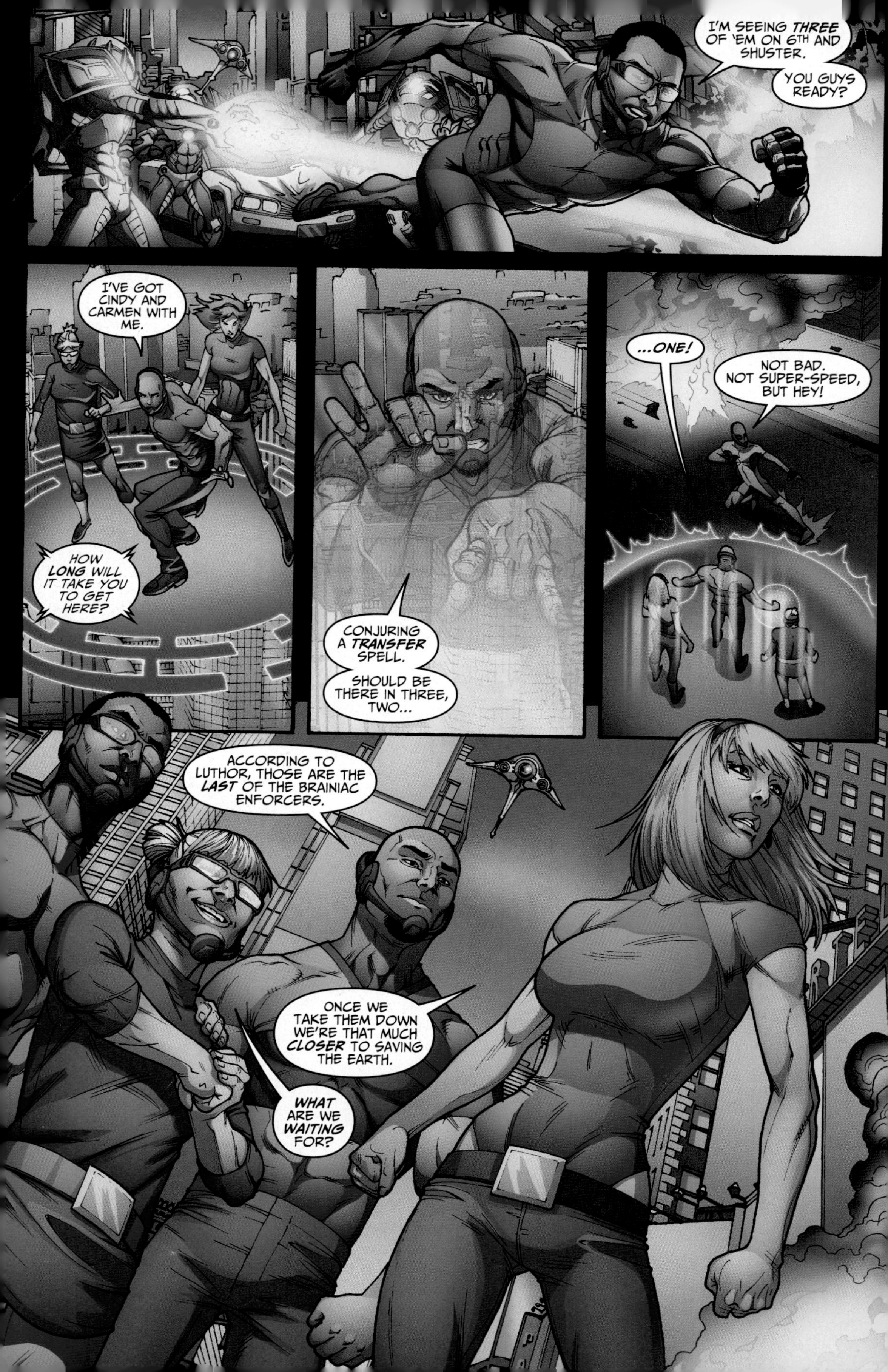
I'M SEEING THREE OF 'EM ON 6TH AND SHUSTER.
YOU GUYS READY?
I'VE GOT CINDY AND CARMEN WITH ME.
HOW LONG WILL IT TAKE YOU TO GET HERE?
CONJURING A TRANSFER SPELL.
SHOULD BE THERE IN THREE, TWO...
...ONE!
NOT BAD. NOT SUPER-SPEED, BUT HEY!
ACCORDING TO LUTHOR, THOSE ARE THE LAST OF THE BRAINIAC ENFORCERS.
ONCE WE TAKE THEM DOWN WE'RE THAT MUCH CLOSER TO SAVING THE EARTH.
WHAT ARE WE WAITING FOR?

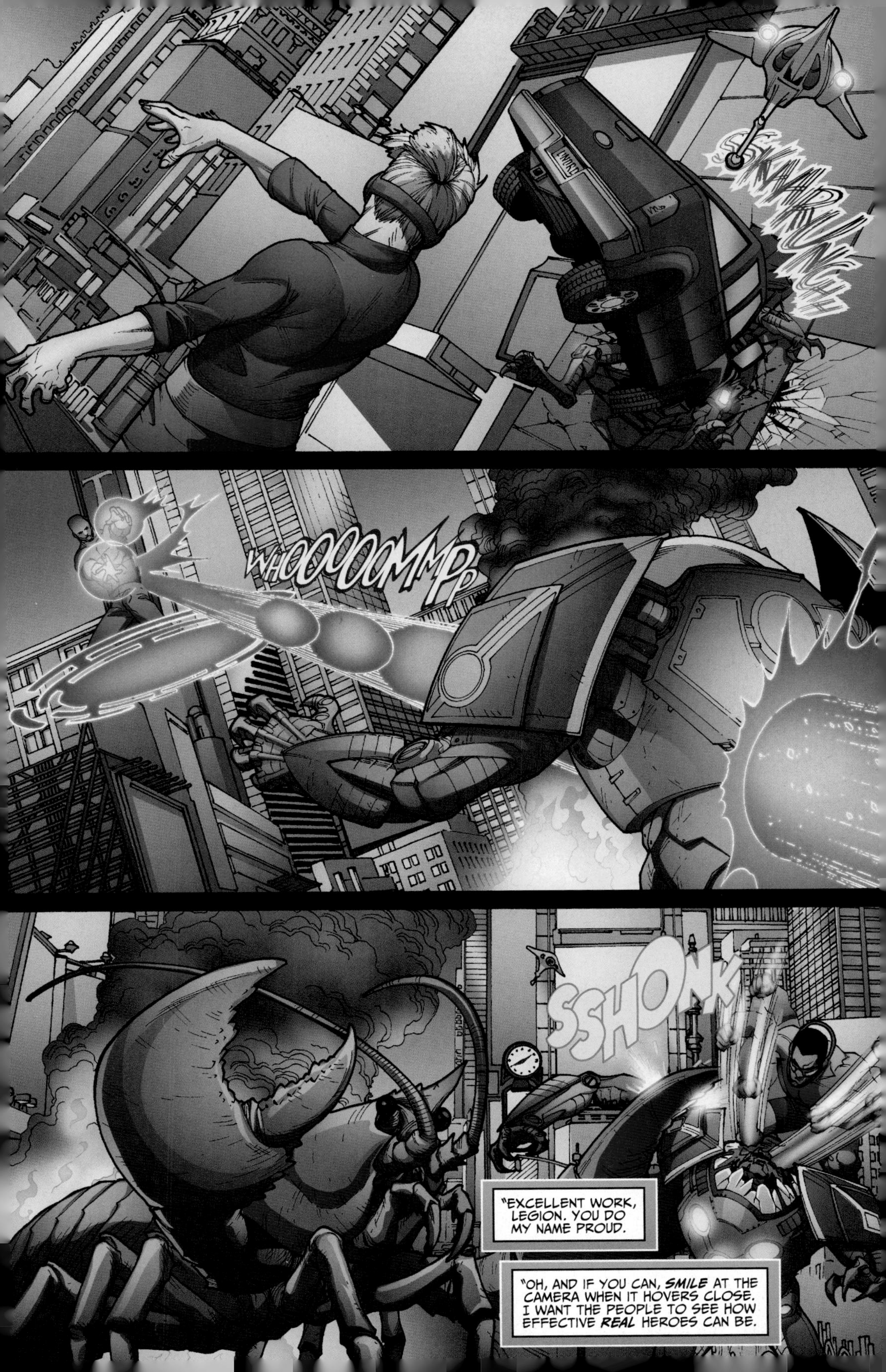

SKKARUNCH
WHOOOOOMMPP
SSHONK
"EXCELLENT WORK, LEGION. YOU DO MY NAME PROUD.
"OH, AND IF YOU CAN, SMILE AT THE CAMERA WHEN IT HOVERS CLOSE. I WANT THE PEOPLE TO SEE HOW EFFECTIVE REAL HEROES CAN BE.

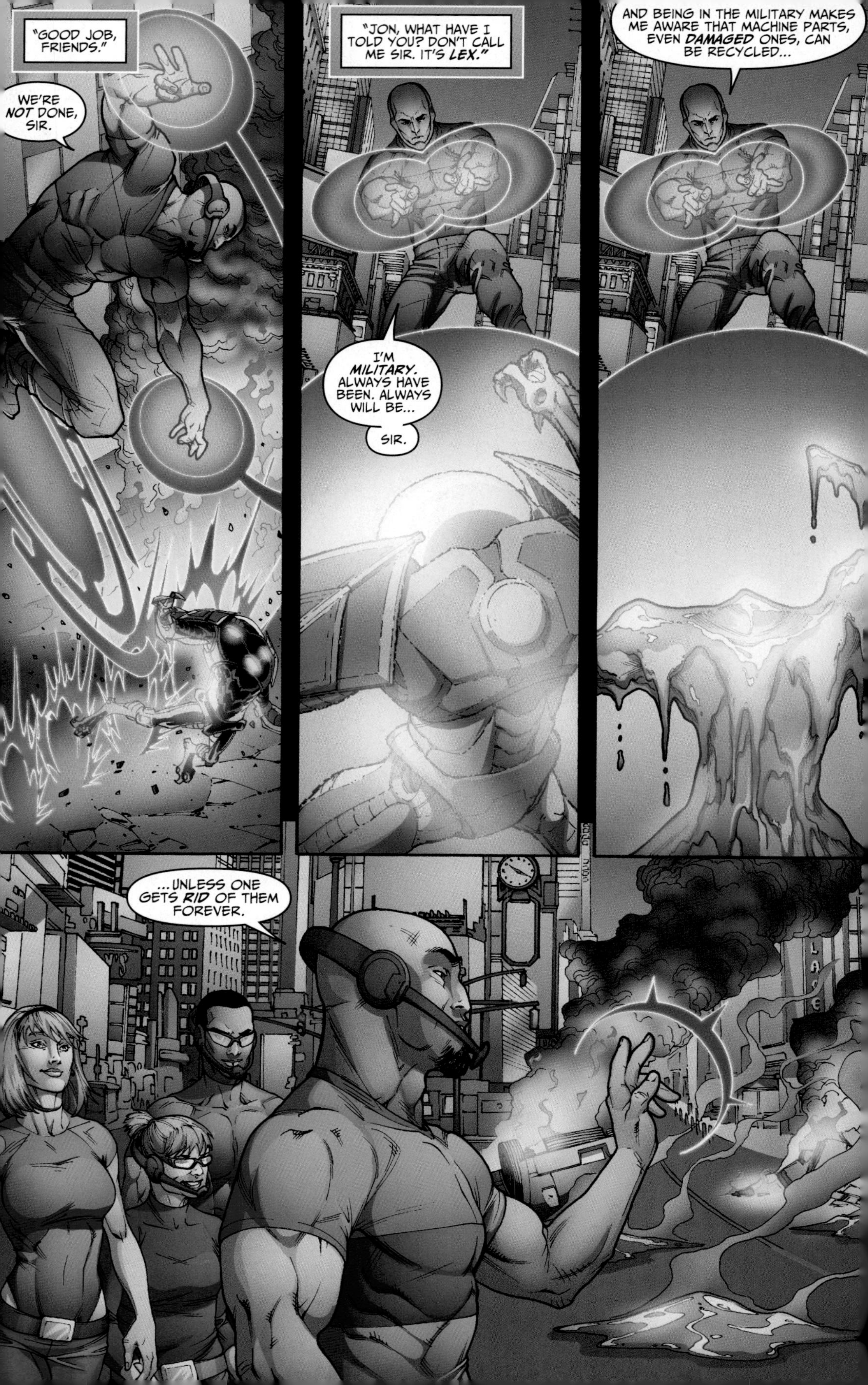
"GOOD JOB, FRIENDS."
WE'RE *NOT* DONE, SIR.
"JON, WHAT HAVE I TOLD YOU? DON'T CALL ME SIR. IT'S *LEX.*"
I'M *MILITARY.* ALWAYS HAVE BEEN. ALWAYS WILL BE...
SIR.
AND BEING IN THE MILITARY MAKES ME AWARE THAT MACHINE PARTS, EVEN *DAMAGED* ONES, CAN BE RECYCLED...
...UNLESS ONE GETS *RID* OF THEM FOREVER.

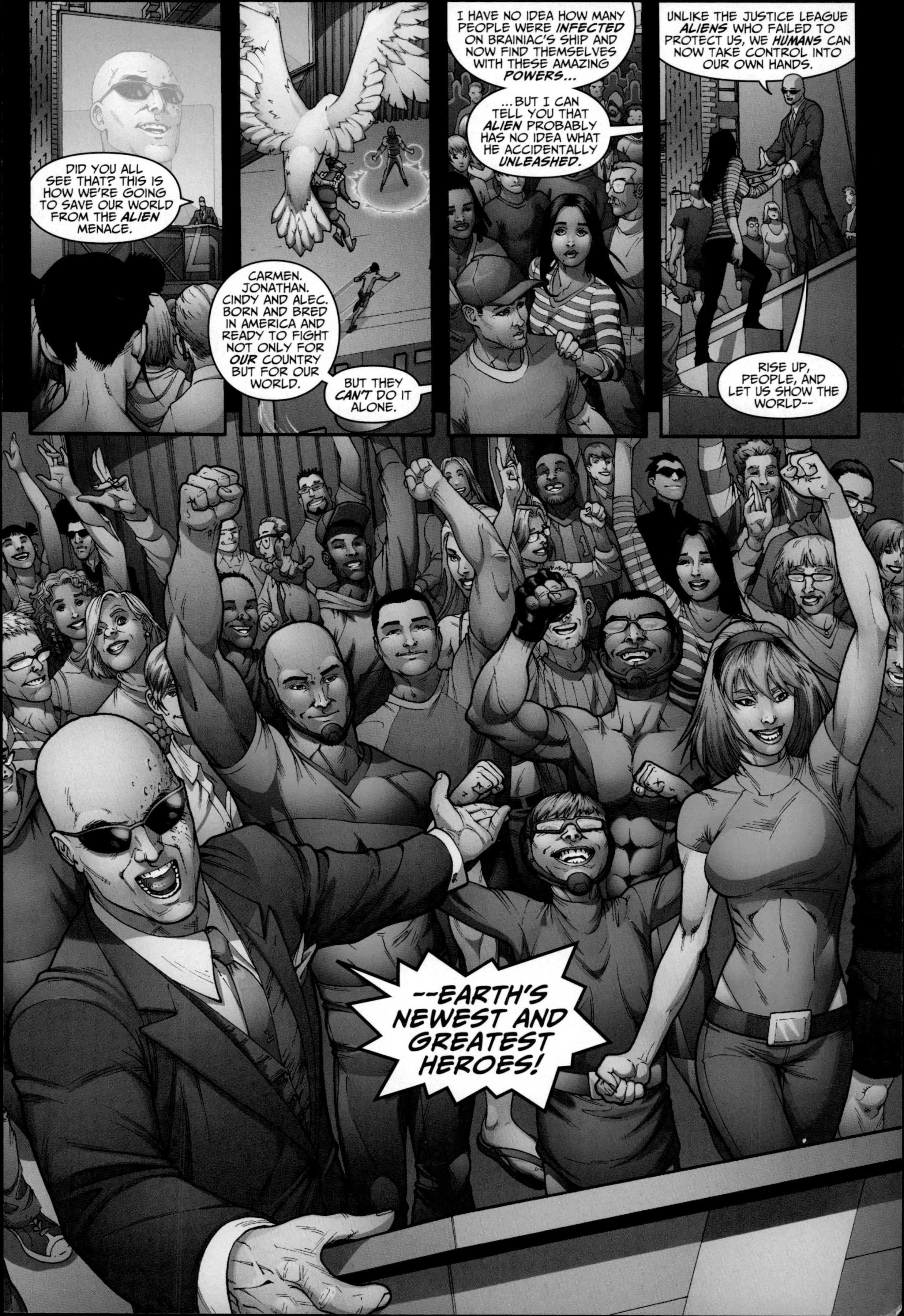
DID YOU ALL SEE THAT? THIS IS HOW WE'RE GOING TO SAVE OUR WORLD FROM THE *ALIEN* MENACE.
CARMEN. JONATHAN. CINDY AND ALEC. BORN AND BRED IN AMERICA AND READY TO FIGHT NOT ONLY FOR *OUR* COUNTRY BUT FOR OUR WORLD.
BUT THEY *CAN'T* DO IT ALONE.
I HAVE NO IDEA HOW MANY PEOPLE WERE *INFECTED* ON BRAINIAC'S SHIP AND NOW FIND THEMSELVES WITH THESE AMAZING *POWERS...*
...BUT I CAN TELL YOU THAT *ALIEN* PROBABLY HAS NO IDEA WHAT HE ACCIDENTALLY *UNLEASHED.*
UNLIKE THE JUSTICE LEAGUE *ALIENS* WHO FAILED TO PROTECT US, WE *HUMANS* CAN NOW TAKE CONTROL INTO OUR OWN HANDS.
RISE UP, PEOPLE, AND LET US SHOW THE WORLD--
--EARTH'S NEWEST AND GREATEST HEROES!

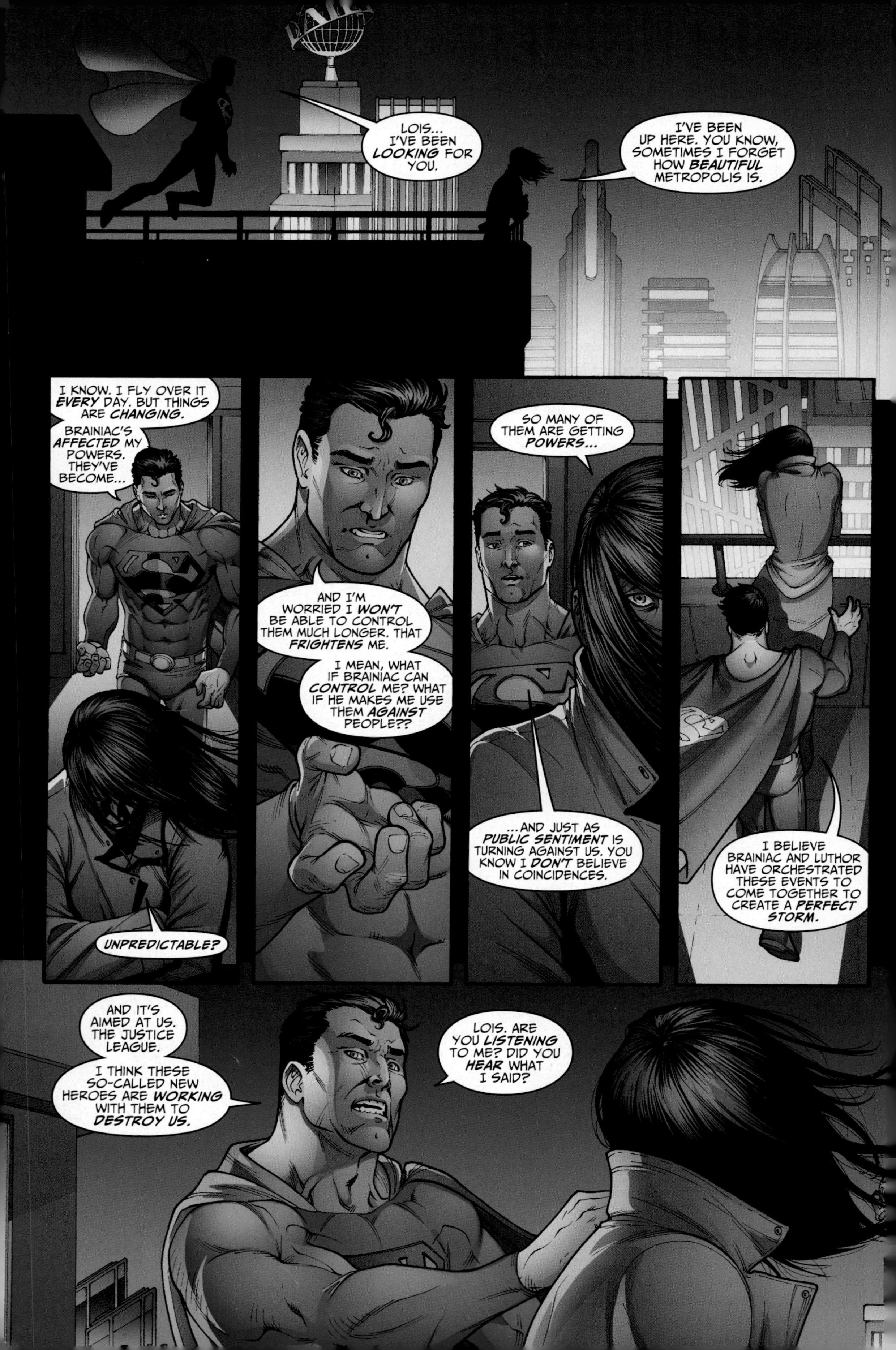
LOIS... I'VE BEEN LOOKING FOR YOU.
I'VE BEEN UP HERE. YOU KNOW, SOMETIMES I FORGET HOW BEAUTIFUL METROPOLIS IS.
I KNOW. I FLY OVER IT EVERY DAY. BUT THINGS ARE CHANGING.
BRAINIAC'S AFFECTED MY POWERS. THEY'VE BECOME...
UNPREDICTABLE?
AND I'M WORRIED I WON'T BE ABLE TO CONTROL THEM MUCH LONGER. THAT FRIGHTENS ME.
I MEAN, WHAT IF BRAINIAC CAN CONTROL ME? WHAT IF HE MAKES ME USE THEM AGAINST PEOPLE??
SO MANY OF THEM ARE GETTING POWERS...
...AND JUST AS PUBLIC SENTIMENT IS TURNING AGAINST US. YOU KNOW I DON'T BELIEVE IN COINCIDENCES.
I BELIEVE BRAINIAC AND LUTHOR HAVE ORCHESTRATED THESE EVENTS TO COME TOGETHER TO CREATE A PERFECT STORM.
AND IT'S AIMED AT US. THE JUSTICE LEAGUE.
I THINK THESE SO-CALLED NEW HEROES ARE WORKING WITH THEM TO DESTROY US.
LOIS. ARE YOU LISTENING TO ME? DID YOU HEAR WHAT I SAID?

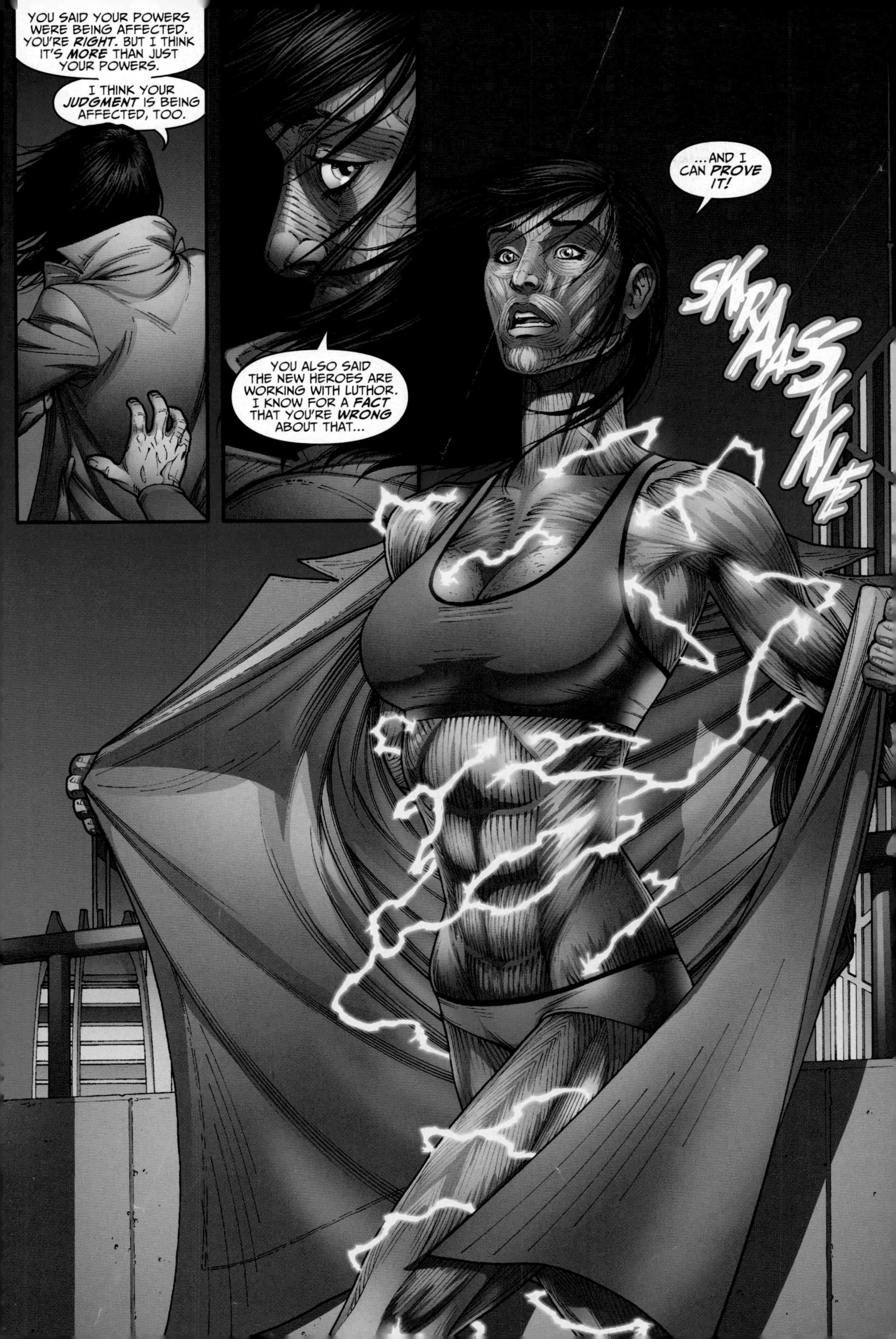
YOU SAID YOUR POWERS WERE BEING AFFECTED. YOU'RE RIGHT. BUT I THINK IT'S MORE THAN JUST YOUR POWERS.
I THINK YOUR JUDGMENT IS BEING AFFECTED, TOO.
YOU ALSO SAID THE NEW HEROES ARE WORKING WITH LUTHOR. I KNOW FOR A FACT THAT YOU'RE WRONG ABOUT THAT...
...AND I CAN PROVE IT!
SKRAASSKKLE

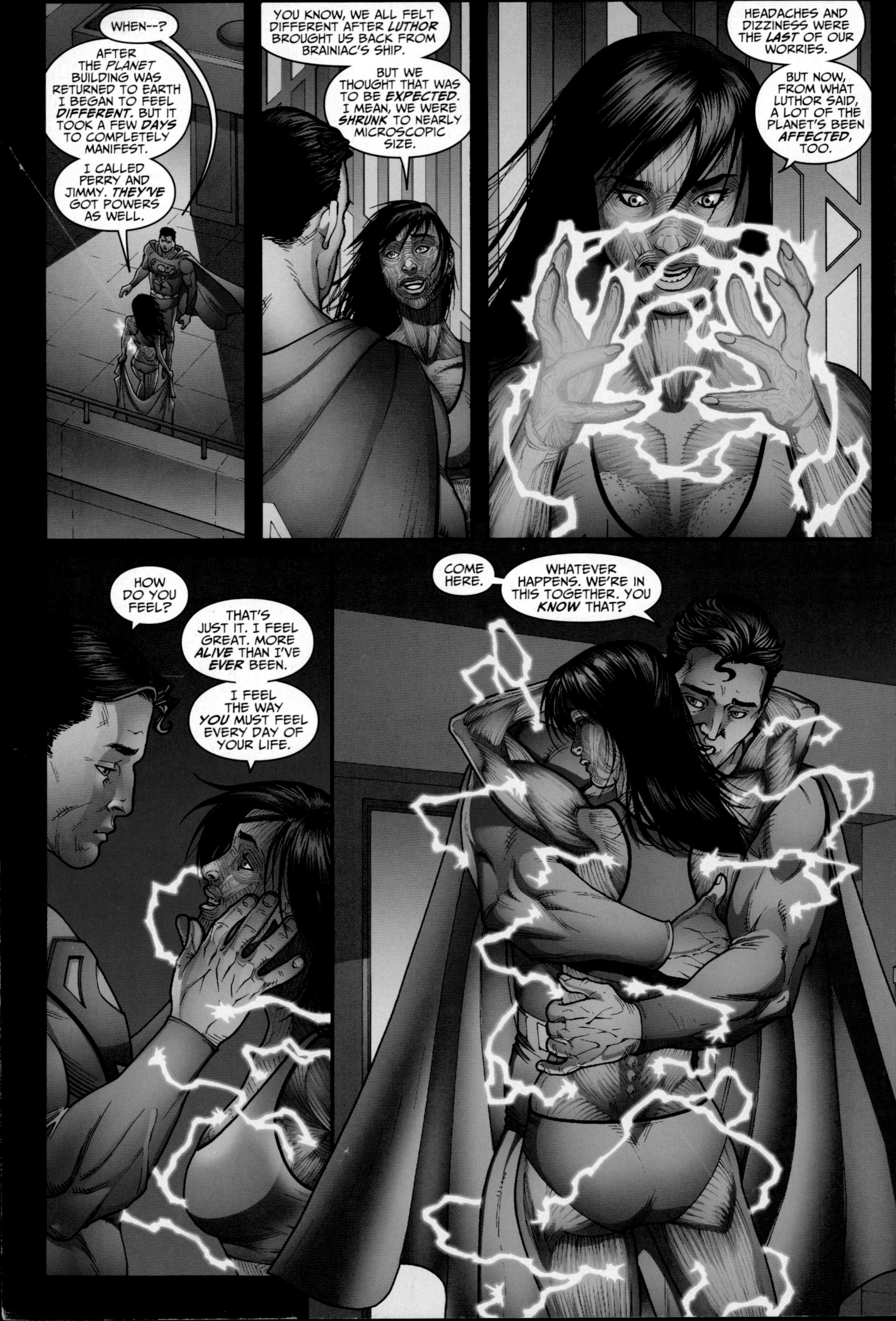
WHEN--?
AFTER THE PLANET BUILDING WAS RETURNED TO EARTH I BEGAN TO FEEL DIFFERENT. BUT IT TOOK A FEW DAYS TO COMPLETELY MANIFEST.
I CALLED PERRY AND JIMMY. THEY'VE GOT POWERS AS WELL.
YOU KNOW, WE ALL FELT DIFFERENT AFTER LUTHOR BROUGHT US BACK FROM BRAINIAC'S SHIP.
BUT WE THOUGHT THAT WAS TO BE EXPECTED. I MEAN, WE WERE SHRUNK TO NEARLY MICROSCOPIC SIZE.
HEADACHES AND DIZZINESS WERE THE LAST OF OUR WORRIES.
BUT NOW, FROM WHAT LUTHOR SAID, A LOT OF THE PLANET'S BEEN AFFECTED, TOO.
HOW DO YOU FEEL?
THAT'S JUST IT. I FEEL GREAT. MORE ALIVE THAN I'VE EVER BEEN.
I FEEL THE WAY YOU MUST FEEL EVERY DAY OF YOUR LIFE.
COME HERE.
WHATEVER HAPPENS. WE'RE IN THIS TOGETHER. YOU KNOW THAT?

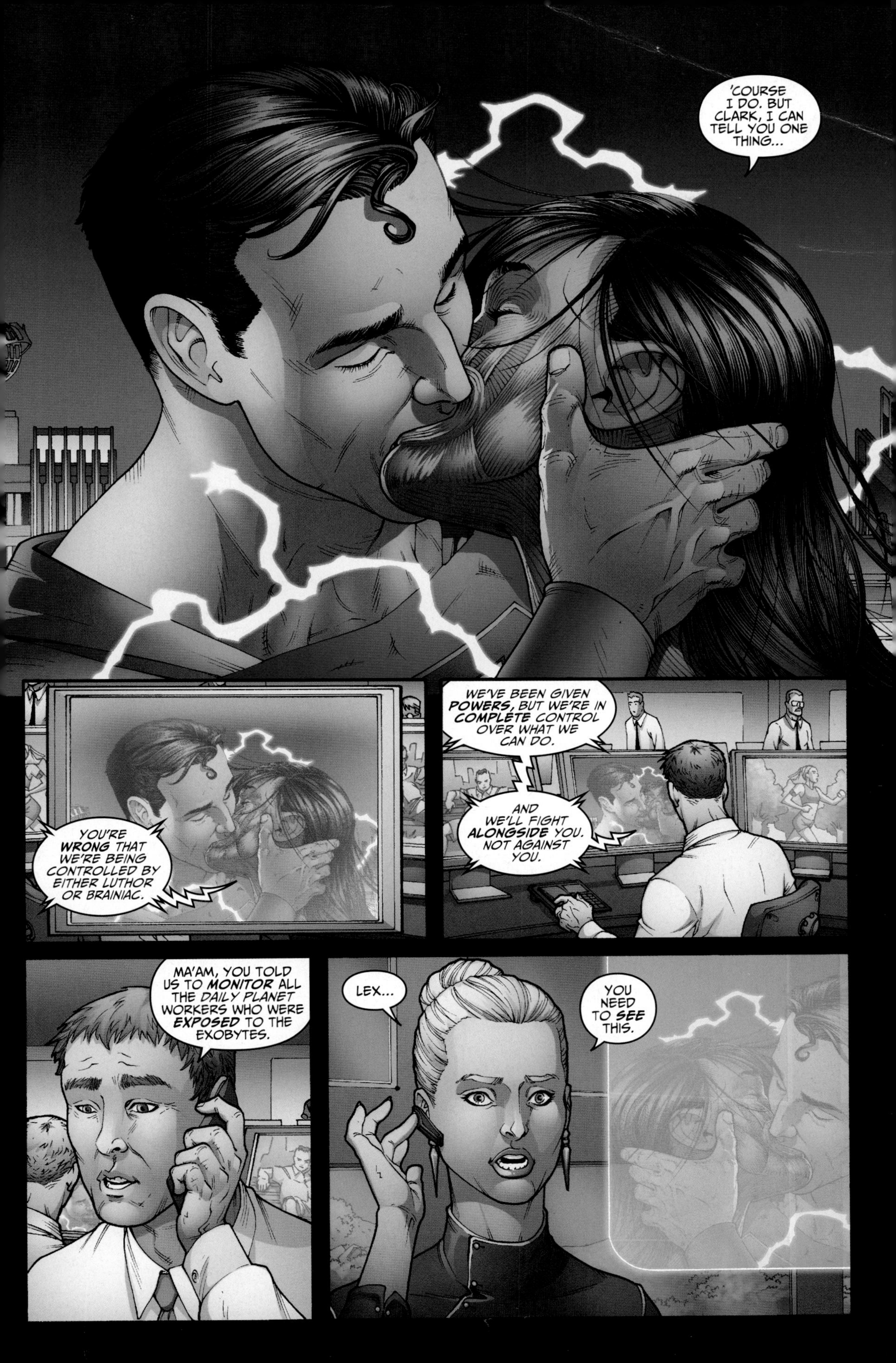
'COURSE I DO. BUT CLARK, I CAN TELL YOU ONE THING...
YOU'RE WRONG THAT WE'RE BEING CONTROLLED BY EITHER LUTHOR OR BRAINIAC.
WE'VE BEEN GIVEN POWERS, BUT WE'RE IN COMPLETE CONTROL OVER WHAT WE CAN DO.
AND WE'LL FIGHT ALONGSIDE YOU. NOT AGAINST YOU.
MA'AM, YOU TOLD US TO MONITOR ALL THE DAILY PLANET WORKERS WHO WERE EXPOSED TO THE EXOBYTES.
LEX...
YOU NEED TO SEE THIS.

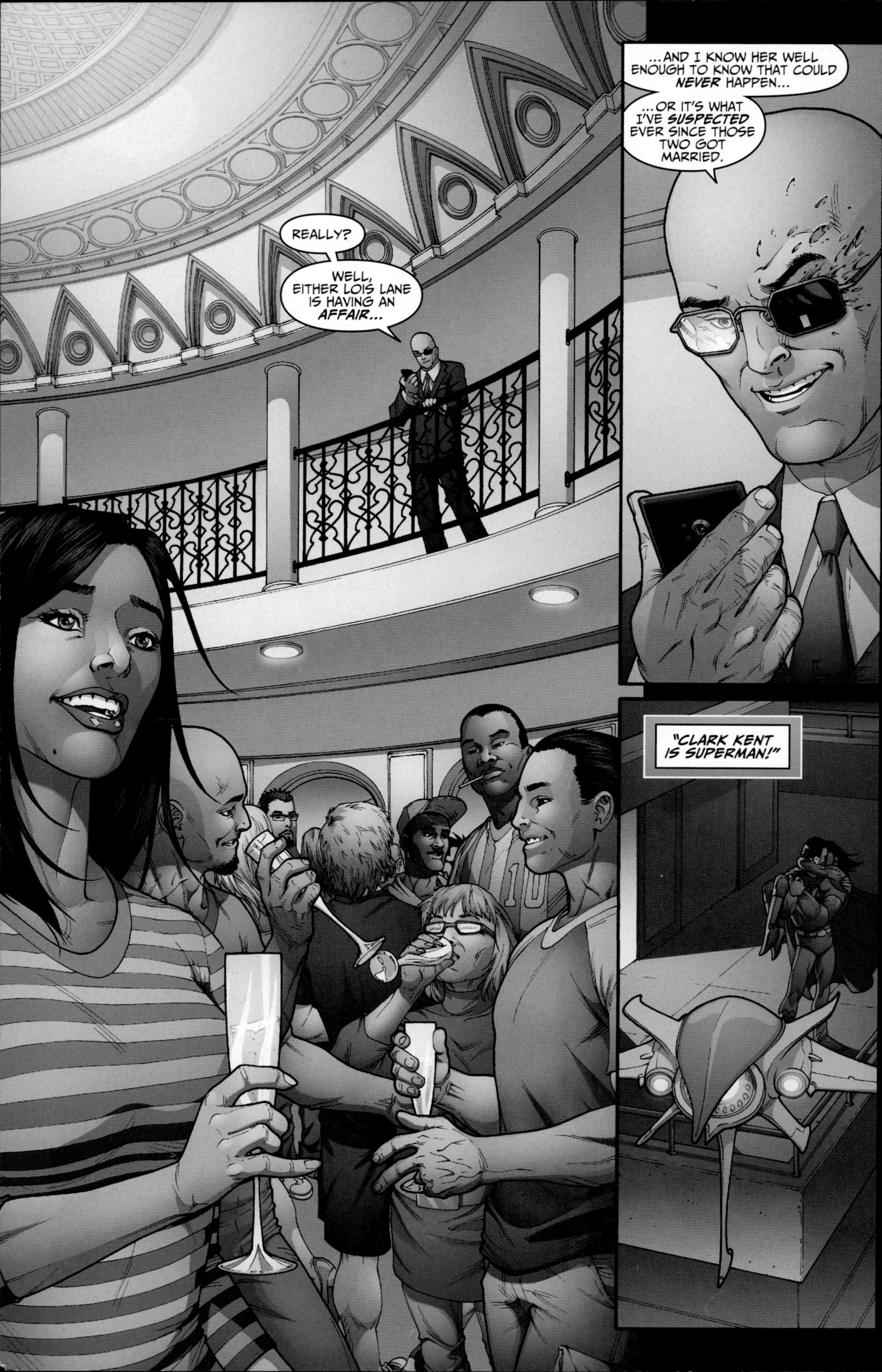
REALLY?
WELL, EITHER LOIS LANE IS HAVING AN AFFAIR...
...AND I KNOW HER WELL ENOUGH TO KNOW THAT COULD NEVER HAPPEN...
...OR IT'S WHAT I'VE SUSPECTED EVER SINCE THOSE TWO GOT MARRIED.
"CLARK KENT IS SUPERMAN!"

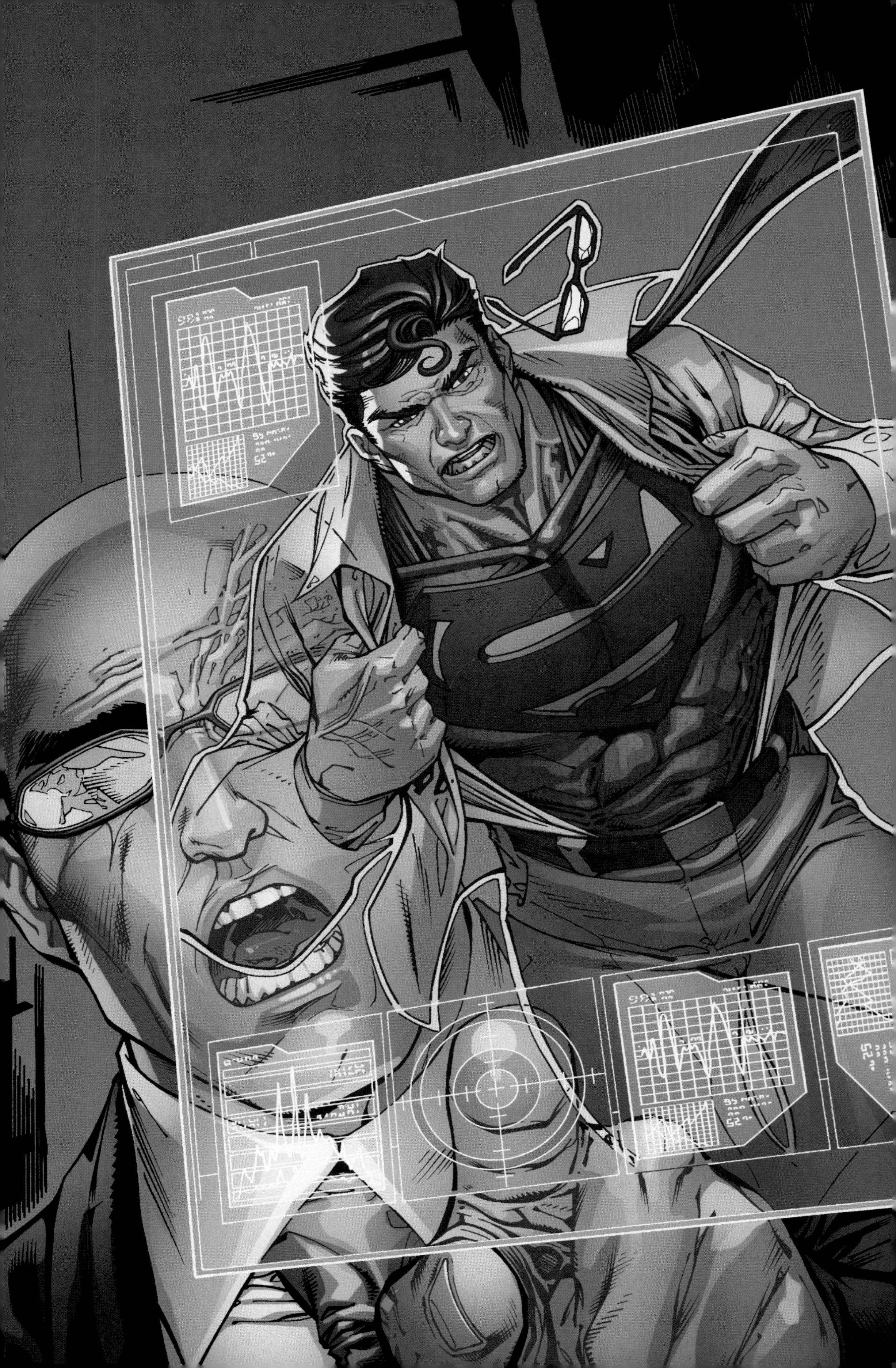

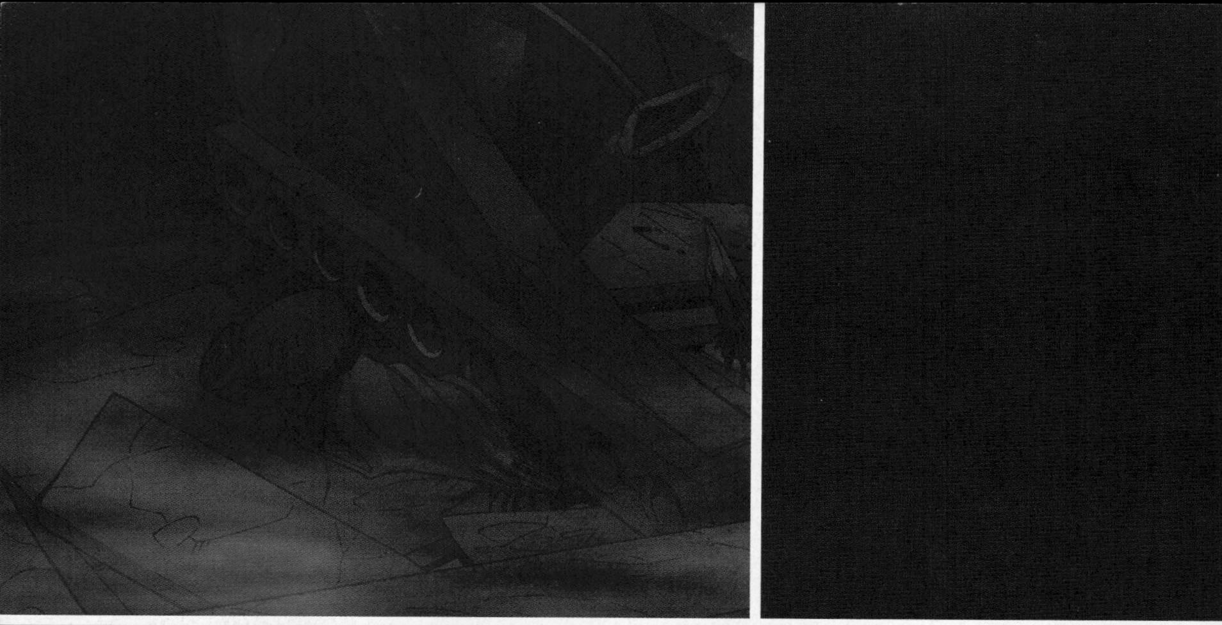

"...CLARK KENT IS SUPERMAN!"

Tony Bedard
Writer

Howard Porter & John Livesay
Artists

Cover by Ed Benes & Jorge Gonzalez

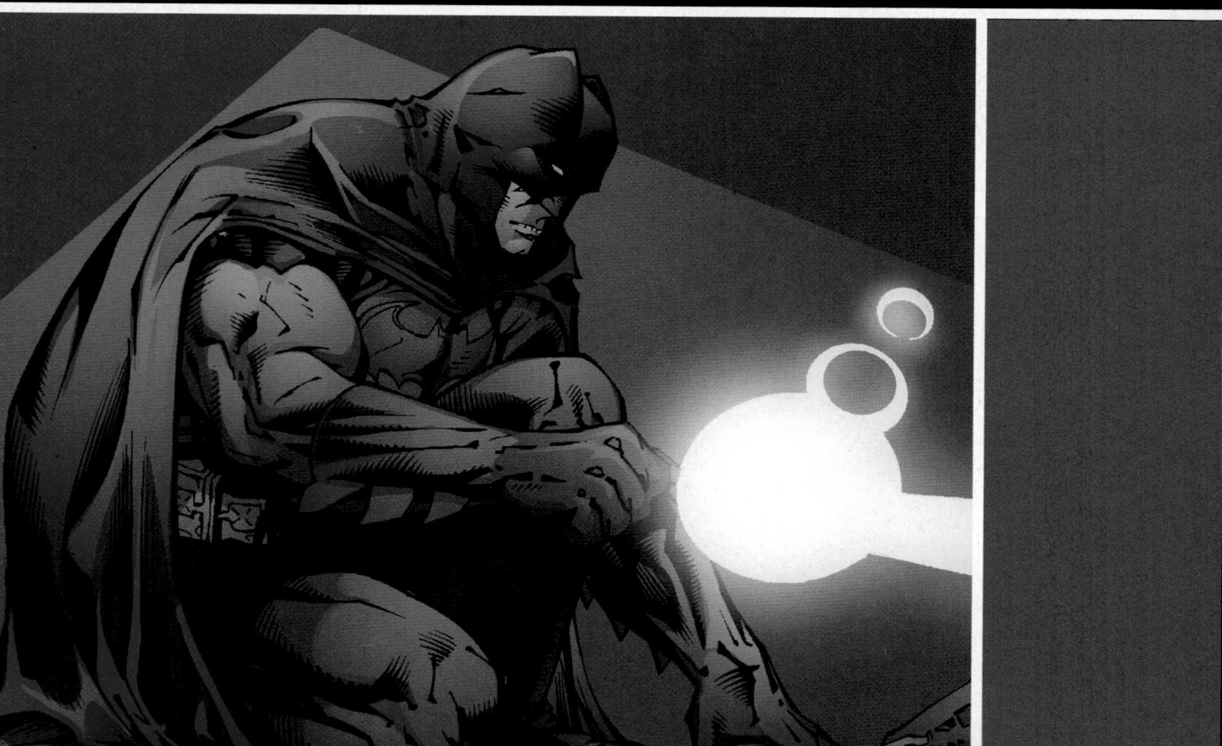

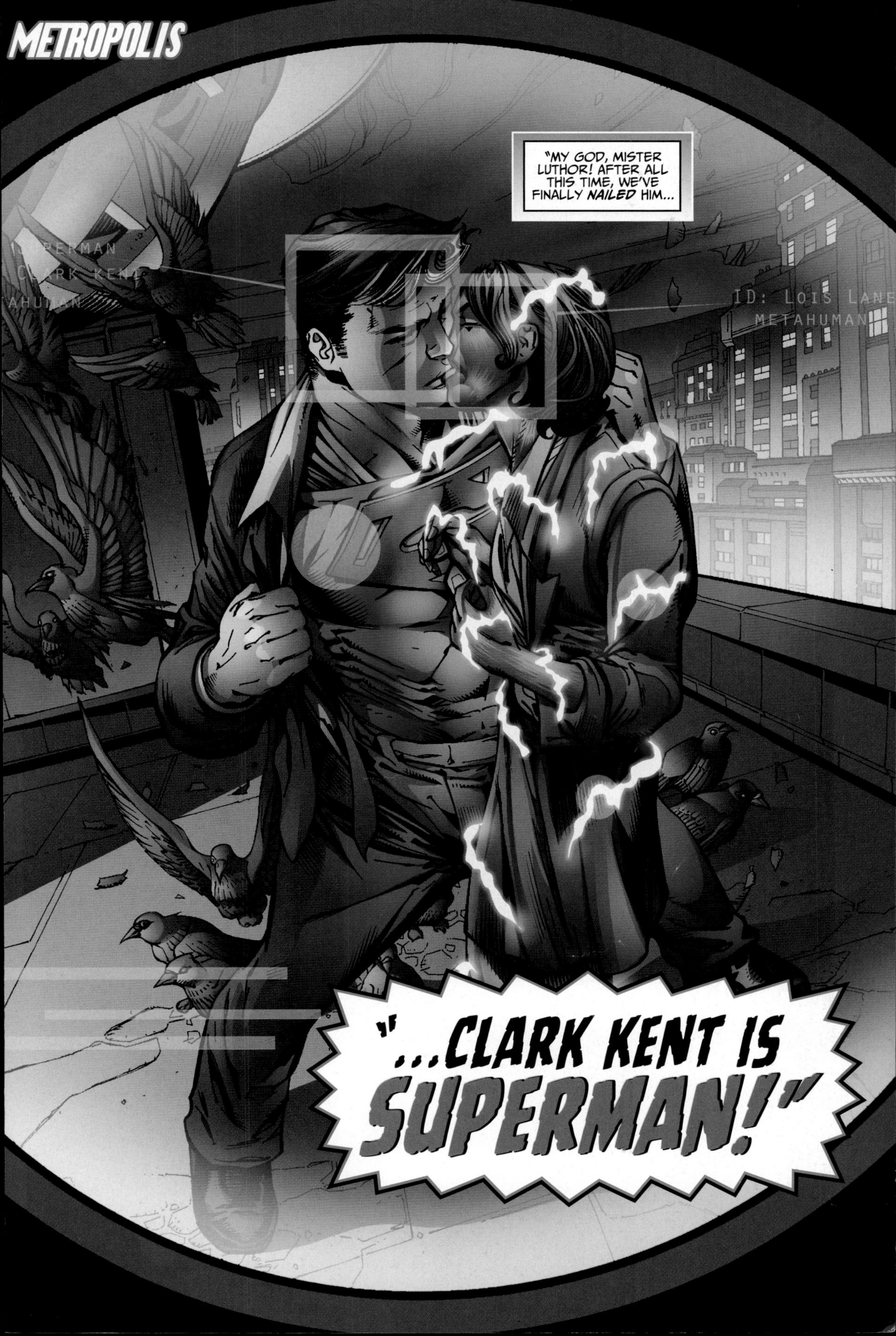
METROPOLIS
"MY GOD, MISTER LUTHOR! AFTER ALL THIS TIME, WE'VE FINALLY *NAILED* HIM...
ID: LOIS LANE
METAHUMAN
"...CLARK KENT IS SUPERMAN!"

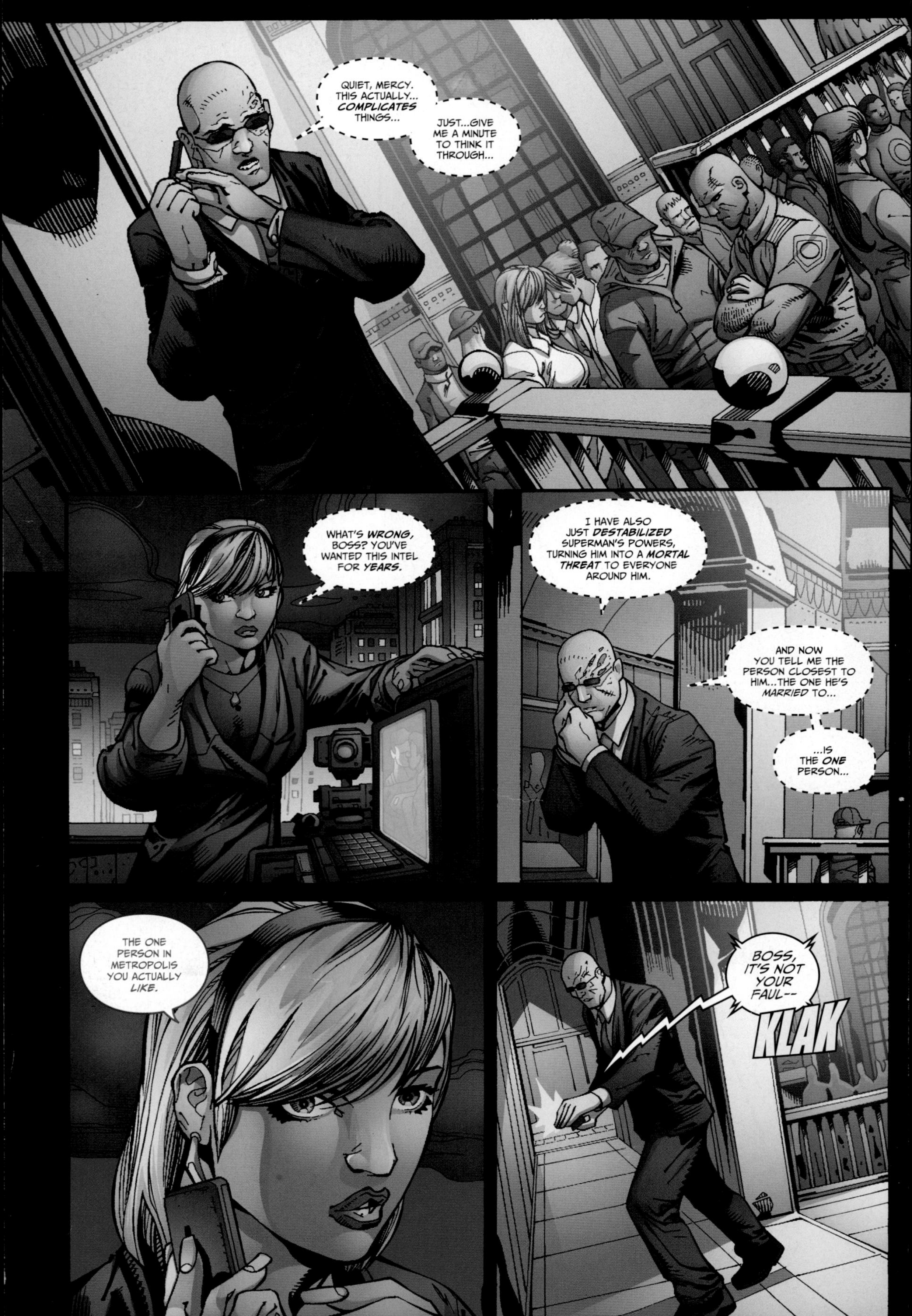
QUIET, MERCY. THIS ACTUALLY... COMPLICATES THINGS...
JUST...GIVE ME A MINUTE TO THINK IT THROUGH...
WHAT'S WRONG, BOSS? YOU'VE WANTED THIS INTEL FOR YEARS.
I HAVE ALSO JUST DESTABILIZED SUPERMAN'S POWERS, TURNING HIM INTO A MORTAL THREAT TO EVERYONE AROUND HIM.
AND NOW YOU TELL ME THE PERSON CLOSEST TO HIM...THE ONE HE'S MARRIED TO...
...IS THE ONE PERSON...
THE ONE PERSON IN METROPOLIS YOU ACTUALLY LIKE.
BOSS, IT'S NOT YOUR FAUL--
KLAK

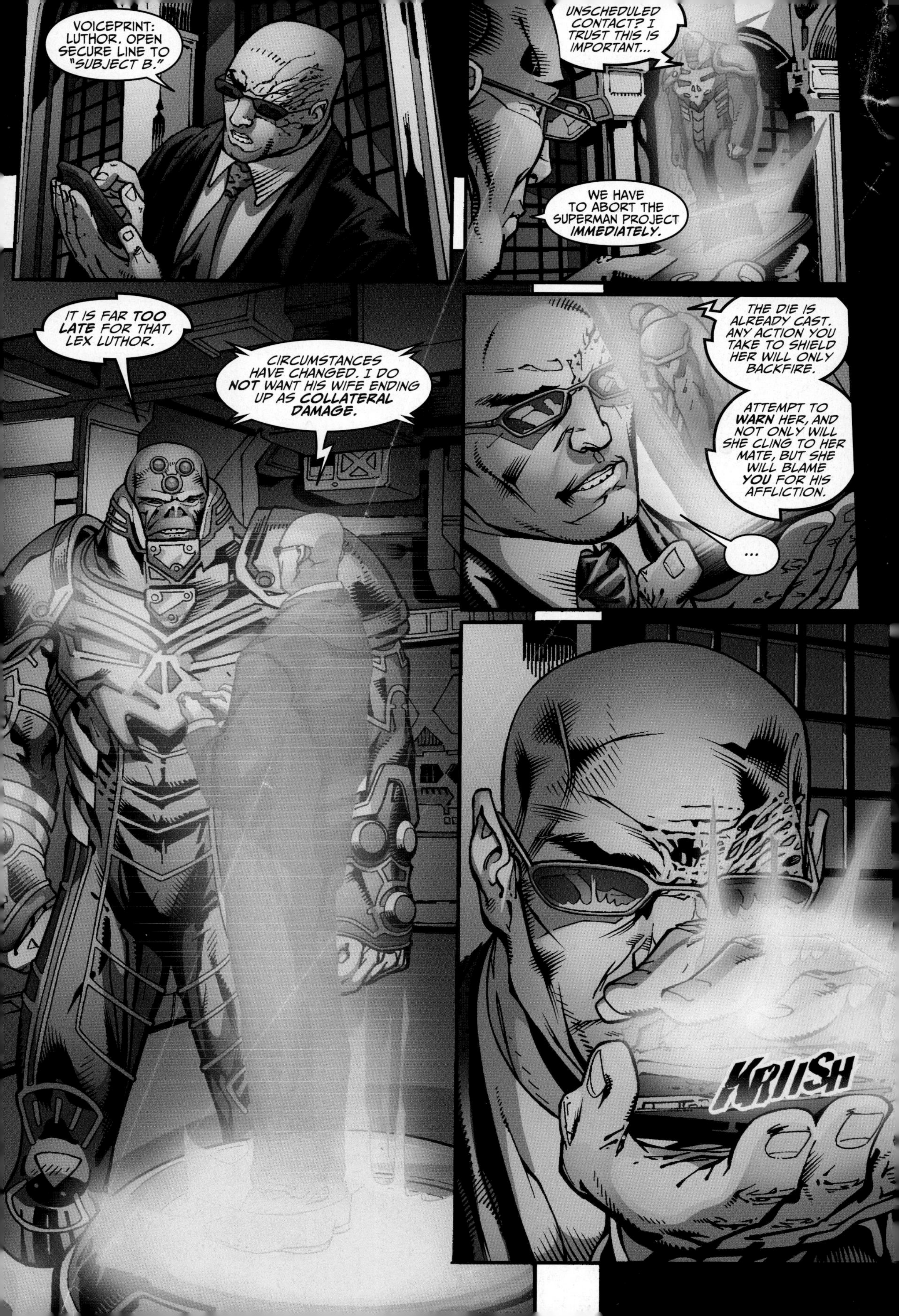
VOICEPRINT: LUTHOR. OPEN SECURE LINE TO "SUBJECT B."
UNSCHEDULED CONTACT? I TRUST THIS IS IMPORTANT...
WE HAVE TO ABORT THE SUPERMAN PROJECT IMMEDIATELY.
IT IS FAR TOO LATE FOR THAT, LEX LUTHOR.
CIRCUMSTANCES HAVE CHANGED. I DO NOT WANT HIS WIFE ENDING UP AS COLLATERAL DAMAGE.
THE DIE IS ALREADY CAST. ANY ACTION YOU TAKE TO SHIELD HER WILL ONLY BACKFIRE.
ATTEMPT TO WARN HER, AND NOT ONLY WILL SHE CLING TO HER MATE, BUT SHE WILL BLAME YOU FOR HIS AFFLICTION.
...
KRIISH

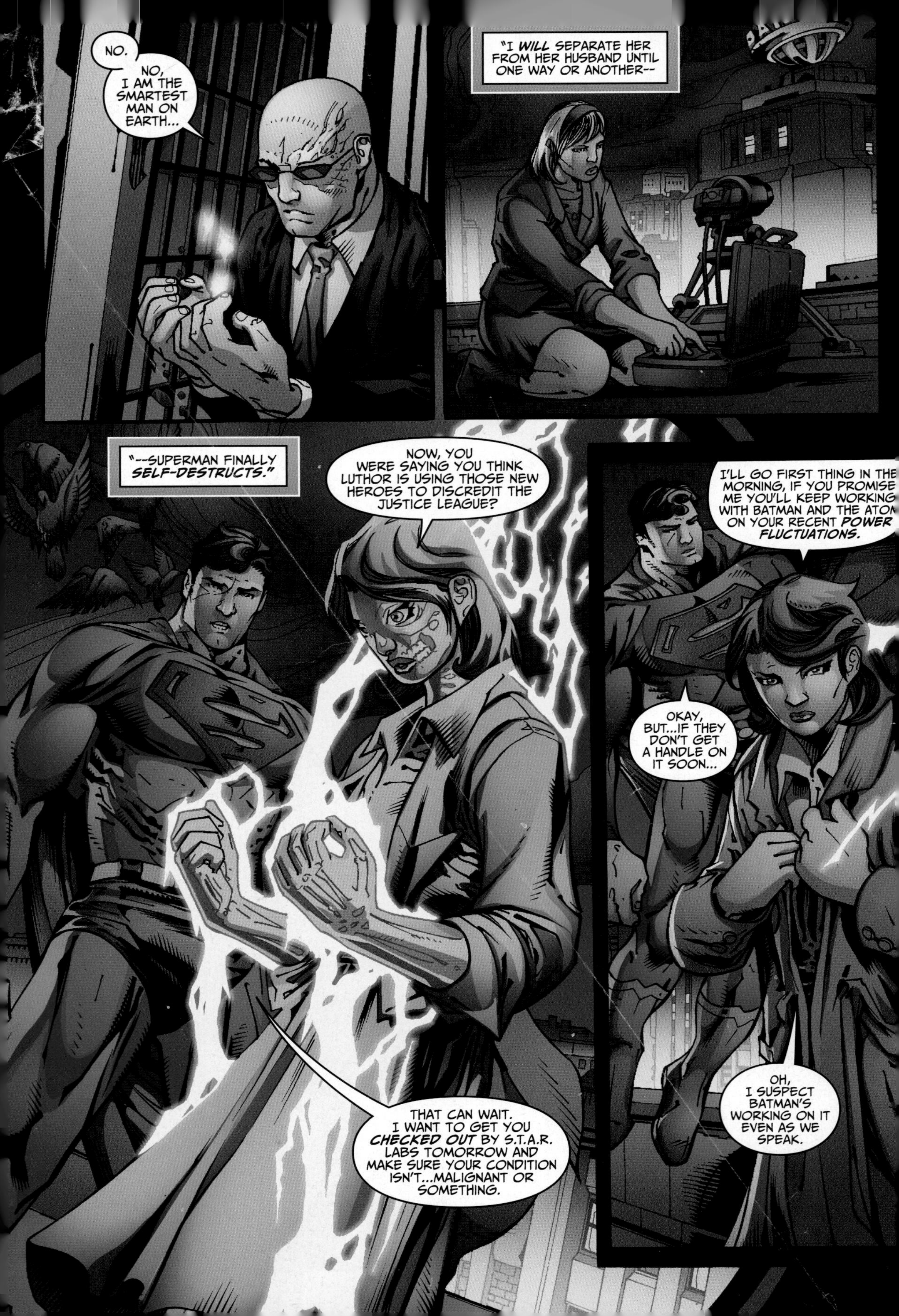
NO.
NO, I AM THE SMARTEST MAN ON EARTH...
"I WILL SEPARATE HER FROM HER HUSBAND UNTIL ONE WAY OR ANOTHER--
"--SUPERMAN FINALLY SELF-DESTRUCTS."
NOW, YOU WERE SAYING YOU THINK LUTHOR IS USING THOSE NEW HEROES TO DISCREDIT THE JUSTICE LEAGUE?
THAT CAN WAIT. I WANT TO GET YOU CHECKED OUT BY S.T.A.R. LABS TOMORROW AND MAKE SURE YOUR CONDITION ISN'T...MALIGNANT OR SOMETHING.
I'LL GO FIRST THING IN THE MORNING, IF YOU PROMISE ME YOU'LL KEEP WORKING WITH BATMAN AND THE ATOM ON YOUR RECENT POWER FLUCTUATIONS.
OKAY, BUT...IF THEY DON'T GET A HANDLE ON IT SOON...
OH, I SUSPECT BATMAN'S WORKING ON IT EVEN AS WE SPEAK.

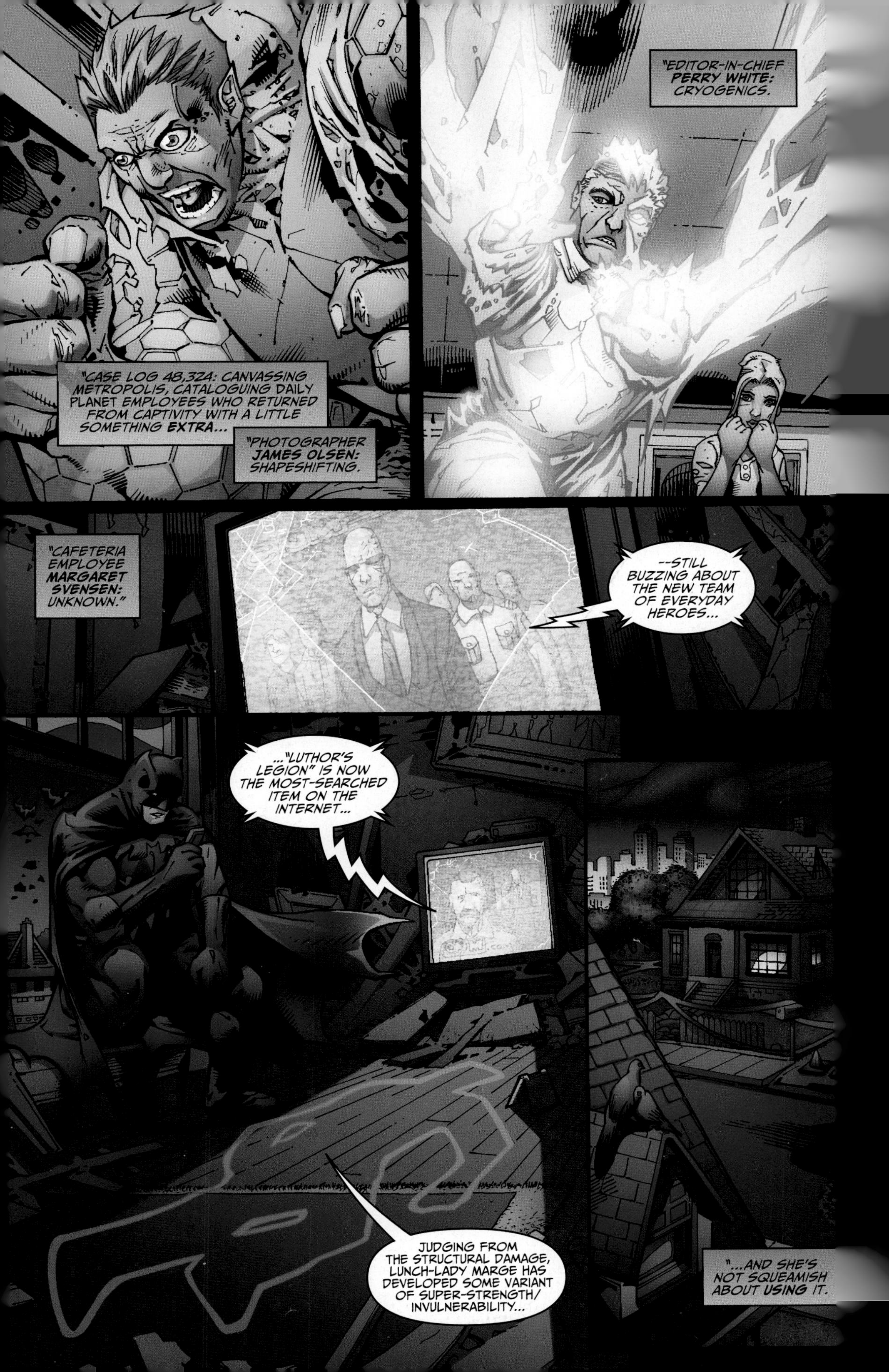
"CASE LOG 48,324: CANVASSING METROPOLIS, CATALOGUING DAILY PLANET EMPLOYEES WHO RETURNED FROM CAPTIVITY WITH A LITTLE SOMETHING EXTRA...
"PHOTOGRAPHER JAMES OLSEN: SHAPESHIFTING.
"EDITOR-IN-CHIEF PERRY WHITE: CRYOGENICS.
"CAFETERIA EMPLOYEE MARGARET SVENSEN: UNKNOWN."
--STILL BUZZING ABOUT THE NEW TEAM OF EVERYDAY HEROES...
..."LUTHOR'S LEGION" IS NOW THE MOST-SEARCHED ITEM ON THE INTERNET...
JUDGING FROM THE STRUCTURAL DAMAGE, LUNCH-LADY MARGE HAS DEVELOPED SOME VARIANT OF SUPER-STRENGTH/ INVULNERABILITY...
"...AND SHE'S NOT SQUEAMISH ABOUT USING IT.

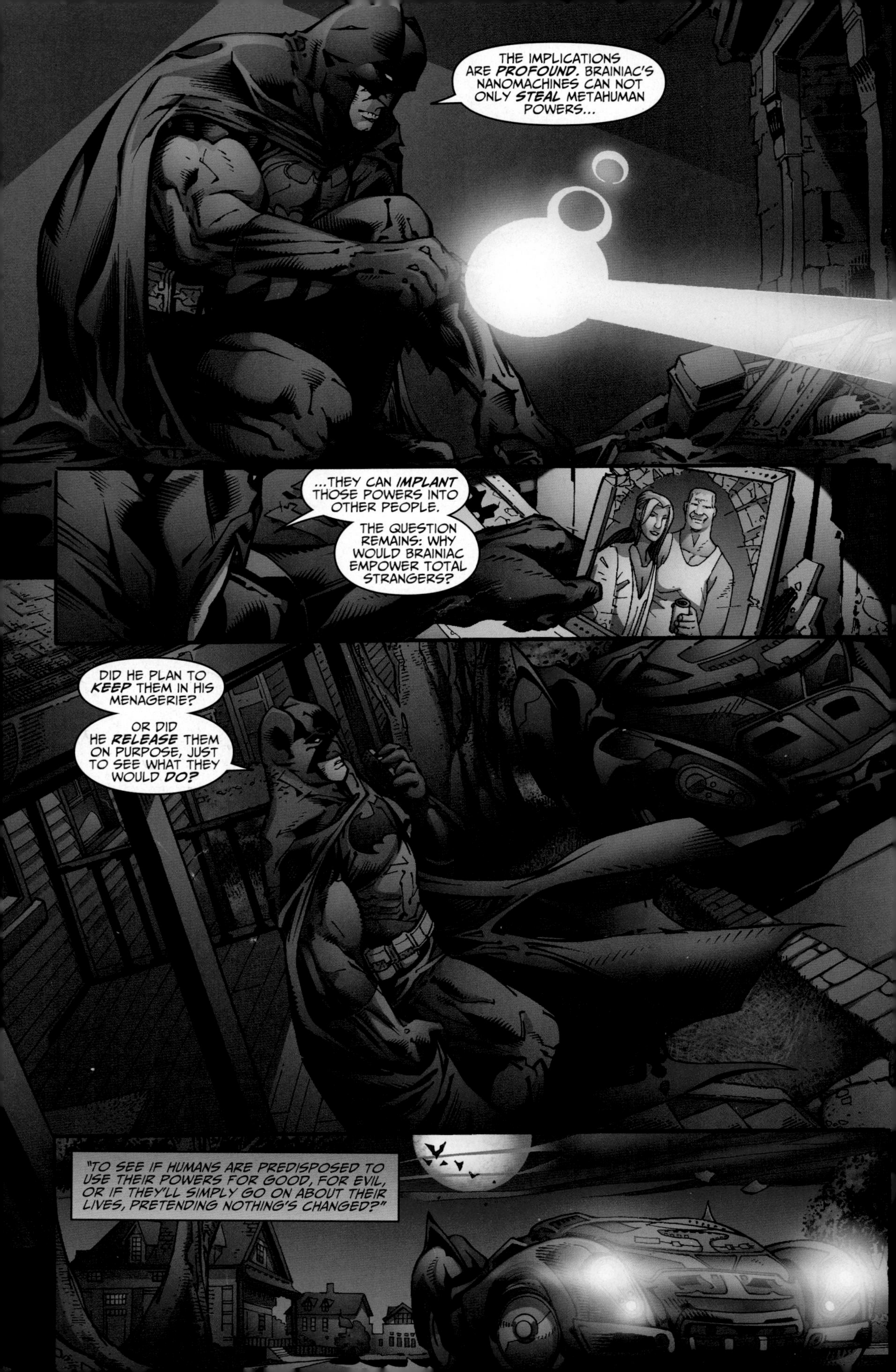
THE IMPLICATIONS ARE PROFOUND. BRAINIAC'S NANOMACHINES CAN NOT ONLY STEAL METAHUMAN POWERS...
...THEY CAN IMPLANT THOSE POWERS INTO OTHER PEOPLE.
THE QUESTION REMAINS: WHY WOULD BRAINIAC EMPOWER TOTAL STRANGERS?
DID HE PLAN TO KEEP THEM IN HIS MENAGERIE?
OR DID HE RELEASE THEM ON PURPOSE, JUST TO SEE WHAT THEY WOULD DO?
"TO SEE IF HUMANS ARE PREDISPOSED TO USE THEIR POWERS FOR GOOD, FOR EVIL, OR IF THEY'LL SIMPLY GO ON ABOUT THEIR LIVES, PRETENDING NOTHING'S CHANGED?"

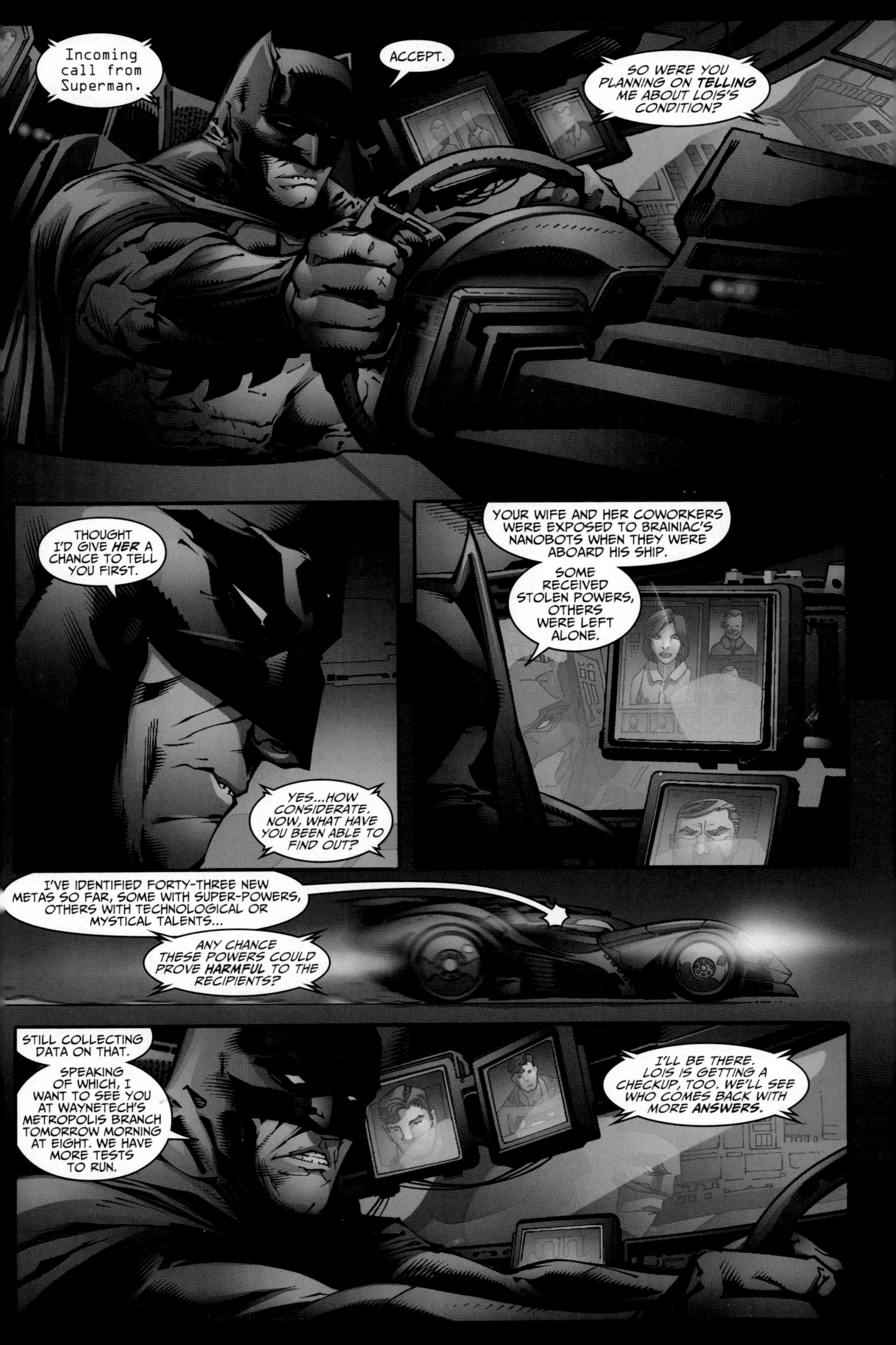
Incoming call from Superman.
ACCEPT.
SO WERE YOU PLANNING ON TELLING ME ABOUT LOIS'S CONDITION?
THOUGHT I'D GIVE HER A CHANCE TO TELL YOU FIRST.
YES...HOW CONSIDERATE. NOW, WHAT HAVE YOU BEEN ABLE TO FIND OUT?
YOUR WIFE AND HER COWORKERS WERE EXPOSED TO BRAINIAC'S NANOBOTS WHEN THEY WERE ABOARD HIS SHIP.
SOME RECEIVED STOLEN POWERS, OTHERS WERE LEFT ALONE.
I'VE IDENTIFIED FORTY-THREE NEW METAS SO FAR, SOME WITH SUPER-POWERS, OTHERS WITH TECHNOLOGICAL OR MYSTICAL TALENTS...
ANY CHANCE THESE POWERS COULD PROVE HARMFUL TO THE RECIPIENTS?
STILL COLLECTING DATA ON THAT.
SPEAKING OF WHICH, I WANT TO SEE YOU AT WAYNETECH'S METROPOLIS BRANCH TOMORROW MORNING AT EIGHT. WE HAVE MORE TESTS TO RUN.
I'LL BE THERE. LOIS IS GETTING A CHECKUP, TOO. WE'LL SEE WHO COMES BACK WITH MORE ANSWERS.

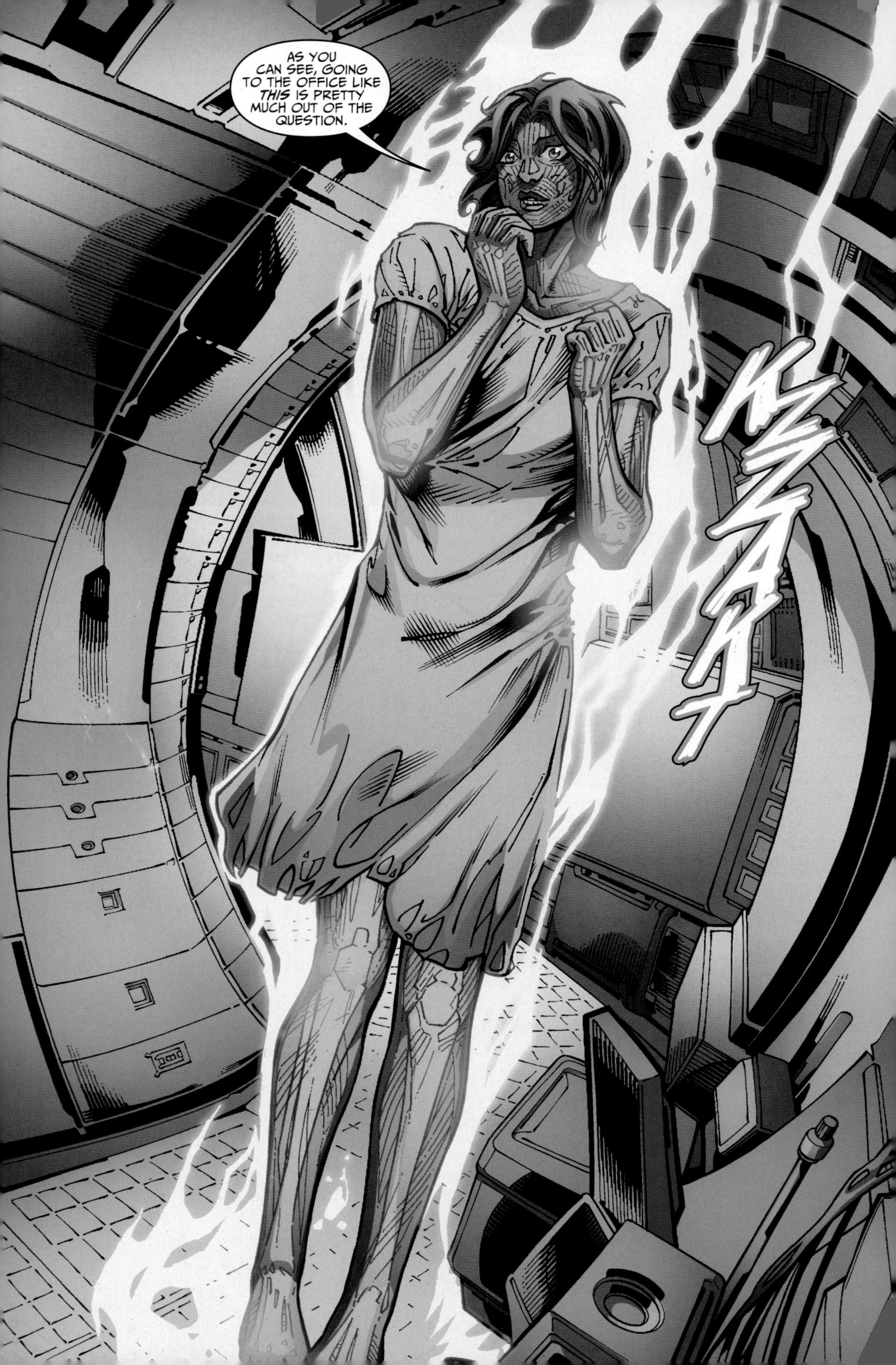
AS YOU CAN SEE, GOING TO THE OFFICE LIKE *THIS* IS PRETTY MUCH OUT OF THE QUESTION.
KZZAAT

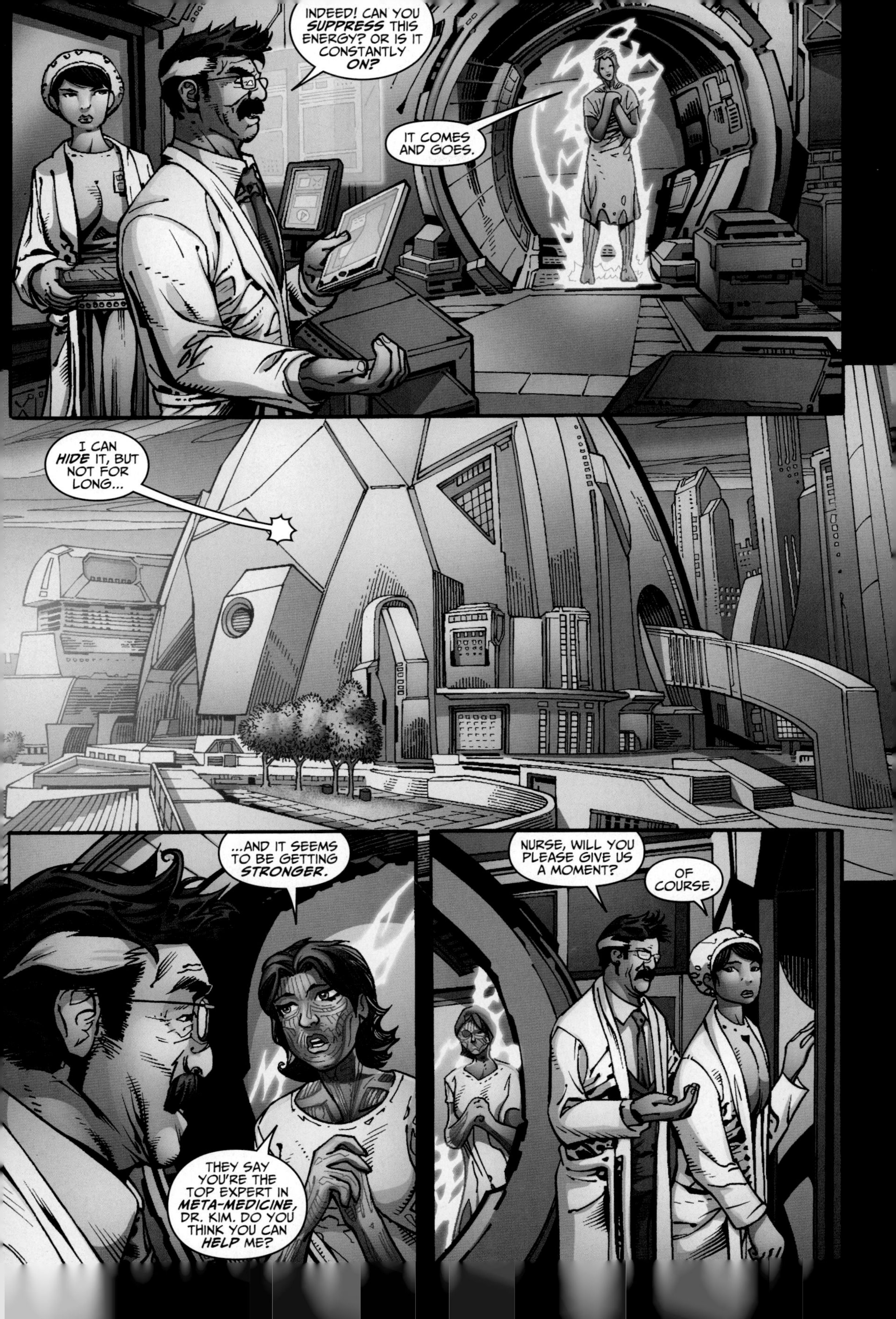

INDEED! CAN YOU SUPPRESS THIS ENERGY? OR IS IT CONSTANTLY ON?
IT COMES AND GOES.
I CAN HIDE IT, BUT NOT FOR LONG...
...AND IT SEEMS TO BE GETTING STRONGER.
THEY SAY YOU'RE THE TOP EXPERT IN META-MEDICINE, DR. KIM. DO YOU THINK YOU CAN HELP ME?
NURSE, WILL YOU PLEASE GIVE US A MOMENT?
OF COURSE.

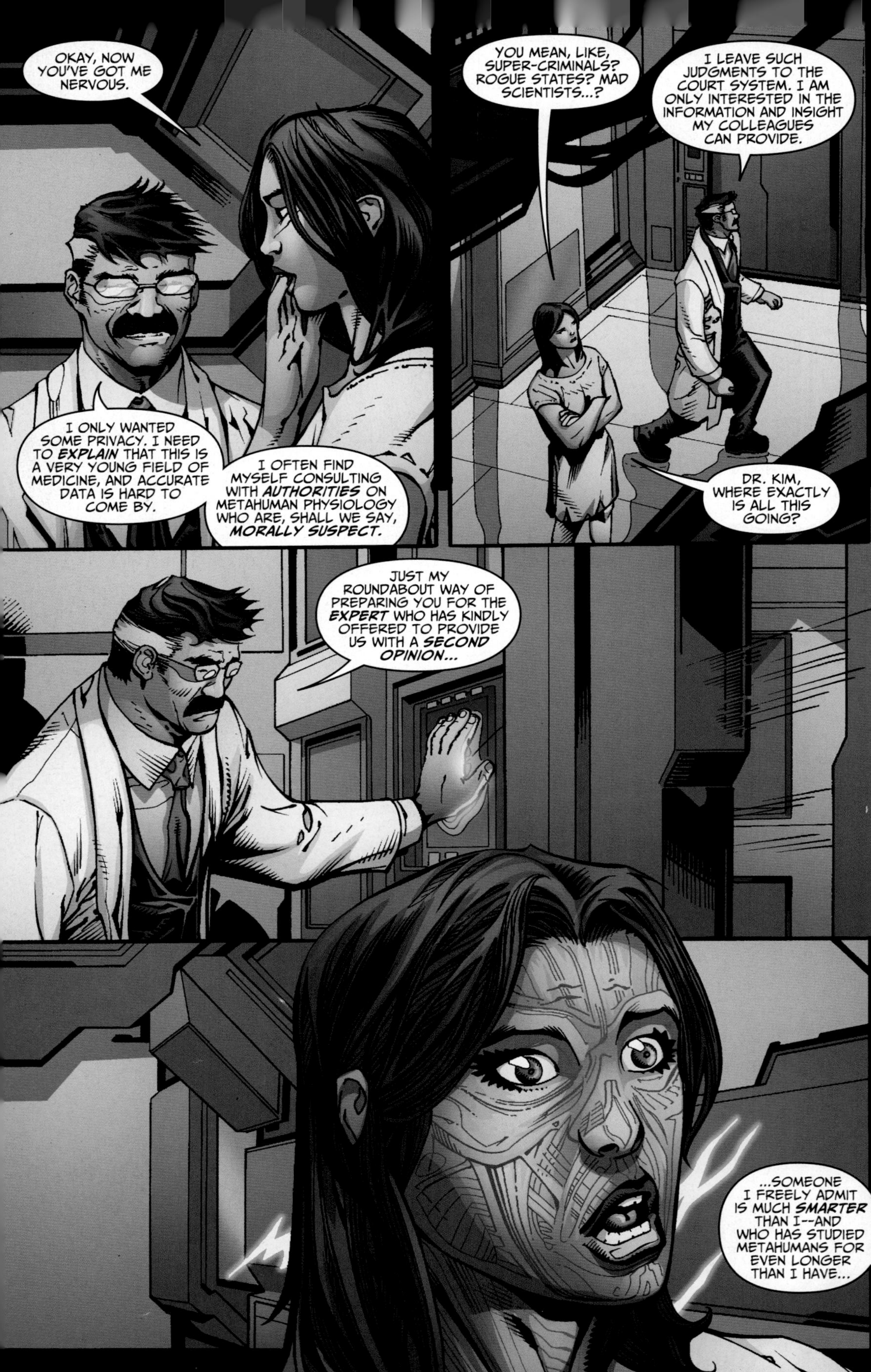
OKAY, NOW YOU'VE GOT ME NERVOUS.
I ONLY WANTED SOME PRIVACY. I NEED TO EXPLAIN THAT THIS IS A VERY YOUNG FIELD OF MEDICINE, AND ACCURATE DATA IS HARD TO COME BY.
I OFTEN FIND MYSELF CONSULTING WITH AUTHORITIES ON METAHUMAN PHYSIOLOGY WHO ARE, SHALL WE SAY, MORALLY SUSPECT.
YOU MEAN, LIKE, SUPER-CRIMINALS? ROGUE STATES? MAD SCIENTISTS...?
I LEAVE SUCH JUDGMENTS TO THE COURT SYSTEM. I AM ONLY INTERESTED IN THE INFORMATION AND INSIGHT MY COLLEAGUES CAN PROVIDE.
DR. KIM, WHERE EXACTLY IS ALL THIS GOING?
JUST MY ROUNDABOUT WAY OF PREPARING YOU FOR THE EXPERT WHO HAS KINDLY OFFERED TO PROVIDE US WITH A SECOND OPINION...
...SOMEONE I FREELY ADMIT IS MUCH SMARTER THAN I--AND WHO HAS STUDIED METAHUMANS FOR EVEN LONGER THAN I HAVE...

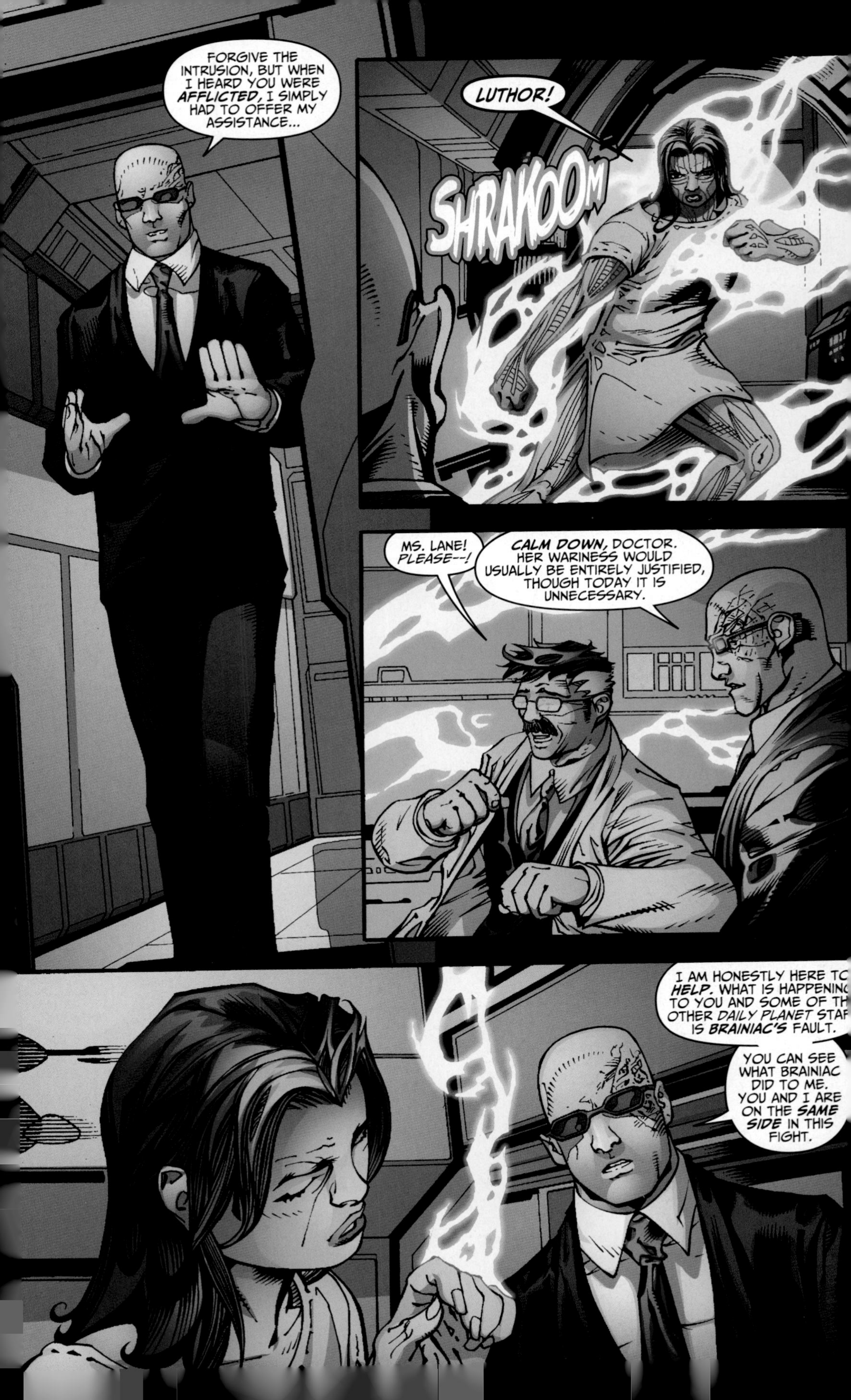
FORGIVE THE INTRUSION, BUT WHEN I HEARD YOU WERE *AFFLICTED,* I SIMPLY HAD TO OFFER MY ASSISTANCE...
LUTHOR!
SHRAKOOM
MS. LANE! *PLEASE--!*
CALM DOWN, DOCTOR. HER WARINESS WOULD USUALLY BE ENTIRELY JUSTIFIED, THOUGH TODAY IT IS UNNECESSARY.
I AM HONESTLY HERE TO *HELP.* WHAT IS HAPPENING TO YOU AND SOME OF THE OTHER *DAILY PLANET* STAFF IS *BRAINIAC'S* FAULT.
YOU CAN SEE WHAT BRAINIAC DID TO ME. YOU AND I ARE ON THE *SAME SIDE* IN THIS FIGHT.

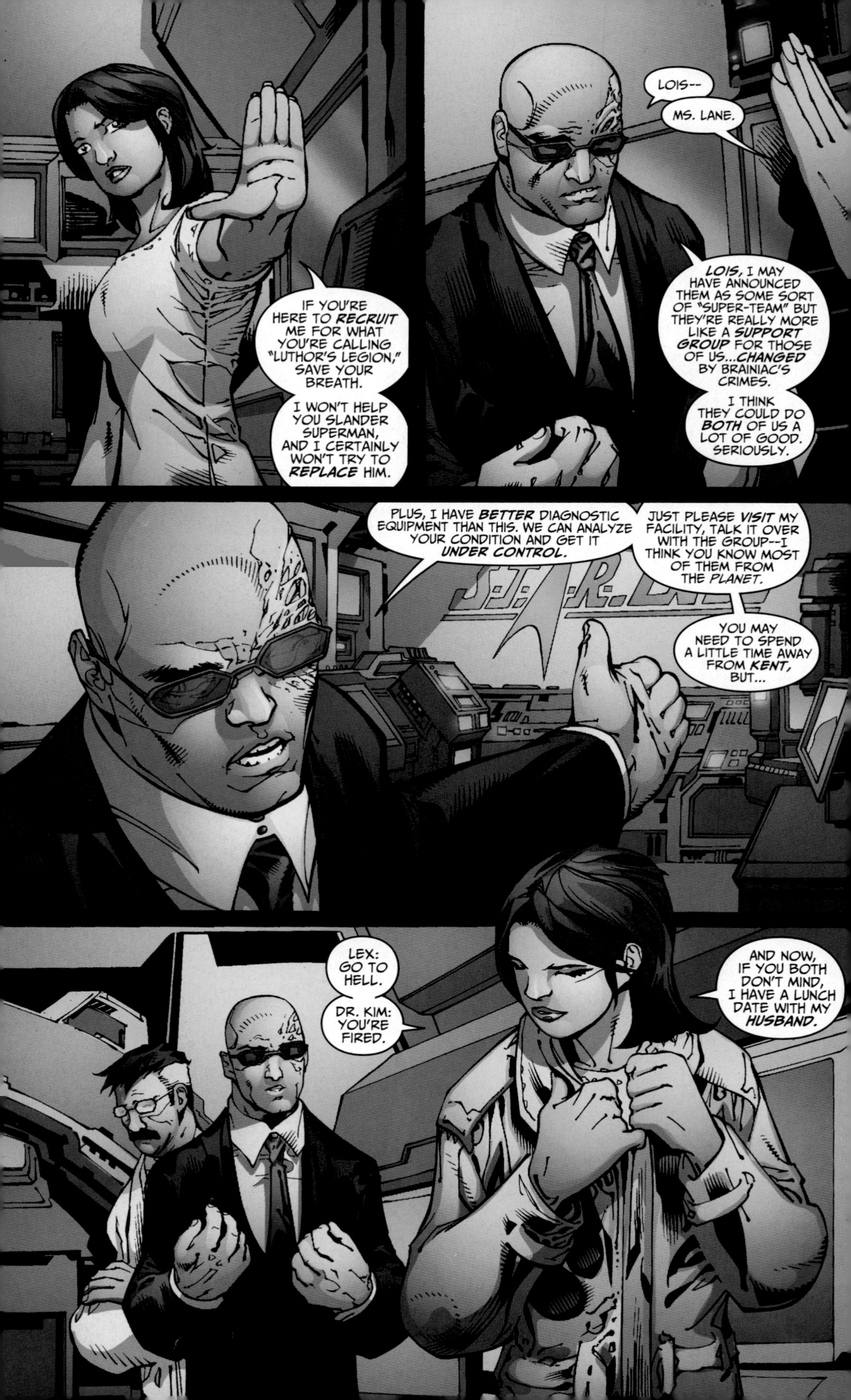
IF YOU'RE HERE TO RECRUIT ME FOR WHAT YOU'RE CALLING "LUTHOR'S LEGION," SAVE YOUR BREATH.
I WON'T HELP YOU SLANDER SUPERMAN, AND I CERTAINLY WON'T TRY TO REPLACE HIM.
LOIS--
MS. LANE.
LOIS, I MAY HAVE ANNOUNCED THEM AS SOME SORT OF "SUPER-TEAM" BUT THEY'RE REALLY MORE LIKE A SUPPORT GROUP FOR THOSE OF US...CHANGED BY BRAINIAC'S CRIMES.
I THINK THEY COULD DO BOTH OF US A LOT OF GOOD. SERIOUSLY.
PLUS, I HAVE BETTER DIAGNOSTIC EQUIPMENT THAN THIS. WE CAN ANALYZE YOUR CONDITION AND GET IT UNDER CONTROL.
JUST PLEASE VISIT MY FACILITY, TALK IT OVER WITH THE GROUP--I THINK YOU KNOW MOST OF THEM FROM THE PLANET.
YOU MAY NEED TO SPEND A LITTLE TIME AWAY FROM KENT, BUT...
LEX: GO TO HELL.
DR. KIM: YOU'RE FIRED.
AND NOW, IF YOU BOTH DON'T MIND, I HAVE A LUNCH DATE WITH MY HUSBAND.

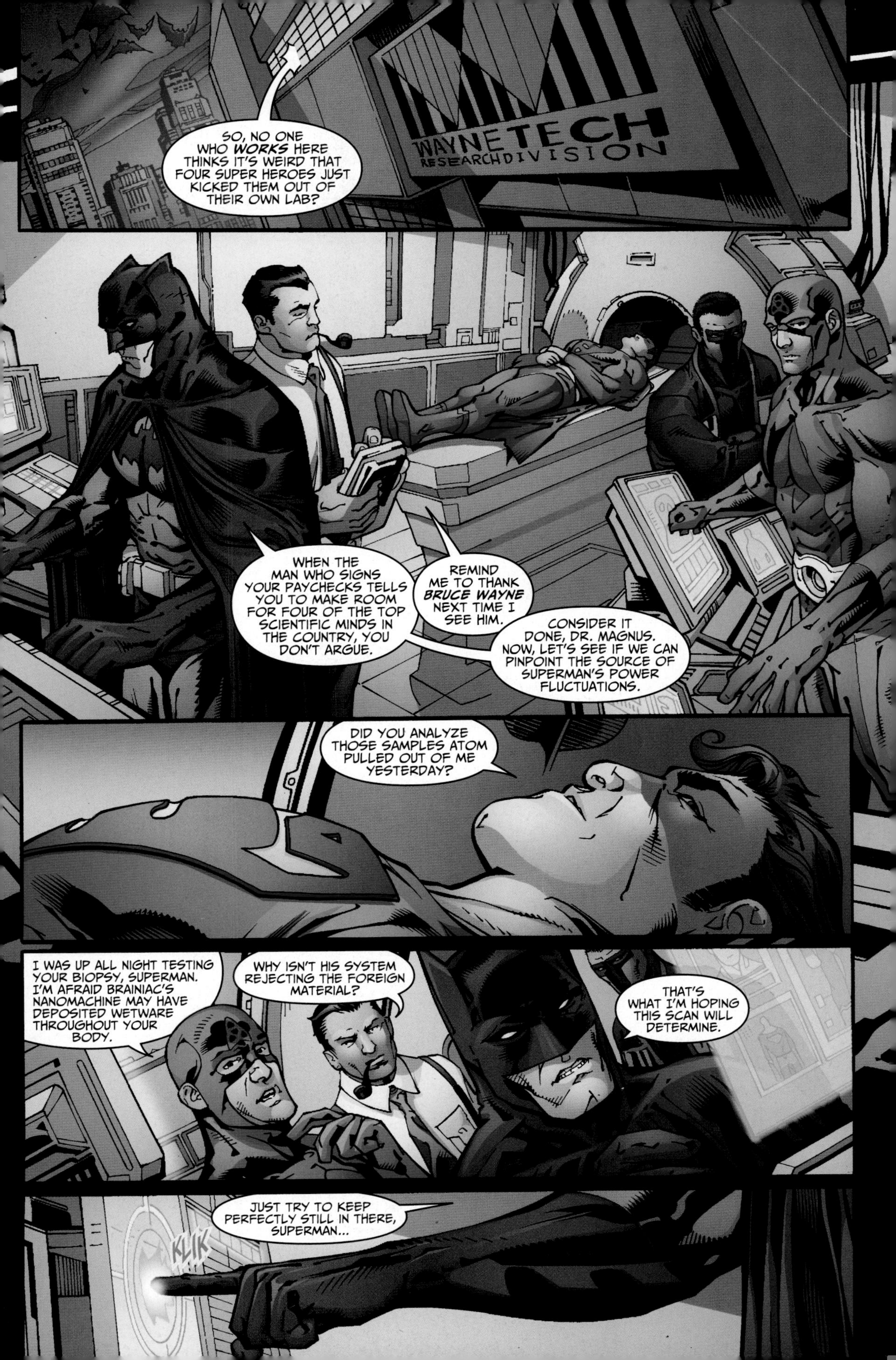
SO, NO ONE WHO WORKS HERE THINKS IT'S WEIRD THAT FOUR SUPER HEROES JUST KICKED THEM OUT OF THEIR OWN LAB?
WAYNETECH RESEARCH DIVISION
WHEN THE MAN WHO SIGNS YOUR PAYCHECKS TELLS YOU TO MAKE ROOM FOR FOUR OF THE TOP SCIENTIFIC MINDS IN THE COUNTRY, YOU DON'T ARGUE.
REMIND ME TO THANK BRUCE WAYNE NEXT TIME I SEE HIM.
CONSIDER IT DONE, DR. MAGNUS. NOW, LET'S SEE IF WE CAN PINPOINT THE SOURCE OF SUPERMAN'S POWER FLUCTUATIONS.
DID YOU ANALYZE THOSE SAMPLES ATOM PULLED OUT OF ME YESTERDAY?
I WAS UP ALL NIGHT TESTING YOUR BIOPSY, SUPERMAN. I'M AFRAID BRAINIAC'S NANOMACHINE MAY HAVE DEPOSITED WETWARE THROUGHOUT YOUR BODY.
WHY ISN'T HIS SYSTEM REJECTING THE FOREIGN MATERIAL?
THAT'S WHAT I'M HOPING THIS SCAN WILL DETERMINE.
JUST TRY TO KEEP PERFECTLY STILL IN THERE, SUPERMAN...
KLIK

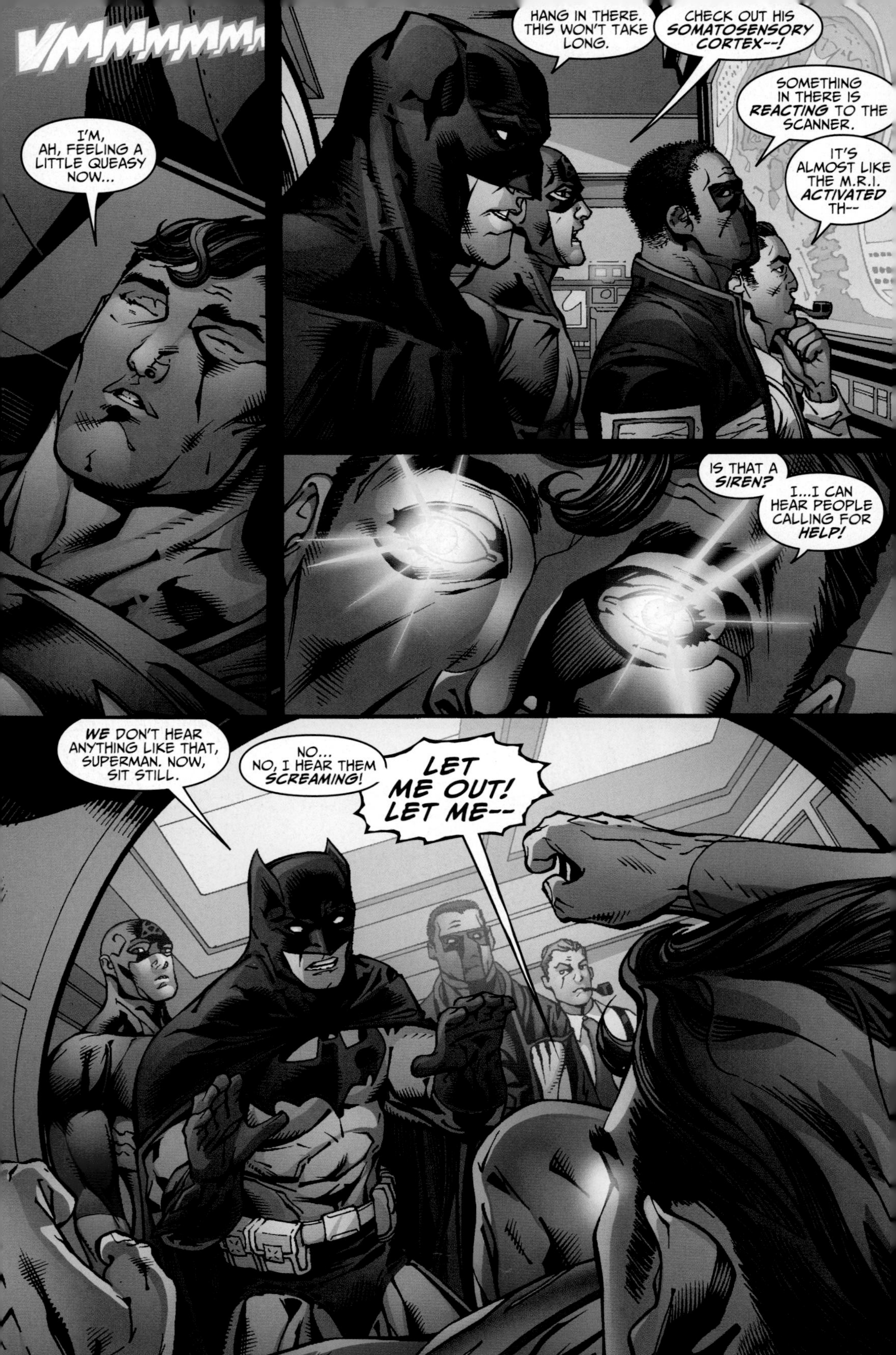
VMMMMMM
I'M, AH, FEELING A LITTLE QUEASY NOW...
HANG IN THERE. THIS WON'T TAKE LONG.
CHECK OUT HIS SOMATOSENSORY CORTEX--!
SOMETHING IN THERE IS REACTING TO THE SCANNER.
IT'S ALMOST LIKE THE M.R.I. ACTIVATED TH--
IS THAT A SIREN?
I...I CAN HEAR PEOPLE CALLING FOR HELP!
WE DON'T HEAR ANYTHING LIKE THAT, SUPERMAN. NOW, SIT STILL.
NO... NO, I HEAR THEM SCREAMING!
LET ME OUT! LET ME--

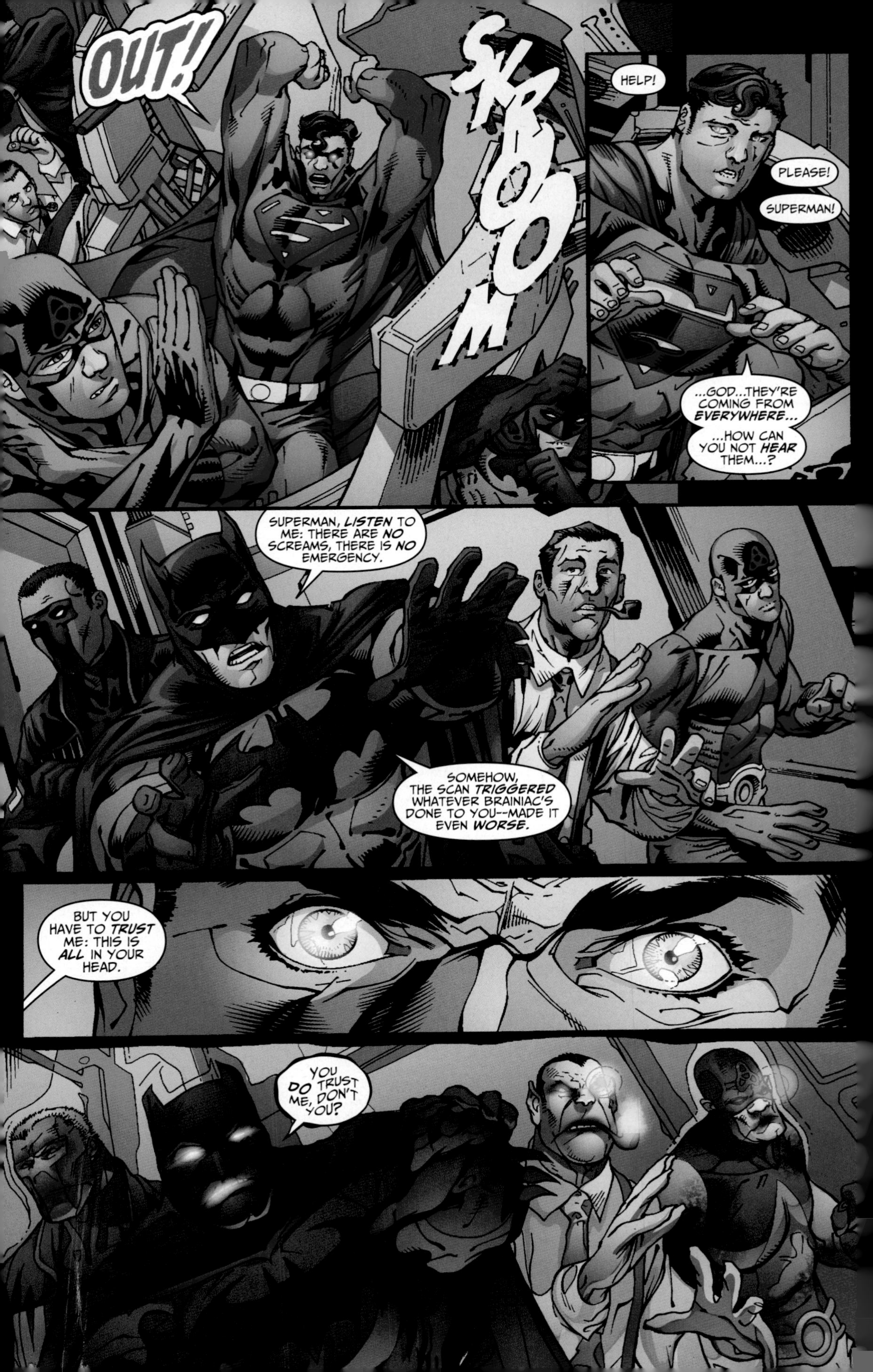
OUT!
SKROOOM
HELP!
PLEASE!
SUPERMAN!
...GOD...THEY'RE COMING FROM EVERYWHERE...
...HOW CAN YOU NOT HEAR THEM...?
SUPERMAN, LISTEN TO ME: THERE ARE NO SCREAMS, THERE IS NO EMERGENCY.
SOMEHOW, THE SCAN TRIGGERED WHATEVER BRAINIAC'S DONE TO YOU--MADE IT EVEN WORSE.
BUT YOU HAVE TO TRUST ME: THIS IS ALL IN YOUR HEAD.
YOU DO TRUST ME, DON'T YOU?

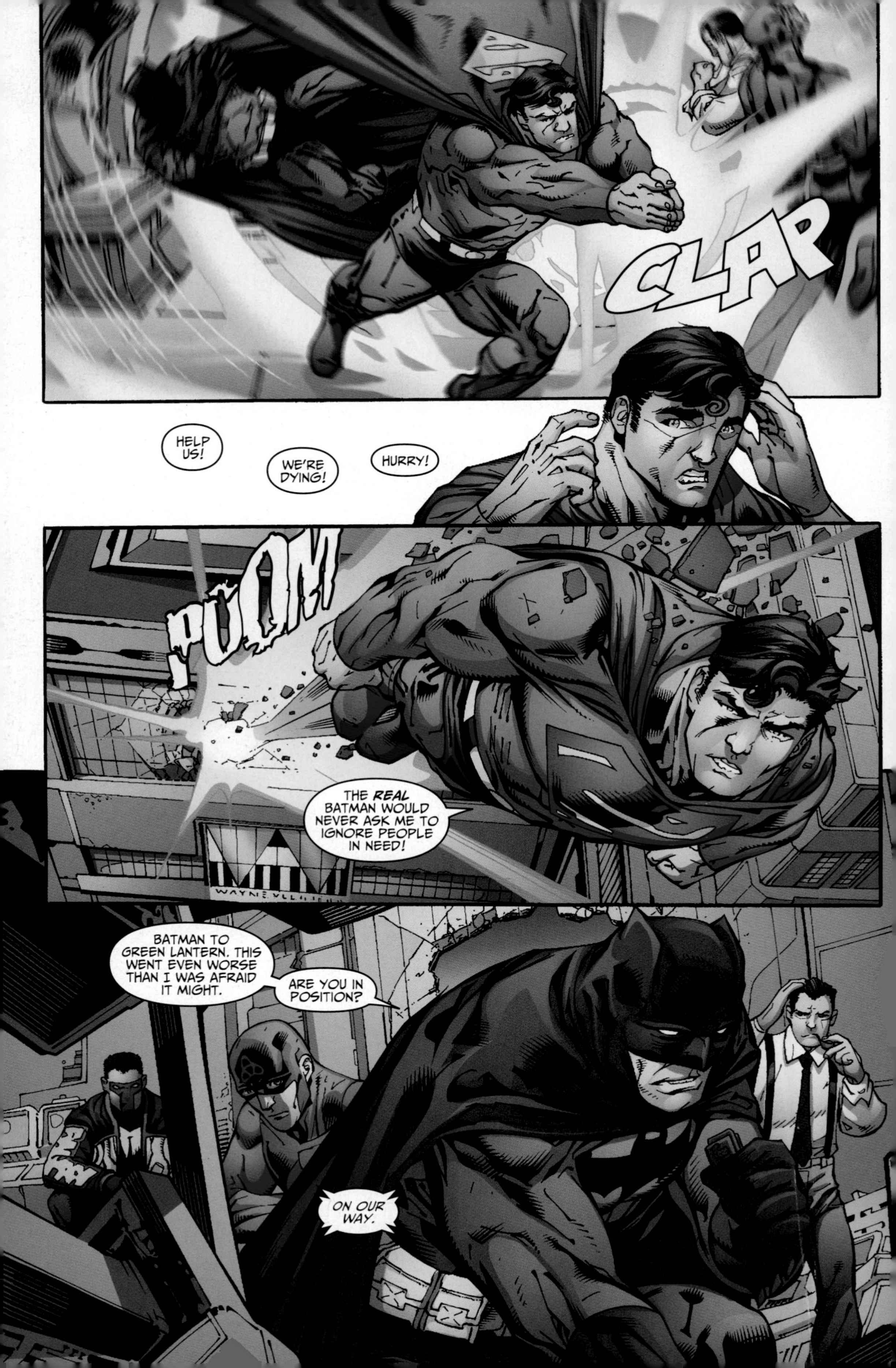
CLAP
HELP US!
WE'RE DYING!
HURRY!
POOM
THE REAL BATMAN WOULD NEVER ASK ME TO IGNORE PEOPLE IN NEED!
BATMAN TO GREEN LANTERN. THIS WENT EVEN WORSE THAN I WAS AFRAID IT MIGHT.
ARE YOU IN POSITION?
ON OUR WAY.

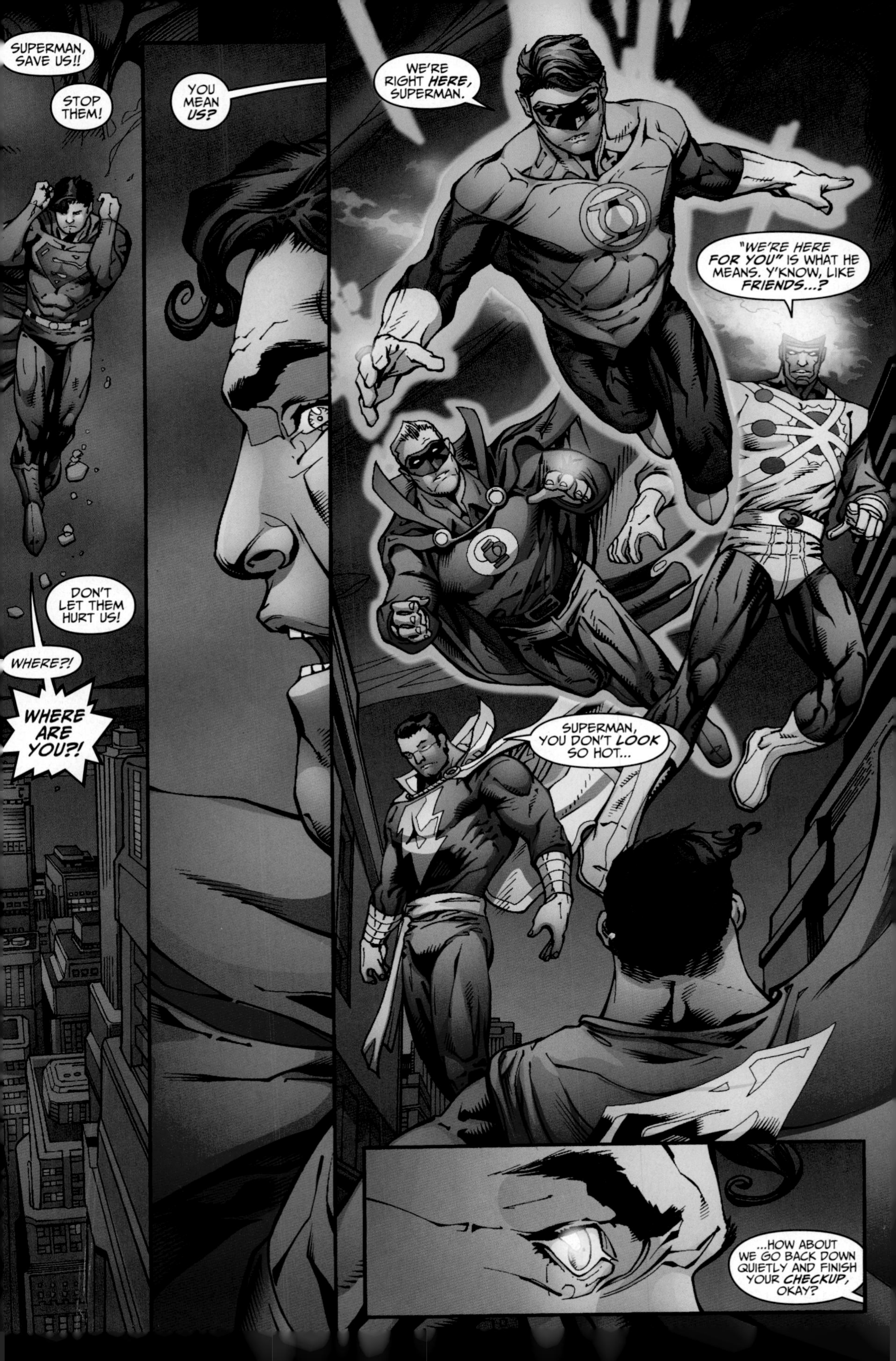
SUPERMAN, SAVE US!!
STOP THEM!
YOU MEAN US?
WE'RE RIGHT HERE, SUPERMAN.
"WE'RE HERE FOR YOU" IS WHAT HE MEANS. Y'KNOW, LIKE FRIENDS...?
DON'T LET THEM HURT US!
WHERE?!
WHERE ARE YOU?!
SUPERMAN, YOU DON'T LOOK SO HOT...
...HOW ABOUT WE GO BACK DOWN QUIETLY AND FINISH YOUR CHECKUP, OKAY?

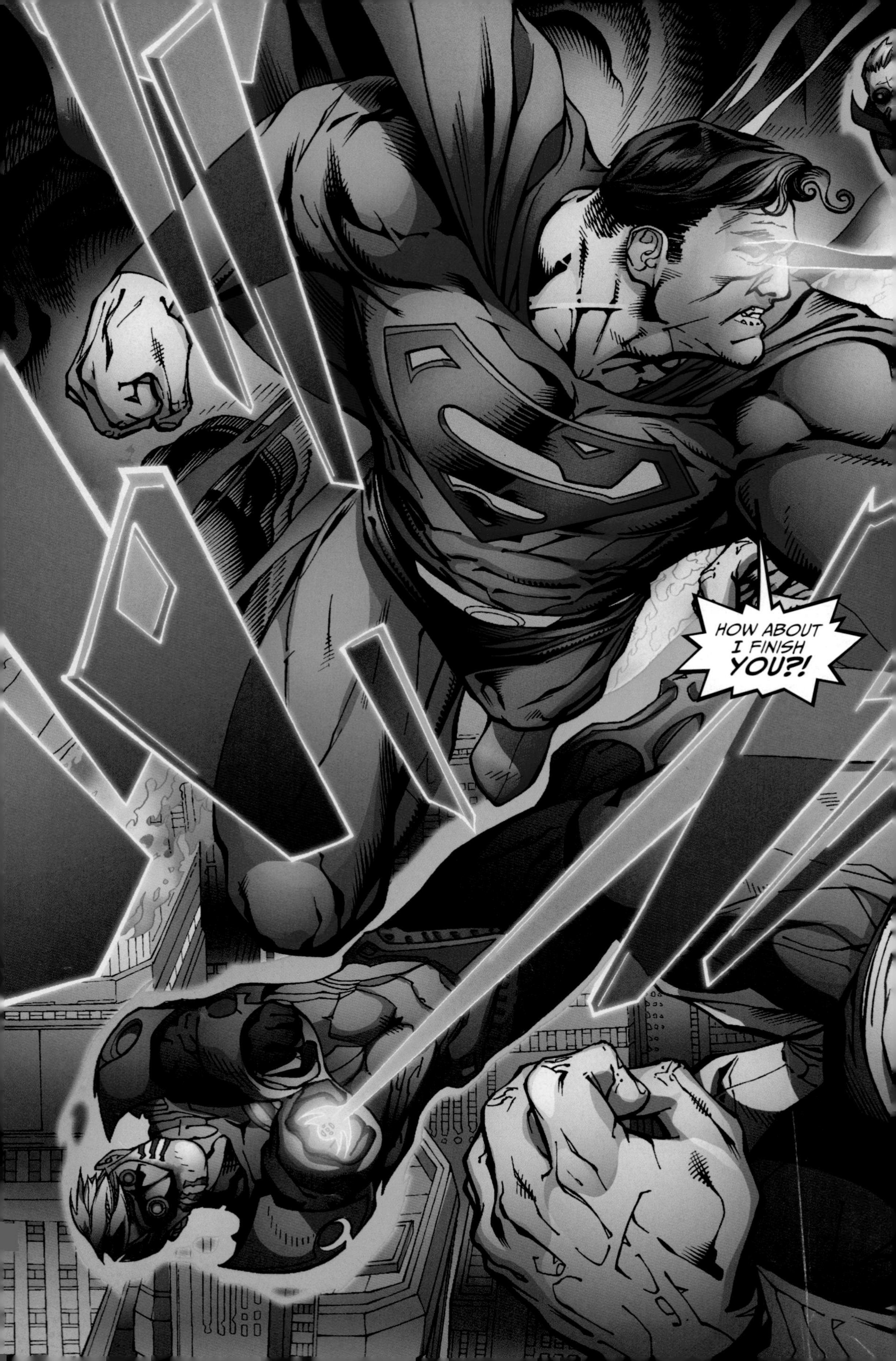
HOW ABOUT I FINISH YOU?!

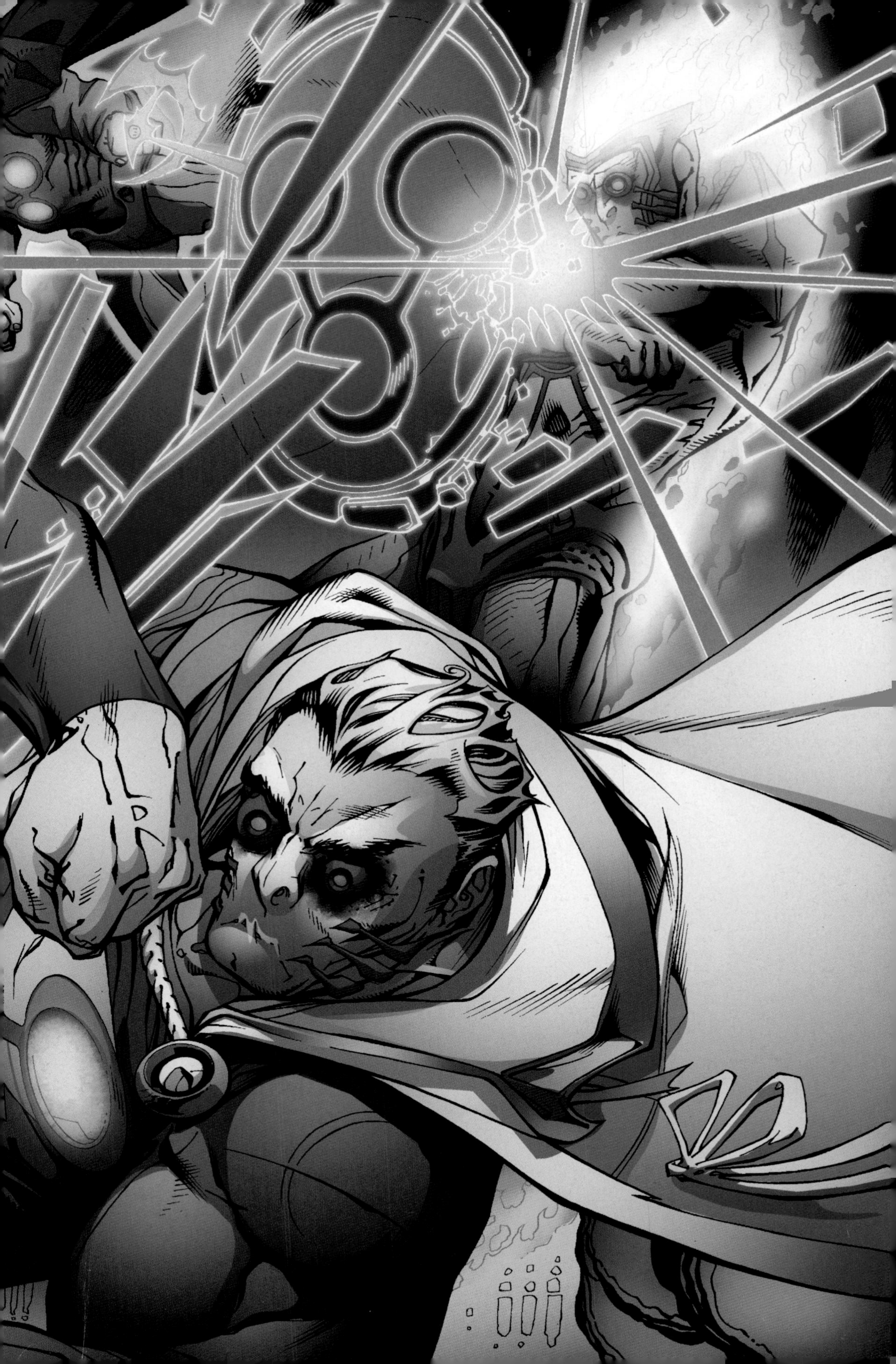

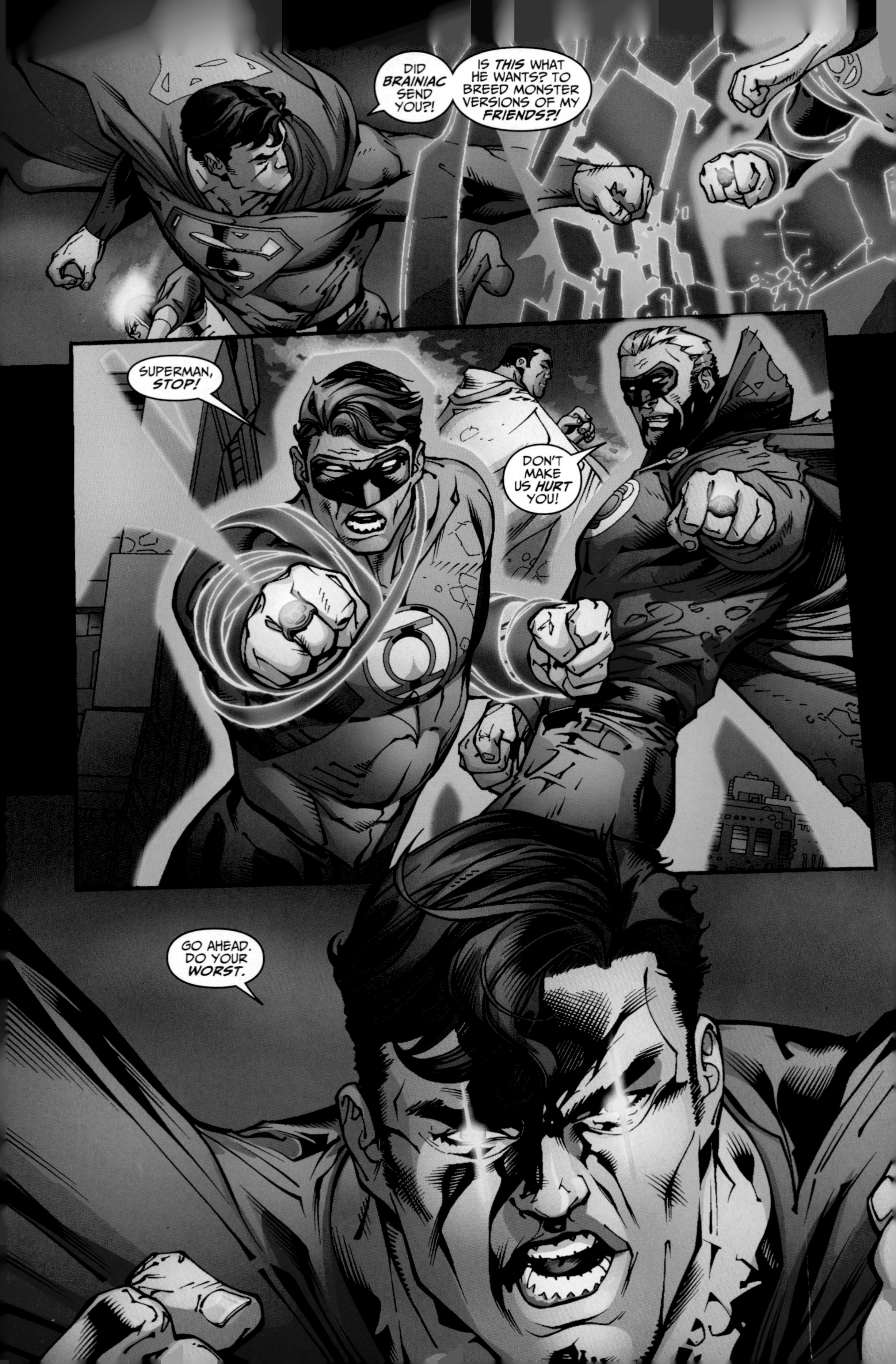
DID BRAINIAC SEND YOU?!
IS THIS WHAT HE WANTS? TO BREED MONSTER VERSIONS OF MY FRIENDS?!
SUPERMAN, STOP!
DON'T MAKE US HURT YOU!
GO AHEAD. DO YOUR WORST.

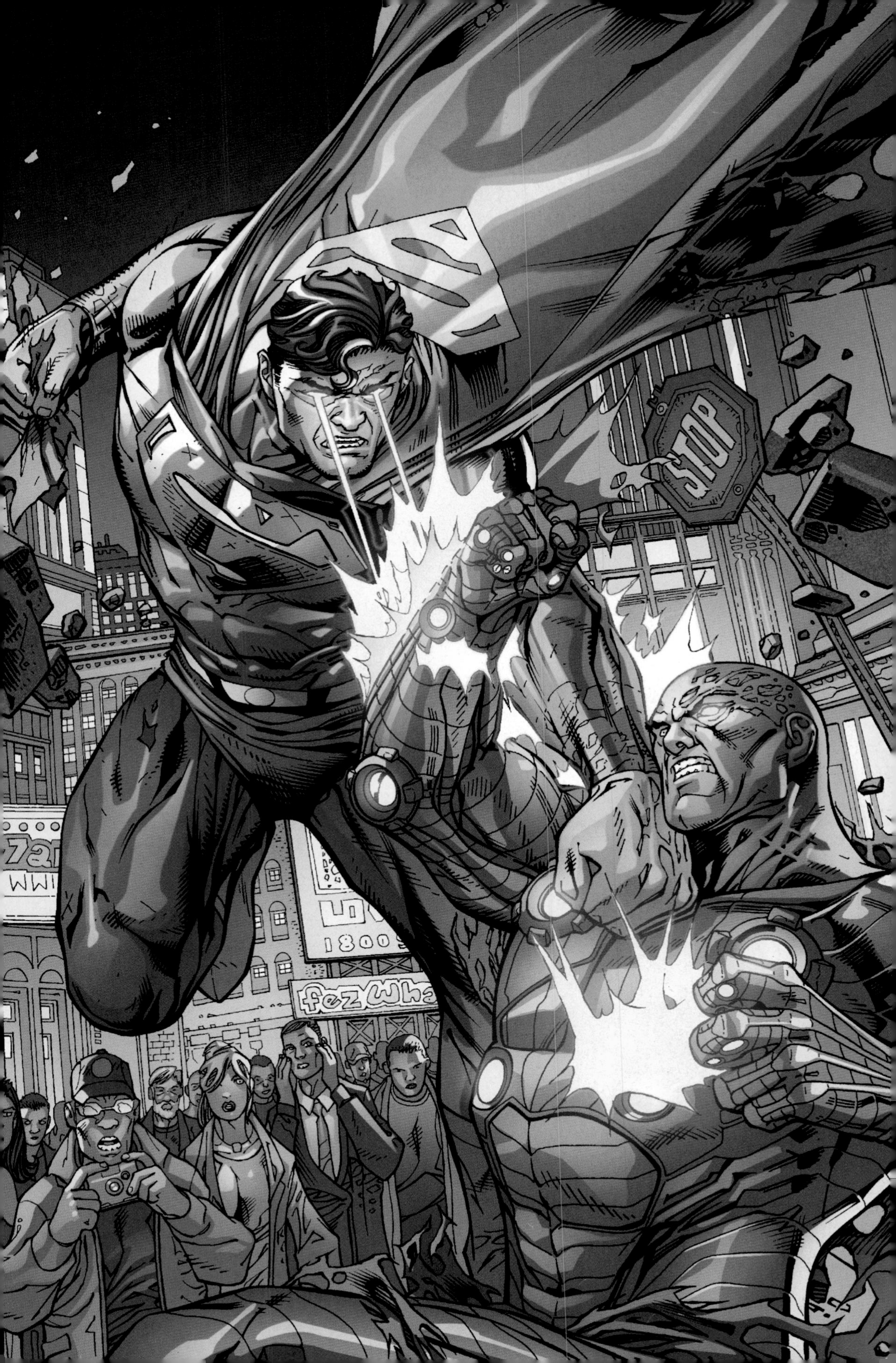
STOP

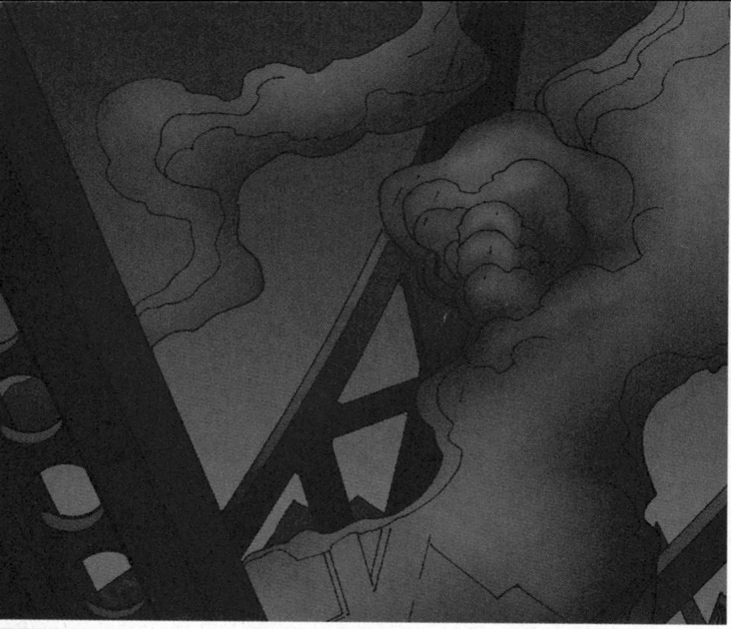

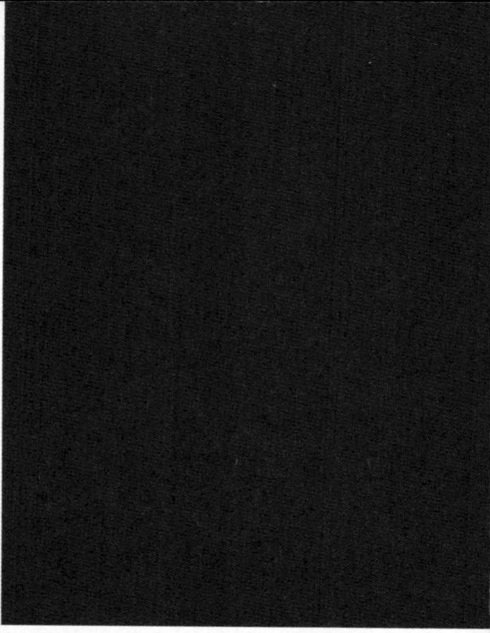

ENEMIES

Marv Wolfman
Writer

Mike S. Miller
Artist

Cover by Howard Porter, John Livesay & Jorge Gonzalez

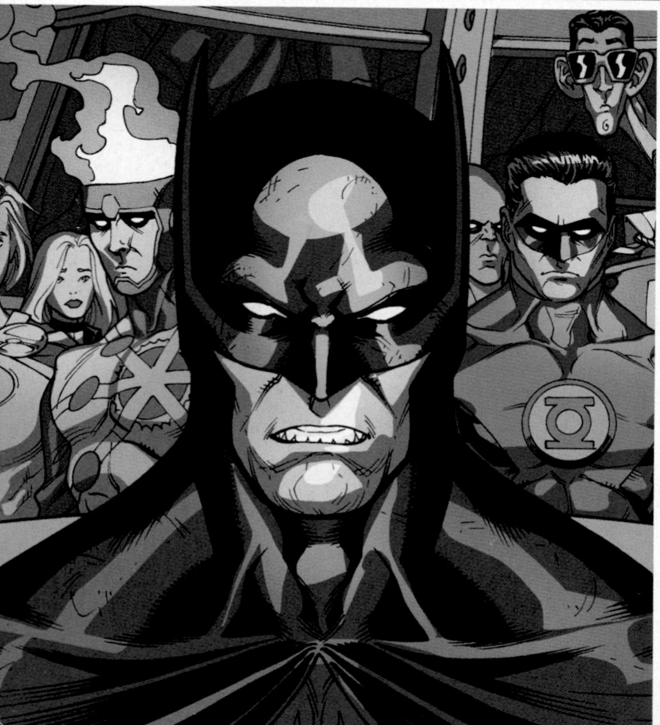

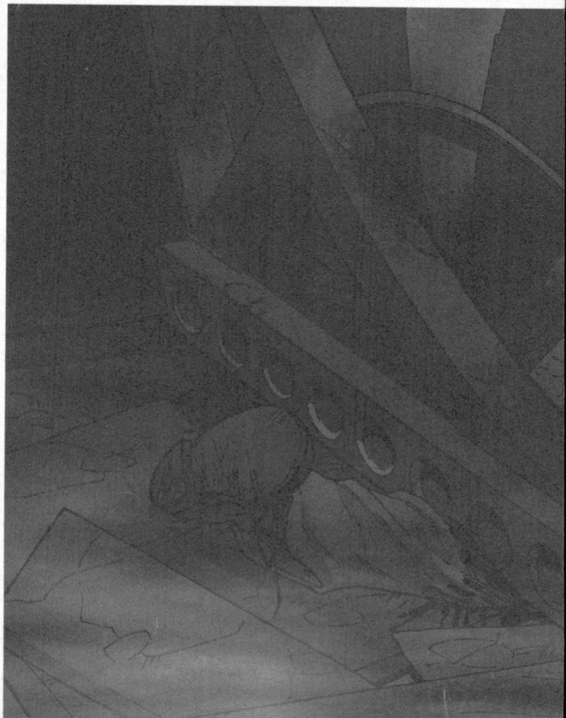

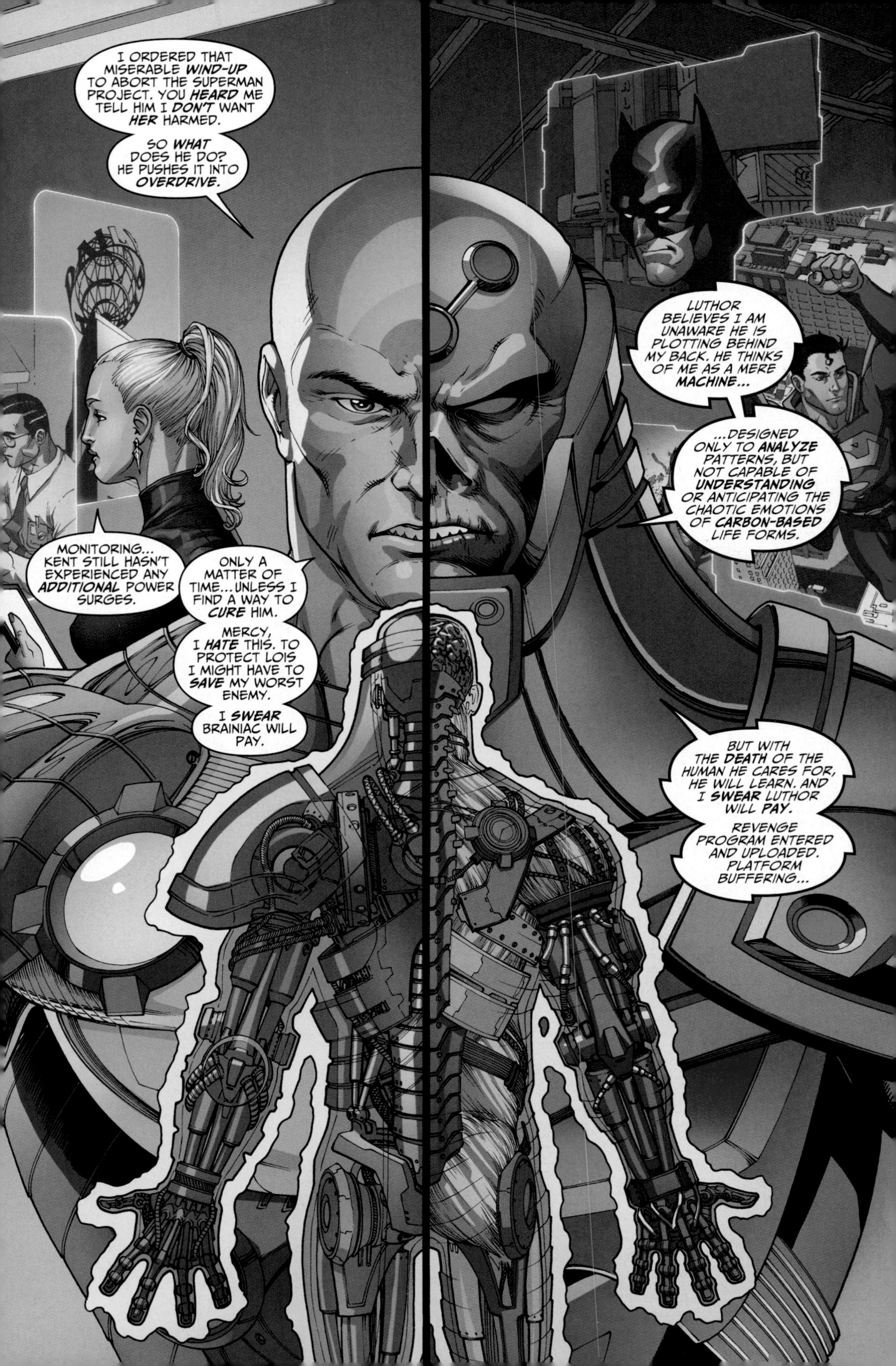
I ORDERED THAT MISERABLE WIND-UP TO ABORT THE SUPERMAN PROJECT. YOU HEARD ME TELL HIM I DON'T WANT HER HARMED.
SO WHAT DOES HE DO? HE PUSHES IT INTO OVERDRIVE.
MONITORING... KENT STILL HASN'T EXPERIENCED ANY ADDITIONAL POWER SURGES.
ONLY A MATTER OF TIME...UNLESS I FIND A WAY TO CURE HIM.
MERCY, I HATE THIS. TO PROTECT LOIS I MIGHT HAVE TO SAVE MY WORST ENEMY.
I SWEAR BRAINIAC WILL PAY.
LUTHOR BELIEVES I AM UNAWARE HE IS PLOTTING BEHIND MY BACK. HE THINKS OF ME AS A MERE MACHINE...
...DESIGNED ONLY TO ANALYZE PATTERNS, BUT NOT CAPABLE OF UNDERSTANDING OR ANTICIPATING THE CHAOTIC EMOTIONS OF CARBON-BASED LIFE FORMS.
BUT WITH THE DEATH OF THE HUMAN HE CARES FOR, HE WILL LEARN. AND I SWEAR LUTHOR WILL PAY.
REVENGE PROGRAM ENTERED AND UPLOADED. PLATFORM BUFFERING...

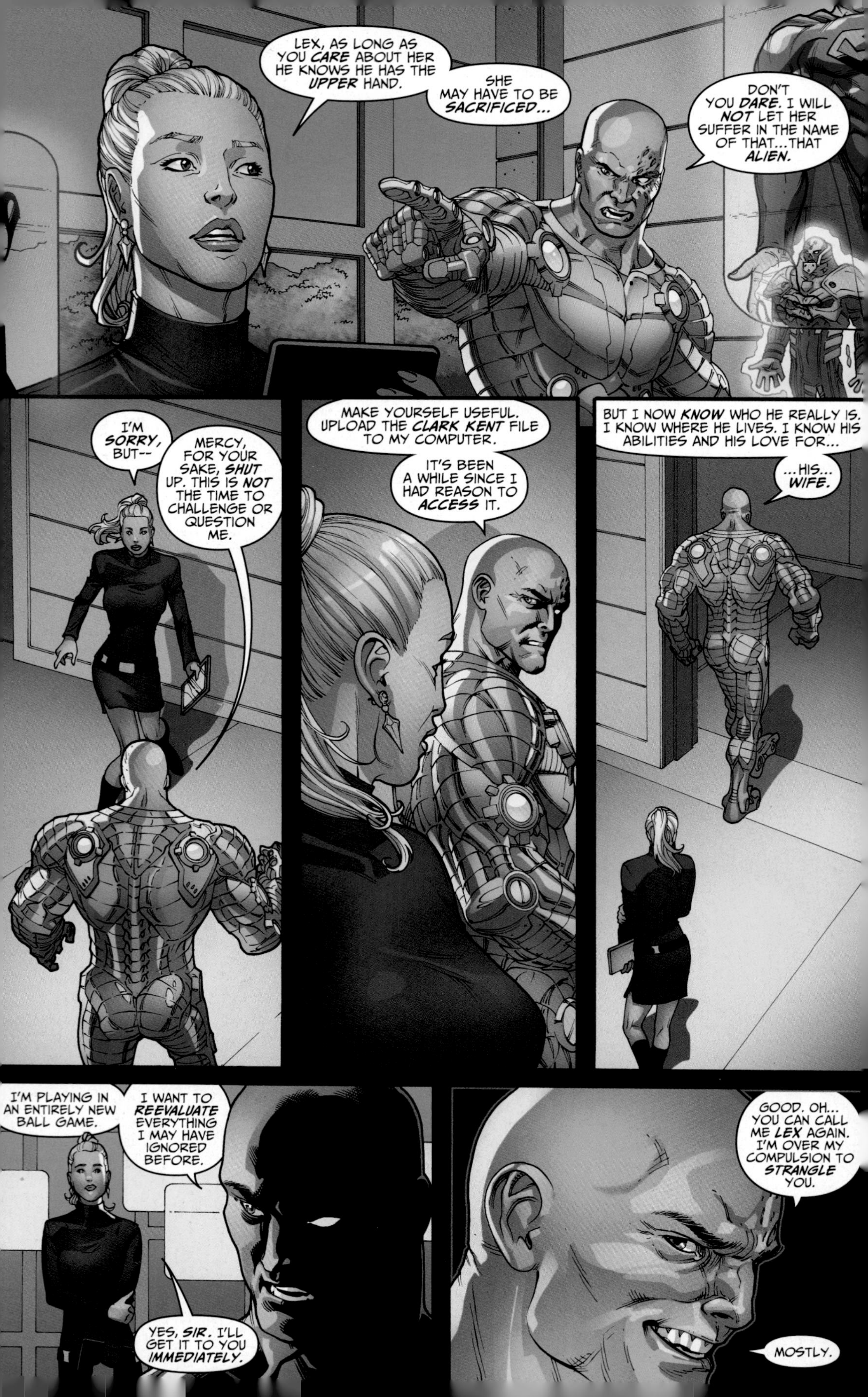
LEX, AS LONG AS YOU CARE ABOUT HER HE KNOWS HE HAS THE UPPER HAND.
SHE MAY HAVE TO BE SACRIFICED...
DON'T YOU DARE. I WILL NOT LET HER SUFFER IN THE NAME OF THAT...THAT ALIEN.
I'M SORRY, BUT--
MERCY, FOR YOUR SAKE, SHUT UP. THIS IS NOT THE TIME TO CHALLENGE OR QUESTION ME.
MAKE YOURSELF USEFUL. UPLOAD THE CLARK KENT FILE TO MY COMPUTER.
IT'S BEEN A WHILE SINCE I HAD REASON TO ACCESS IT.
BUT I NOW KNOW WHO HE REALLY IS. I KNOW WHERE HE LIVES. I KNOW HIS ABILITIES AND HIS LOVE FOR...
...HIS... WIFE.
I'M PLAYING IN AN ENTIRELY NEW BALL GAME.
I WANT TO REEVALUATE EVERYTHING I MAY HAVE IGNORED BEFORE.
YES, SIR. I'LL GET IT TO YOU IMMEDIATELY.
GOOD. OH... YOU CAN CALL ME LEX AGAIN. I'M OVER MY COMPULSION TO STRANGLE YOU.
MOSTLY.

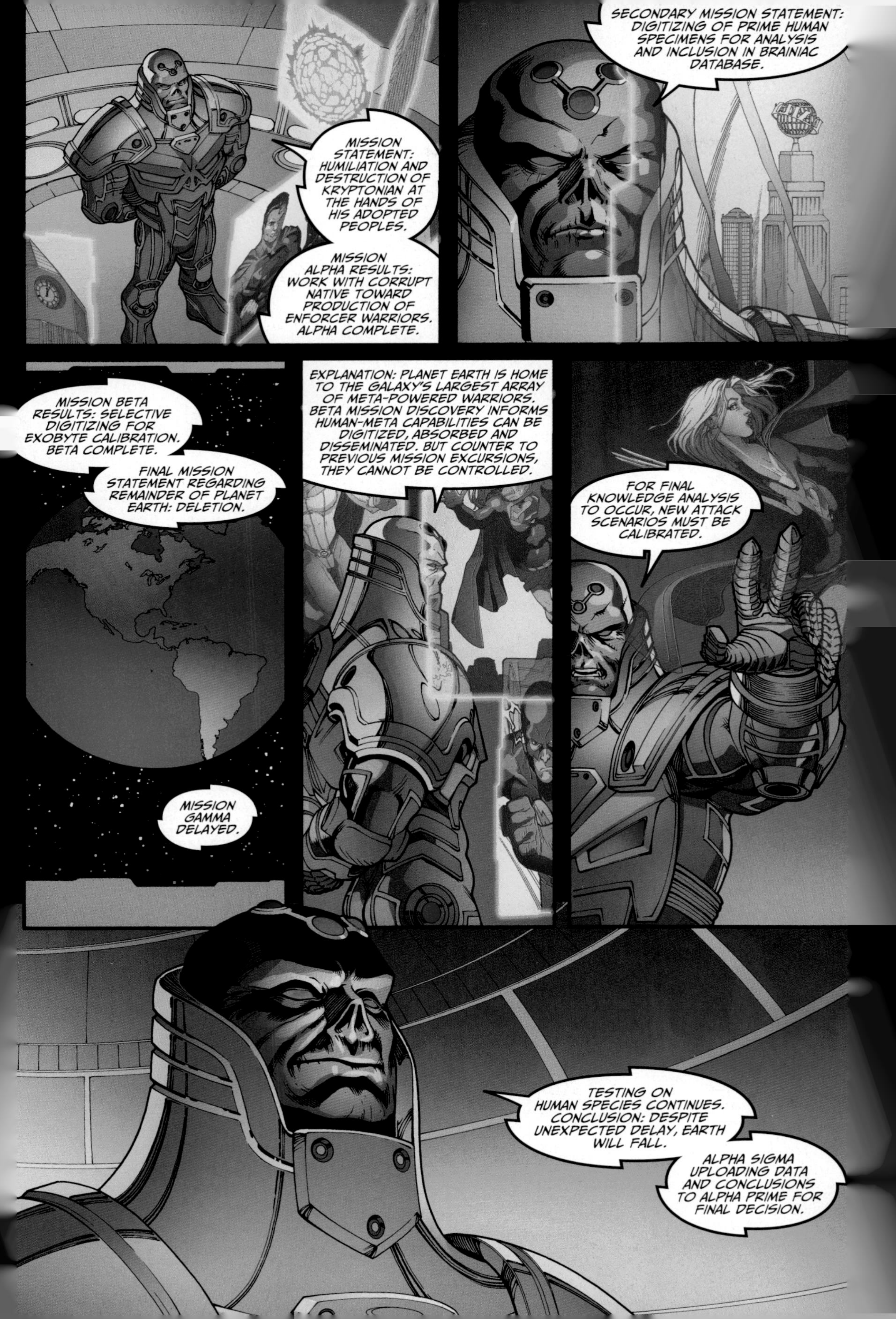
MISSION STATEMENT: HUMILIATION AND DESTRUCTION OF KRYPTONIAN AT THE HANDS OF HIS ADOPTED PEOPLES.
MISSION ALPHA RESULTS: WORK WITH CORRUPT NATIVE TOWARD PRODUCTION OF ENFORCER WARRIORS. ALPHA COMPLETE.
SECONDARY MISSION STATEMENT: DIGITIZING OF PRIME HUMAN SPECIMENS FOR ANALYSIS AND INCLUSION IN BRAINIAC DATABASE.
MISSION BETA RESULTS: SELECTIVE DIGITIZING FOR EXOBYTE CALIBRATION. BETA COMPLETE.
FINAL MISSION STATEMENT REGARDING REMAINDER OF PLANET EARTH: DELETION.
MISSION GAMMA DELAYED.
EXPLANATION: PLANET EARTH IS HOME TO THE GALAXY'S LARGEST ARRAY OF META-POWERED WARRIORS. BETA MISSION DISCOVERY INFORMS HUMAN-META CAPABILITIES CAN BE DIGITIZED, ABSORBED AND DISSEMINATED. BUT COUNTER TO PREVIOUS MISSION EXCURSIONS, THEY CANNOT BE CONTROLLED.
FOR FINAL KNOWLEDGE ANALYSIS TO OCCUR, NEW ATTACK SCENARIOS MUST BE CALIBRATED.
TESTING ON HUMAN SPECIES CONTINUES. CONCLUSION: DESPITE UNEXPECTED DELAY, EARTH WILL FALL.
ALPHA SIGMA UPLOADING DATA AND CONCLUSIONS TO ALPHA PRIME FOR FINAL DECISION.

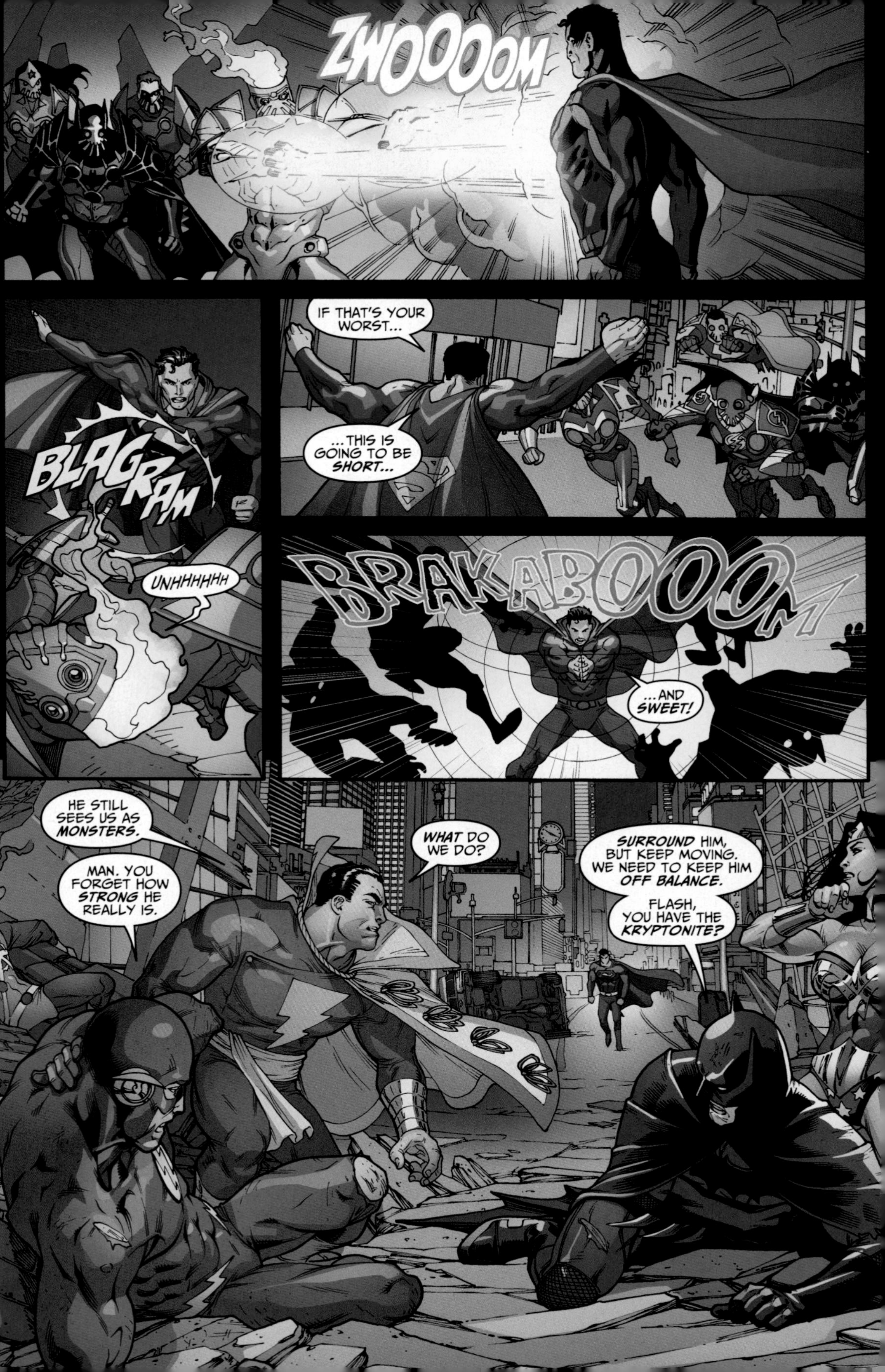
ZWOOOOM
BLAGRAM
UNHHHHHH
IF THAT'S YOUR WORST...
...THIS IS GOING TO BE SHORT...
BRAKABOOOOM
...AND SWEET!
HE STILL SEES US AS MONSTERS.
MAN. YOU FORGET HOW STRONG HE REALLY IS.
WHAT DO WE DO?
SURROUND HIM, BUT KEEP MOVING. WE NEED TO KEEP HIM OFF BALANCE.
FLASH, YOU HAVE THE KRYPTONITE?

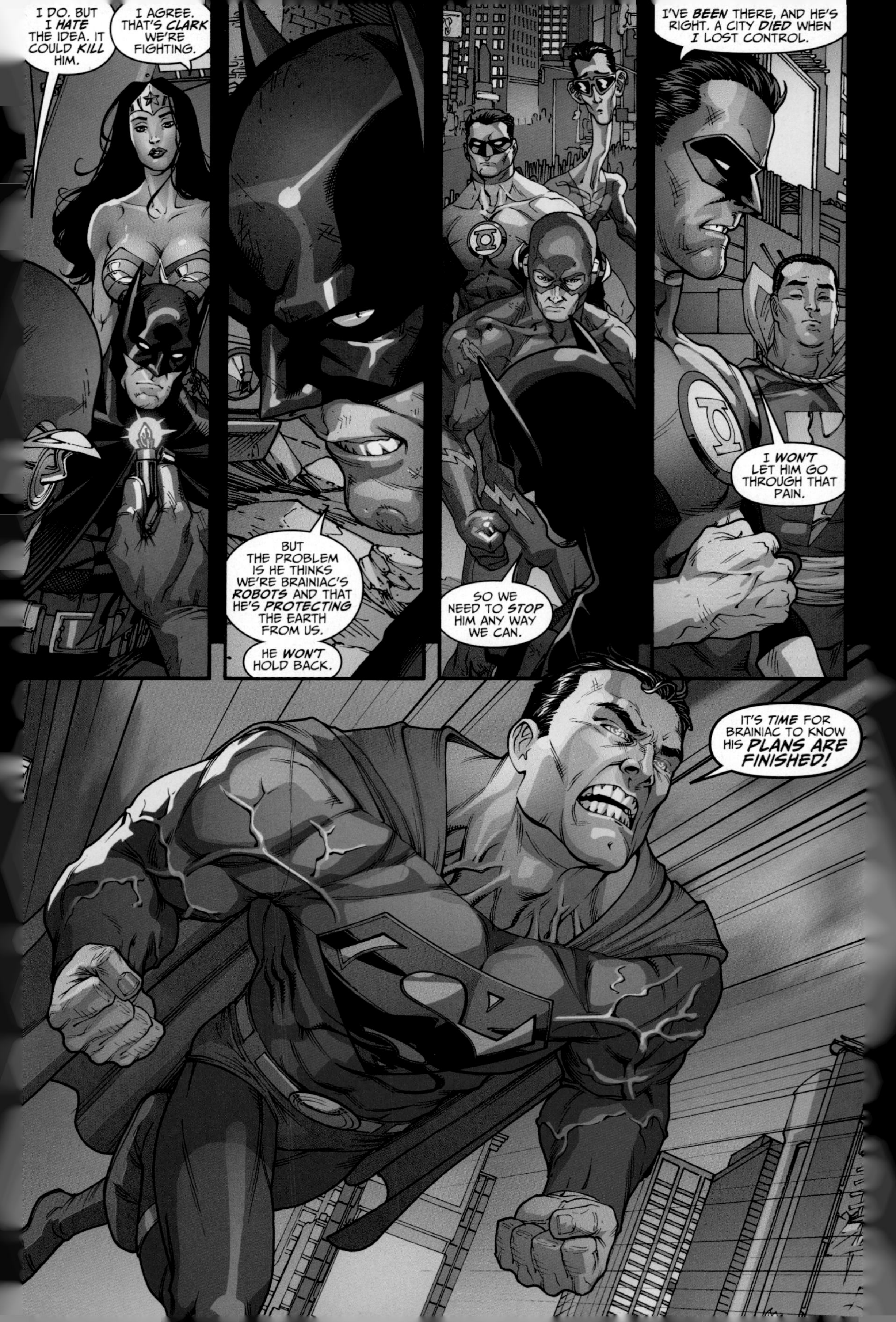
I DO. BUT I HATE THE IDEA. IT COULD KILL HIM.
I AGREE. THAT'S CLARK WE'RE FIGHTING.
BUT THE PROBLEM IS HE THINKS WE'RE BRAINIAC'S ROBOTS AND THAT HE'S PROTECTING THE EARTH FROM US.
HE WON'T HOLD BACK.
SO WE NEED TO STOP HIM ANY WAY WE CAN.
I'VE BEEN THERE, AND HE'S RIGHT. A CITY DIED WHEN I LOST CONTROL.
I WON'T LET HIM GO THROUGH THAT PAIN.
IT'S TIME FOR BRAINIAC TO KNOW HIS PLANS ARE FINISHED!

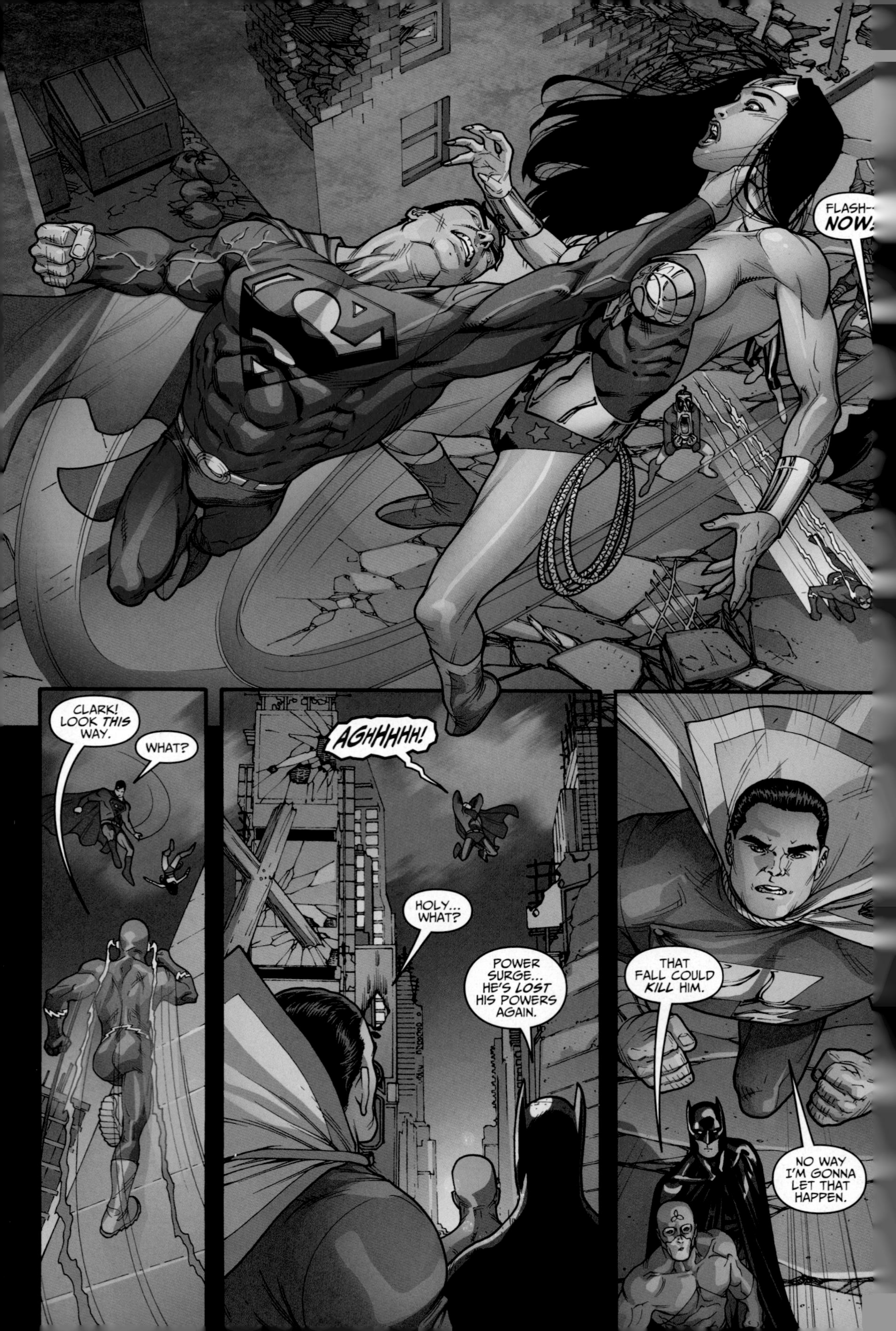
FLASH-- NOW!
CLARK! LOOK THIS WAY.
WHAT?
AGHHHHH!
HOLY... WHAT?
POWER SURGE... HE'S LOST HIS POWERS AGAIN.
THAT FALL COULD KILL HIM.
NO WAY I'M GONNA LET THAT HAPPEN.

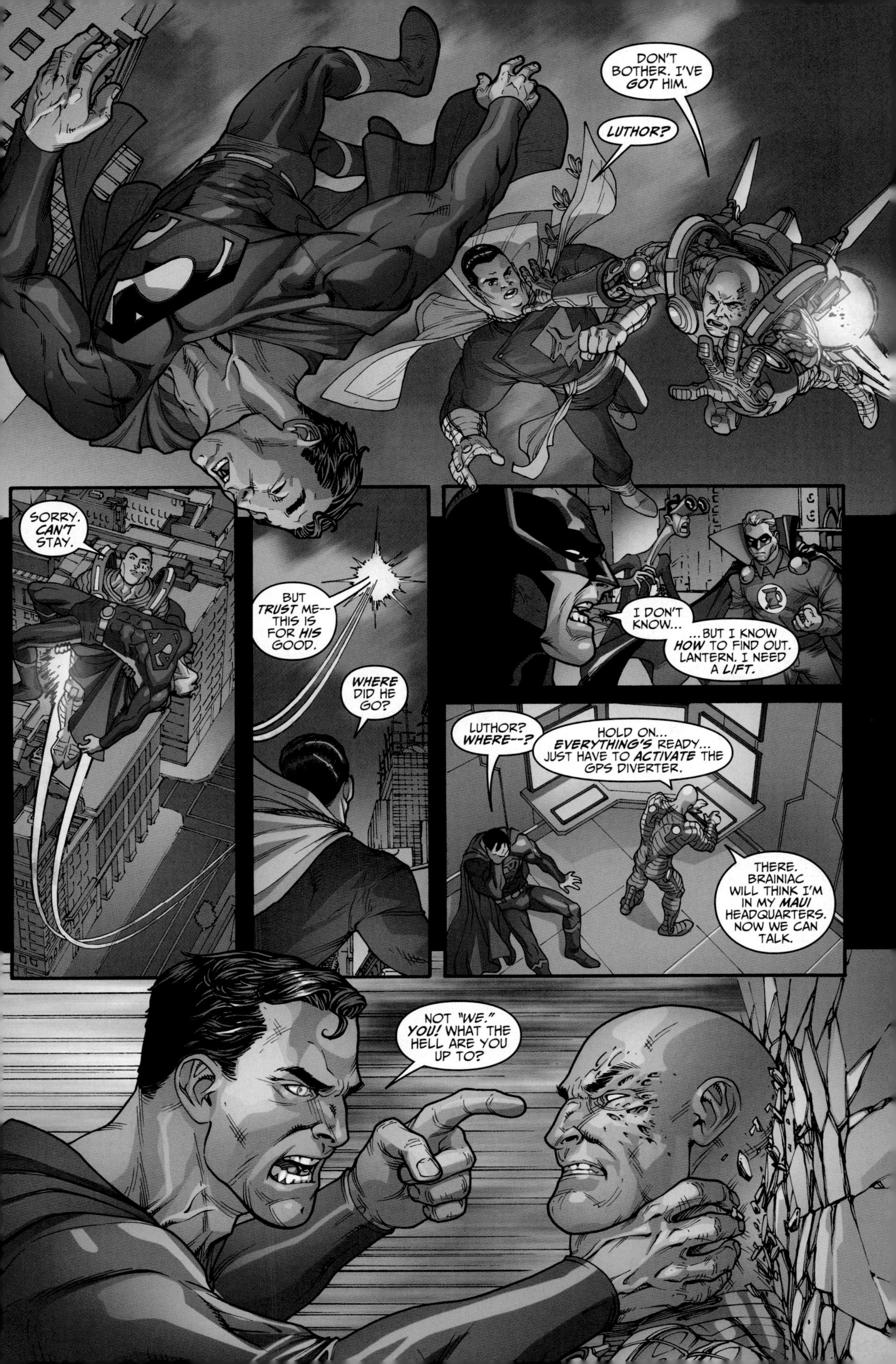
DON'T BOTHER. I'VE GOT HIM.
LUTHOR?
SORRY. CAN'T STAY.
BUT TRUST ME-- THIS IS FOR HIS GOOD.
WHERE DID HE GO?
I DON'T KNOW...
...BUT I KNOW HOW TO FIND OUT. LANTERN. I NEED A LIFT.
LUTHOR? WHERE--?
HOLD ON... EVERYTHING'S READY... JUST HAVE TO ACTIVATE THE GPS DIVERTER.
THERE. BRAINIAC WILL THINK I'M IN MY MAUI HEADQUARTERS. NOW WE CAN TALK.
NOT "WE." YOU! WHAT THE HELL ARE YOU UP TO?

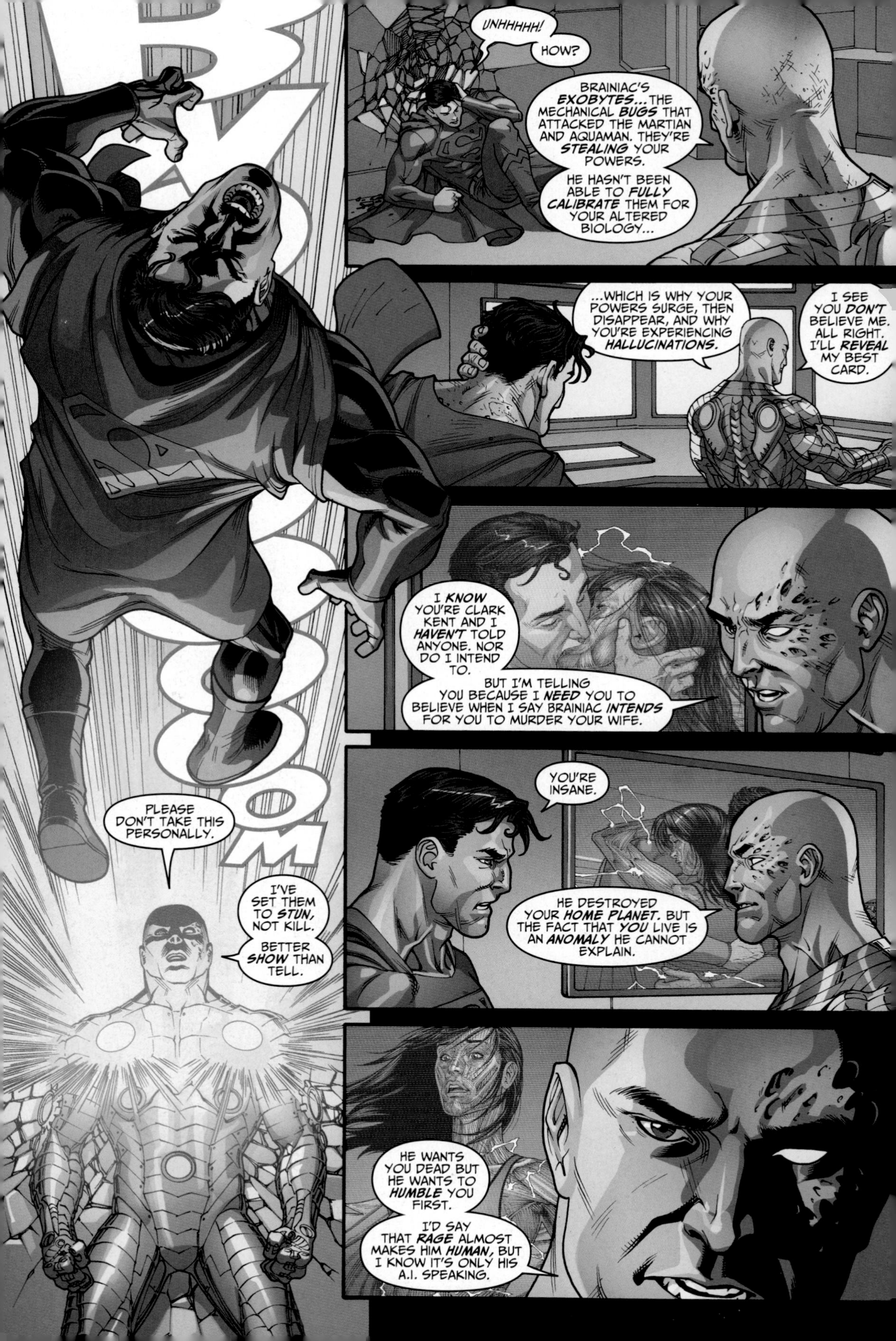
PLEASE DON'T TAKE THIS PERSONALLY.
I'VE SET THEM TO STUN, NOT KILL.
BETTER SHOW THAN TELL.
UNHHHHH!
HOW?
BRAINIAC'S EXOBYTES... THE MECHANICAL BUGS THAT ATTACKED THE MARTIAN AND AQUAMAN. THEY'RE STEALING YOUR POWERS.
HE HASN'T BEEN ABLE TO FULLY CALIBRATE THEM FOR YOUR ALTERED BIOLOGY...
...WHICH IS WHY YOUR POWERS SURGE, THEN DISAPPEAR, AND WHY YOU'RE EXPERIENCING HALLUCINATIONS.
I SEE YOU DON'T BELIEVE ME. ALL RIGHT. I'LL REVEAL MY BEST CARD.
I KNOW YOU'RE CLARK KENT AND I HAVEN'T TOLD ANYONE. NOR DO I INTEND TO.
BUT I'M TELLING YOU BECAUSE I NEED YOU TO BELIEVE WHEN I SAY BRAINIAC INTENDS FOR YOU TO MURDER YOUR WIFE.
YOU'RE INSANE.
HE DESTROYED YOUR HOME PLANET. BUT THE FACT THAT YOU LIVE IS AN ANOMALY HE CANNOT EXPLAIN.
HE WANTS YOU DEAD BUT HE WANTS TO HUMBLE YOU FIRST.
I'D SAY THAT RAGE ALMOST MAKES HIM HUMAN, BUT I KNOW IT'S ONLY HIS A.I. SPEAKING.

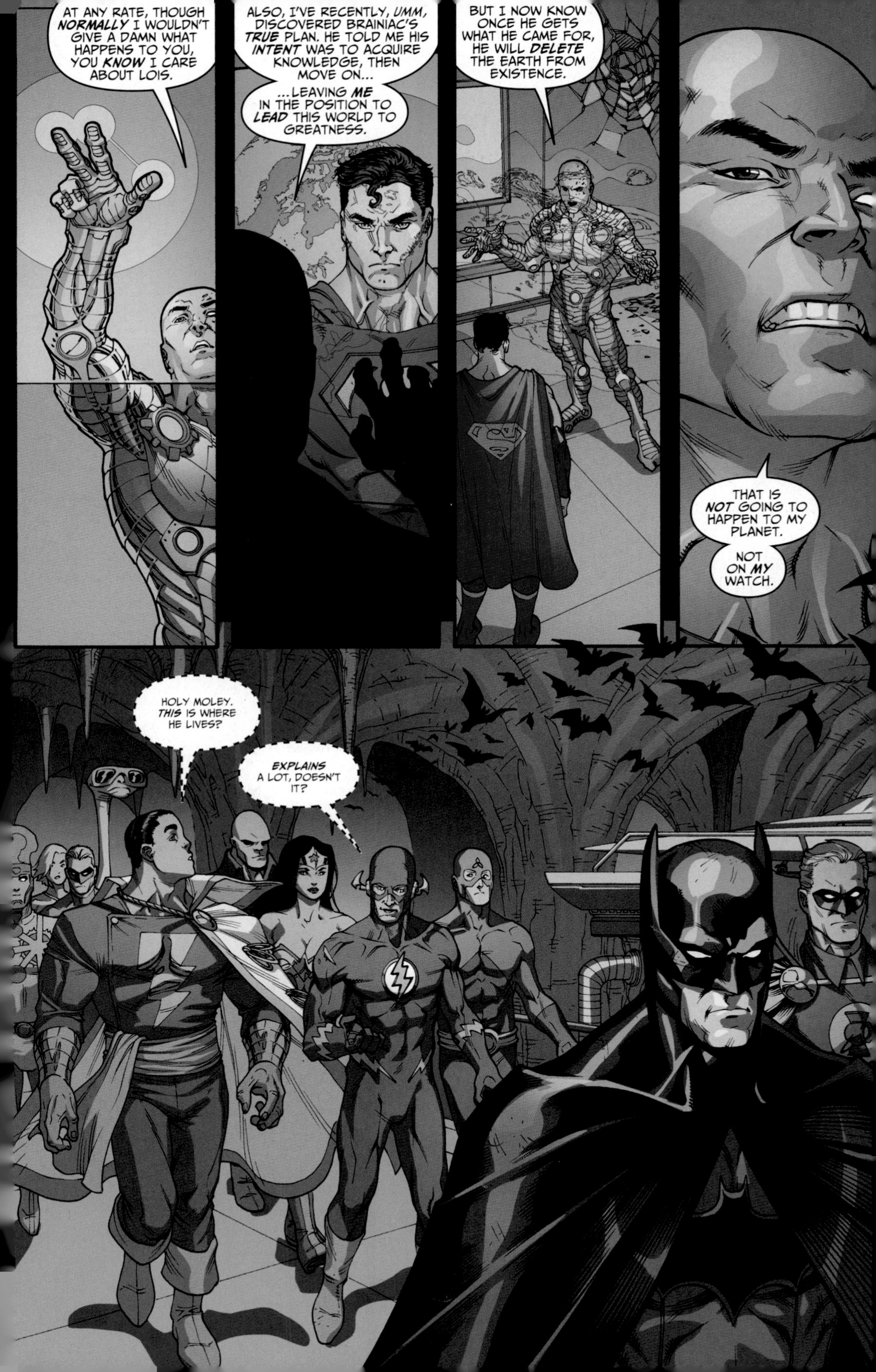
AT ANY RATE, THOUGH NORMALLY I WOULDN'T GIVE A DAMN WHAT HAPPENS TO YOU, YOU KNOW I CARE ABOUT LOIS.
ALSO, I'VE RECENTLY, UMM, DISCOVERED BRAINIAC'S TRUE PLAN. HE TOLD ME HIS INTENT WAS TO ACQUIRE KNOWLEDGE, THEN MOVE ON...
...LEAVING ME IN THE POSITION TO LEAD THIS WORLD TO GREATNESS.
BUT I NOW KNOW ONCE HE GETS WHAT HE CAME FOR, HE WILL DELETE THE EARTH FROM EXISTENCE.
THAT IS NOT GOING TO HAPPEN TO MY PLANET.
NOT ON MY WATCH.
HOLY MOLEY. THIS IS WHERE HE LIVES?
EXPLAINS A LOT, DOESN'T IT?

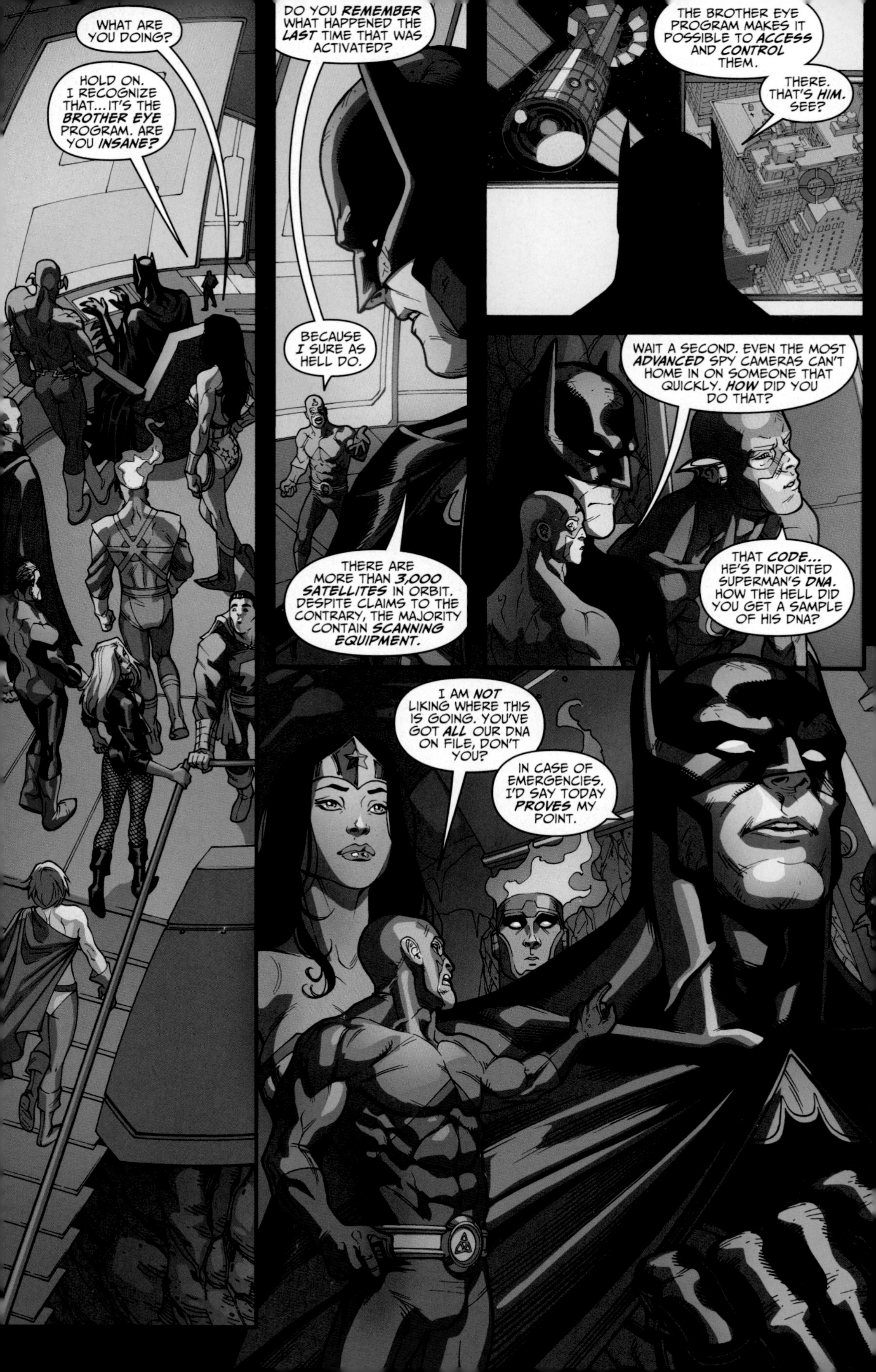
WHAT ARE YOU DOING?
HOLD ON. I RECOGNIZE THAT... IT'S THE BROTHER EYE PROGRAM. ARE YOU INSANE?
DO YOU REMEMBER WHAT HAPPENED THE LAST TIME THAT WAS ACTIVATED?
BECAUSE I SURE AS HELL DO.
THERE ARE MORE THAN 3,000 SATELLITES IN ORBIT. DESPITE CLAIMS TO THE CONTRARY, THE MAJORITY CONTAIN SCANNING EQUIPMENT.
THE BROTHER EYE PROGRAM MAKES IT POSSIBLE TO ACCESS AND CONTROL THEM.
THERE. THAT'S HIM. SEE?
WAIT A SECOND. EVEN THE MOST ADVANCED SPY CAMERAS CAN'T HOME IN ON SOMEONE THAT QUICKLY. HOW DID YOU DO THAT?
THAT CODE... HE'S PINPOINTED SUPERMAN'S DNA. HOW THE HELL DID YOU GET A SAMPLE OF HIS DNA?
I AM NOT LIKING WHERE THIS IS GOING. YOU'VE GOT ALL OUR DNA ON FILE, DON'T YOU?
IN CASE OF EMERGENCIES. I'D SAY TODAY PROVES MY POINT.

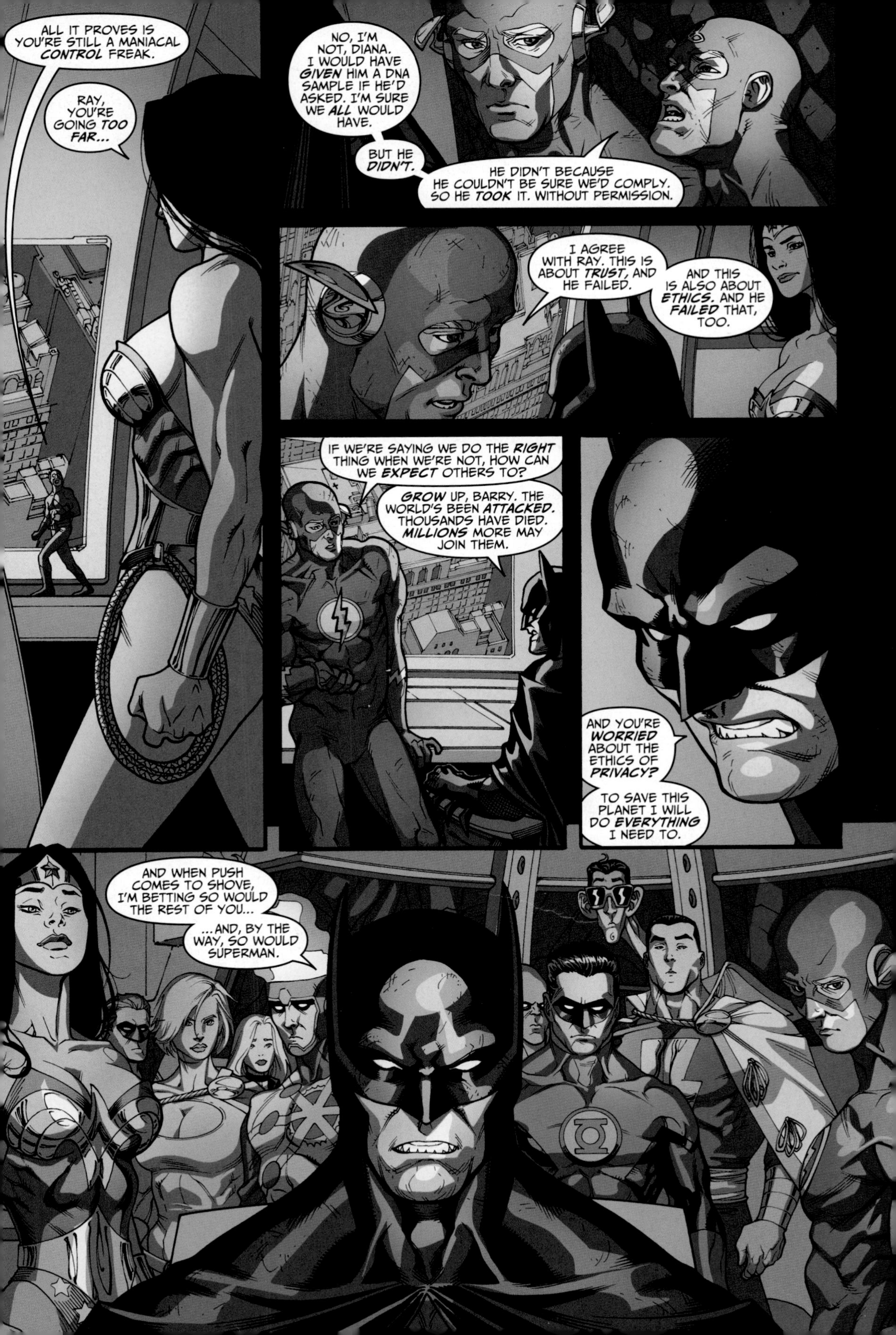
ALL IT PROVES IS YOU'RE STILL A MANIACAL CONTROL FREAK.
RAY, YOU'RE GOING TOO FAR...
NO, I'M NOT, DIANA. I WOULD HAVE GIVEN HIM A DNA SAMPLE IF HE'D ASKED. I'M SURE WE ALL WOULD HAVE.
BUT HE DIDN'T.
HE DIDN'T BECAUSE HE COULDN'T BE SURE WE'D COMPLY. SO HE TOOK IT. WITHOUT PERMISSION.
I AGREE WITH RAY. THIS IS ABOUT TRUST, AND HE FAILED.
AND THIS IS ALSO ABOUT ETHICS. AND HE FAILED THAT, TOO.
IF WE'RE SAYING WE DO THE RIGHT THING WHEN WE'RE NOT, HOW CAN WE EXPECT OTHERS TO?
GROW UP, BARRY. THE WORLD'S BEEN ATTACKED. THOUSANDS HAVE DIED. MILLIONS MORE MAY JOIN THEM.
AND YOU'RE WORRIED ABOUT THE ETHICS OF PRIVACY?
TO SAVE THIS PLANET I WILL DO EVERYTHING I NEED TO.
AND WHEN PUSH COMES TO SHOVE, I'M BETTING SO WOULD THE REST OF YOU...
...AND, BY THE WAY, SO WOULD SUPERMAN.

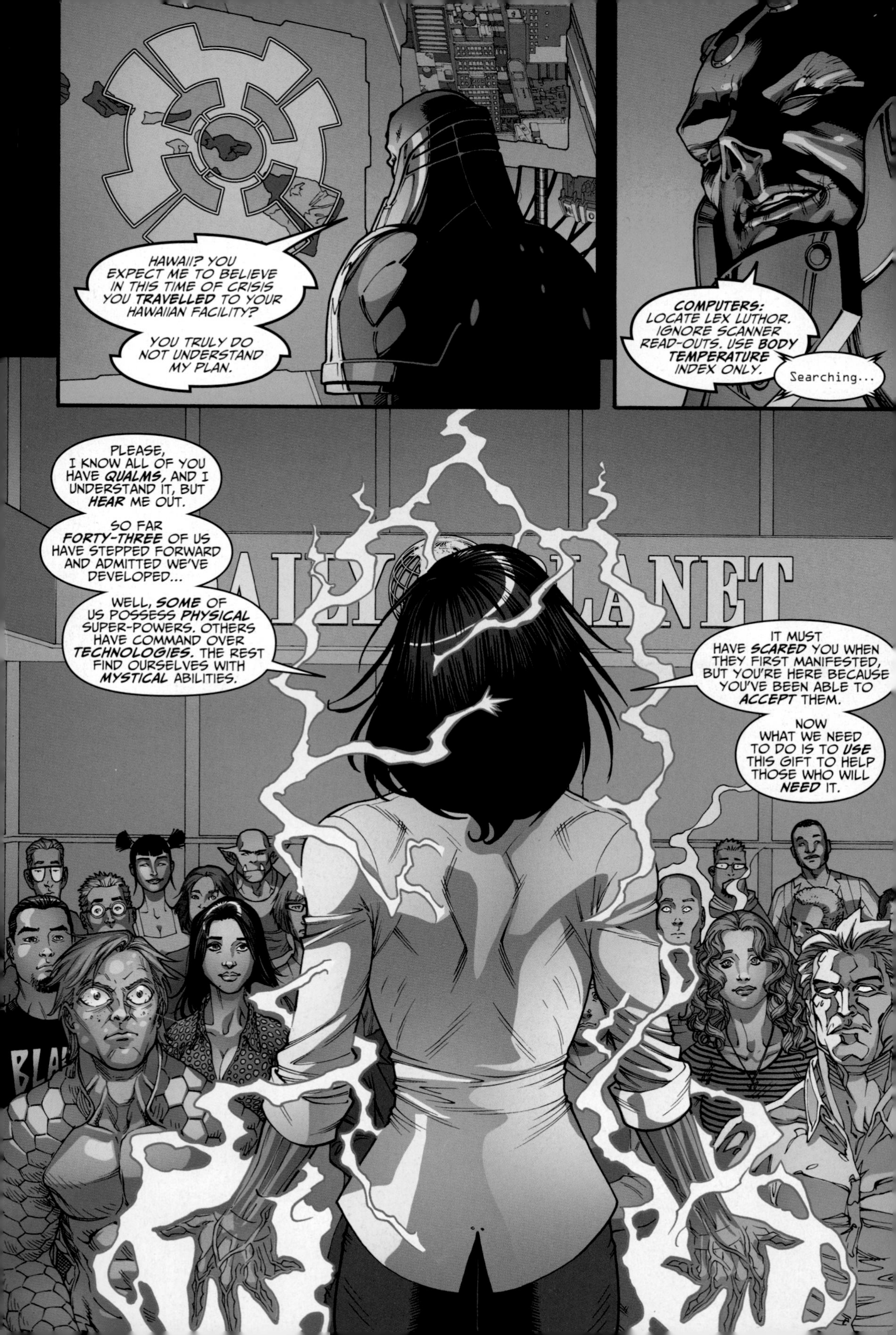

HAWAII? YOU EXPECT ME TO BELIEVE IN THIS TIME OF CRISIS YOU TRAVELLED TO YOUR HAWAIIAN FACILITY?
YOU TRULY DO NOT UNDERSTAND MY PLAN.
COMPUTERS: LOCATE LEX LUTHOR. IGNORE SCANNER READ-OUTS. USE BODY TEMPERATURE INDEX ONLY.
Searching...
PLEASE, I KNOW ALL OF YOU HAVE QUALMS, AND I UNDERSTAND IT, BUT HEAR ME OUT.
SO FAR FORTY-THREE OF US HAVE STEPPED FORWARD AND ADMITTED WE'VE DEVELOPED...
WELL, SOME OF US POSSESS PHYSICAL SUPER-POWERS. OTHERS HAVE COMMAND OVER TECHNOLOGIES. THE REST FIND OURSELVES WITH MYSTICAL ABILITIES.
IT MUST HAVE SCARED YOU WHEN THEY FIRST MANIFESTED, BUT YOU'RE HERE BECAUSE YOU'VE BEEN ABLE TO ACCEPT THEM.
NOW WHAT WE NEED TO DO IS TO USE THIS GIFT TO HELP THOSE WHO WILL NEED IT.

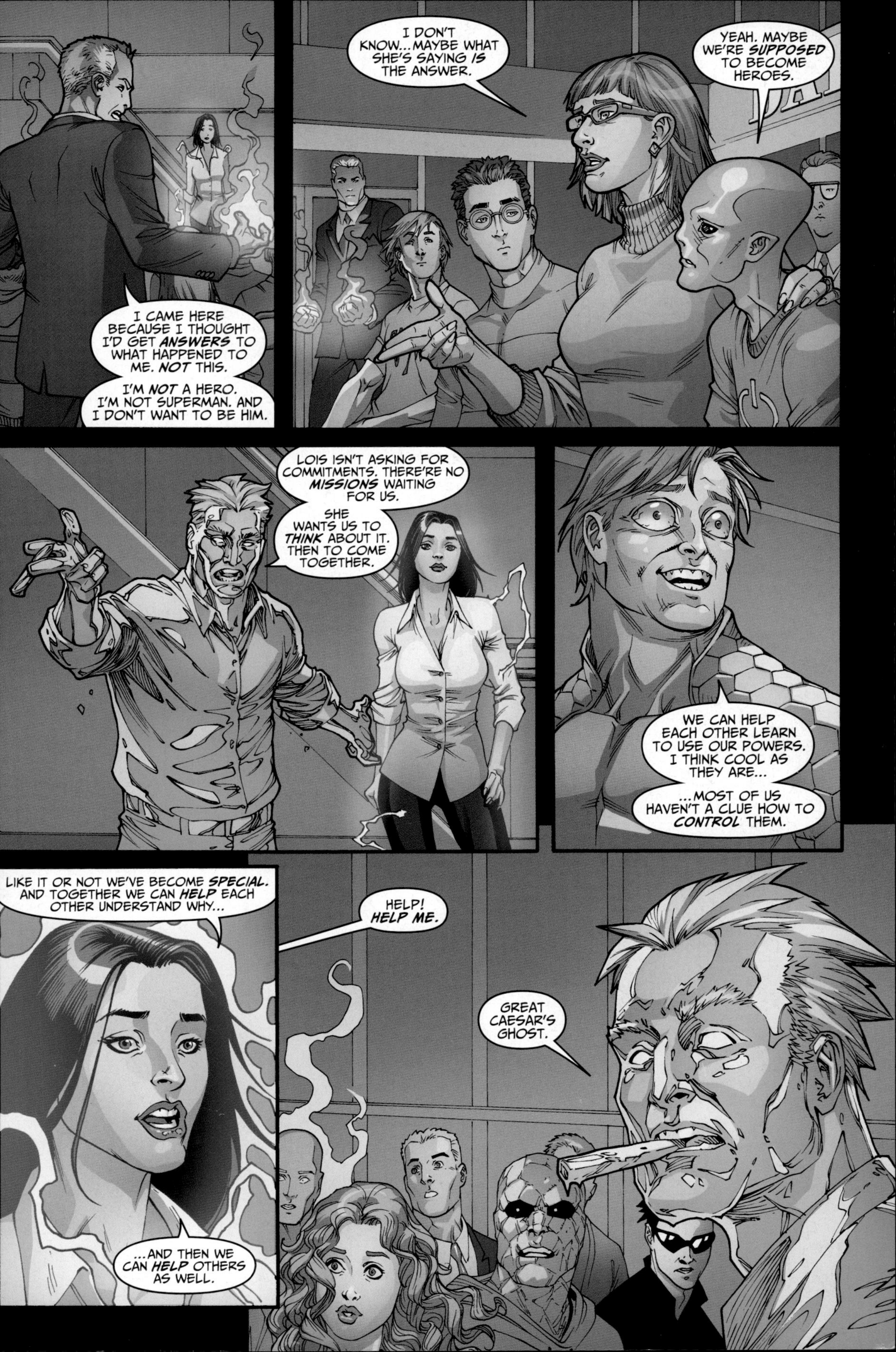
I CAME HERE BECAUSE I THOUGHT I'D GET *ANSWERS* TO WHAT HAPPENED TO ME. *NOT* THIS.
I'M *NOT* A HERO. I'M NOT SUPERMAN. AND I DON'T WANT TO BE HIM.
I DON'T KNOW...MAYBE WHAT SHE'S SAYING *IS* THE ANSWER.
YEAH. MAYBE WE'RE *SUPPOSED* TO BECOME HEROES.
LOIS ISN'T ASKING FOR COMMITMENTS. THERE'RE NO *MISSIONS* WAITING FOR US.
SHE WANTS US TO *THINK* ABOUT IT. THEN TO COME TOGETHER.
WE CAN HELP EACH OTHER LEARN TO USE OUR POWERS. I THINK COOL AS THEY ARE...
...MOST OF US HAVEN'T A CLUE HOW TO *CONTROL* THEM.
LIKE IT OR NOT WE'VE BECOME *SPECIAL*. AND TOGETHER WE CAN *HELP* EACH OTHER UNDERSTAND WHY...
...AND THEN WE CAN *HELP* OTHERS AS WELL.
HELP! *HELP ME.*
GREAT CAESAR'S GHOST.

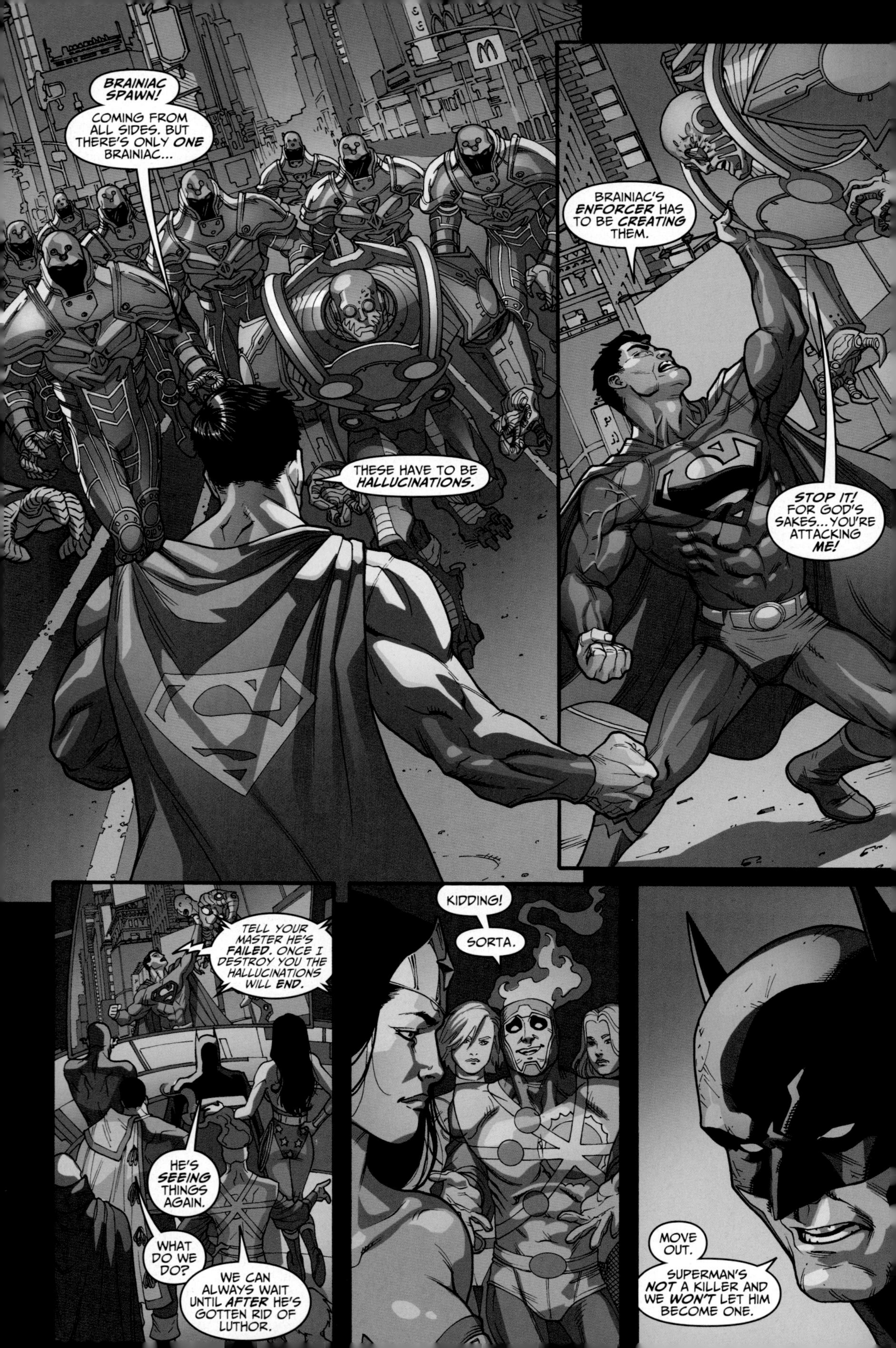

BRAINIAC SPAWN!
COMING FROM ALL SIDES. BUT THERE'S ONLY ONE BRAINIAC...
THESE HAVE TO BE HALLUCINATIONS.
BRAINIAC'S ENFORCER HAS TO BE CREATING THEM.
STOP IT! FOR GOD'S SAKES...YOU'RE ATTACKING ME!
TELL YOUR MASTER HE'S FAILED. ONCE I DESTROY YOU THE HALLUCINATIONS WILL END.
HE'S SEEING THINGS AGAIN.
WHAT DO WE DO?
WE CAN ALWAYS WAIT UNTIL AFTER HE'S GOTTEN RID OF LUTHOR.
KIDDING!
SORTA.
MOVE OUT.
SUPERMAN'S NOT A KILLER AND WE WON'T LET HIM BECOME ONE.

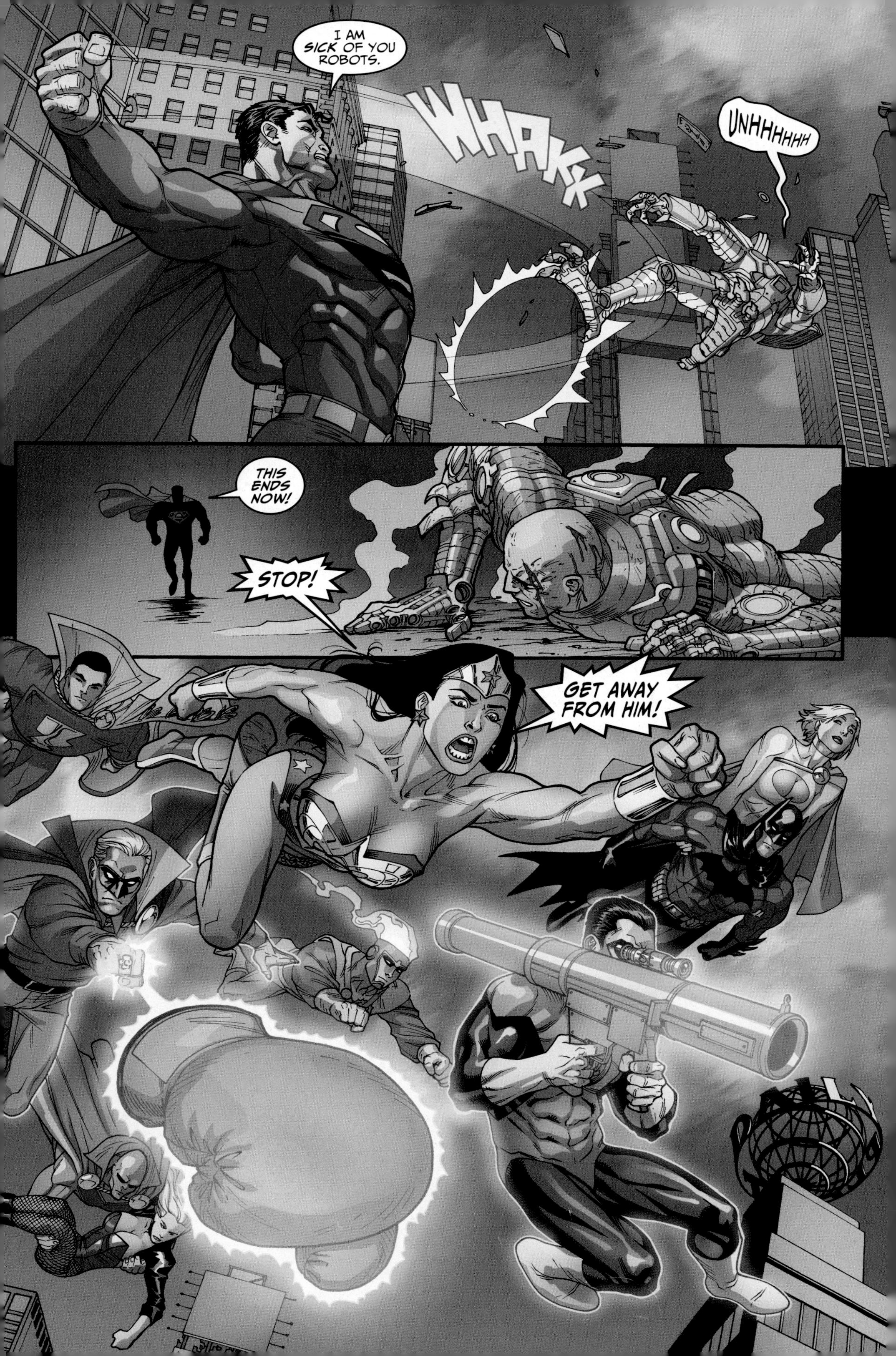
I AM SICK OF YOU ROBOTS.
WHAKK
UNHHHHHH
THIS ENDS NOW!
STOP!
GET AWAY FROM HIM!

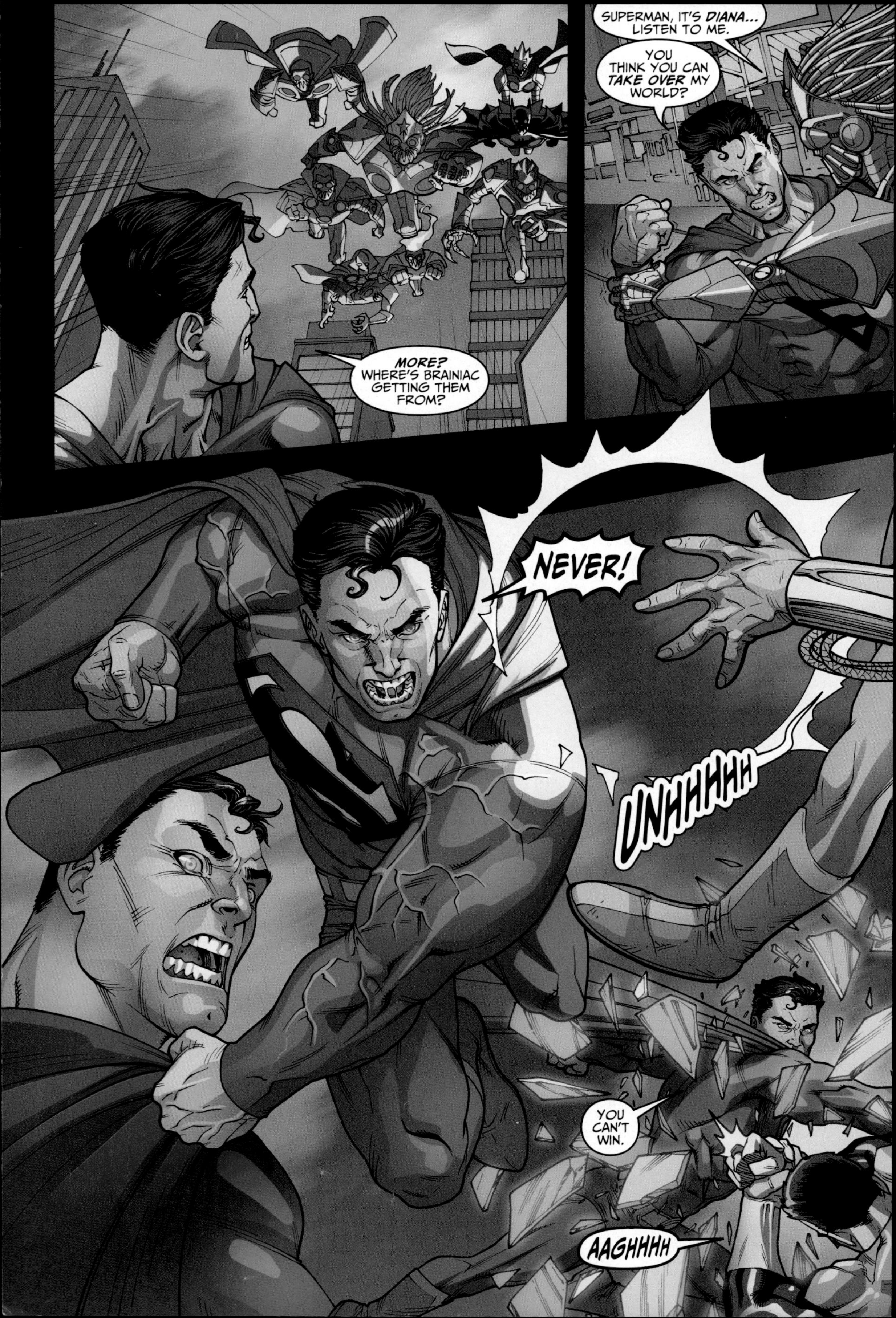
MORE? WHERE'S BRAINIAC GETTING THEM FROM?
SUPERMAN, IT'S DIANA... LISTEN TO ME.
YOU THINK YOU CAN TAKE OVER MY WORLD?
NEVER!
UNHHHHH
YOU CAN'T WIN.
AAGHHHH

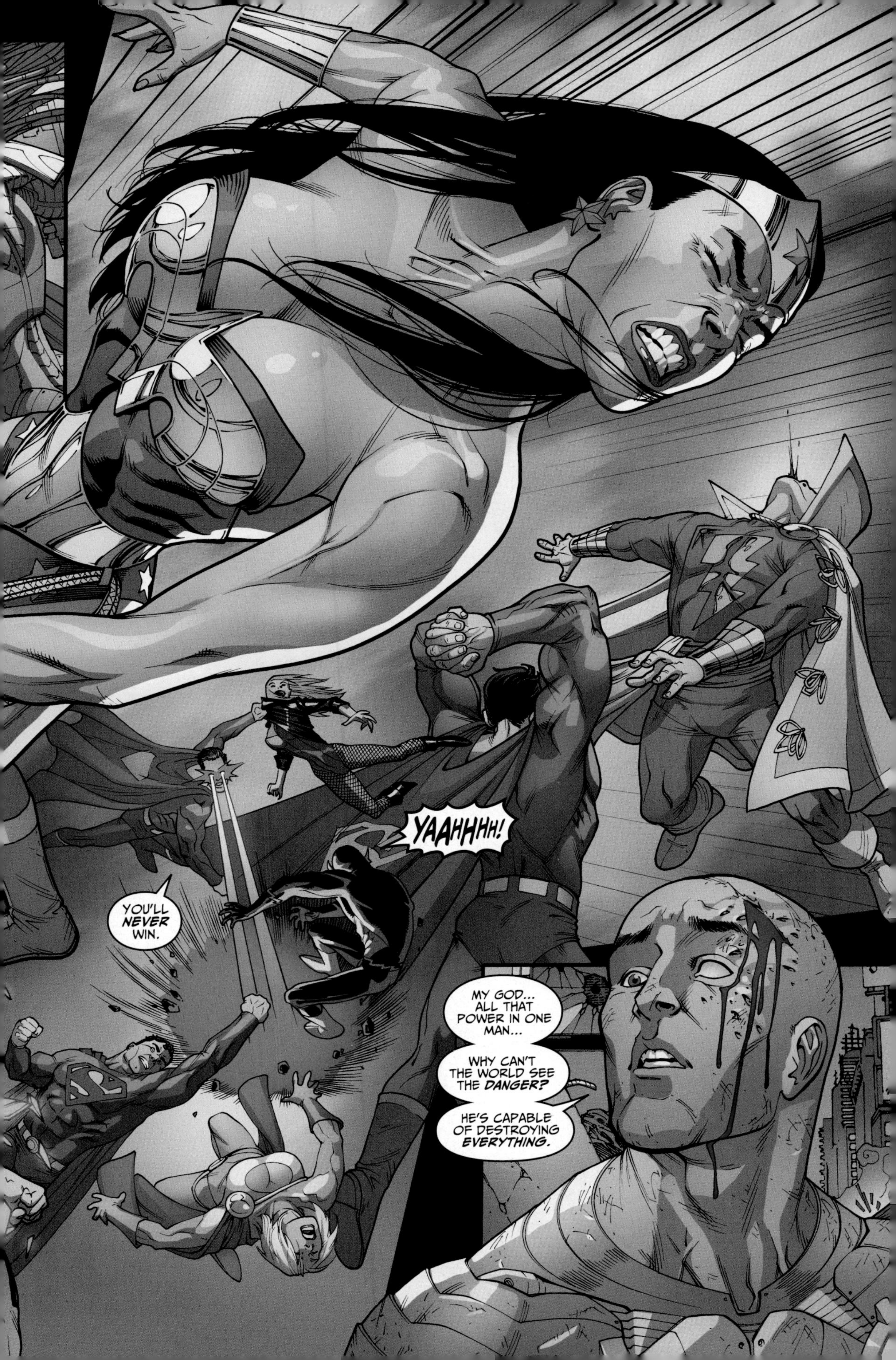
YAAHHHH!
YOU'LL NEVER WIN.
MY GOD... ALL THAT POWER IN ONE MAN...
WHY CAN'T THE WORLD SEE THE DANGER?
HE'S CAPABLE OF DESTROYING EVERYTHING.

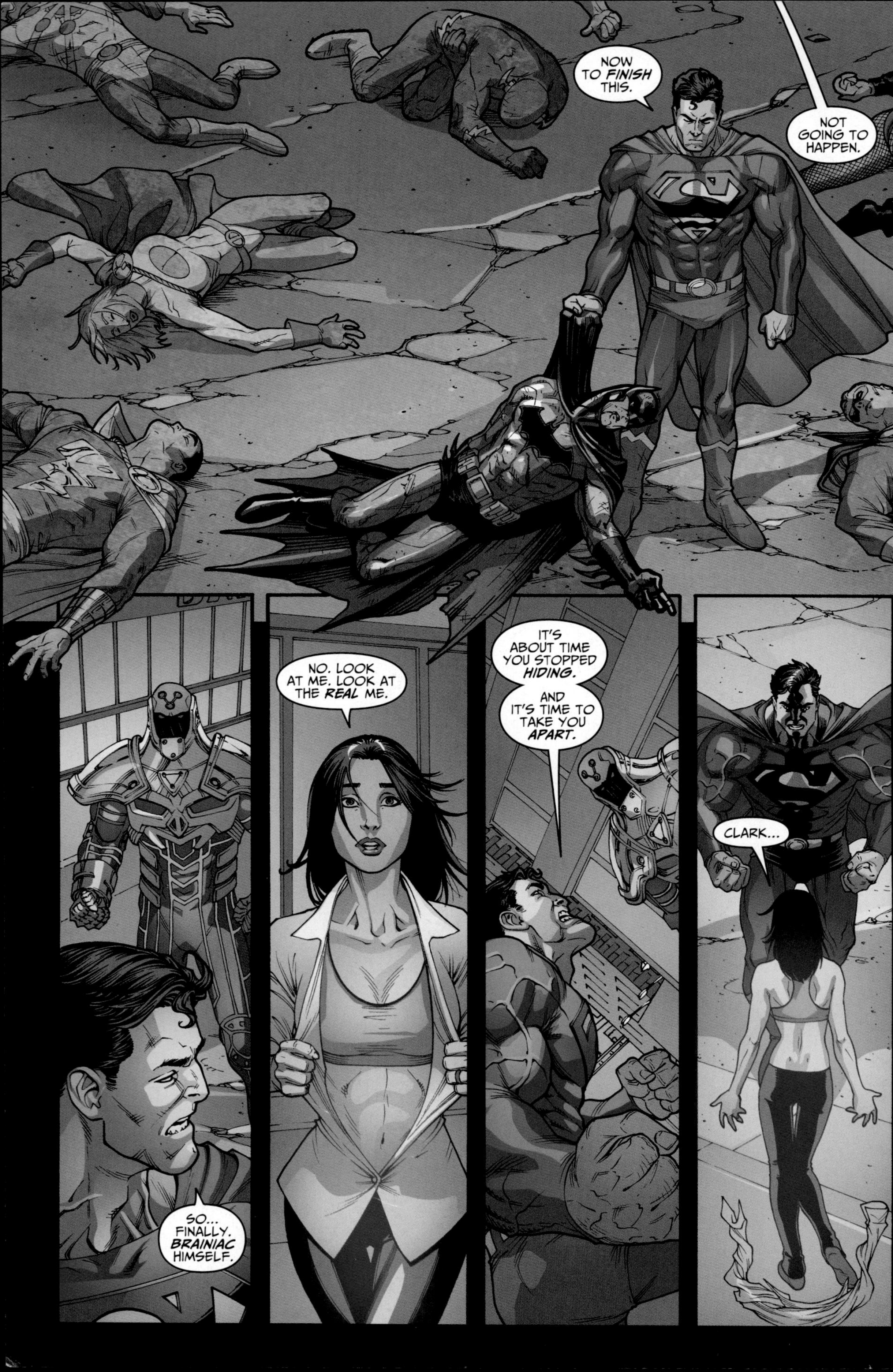
NOW TO FINISH THIS.
NOT GOING TO HAPPEN.
SO... FINALLY. BRAINIAC HIMSELF.
NO. LOOK AT ME. LOOK AT THE REAL ME.
IT'S ABOUT TIME YOU STOPPED HIDING.
AND IT'S TIME TO TAKE YOU APART.
CLARK...

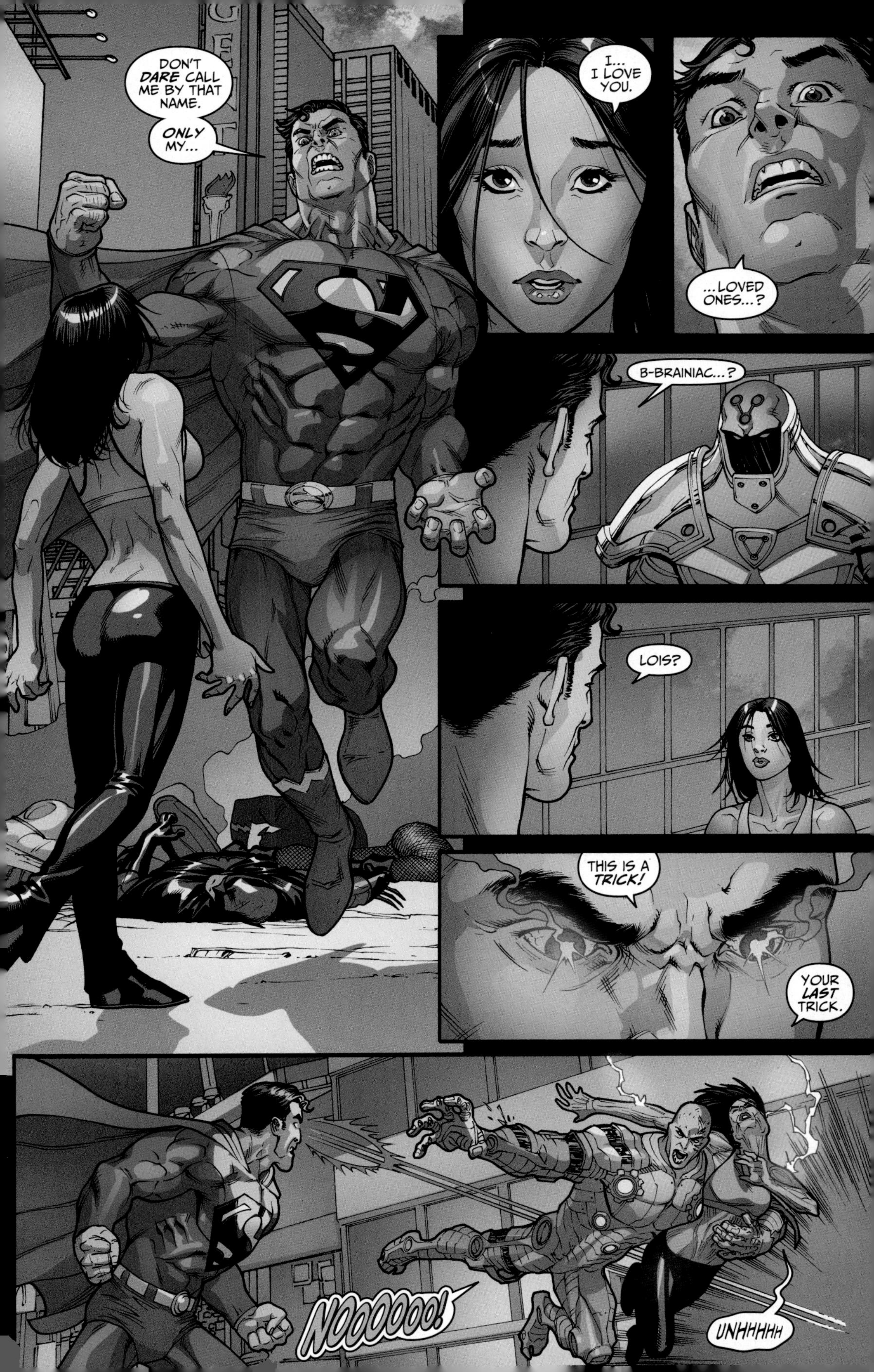
DON'T DARE CALL ME BY THAT NAME.
ONLY MY...
I... I LOVE YOU.
...LOVED ONES...?
B-BRAINIAC...?
LOIS?
THIS IS A TRICK!
YOUR LAST TRICK.
NOOOOOO!
UNHHHHH

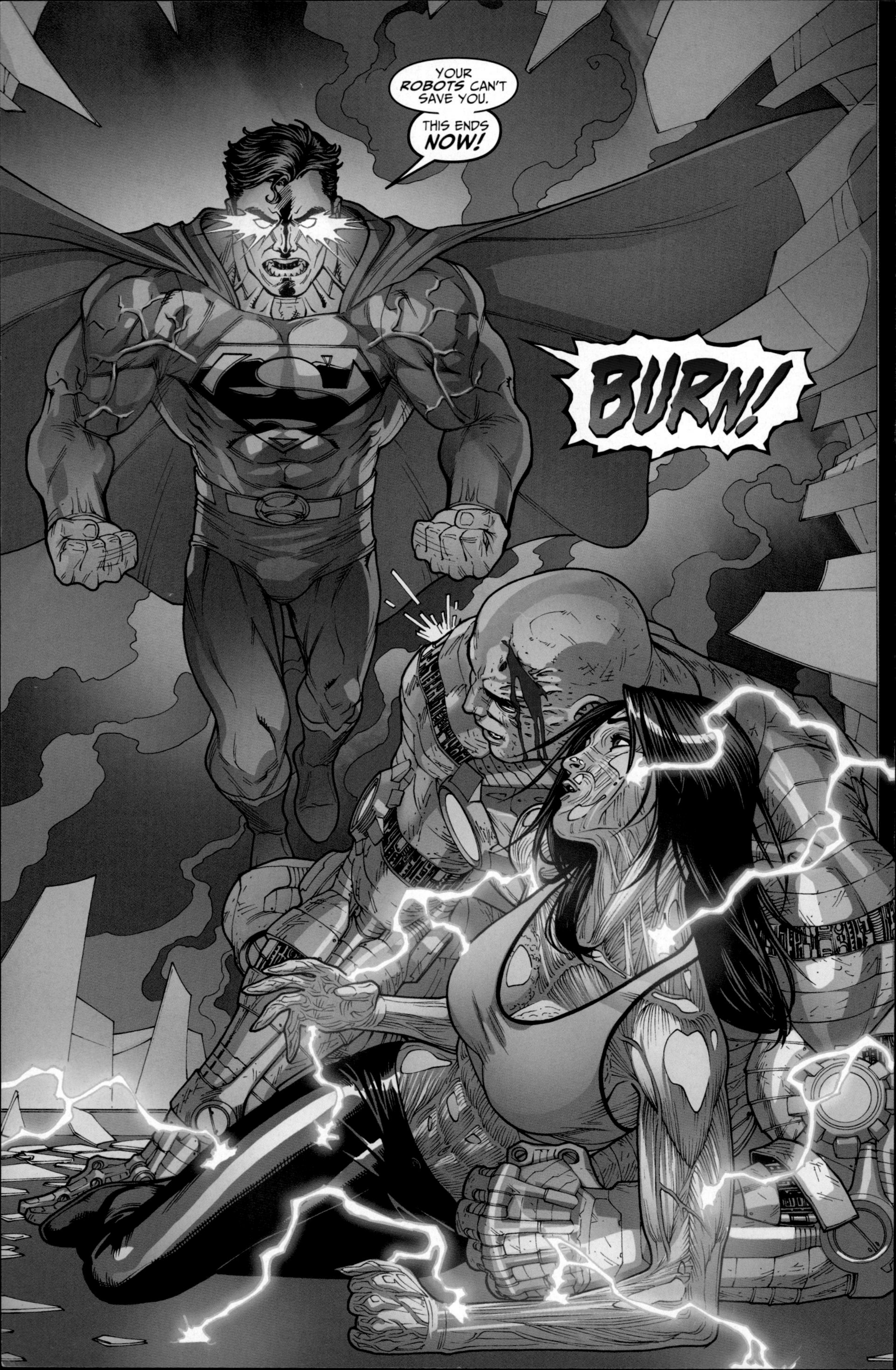
YOUR ROBOTS CAN'T SAVE YOU.
THIS ENDS NOW!
BURN!

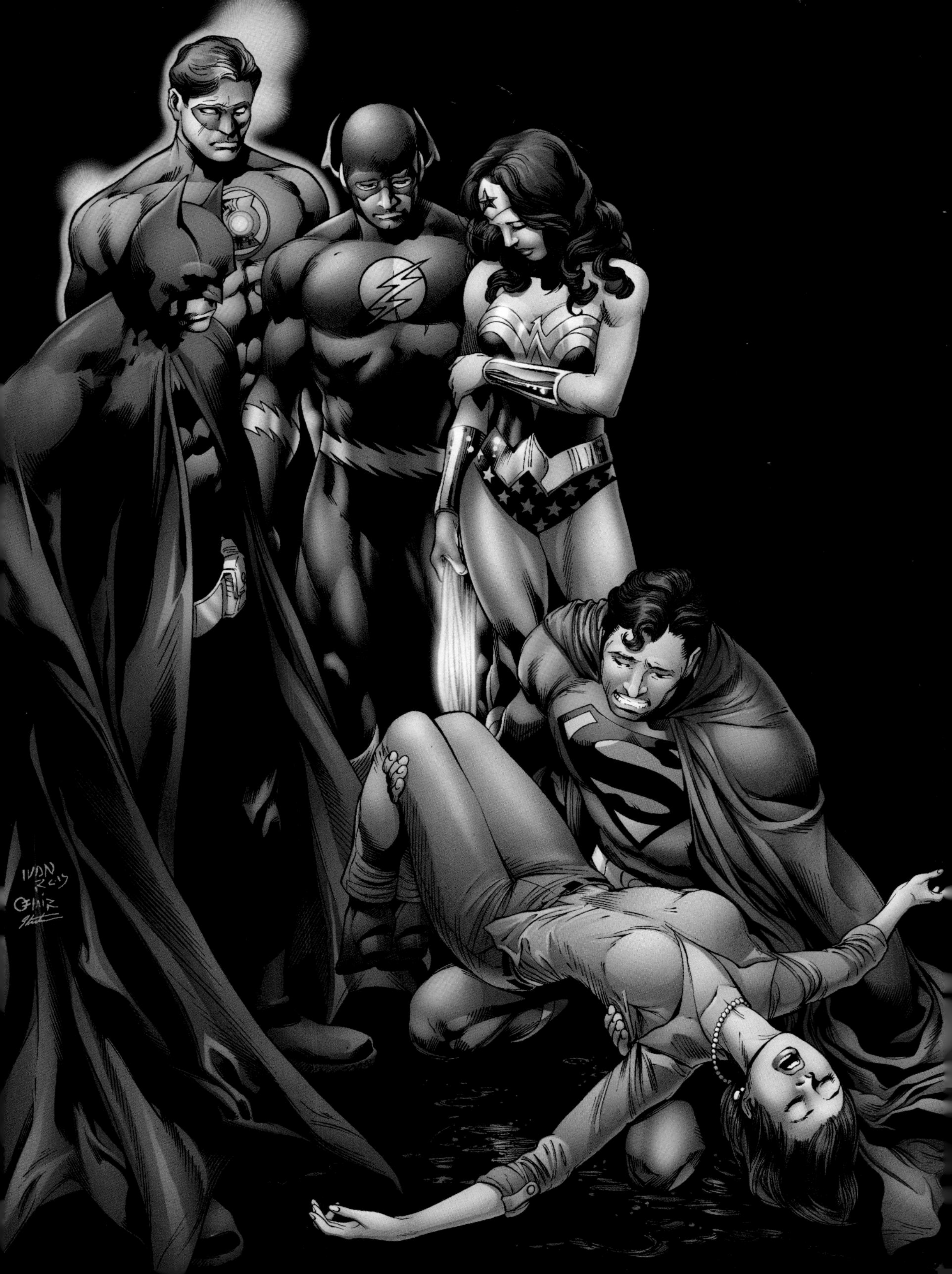

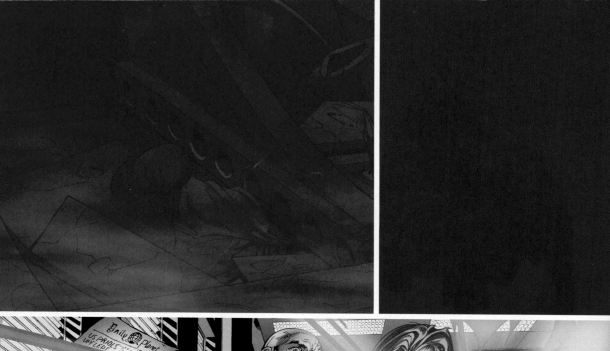

TROJAN HORSE

Tony Bedard
Writer

Howard Porter & John Livesay
Artists

Cover by Ivan Reis, Oclair Albert and Garrie Strachan

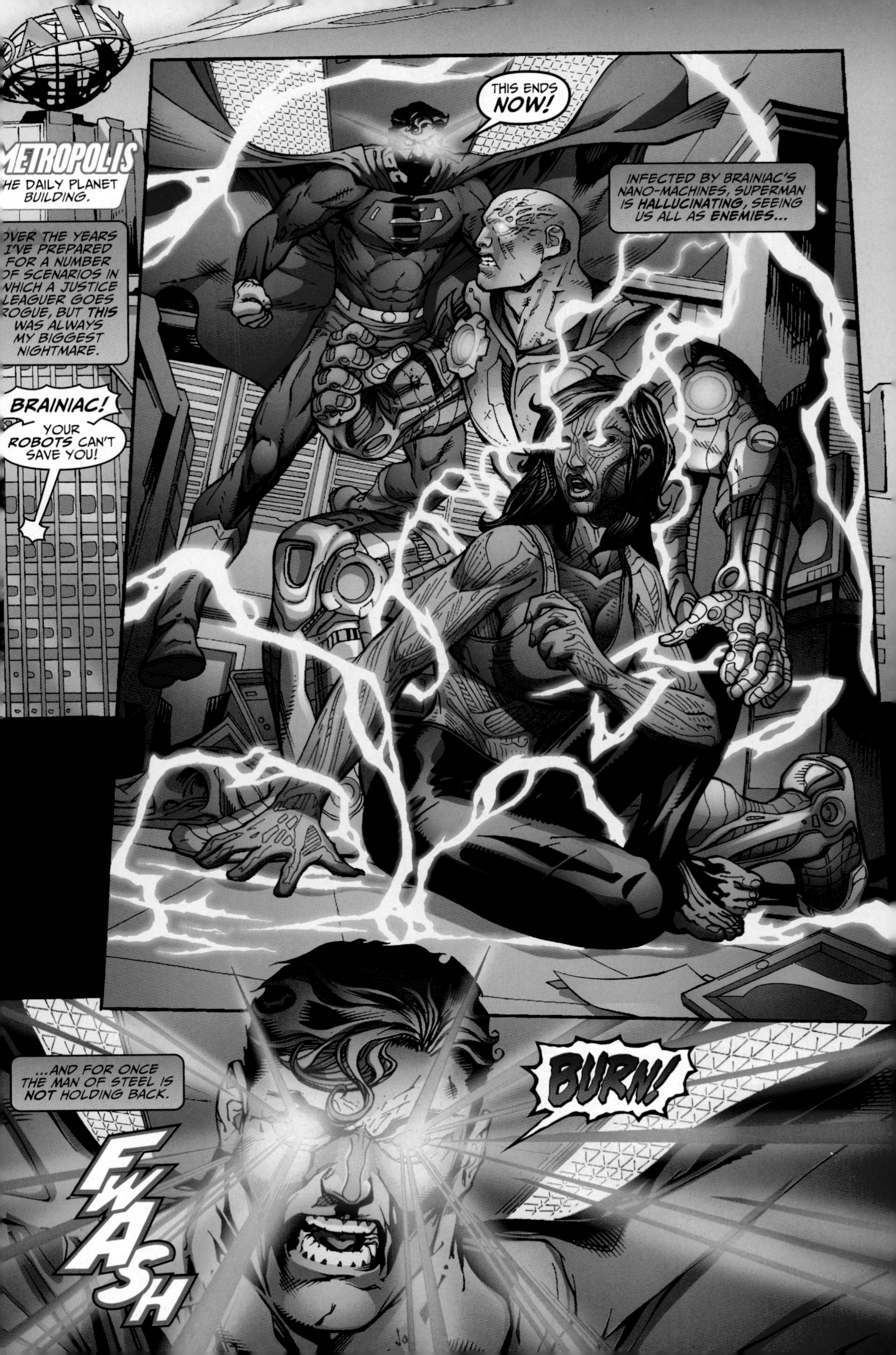
METROPOLIS
THE DAILY PLANET BUILDING.
OVER THE YEARS I'VE PREPARED FOR A NUMBER OF SCENARIOS IN WHICH A JUSTICE LEAGUER GOES ROGUE, BUT THIS WAS ALWAYS MY BIGGEST NIGHTMARE.
BRAINIAC!
YOUR ROBOTS CAN'T SAVE YOU!
THIS ENDS NOW!
INFECTED BY BRAINIAC'S NANO-MACHINES, SUPERMAN IS HALLUCINATING, SEEING US ALL AS ENEMIES...
...AND FOR ONCE THE MAN OF STEEL IS NOT HOLDING BACK.
BURN!
FWASH

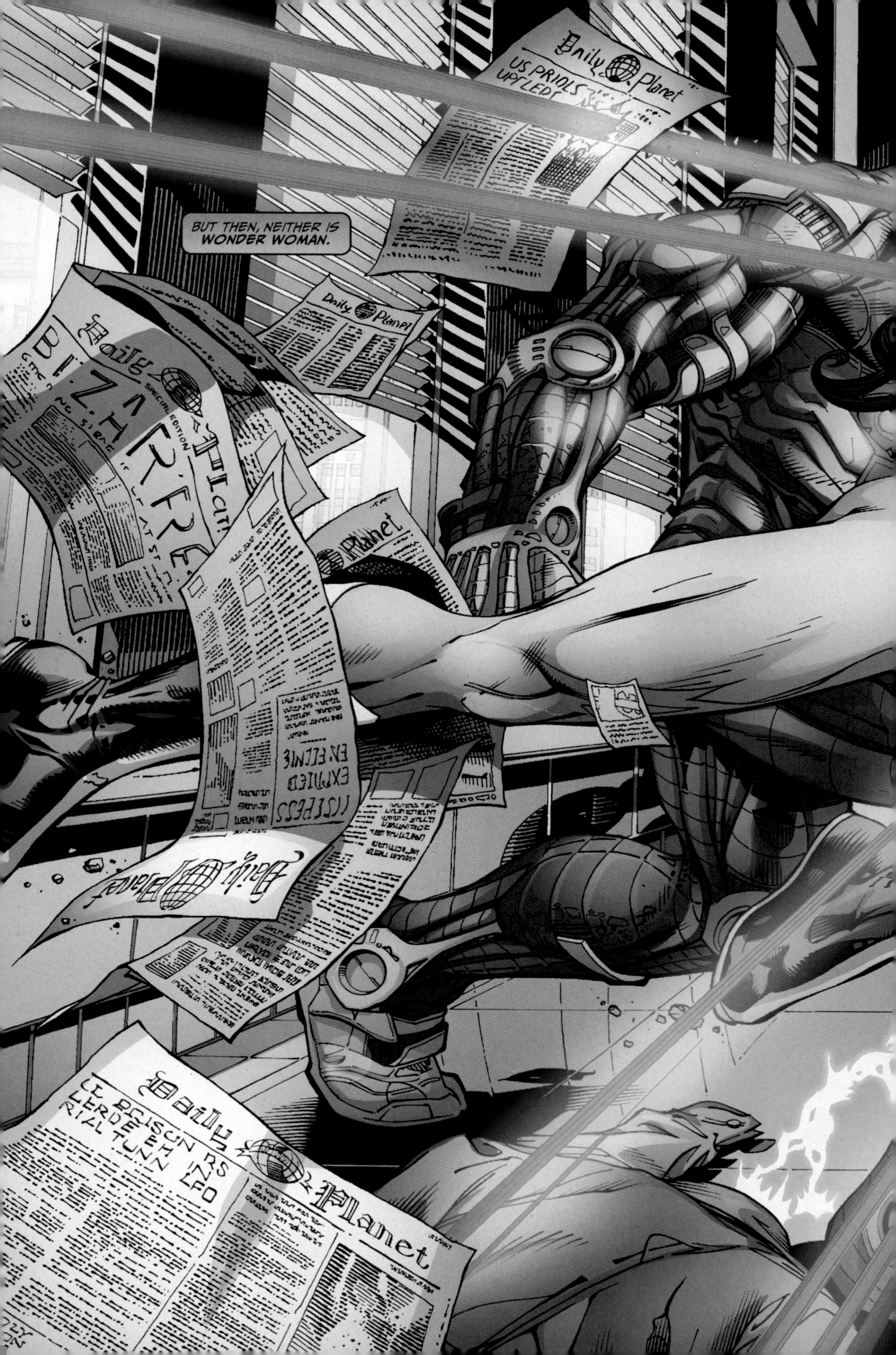
BUT THEN, NEITHER IS WONDER WOMAN.

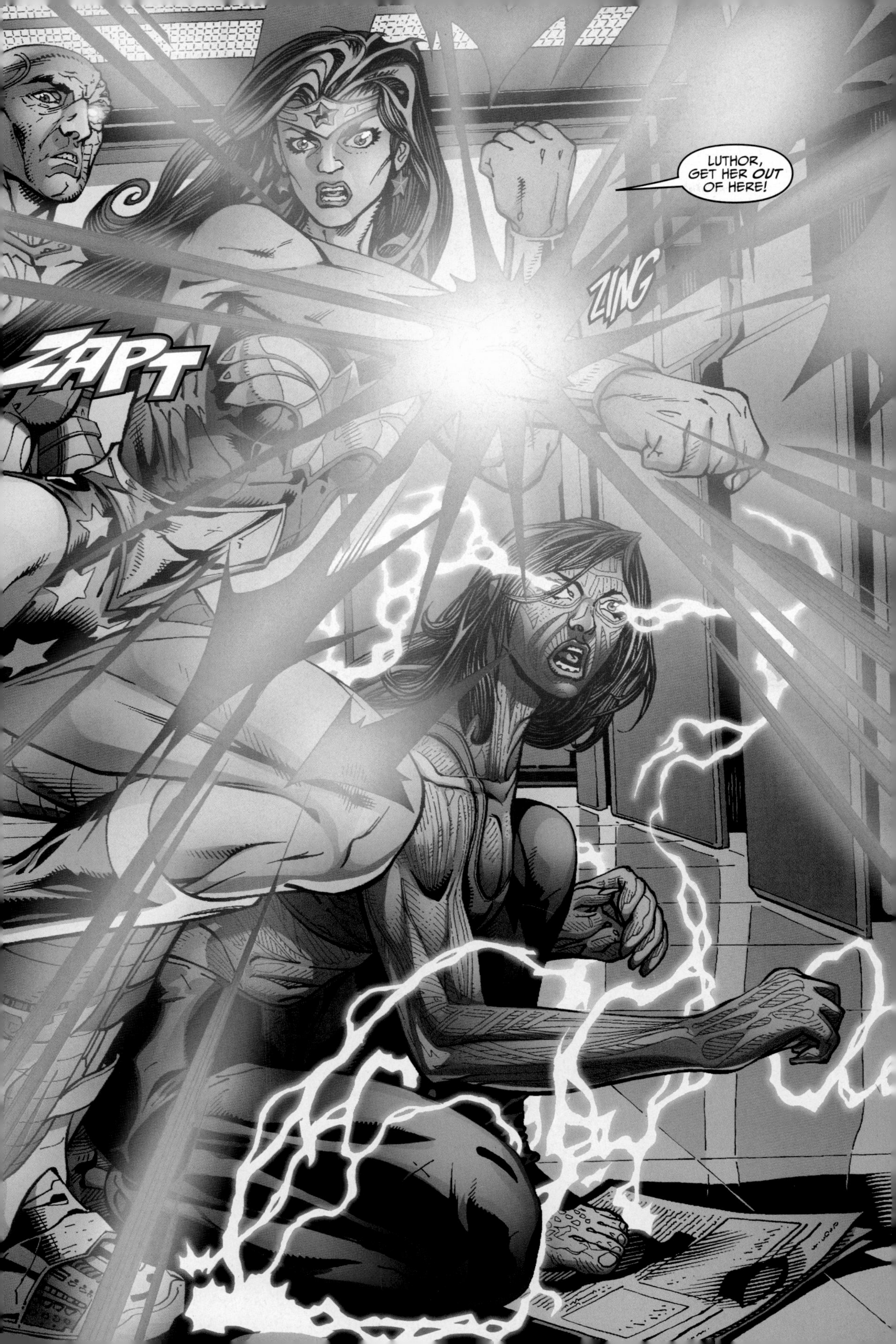
LUTHOR, GET HER OUT OF HERE!
ZING
ZAPT

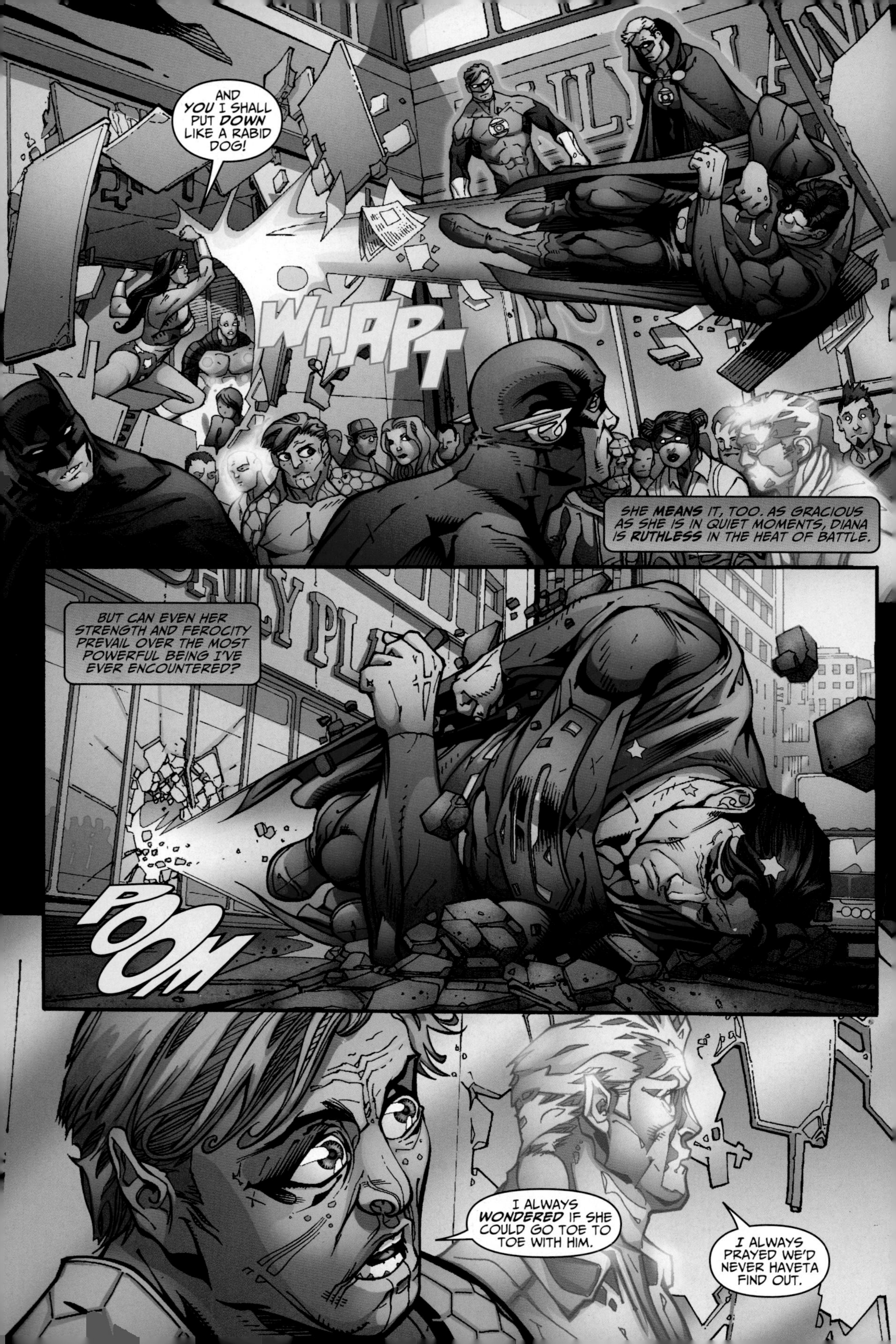
AND YOU I SHALL PUT DOWN LIKE A RABID DOG!
WHAPT
SHE MEANS IT, TOO. AS GRACIOUS AS SHE IS IN QUIET MOMENTS, DIANA IS RUTHLESS IN THE HEAT OF BATTLE.
BUT CAN EVEN HER STRENGTH AND FEROCITY PREVAIL OVER THE MOST POWERFUL BEING I'VE EVER ENCOUNTERED?
POOM
I ALWAYS WONDERED IF SHE COULD GO TOE TO TOE WITH HIM.
I ALWAYS PRAYED WE'D NEVER HAVETA FIND OUT.

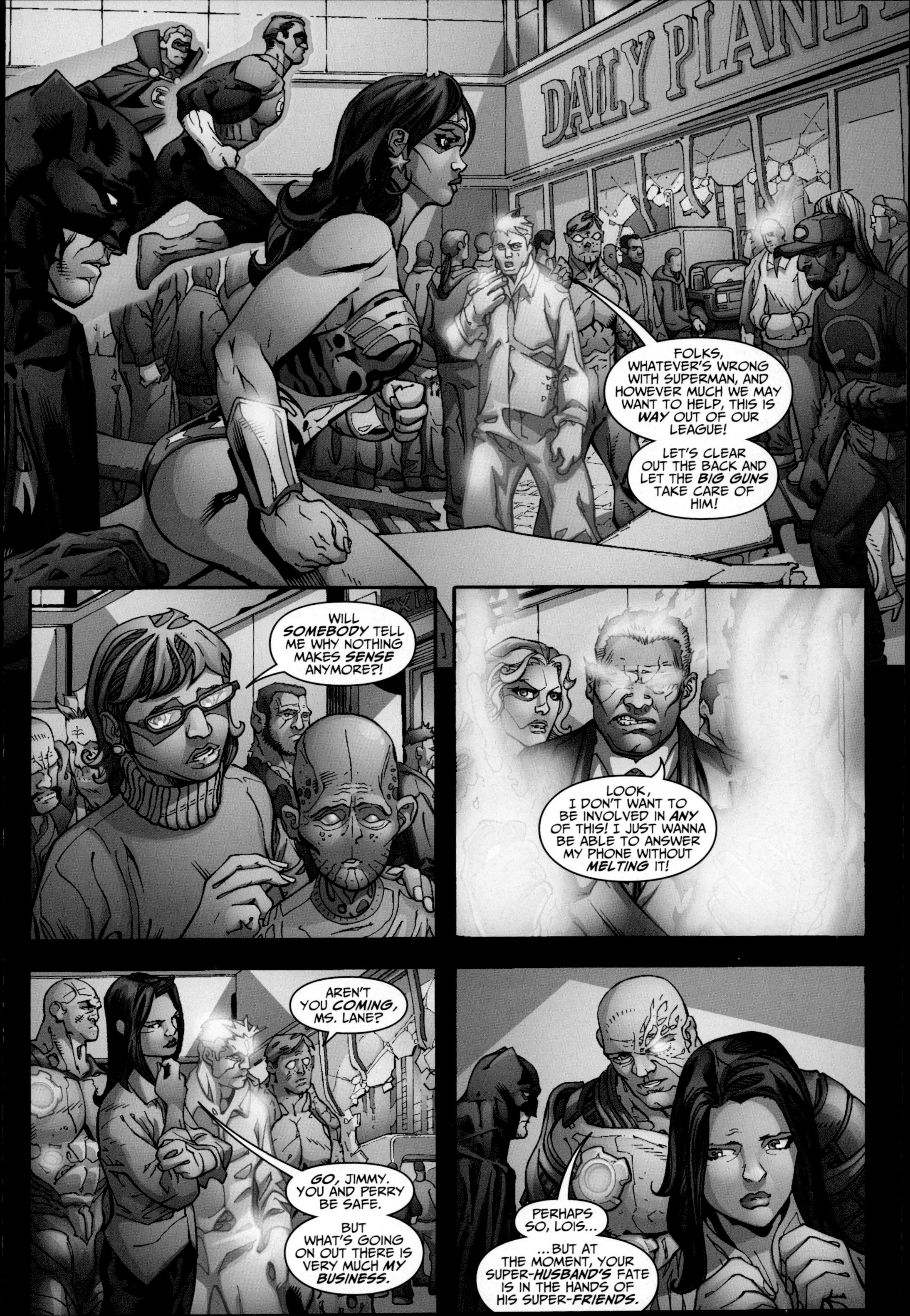
DAILY PLANET
FOLKS, WHATEVER'S WRONG WITH SUPERMAN, AND HOWEVER MUCH WE MAY WANT TO HELP, THIS IS WAY OUT OF OUR LEAGUE!
LET'S CLEAR OUT THE BACK AND LET THE BIG GUNS TAKE CARE OF HIM!
WILL SOMEBODY TELL ME WHY NOTHING MAKES SENSE ANYMORE?!
LOOK, I DON'T WANT TO BE INVOLVED IN ANY OF THIS! I JUST WANNA BE ABLE TO ANSWER MY PHONE WITHOUT MELTING IT!
AREN'T YOU COMING, MS. LANE?
GO, JIMMY. YOU AND PERRY BE SAFE.
BUT WHAT'S GOING ON OUT THERE IS VERY MUCH MY BUSINESS.
PERHAPS SO, LOIS...
...BUT AT THE MOMENT, YOUR SUPER-HUSBAND'S FATE IS IN THE HANDS OF HIS SUPER-FRIENDS.

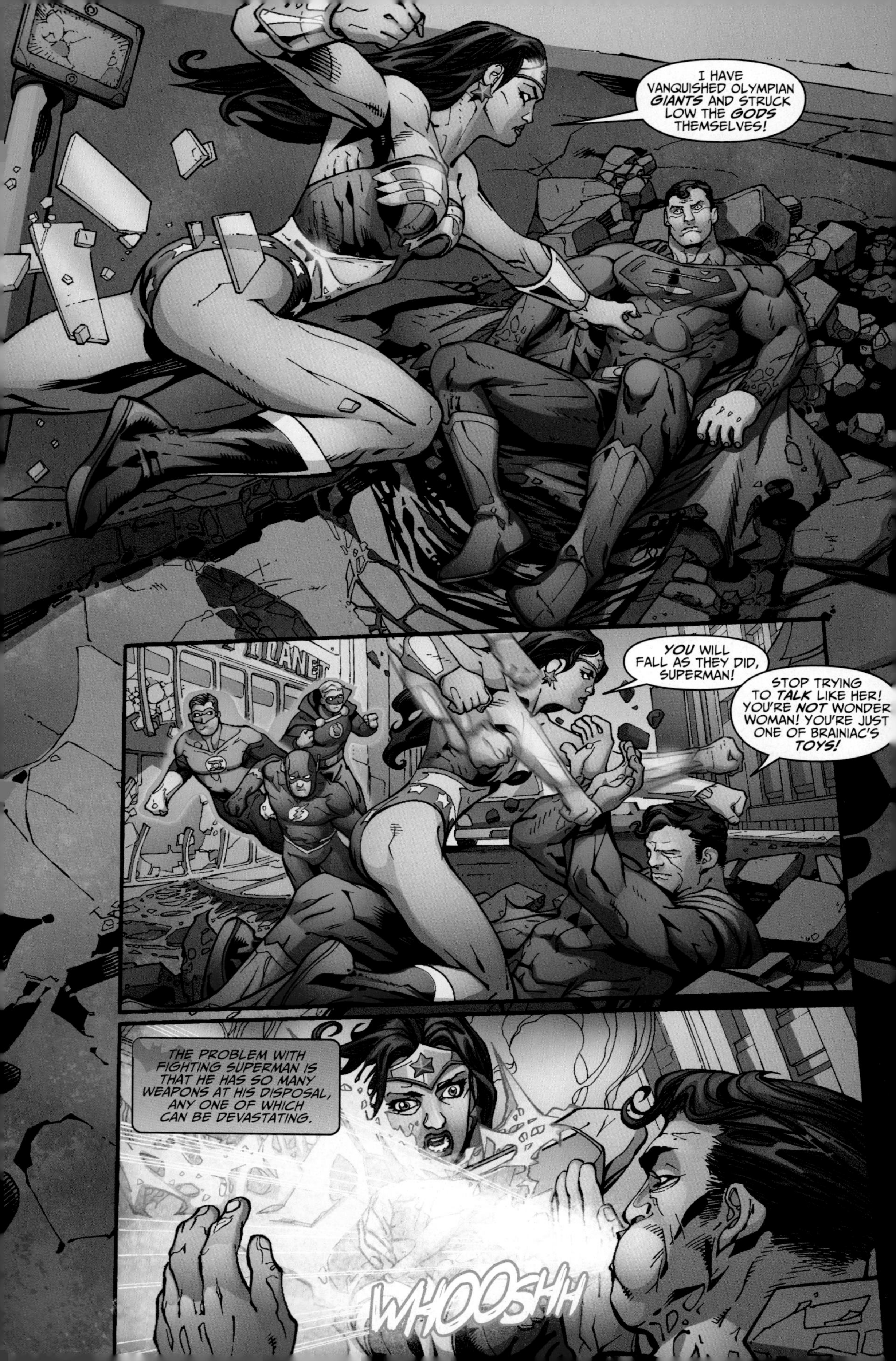
I HAVE VANQUISHED OLYMPIAN GIANTS AND STRUCK LOW THE GODS THEMSELVES!
YOU WILL FALL AS THEY DID, SUPERMAN!
STOP TRYING TO TALK LIKE HER! YOU'RE NOT WONDER WOMAN! YOU'RE JUST ONE OF BRAINIAC'S TOYS!
THE PROBLEM WITH FIGHTING SUPERMAN IS THAT HE HAS SO MANY WEAPONS AT HIS DISPOSAL, ANY ONE OF WHICH CAN BE DEVASTATING.
WHOOSHH

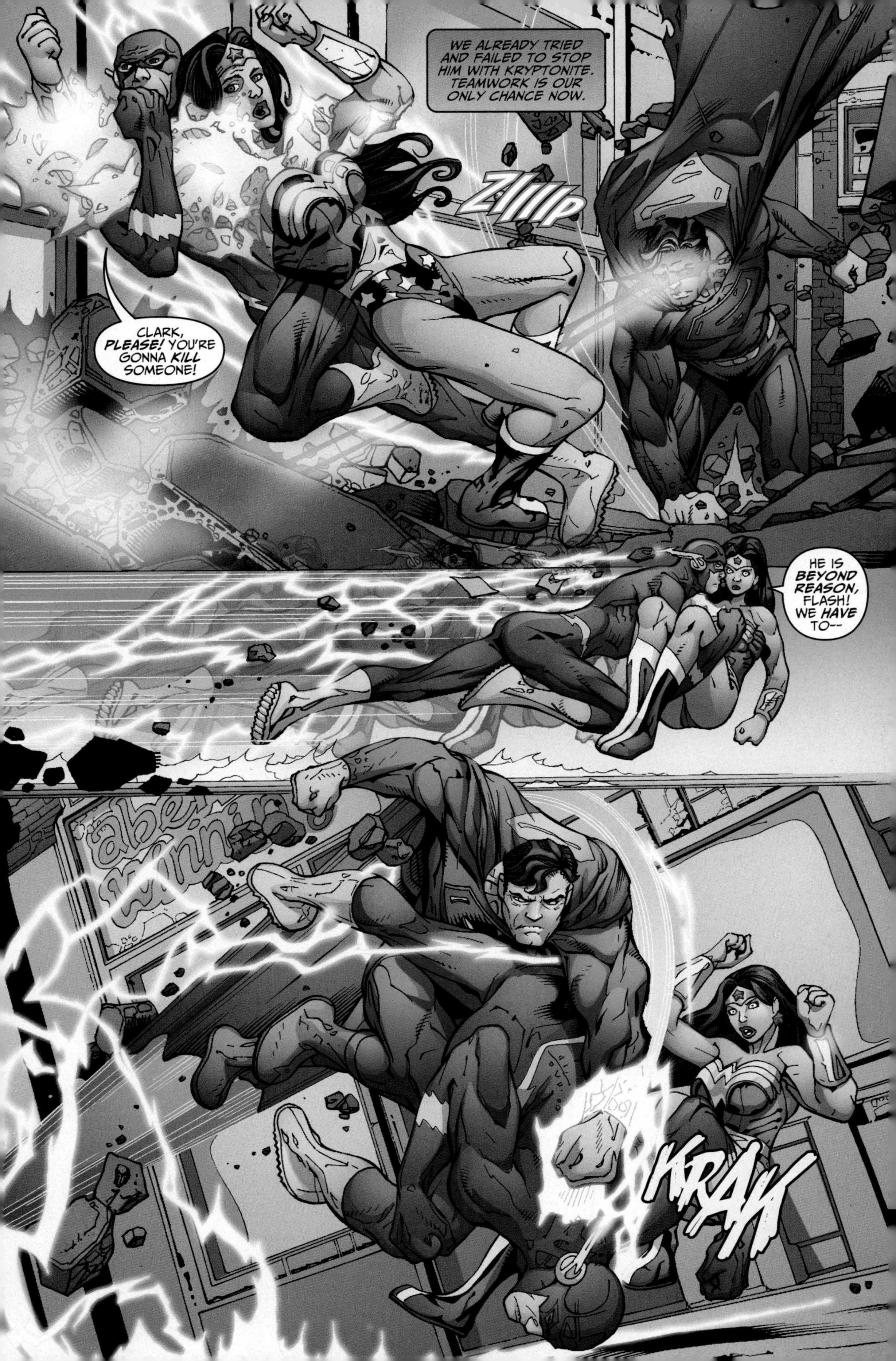
WE ALREADY TRIED AND FAILED TO STOP HIM WITH KRYPTONITE. TEAMWORK IS OUR ONLY CHANCE NOW.
ZIIIIP
CLARK, PLEASE! YOU'RE GONNA KILL SOMEONE!
HE IS BEYOND REASON, FLASH! WE HAVE TO--
KRAK

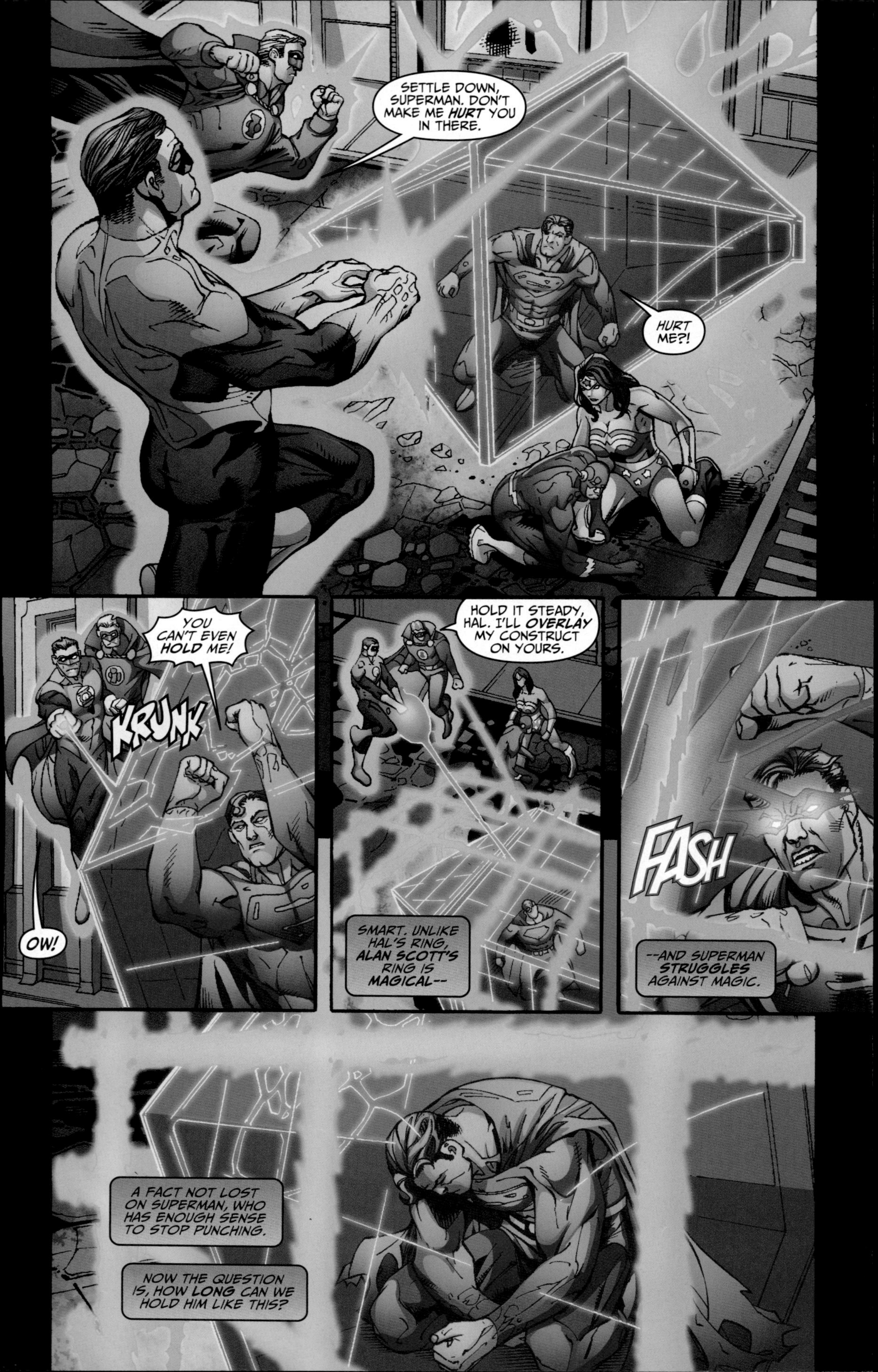
SETTLE DOWN, SUPERMAN. DON'T MAKE ME HURT YOU IN THERE.
HURT ME?!
YOU CAN'T EVEN HOLD ME!
KRUNK
OW!
HOLD IT STEADY, HAL. I'LL OVERLAY MY CONSTRUCT ON YOURS.
SMART. UNLIKE HAL'S RING, ALAN SCOTT'S RING IS MAGICAL--
FASH
--AND SUPERMAN STRUGGLES AGAINST MAGIC.
A FACT NOT LOST ON SUPERMAN, WHO HAS ENOUGH SENSE TO STOP PUNCHING.
NOW THE QUESTION IS, HOW LONG CAN WE HOLD HIM LIKE THIS?

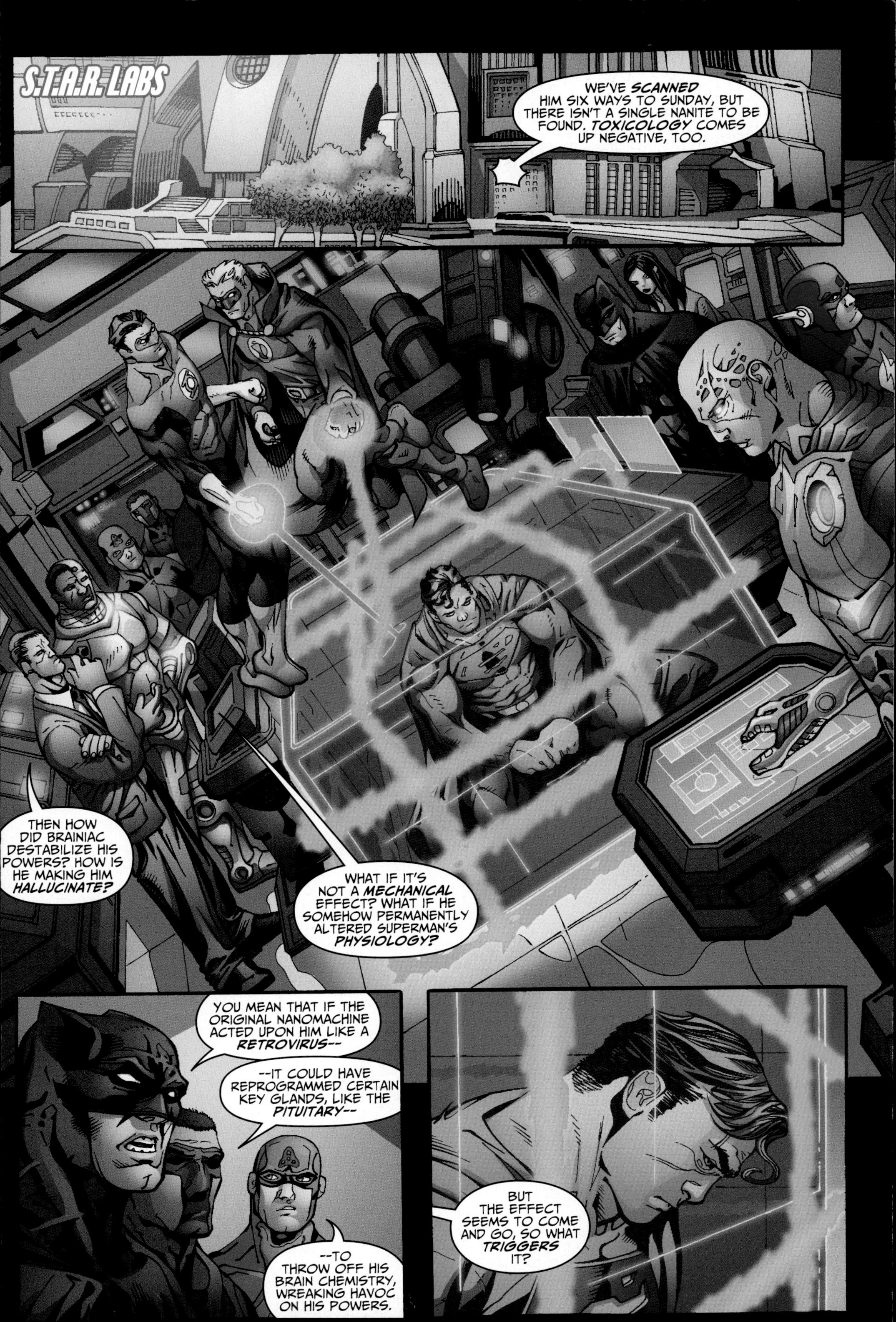
S.T.A.R. LABS
WE'VE SCANNED HIM SIX WAYS TO SUNDAY, BUT THERE ISN'T A SINGLE NANITE TO BE FOUND. TOXICOLOGY COMES UP NEGATIVE, TOO.
THEN HOW DID BRAINIAC DESTABILIZE HIS POWERS? HOW IS HE MAKING HIM HALLUCINATE?
WHAT IF IT'S NOT A MECHANICAL EFFECT? WHAT IF HE SOMEHOW PERMANENTLY ALTERED SUPERMAN'S PHYSIOLOGY?
YOU MEAN THAT IF THE ORIGINAL NANOMACHINE ACTED UPON HIM LIKE A RETROVIRUS--
--IT COULD HAVE REPROGRAMMED CERTAIN KEY GLANDS, LIKE THE PITUITARY--
--TO THROW OFF HIS BRAIN CHEMISTRY, WREAKING HAVOC ON HIS POWERS.
BUT THE EFFECT SEEMS TO COME AND GO, SO WHAT TRIGGERS IT?

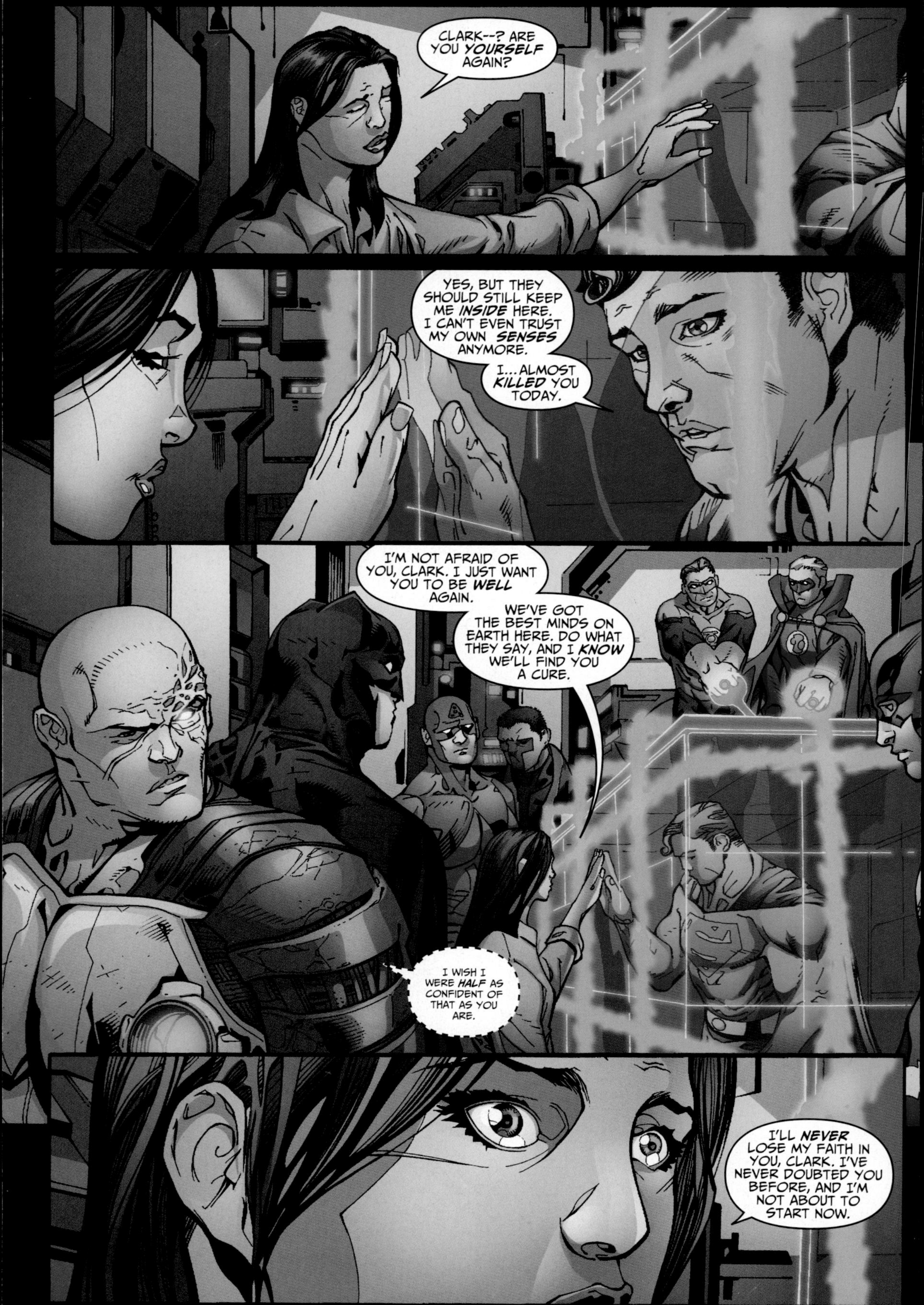
CLARK--? ARE YOU YOURSELF AGAIN?
YES, BUT THEY SHOULD STILL KEEP ME INSIDE HERE. I CAN'T EVEN TRUST MY OWN SENSES ANYMORE.
I...ALMOST KILLED YOU TODAY.
I'M NOT AFRAID OF YOU, CLARK. I JUST WANT YOU TO BE WELL AGAIN.
WE'VE GOT THE BEST MINDS ON EARTH HERE. DO WHAT THEY SAY, AND I KNOW WE'LL FIND YOU A CURE.
I WISH I WERE HALF AS CONFIDENT OF THAT AS YOU ARE.
I'LL NEVER LOSE MY FAITH IN YOU, CLARK. I'VE NEVER DOUBTED YOU BEFORE, AND I'M NOT ABOUT TO START NOW.

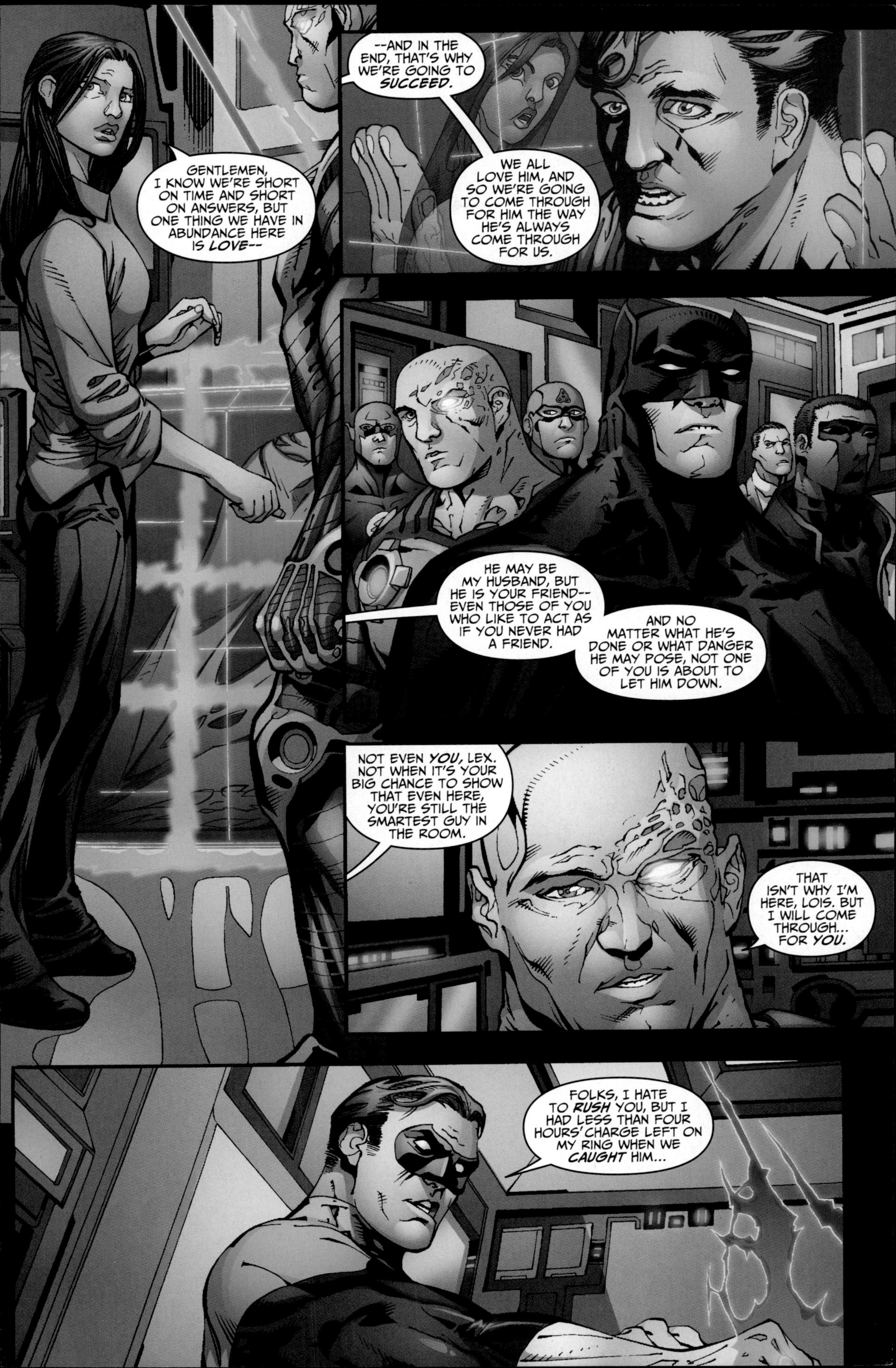
GENTLEMEN, I KNOW WE'RE SHORT ON TIME AND SHORT ON ANSWERS, BUT ONE THING WE HAVE IN ABUNDANCE HERE IS LOVE--
--AND IN THE END, THAT'S WHY WE'RE GOING TO SUCCEED.
WE ALL LOVE HIM, AND SO WE'RE GOING TO COME THROUGH FOR HIM THE WAY HE'S ALWAYS COME THROUGH FOR US.
HE MAY BE MY HUSBAND, BUT HE IS YOUR FRIEND-- EVEN THOSE OF YOU WHO LIKE TO ACT AS IF YOU NEVER HAD A FRIEND.
AND NO MATTER WHAT HE'S DONE OR WHAT DANGER HE MAY POSE, NOT ONE OF YOU IS ABOUT TO LET HIM DOWN.
NOT EVEN YOU, LEX. NOT WHEN IT'S YOUR BIG CHANCE TO SHOW THAT EVEN HERE, YOU'RE STILL THE SMARTEST GUY IN THE ROOM.
THAT ISN'T WHY I'M HERE, LOIS. BUT I WILL COME THROUGH... FOR YOU.
FOLKS, I HATE TO RUSH YOU, BUT I HAD LESS THAN FOUR HOURS' CHARGE LEFT ON MY RING WHEN WE CAUGHT HIM...

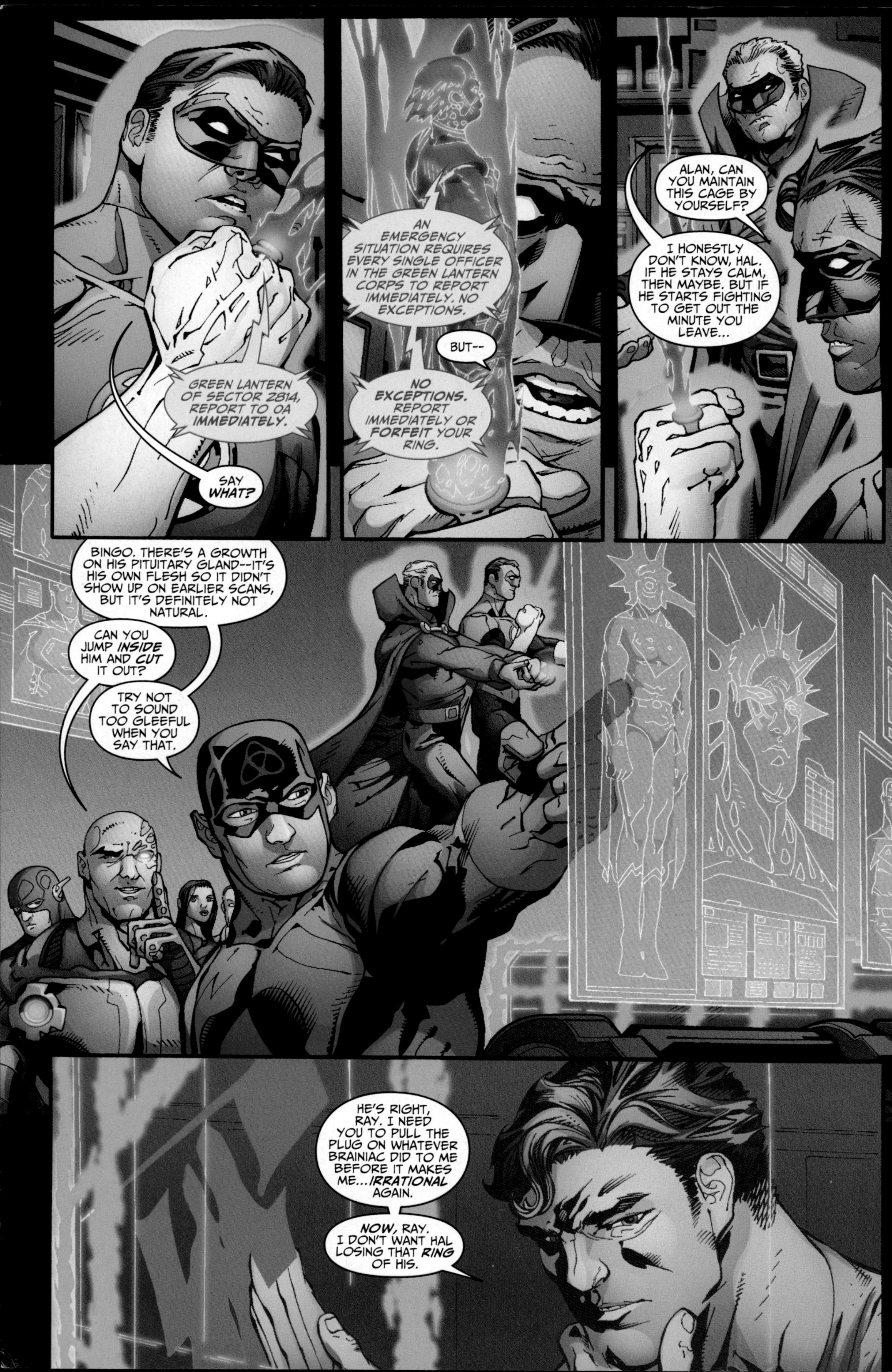
GREEN LANTERN OF SECTOR 2814, REPORT TO OA IMMEDIATELY.
SAY WHAT?
AN EMERGENCY SITUATION REQUIRES EVERY SINGLE OFFICER IN THE GREEN LANTERN CORPS TO REPORT IMMEDIATELY. NO EXCEPTIONS.
BUT--
NO EXCEPTIONS. REPORT IMMEDIATELY OR FORFEIT YOUR RING.
ALAN, CAN YOU MAINTAIN THIS CAGE BY YOURSELF?
I HONESTLY DON'T KNOW, HAL. IF HE STAYS CALM, THEN MAYBE. BUT IF HE STARTS FIGHTING TO GET OUT THE MINUTE YOU LEAVE...
BINGO. THERE'S A GROWTH ON HIS PITUITARY GLAND--IT'S HIS OWN FLESH SO IT DIDN'T SHOW UP ON EARLIER SCANS, BUT IT'S DEFINITELY NOT NATURAL.
CAN YOU JUMP INSIDE HIM AND CUT IT OUT?
TRY NOT TO SOUND TOO GLEEFUL WHEN YOU SAY THAT.
HE'S RIGHT, RAY. I NEED YOU TO PULL THE PLUG ON WHATEVER BRAINIAC DID TO ME BEFORE IT MAKES ME...IRRATIONAL AGAIN.
NOW, RAY. I DON'T WANT HAL LOSING THAT RING OF HIS.

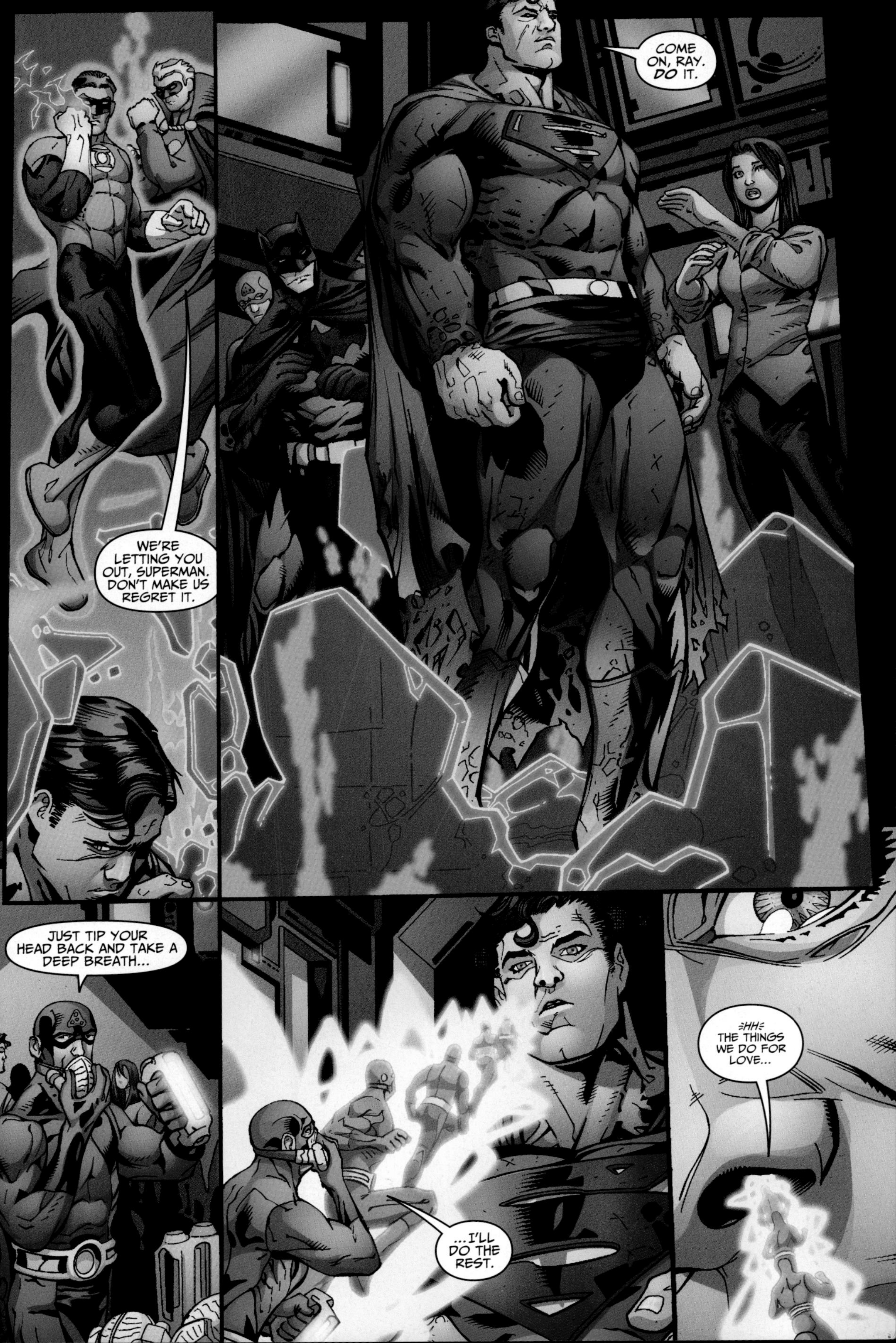
WE'RE LETTING YOU OUT, SUPERMAN. DON'T MAKE US REGRET IT.
COME ON, RAY. DO IT.
JUST TIP YOUR HEAD BACK AND TAKE A DEEP BREATH...
...I'LL DO THE REST.
HH
THE THINGS WE DO FOR LOVE...

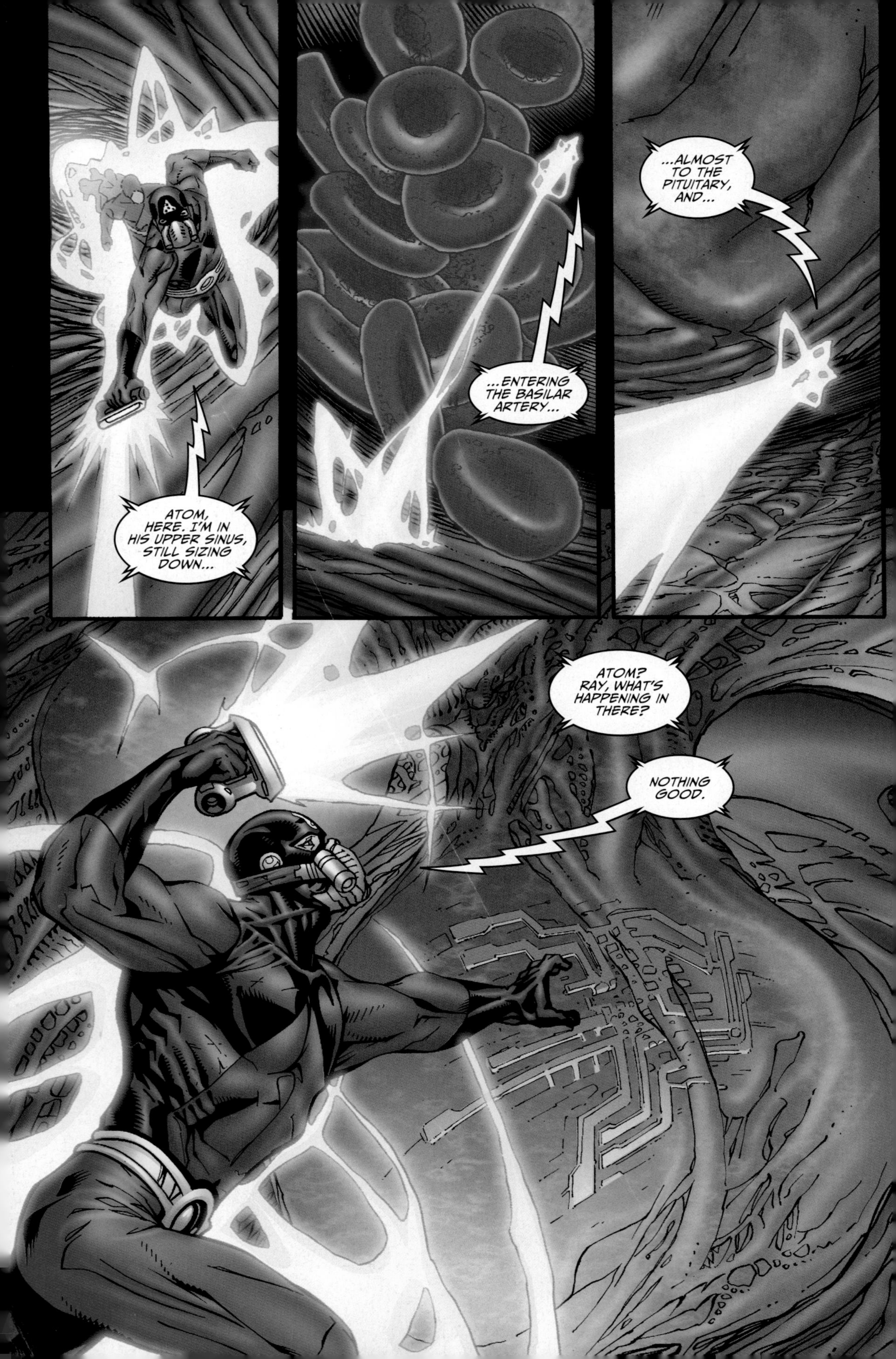
ATOM, HERE. I'M IN HIS UPPER SINUS, STILL SIZING DOWN...
...ENTERING THE BASILAR ARTERY...
...ALMOST TO THE PITUITARY, AND...
ATOM? RAY, WHAT'S HAPPENING IN THERE?
NOTHING GOOD.

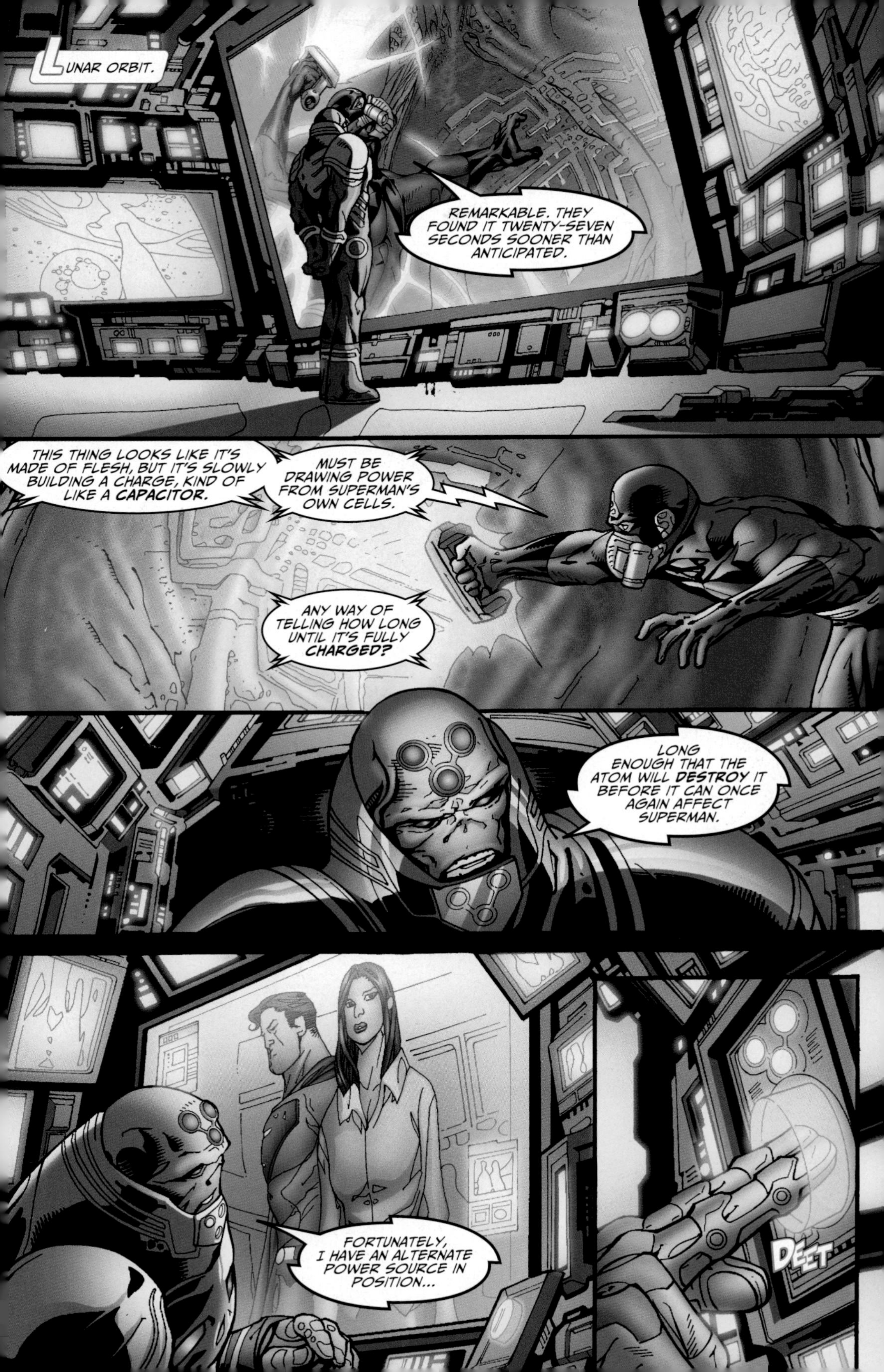
LUNAR ORBIT.
REMARKABLE. THEY FOUND IT TWENTY-SEVEN SECONDS SOONER THAN ANTICIPATED.
THIS THING LOOKS LIKE IT'S MADE OF FLESH, BUT IT'S SLOWLY BUILDING A CHARGE, KIND OF LIKE A CAPACITOR.
MUST BE DRAWING POWER FROM SUPERMAN'S OWN CELLS.
ANY WAY OF TELLING HOW LONG UNTIL IT'S FULLY CHARGED?
LONG ENOUGH THAT THE ATOM WILL DESTROY IT BEFORE IT CAN ONCE AGAIN AFFECT SUPERMAN.
FORTUNATELY, I HAVE AN ALTERNATE POWER SOURCE IN POSITION...
DEET

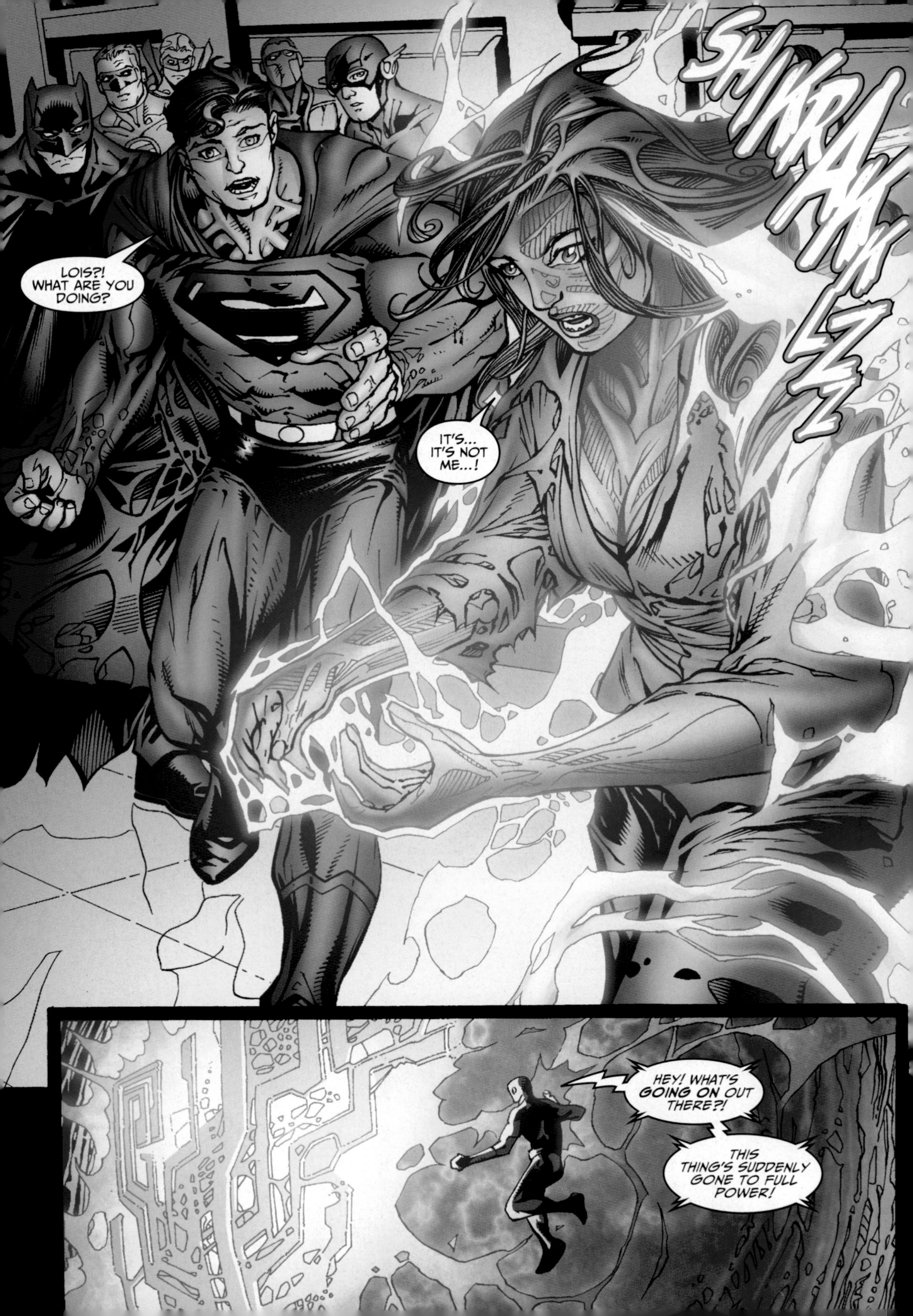
SHKRAKAKKLZZZ
LOIS?! WHAT ARE YOU DOING?
IT'S... IT'S NOT ME...!
HEY! WHAT'S GOING ON OUT THERE?!
THIS THING'S SUDDENLY GONE TO FULL POWER!

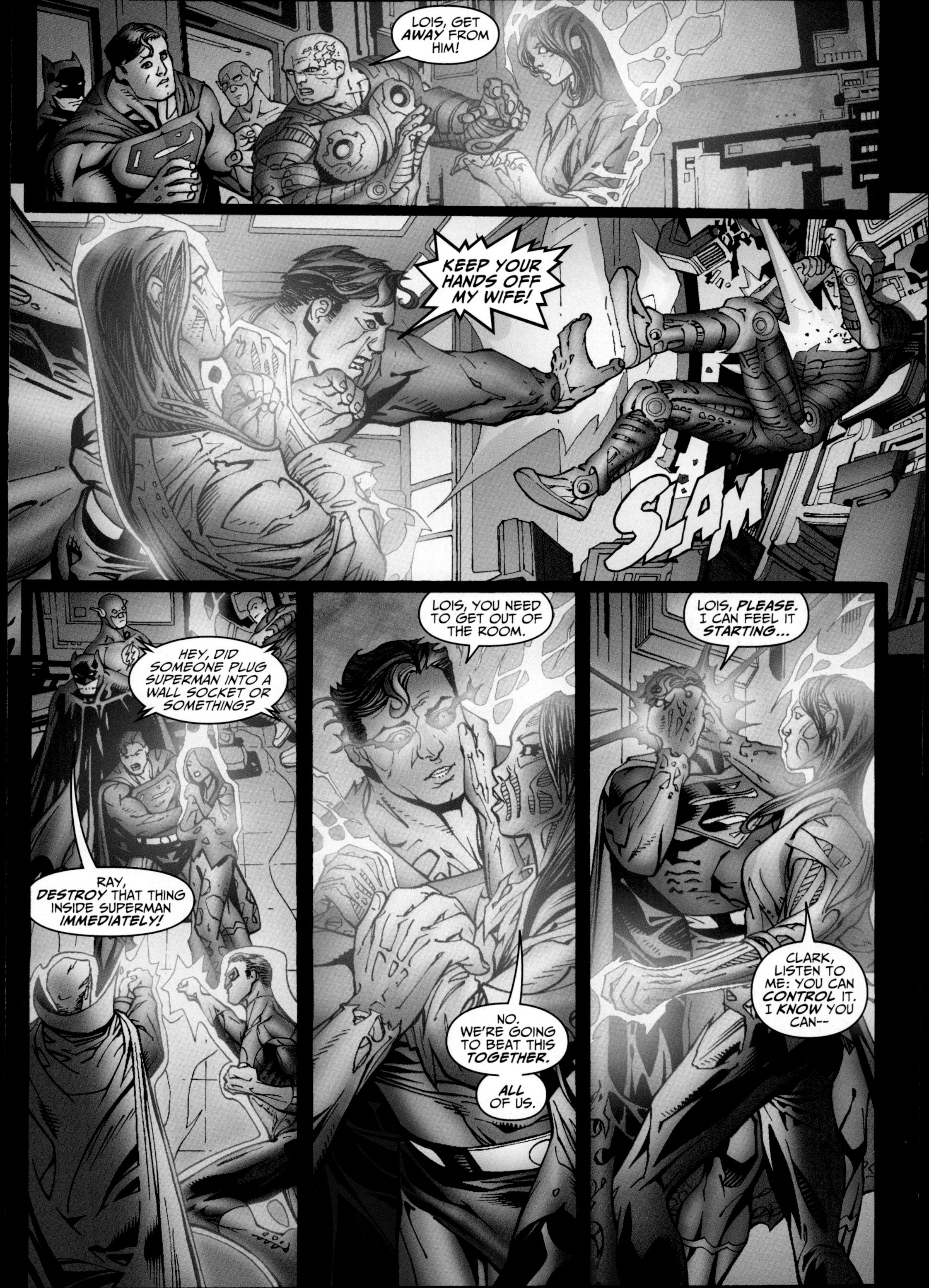

LOIS, GET AWAY FROM HIM!
KEEP YOUR HANDS OFF MY WIFE!
SLAM
HEY, DID SOMEONE PLUG SUPERMAN INTO A WALL SOCKET OR SOMETHING?
RAY, DESTROY THAT THING INSIDE SUPERMAN IMMEDIATELY!
LOIS, YOU NEED TO GET OUT OF THE ROOM.
NO. WE'RE GOING TO BEAT THIS TOGETHER.
ALL OF US.
LOIS, PLEASE. I CAN FEEL IT STARTING...
CLARK, LISTEN TO ME: YOU CAN CONTROL IT. I KNOW YOU CAN--

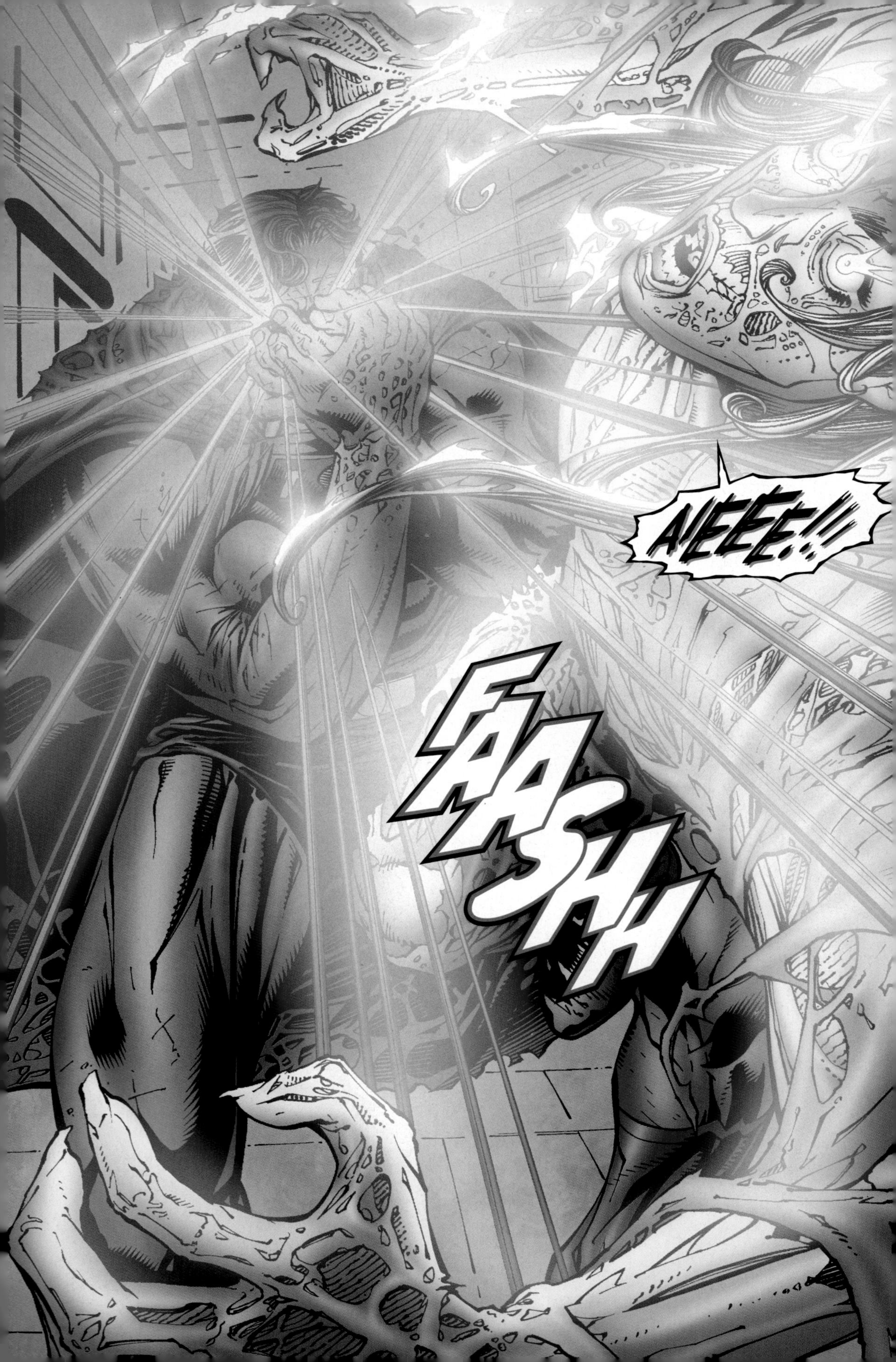
AIEEEE!!!
FAASHH

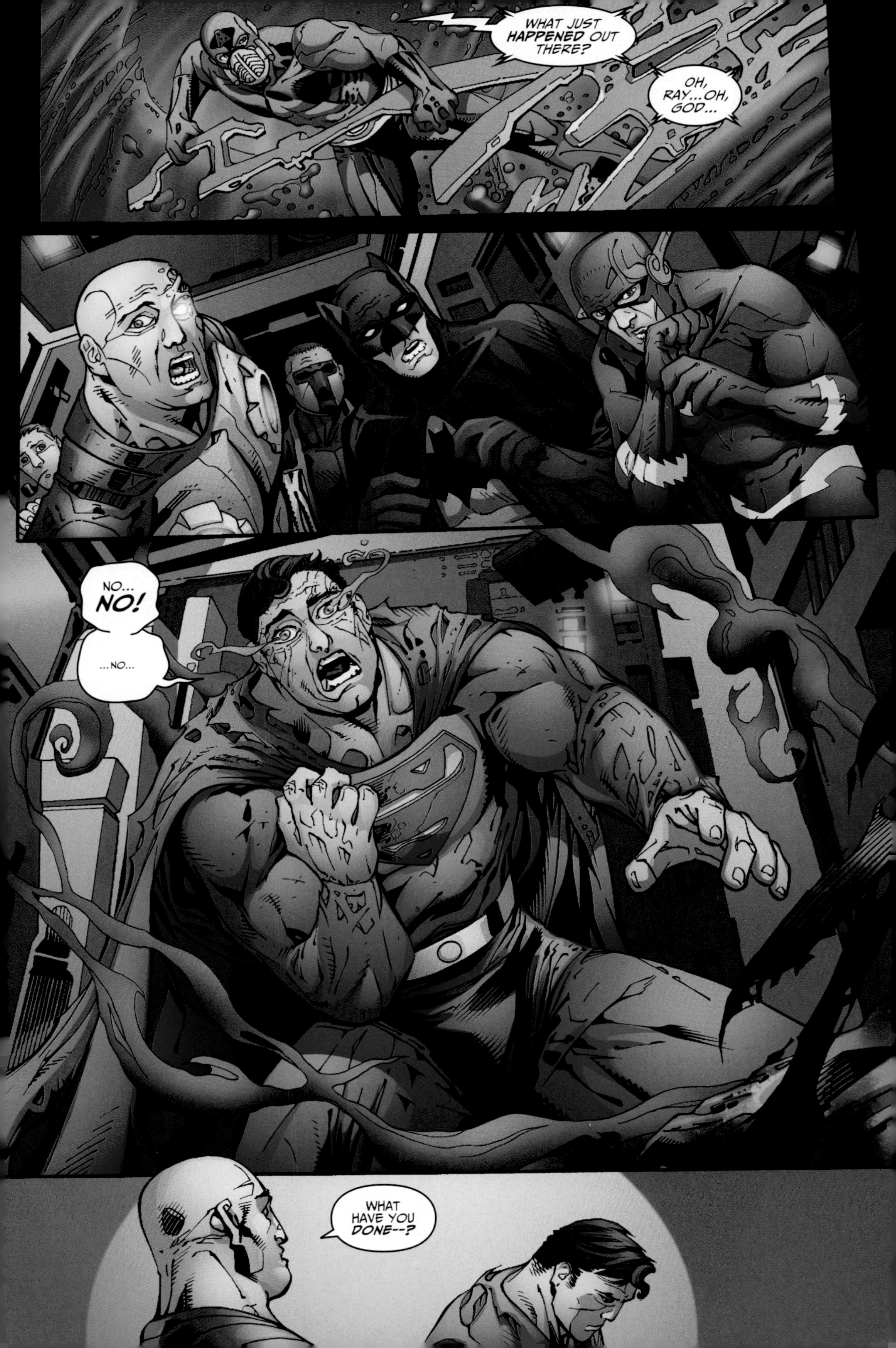
WHAT JUST HAPPENED OUT THERE?
OH, RAY...OH, GOD...
NO... NO!
...NO...
WHAT HAVE YOU DONE--?

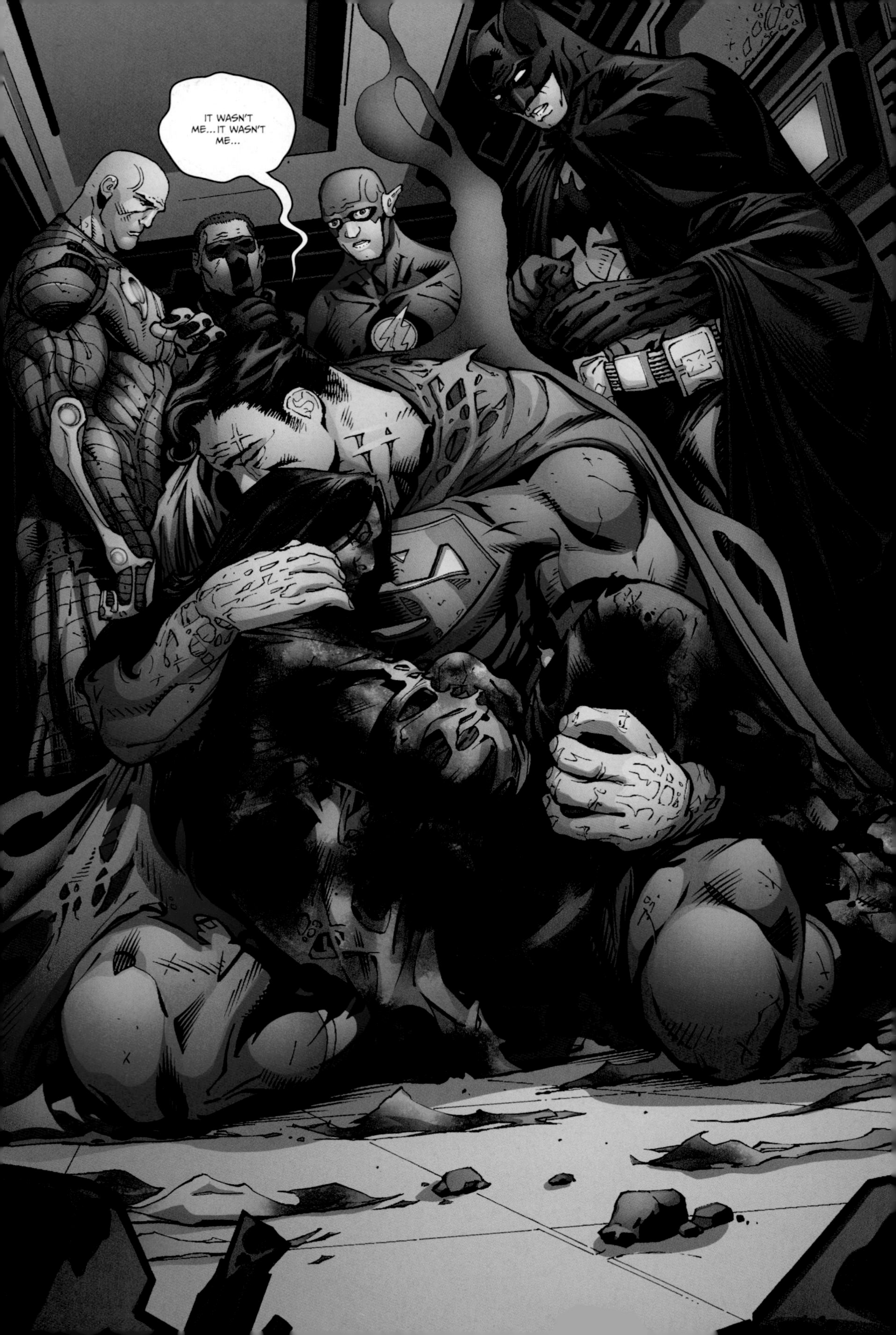
IT WASN'T ME... IT WASN'T ME...

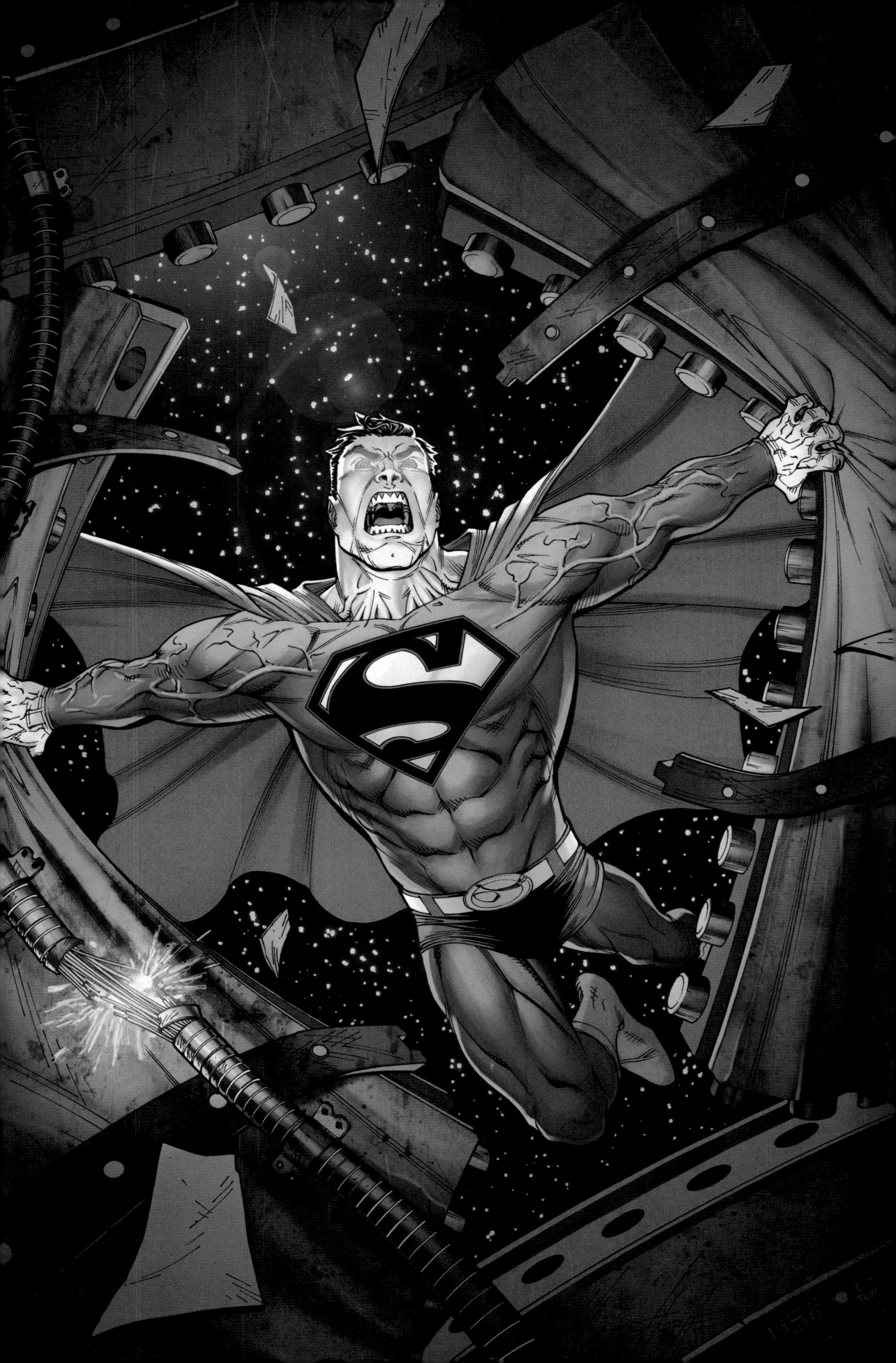

CROSSING THE LINE

Marv Wolfman
Writer

Mike S. Miller
Artist

Cover by Mike S. Miller and Luis Gonzalez

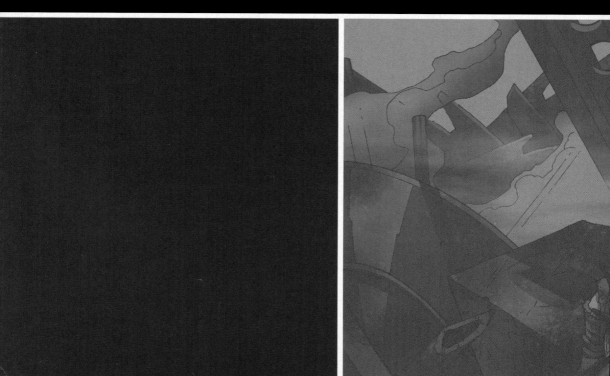

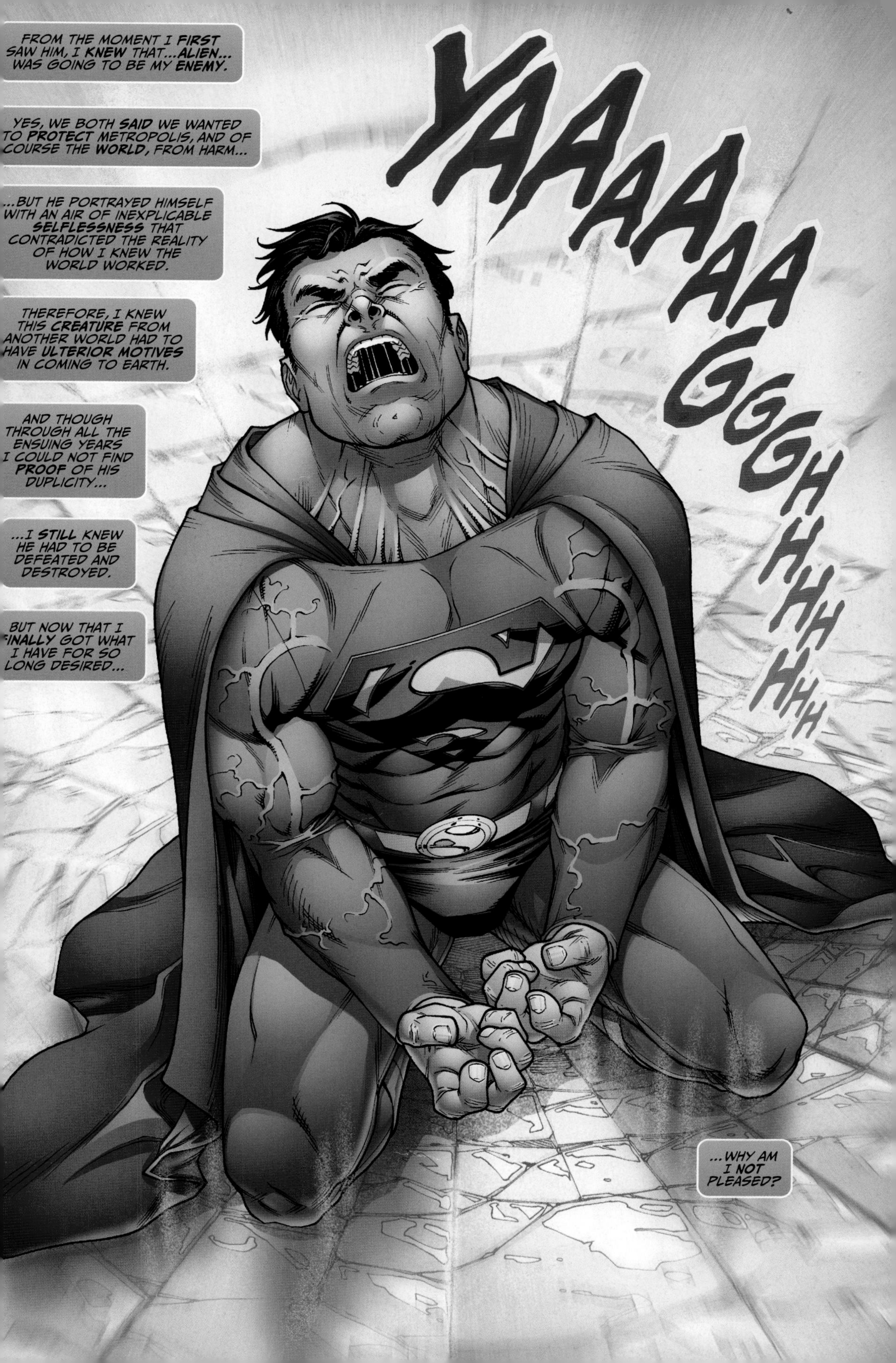
FROM THE MOMENT I FIRST SAW HIM, I KNEW THAT...ALIEN... WAS GOING TO BE MY ENEMY.
YES, WE BOTH SAID WE WANTED TO PROTECT METROPOLIS, AND OF COURSE THE WORLD, FROM HARM...
...BUT HE PORTRAYED HIMSELF WITH AN AIR OF INEXPLICABLE SELFLESSNESS THAT CONTRADICTED THE REALITY OF HOW I KNEW THE WORLD WORKED.
THEREFORE, I KNEW THIS CREATURE FROM ANOTHER WORLD HAD TO HAVE ULTERIOR MOTIVES IN COMING TO EARTH.
AND THOUGH THROUGH ALL THE ENSUING YEARS I COULD NOT FIND PROOF OF HIS DUPLICITY...
...I STILL KNEW HE HAD TO BE DEFEATED AND DESTROYED.
BUT NOW THAT I FINALLY GOT WHAT I HAVE FOR SO LONG DESIRED...
YAAAAAAAGGGHHHHHHH
...WHY AM I NOT PLEASED?

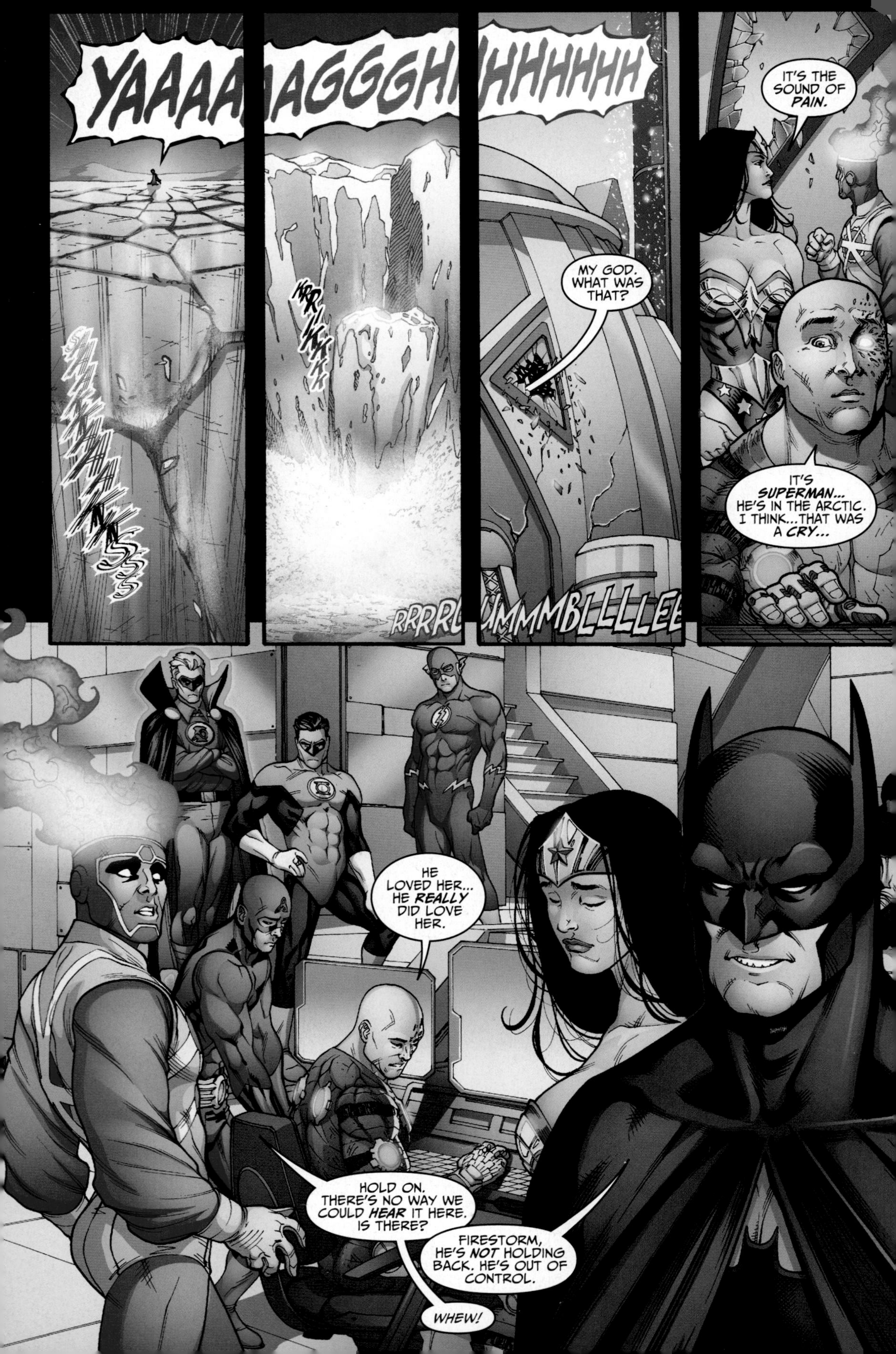
YAAAAAGGGGHHHHHHHH
RRRRUMMMBLLLLEE
MY GOD. WHAT WAS THAT?
IT'S THE SOUND OF *PAIN.*
IT'S *SUPERMAN...* HE'S IN THE ARCTIC. I THINK...THAT WAS A *CRY...*
HE LOVED HER... HE *REALLY* DID LOVE HER.
HOLD ON. THERE'S NO WAY WE COULD *HEAR* IT HERE. IS THERE?
FIRESTORM, HE'S *NOT* HOLDING BACK. HE'S OUT OF CONTROL.
WHEW!

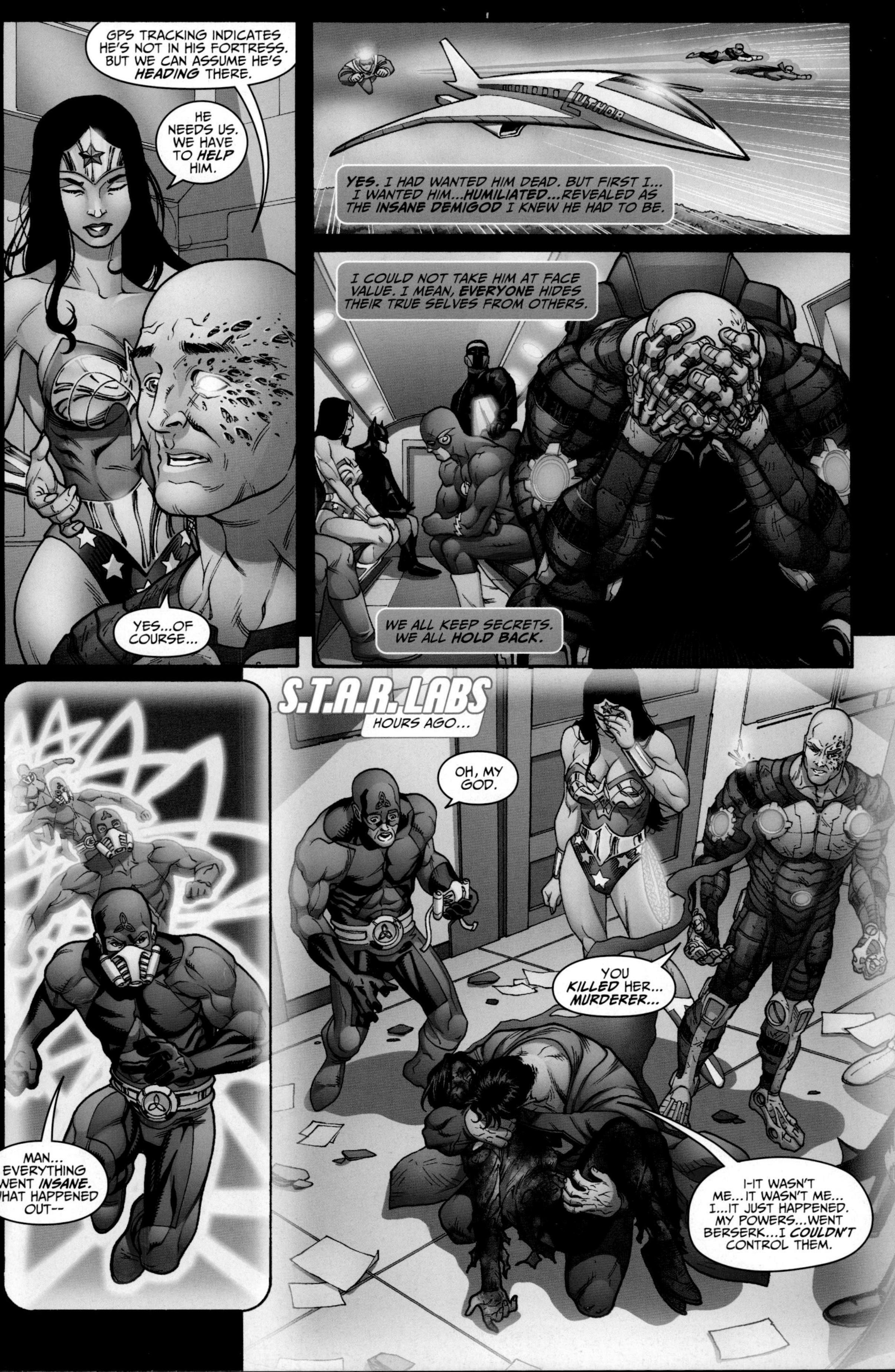
GPS TRACKING INDICATES HE'S NOT IN HIS FORTRESS. BUT WE CAN ASSUME HE'S **HEADING** THERE.
HE NEEDS US. WE HAVE TO **HELP** HIM.
YES...OF COURSE...
LUTHOR
YES. *I HAD WANTED HIM DEAD. BUT FIRST I... I WANTED HIM...* ***HUMILIATED****...REVEALED AS THE* ***INSANE DEMIGOD*** *I KNEW HE HAD TO BE.*
I COULD NOT TAKE HIM AT FACE VALUE. I MEAN, ***EVERYONE*** *HIDES THEIR TRUE SELVES FROM OTHERS.*
WE ALL KEEP SECRETS. WE ALL ***HOLD BACK.***
S.T.A.R. LABS
HOURS AGO...
MAN... EVERYTHING WENT ***INSANE.*** WHAT HAPPENED OUT--
OH, MY GOD.
YOU ***KILLED*** HER... ***MURDERER...***
I-IT WASN'T ME...IT WASN'T ME... I...IT JUST HAPPENED. MY POWERS...WENT BERSERK...I ***COULDN'T*** CONTROL THEM.

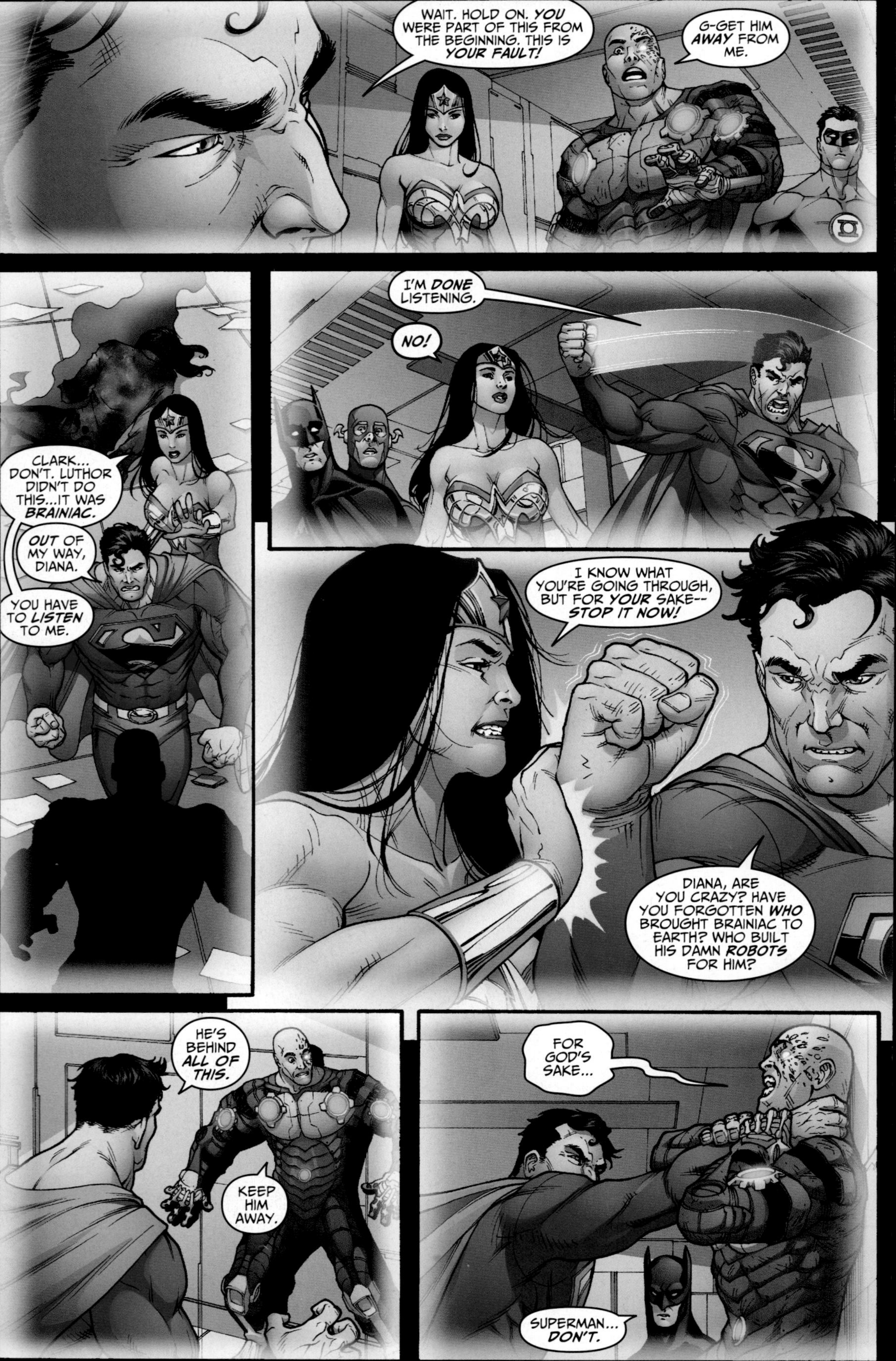
WAIT. HOLD ON. YOU WERE PART OF THIS FROM THE BEGINNING. THIS IS YOUR FAULT!
G-GET HIM AWAY FROM ME.
CLARK... DON'T. LUTHOR DIDN'T DO THIS...IT WAS BRAINIAC.
OUT OF MY WAY, DIANA.
YOU HAVE TO LISTEN TO ME.
I'M DONE LISTENING.
NO!
I KNOW WHAT YOU'RE GOING THROUGH, BUT FOR YOUR SAKE-- STOP IT NOW!
DIANA, ARE YOU CRAZY? HAVE YOU FORGOTTEN WHO BROUGHT BRAINIAC TO EARTH? WHO BUILT HIS DAMN ROBOTS FOR HIM?
HE'S BEHIND ALL OF THIS.
KEEP HIM AWAY.
FOR GOD'S SAKE...
SUPERMAN... DON'T.

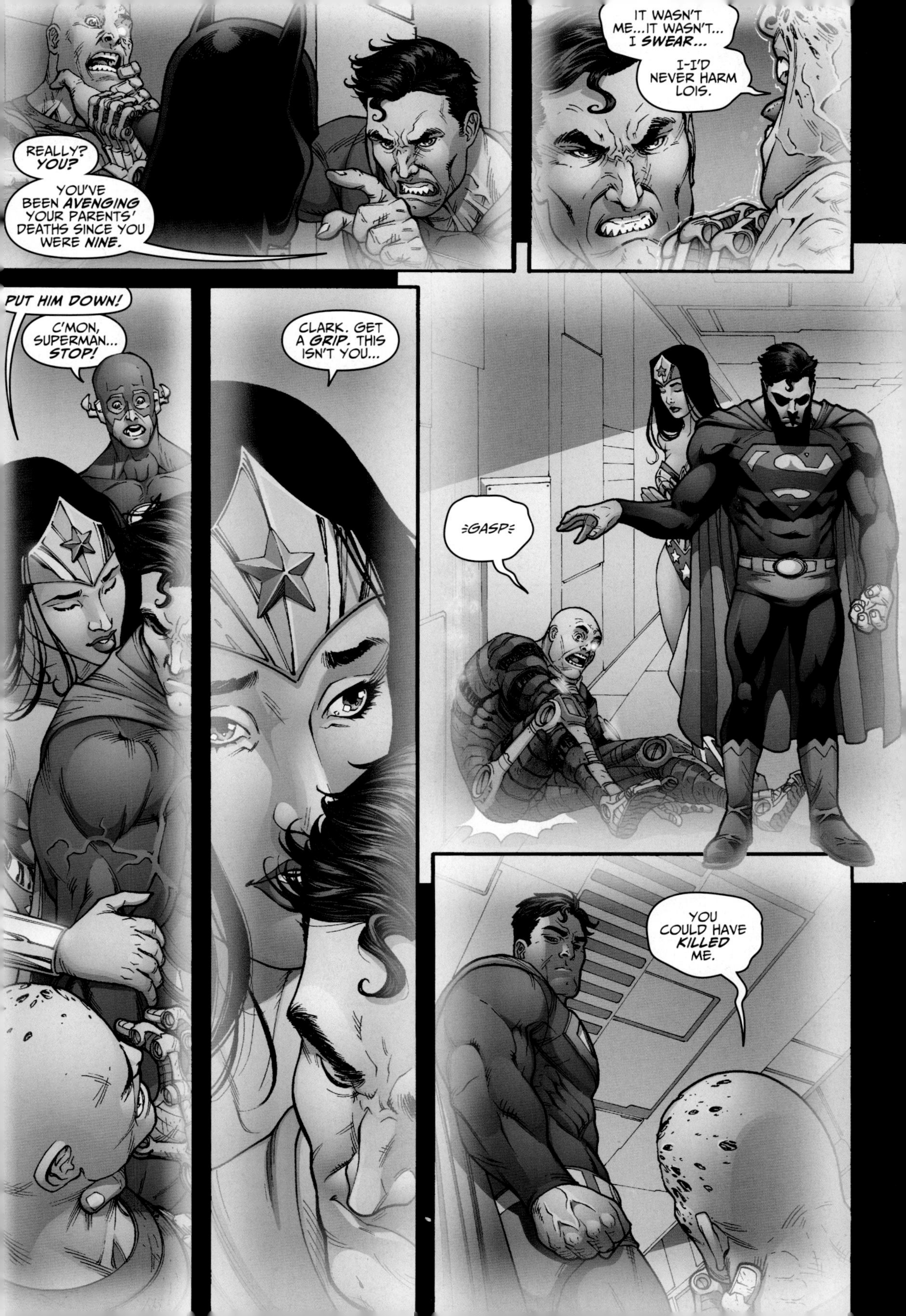
REALLY? *YOU?*
YOU'VE BEEN *AVENGING* YOUR PARENTS' DEATHS SINCE YOU WERE *NINE*.
IT WASN'T ME...IT WASN'T... I *SWEAR*...
I-I'D NEVER HARM LOIS.
PUT HIM DOWN!
C'MON, SUPERMAN... *STOP!*
CLARK. GET A *GRIP*. THIS ISN'T YOU...
GASP
YOU COULD HAVE *KILLED* ME.

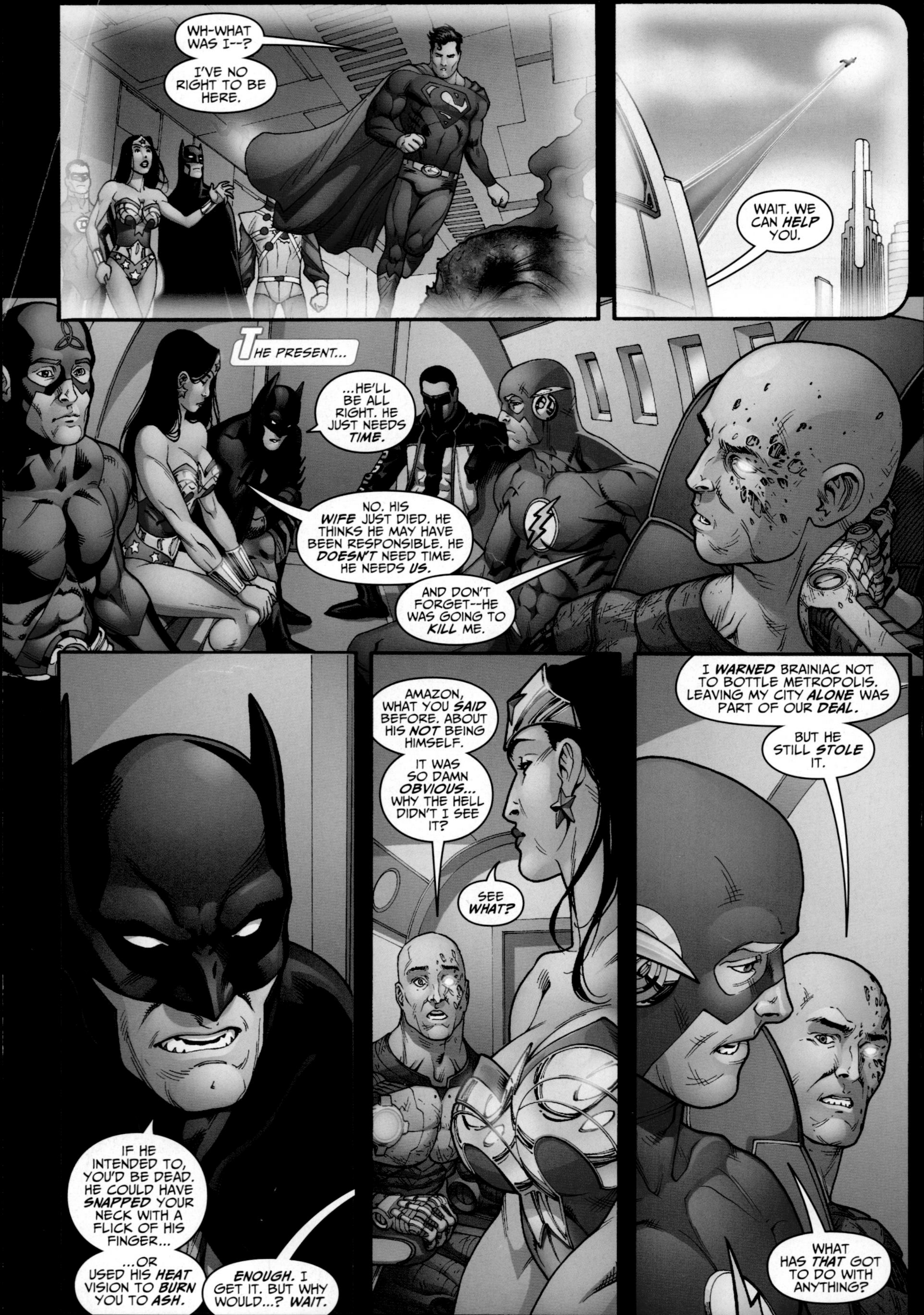
WH-WHAT WAS I--?
I'VE NO RIGHT TO BE HERE.
WAIT. WE CAN HELP YOU.
THE PRESENT...
...HE'LL BE ALL RIGHT. HE JUST NEEDS TIME.
NO. HIS WIFE JUST DIED. HE THINKS HE MAY HAVE BEEN RESPONSIBLE. HE DOESN'T NEED TIME. HE NEEDS US.
AND DON'T FORGET--HE WAS GOING TO KILL ME.
IF HE INTENDED TO, YOU'D BE DEAD. HE COULD HAVE SNAPPED YOUR NECK WITH A FLICK OF HIS FINGER...
...OR USED HIS HEAT VISION TO BURN YOU TO ASH.
ENOUGH. I GET IT. BUT WHY WOULD...? WAIT.
AMAZON, WHAT YOU SAID BEFORE. ABOUT HIS NOT BEING HIMSELF.
IT WAS SO DAMN OBVIOUS... WHY THE HELL DIDN'T I SEE IT?
SEE WHAT?
I WARNED BRAINIAC NOT TO BOTTLE METROPOLIS. LEAVING MY CITY ALONE WAS PART OF OUR DEAL.
BUT HE STILL STOLE IT.
WHAT HAS THAT GOT TO DO WITH ANYTHING?

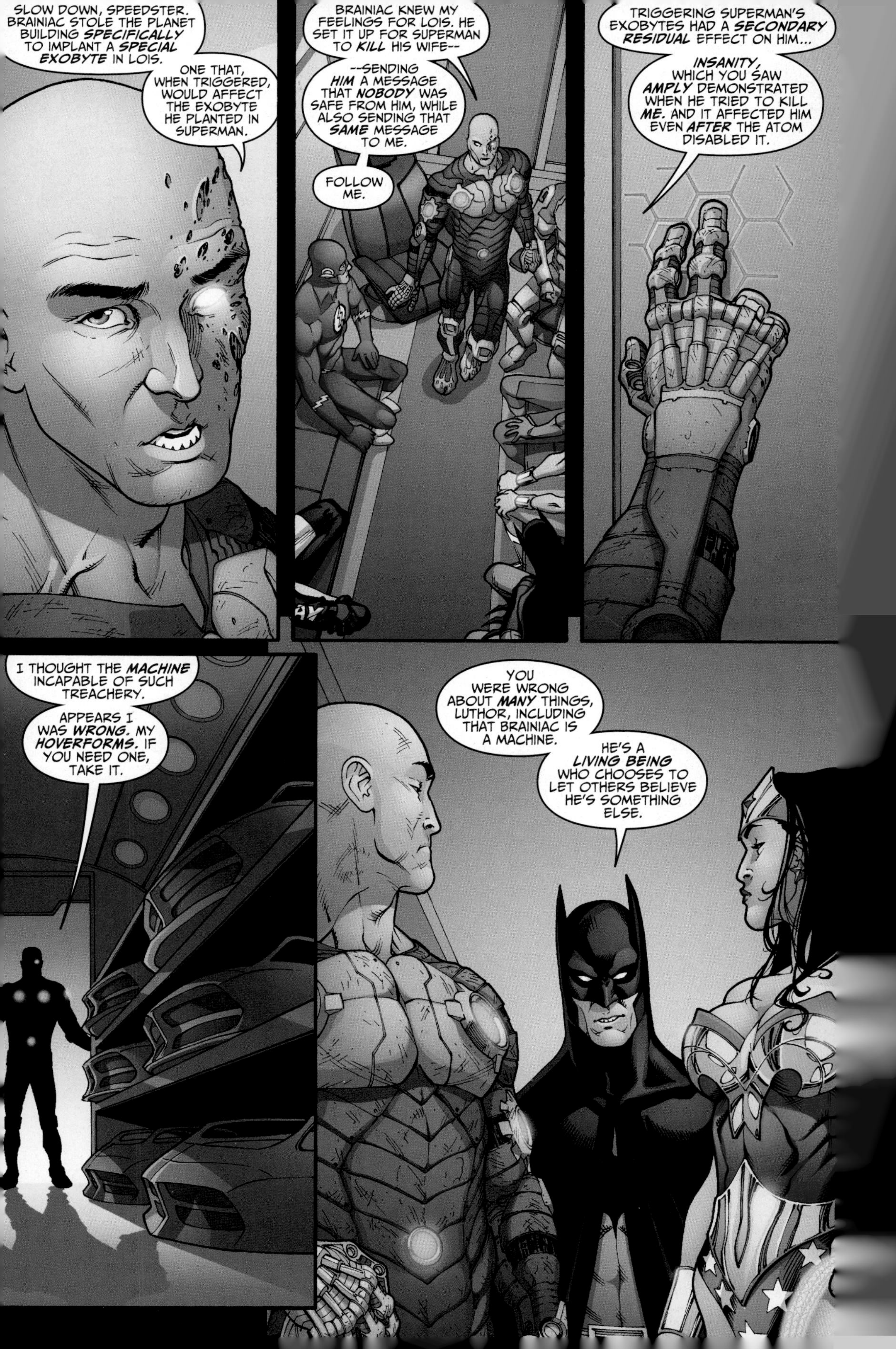
SLOW DOWN, SPEEDSTER. BRAINIAC STOLE THE PLANET BUILDING SPECIFICALLY TO IMPLANT A SPECIAL EXOBYTE IN LOIS.
ONE THAT, WHEN TRIGGERED, WOULD AFFECT THE EXOBYTE HE PLANTED IN SUPERMAN.
BRAINIAC KNEW MY FEELINGS FOR LOIS. HE SET IT UP FOR SUPERMAN TO KILL HIS WIFE--
--SENDING HIM A MESSAGE THAT NOBODY WAS SAFE FROM HIM, WHILE ALSO SENDING THAT SAME MESSAGE TO ME.
FOLLOW ME.
TRIGGERING SUPERMAN'S EXOBYTES HAD A SECONDARY RESIDUAL EFFECT ON HIM...
INSANITY, WHICH YOU SAW AMPLY DEMONSTRATED WHEN HE TRIED TO KILL ME. AND IT AFFECTED HIM EVEN AFTER THE ATOM DISABLED IT.
I THOUGHT THE MACHINE INCAPABLE OF SUCH TREACHERY.
APPEARS I WAS WRONG. MY HOVERFORMS. IF YOU NEED ONE, TAKE IT.
YOU WERE WRONG ABOUT MANY THINGS, LUTHOR, INCLUDING THAT BRAINIAC IS A MACHINE.
HE'S A LIVING BEING WHO CHOOSES TO LET OTHERS BELIEVE HE'S SOMETHING ELSE.

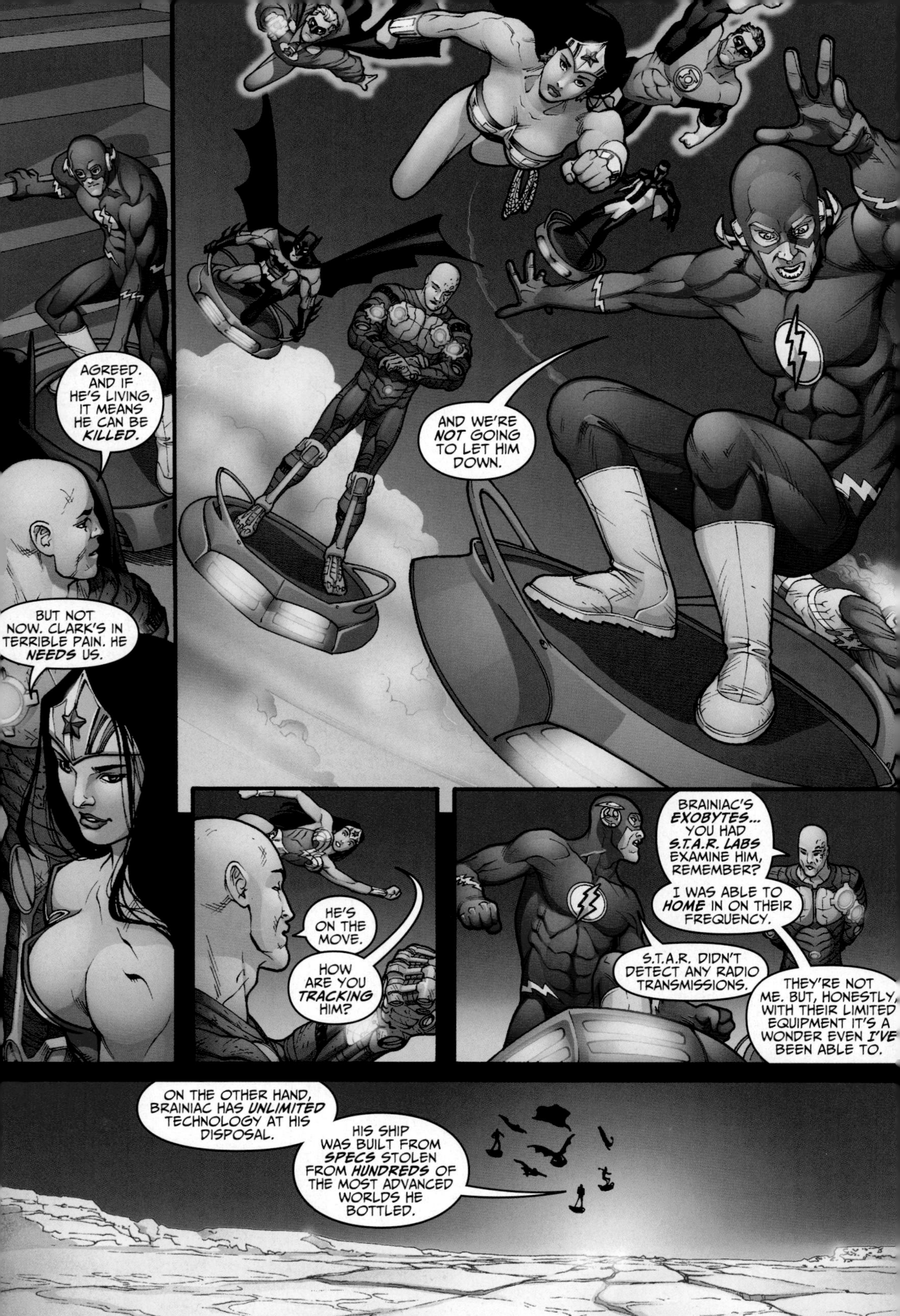
AGREED. AND IF HE'S LIVING, IT MEANS HE CAN BE KILLED.
BUT NOT NOW. CLARK'S IN TERRIBLE PAIN. HE NEEDS US.
AND WE'RE NOT GOING TO LET HIM DOWN.
HE'S ON THE MOVE.
HOW ARE YOU TRACKING HIM?
BRAINIAC'S EXOBYTES... YOU HAD S.T.A.R. LABS EXAMINE HIM, REMEMBER?
I WAS ABLE TO HOME IN ON THEIR FREQUENCY.
S.T.A.R. DIDN'T DETECT ANY RADIO TRANSMISSIONS.
THEY'RE NOT ME. BUT, HONESTLY, WITH THEIR LIMITED EQUIPMENT IT'S A WONDER EVEN I'VE BEEN ABLE TO.
ON THE OTHER HAND, BRAINIAC HAS UNLIMITED TECHNOLOGY AT HIS DISPOSAL.
HIS SHIP WAS BUILT FROM SPECS STOLEN FROM HUNDREDS OF THE MOST ADVANCED WORLDS HE BOTTLED.

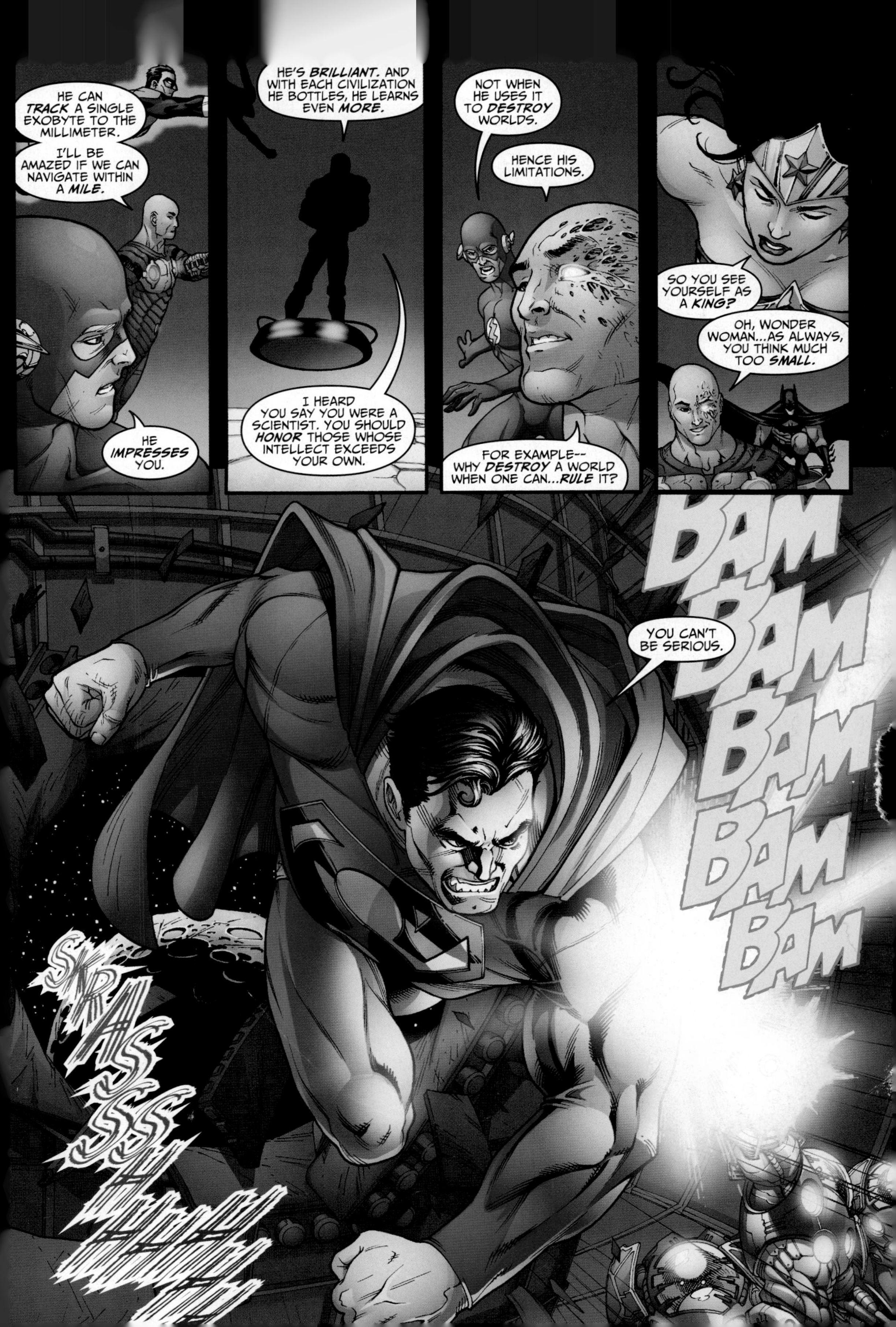
HE CAN TRACK A SINGLE EXOBYTE TO THE MILLIMETER.
I'LL BE AMAZED IF WE CAN NAVIGATE WITHIN A MILE.
HE IMPRESSES YOU.
HE'S BRILLIANT. AND WITH EACH CIVILIZATION HE BOTTLES, HE LEARNS EVEN MORE.
I HEARD YOU SAY YOU WERE A SCIENTIST. YOU SHOULD HONOR THOSE WHOSE INTELLECT EXCEEDS YOUR OWN.
NOT WHEN HE USES IT TO DESTROY WORLDS.
HENCE HIS LIMITATIONS.
FOR EXAMPLE-- WHY DESTROY A WORLD WHEN ONE CAN...RULE IT?
SO YOU SEE YOURSELF AS A KING?
OH, WONDER WOMAN...AS ALWAYS, YOU THINK MUCH TOO SMALL.
BAM BAM BAM BAM BAM BAM BAM
YOU CAN'T BE SERIOUS.

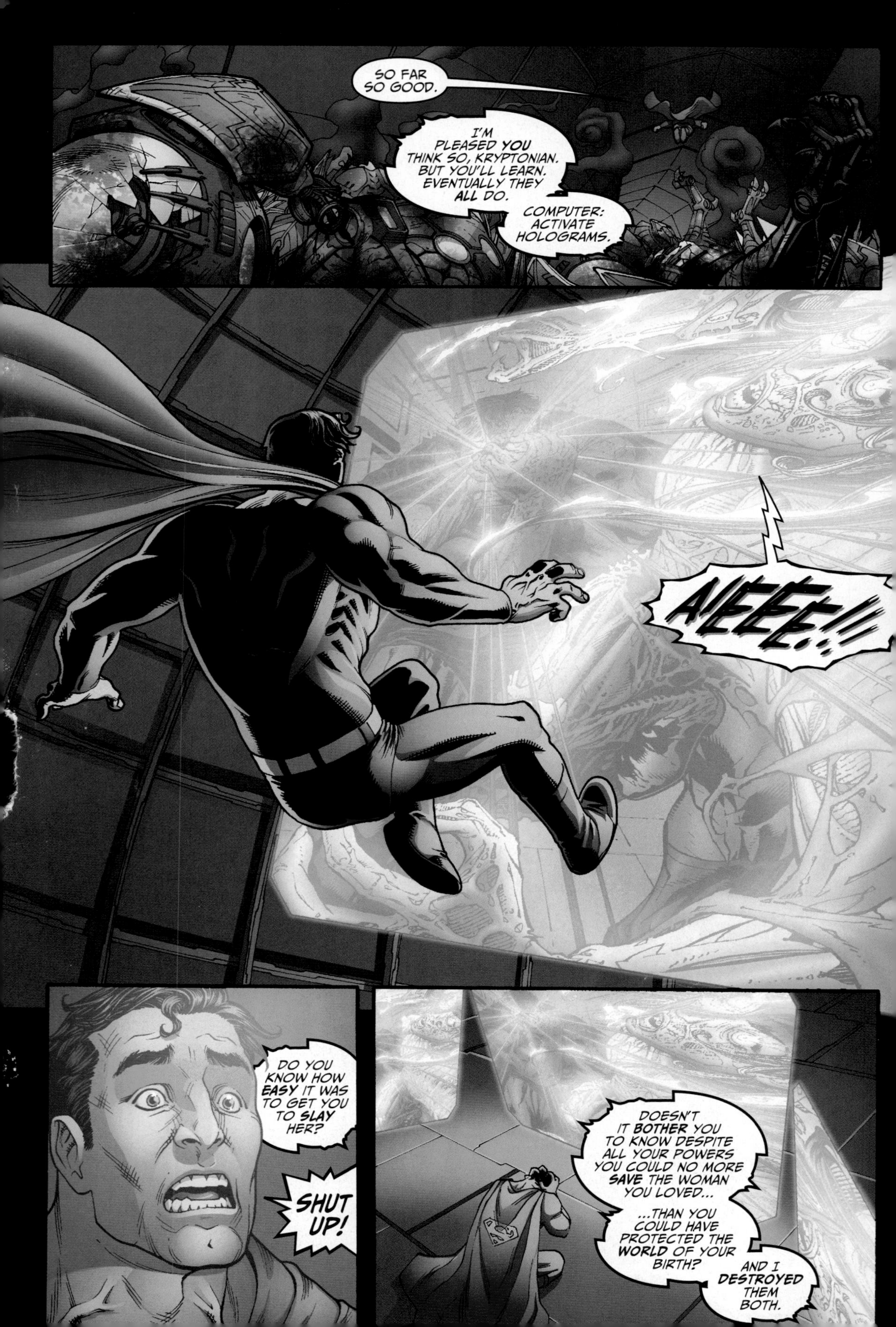
SO FAR SO GOOD.
I'M PLEASED YOU THINK SO, KRYPTONIAN. BUT YOU'LL LEARN. EVENTUALLY THEY ALL DO.
COMPUTER: ACTIVATE HOLOGRAMS.
AIEEEE!!!
DO YOU KNOW HOW EASY IT WAS TO GET YOU TO SLAY HER?
SHUT UP!
DOESN'T IT BOTHER YOU TO KNOW DESPITE ALL YOUR POWERS YOU COULD NO MORE SAVE THE WOMAN YOU LOVED...
...THAN YOU COULD HAVE PROTECTED THE WORLD OF YOUR BIRTH?
AND I DESTROYED THEM BOTH.

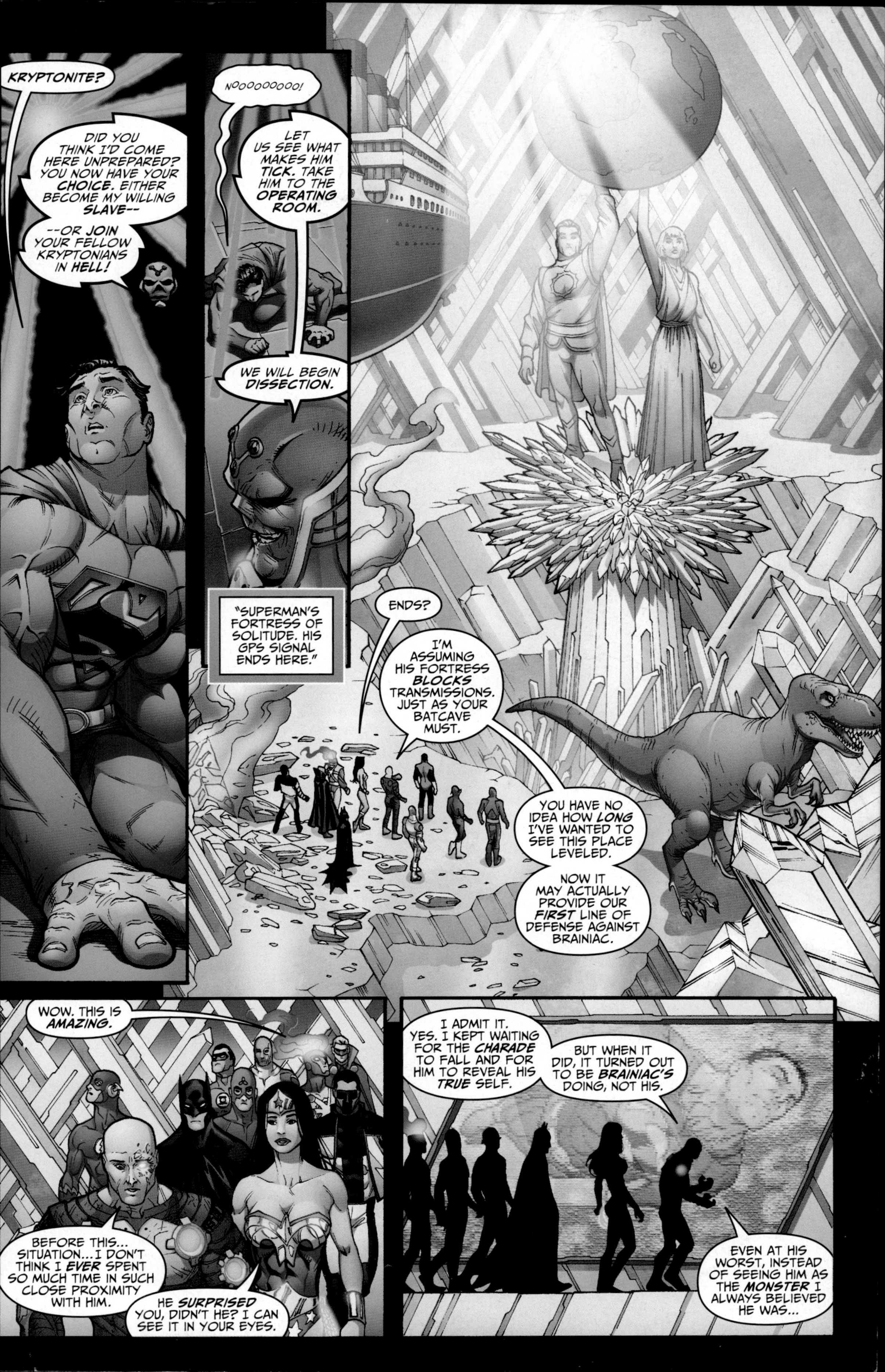
KRYPTONITE?
DID YOU THINK I'D COME HERE UNPREPARED? YOU NOW HAVE YOUR CHOICE. EITHER BECOME MY WILLING SLAVE--
--OR JOIN YOUR FELLOW KRYPTONIANS IN HELL!
NOOOOOOOOO!
LET US SEE WHAT MAKES HIM TICK. TAKE HIM TO THE OPERATING ROOM.
WE WILL BEGIN DISSECTION.
"SUPERMAN'S FORTRESS OF SOLITUDE. HIS GPS SIGNAL ENDS HERE."
ENDS?
I'M ASSUMING HIS FORTRESS BLOCKS TRANSMISSIONS. JUST AS YOUR BATCAVE MUST.
YOU HAVE NO IDEA HOW LONG I'VE WANTED TO SEE THIS PLACE LEVELED.
NOW IT MAY ACTUALLY PROVIDE OUR FIRST LINE OF DEFENSE AGAINST BRAINIAC.
WOW. THIS IS AMAZING.
BEFORE THIS... SITUATION... I DON'T THINK I EVER SPENT SO MUCH TIME IN SUCH CLOSE PROXIMITY WITH HIM.
HE SURPRISED YOU, DIDN'T HE? I CAN SEE IT IN YOUR EYES.
I ADMIT IT. YES. I KEPT WAITING FOR THE CHARADE TO FALL AND FOR HIM TO REVEAL HIS TRUE SELF.
BUT WHEN IT DID, IT TURNED OUT TO BE BRAINIAC'S DOING, NOT HIS.
EVEN AT HIS WORST, INSTEAD OF SEEING HIM AS THE MONSTER I ALWAYS BELIEVED HE WAS...

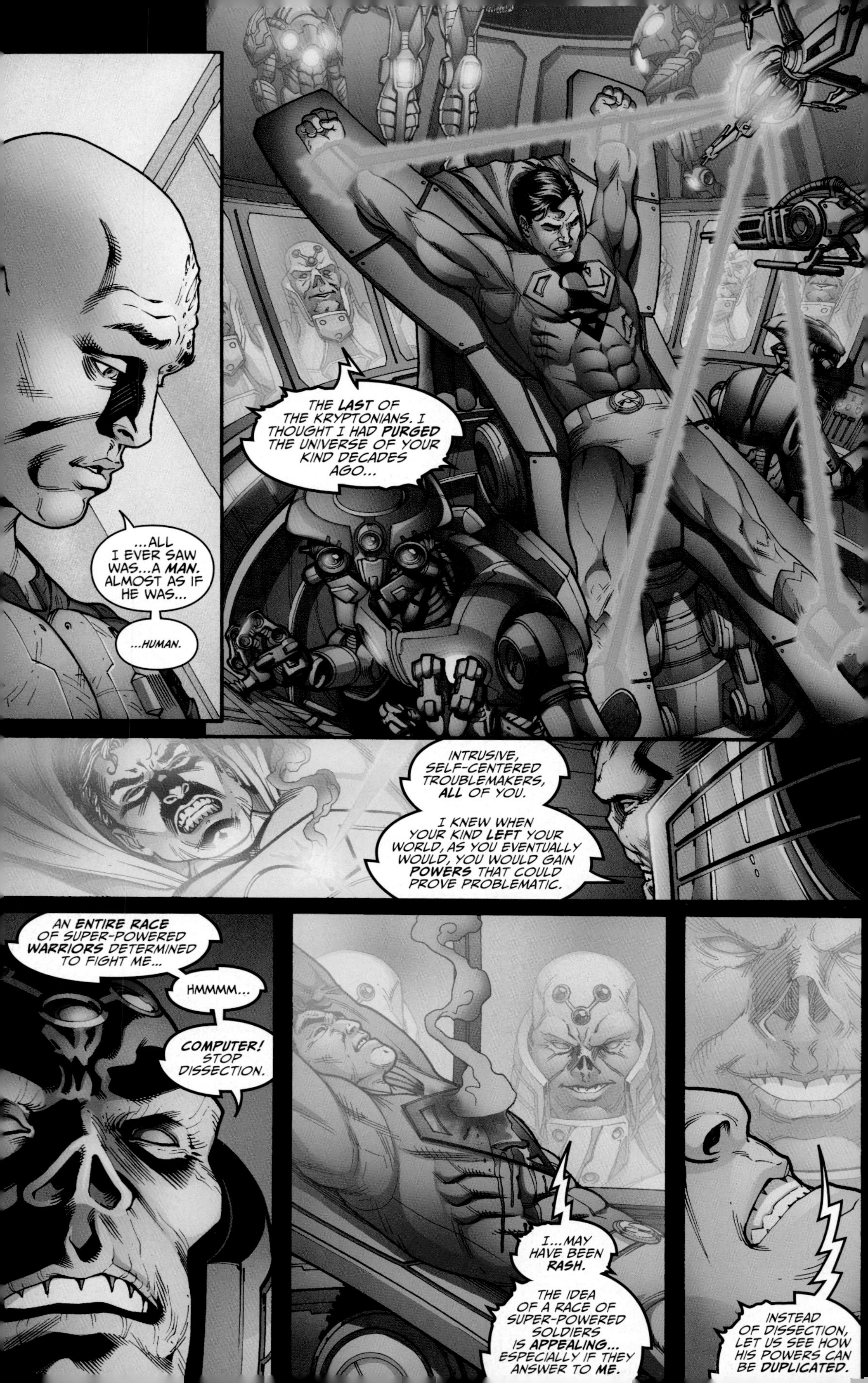

THE LAST OF THE KRYPTONIANS. I THOUGHT I HAD PURGED THE UNIVERSE OF YOUR KIND DECADES AGO...
...ALL I EVER SAW WAS...A MAN. ALMOST AS IF HE WAS...
...HUMAN.
INTRUSIVE, SELF-CENTERED TROUBLEMAKERS, ALL OF YOU.
I KNEW WHEN YOUR KIND LEFT YOUR WORLD, AS YOU EVENTUALLY WOULD, YOU WOULD GAIN POWERS THAT COULD PROVE PROBLEMATIC.
AN ENTIRE RACE OF SUPER-POWERED WARRIORS DETERMINED TO FIGHT ME...
HMMMM...
COMPUTER! STOP DISSECTION.
I...MAY HAVE BEEN RASH.
THE IDEA OF A RACE OF SUPER-POWERED SOLDIERS IS APPEALING... ESPECIALLY IF THEY ANSWER TO ME.
INSTEAD OF DISSECTION, LET US SEE HOW HIS POWERS CAN BE DUPLICATED.

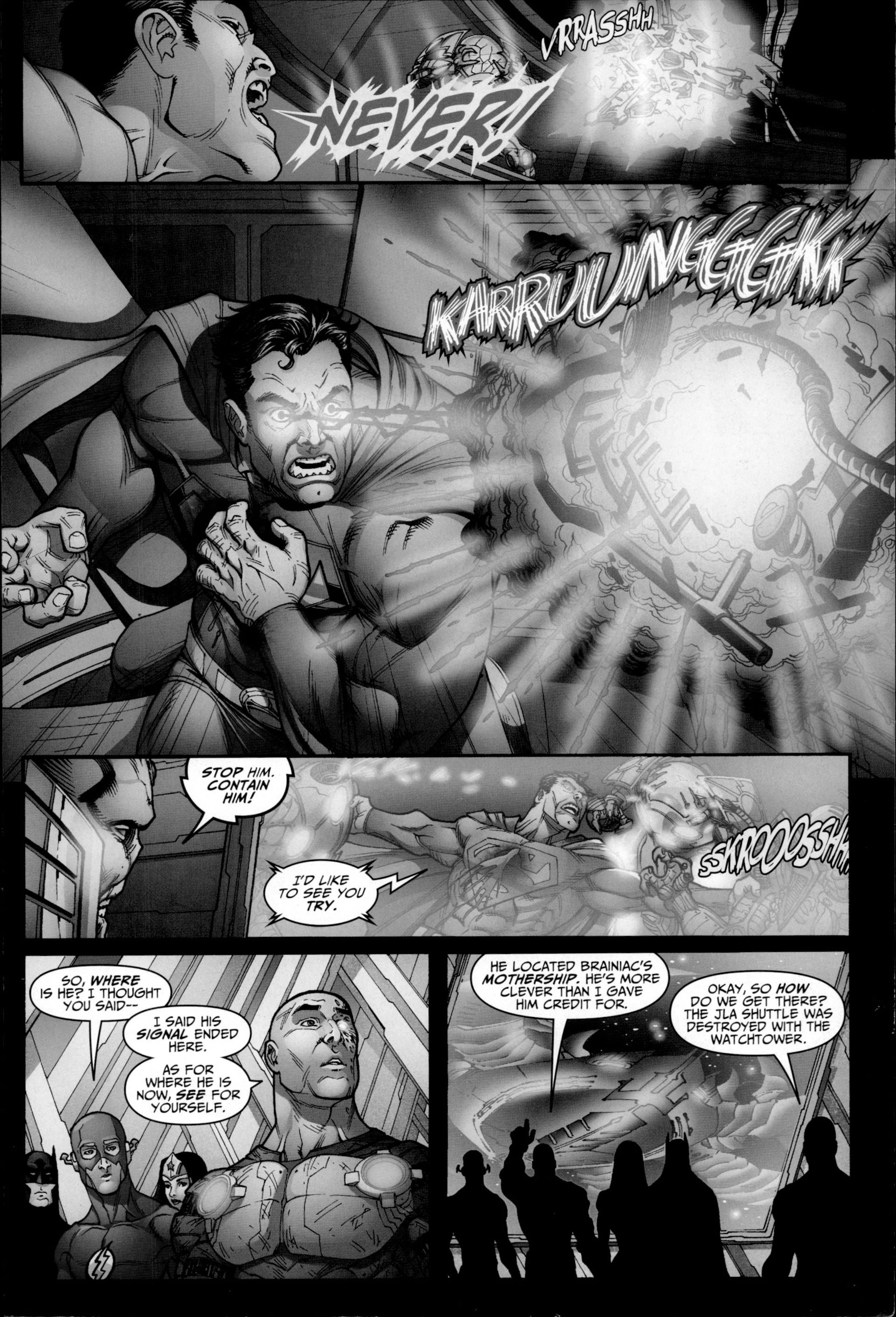
VRRASSHH
NEVER!
KARRUUNGGGKK
STOP HIM. CONTAIN HIM!
I'D LIKE TO SEE YOU TRY.
SSKROOOSSHH
SO, WHERE IS HE? I THOUGHT YOU SAID--
I SAID HIS SIGNAL ENDED HERE.
AS FOR WHERE HE IS NOW, SEE FOR YOURSELF.
HE LOCATED BRAINIAC'S MOTHERSHIP. HE'S MORE CLEVER THAN I GAVE HIM CREDIT FOR.
OKAY, SO HOW DO WE GET THERE? THE JLA SHUTTLE WAS DESTROYED WITH THE WATCHTOWER.

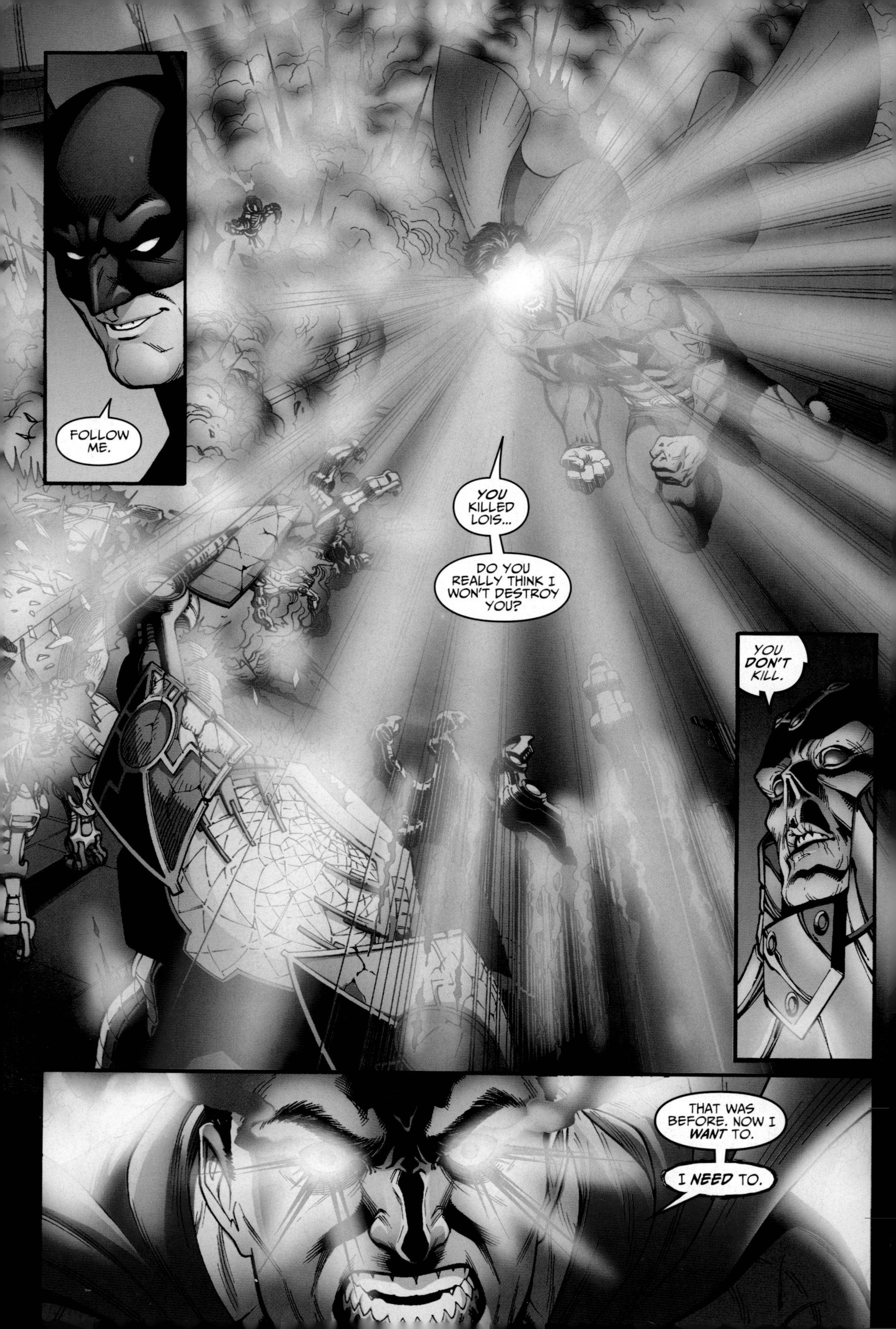
FOLLOW ME.
YOU KILLED LOIS...
DO YOU REALLY THINK I WON'T DESTROY YOU?
YOU DON'T KILL.
THAT WAS BEFORE. NOW I WANT TO.
I NEED TO.

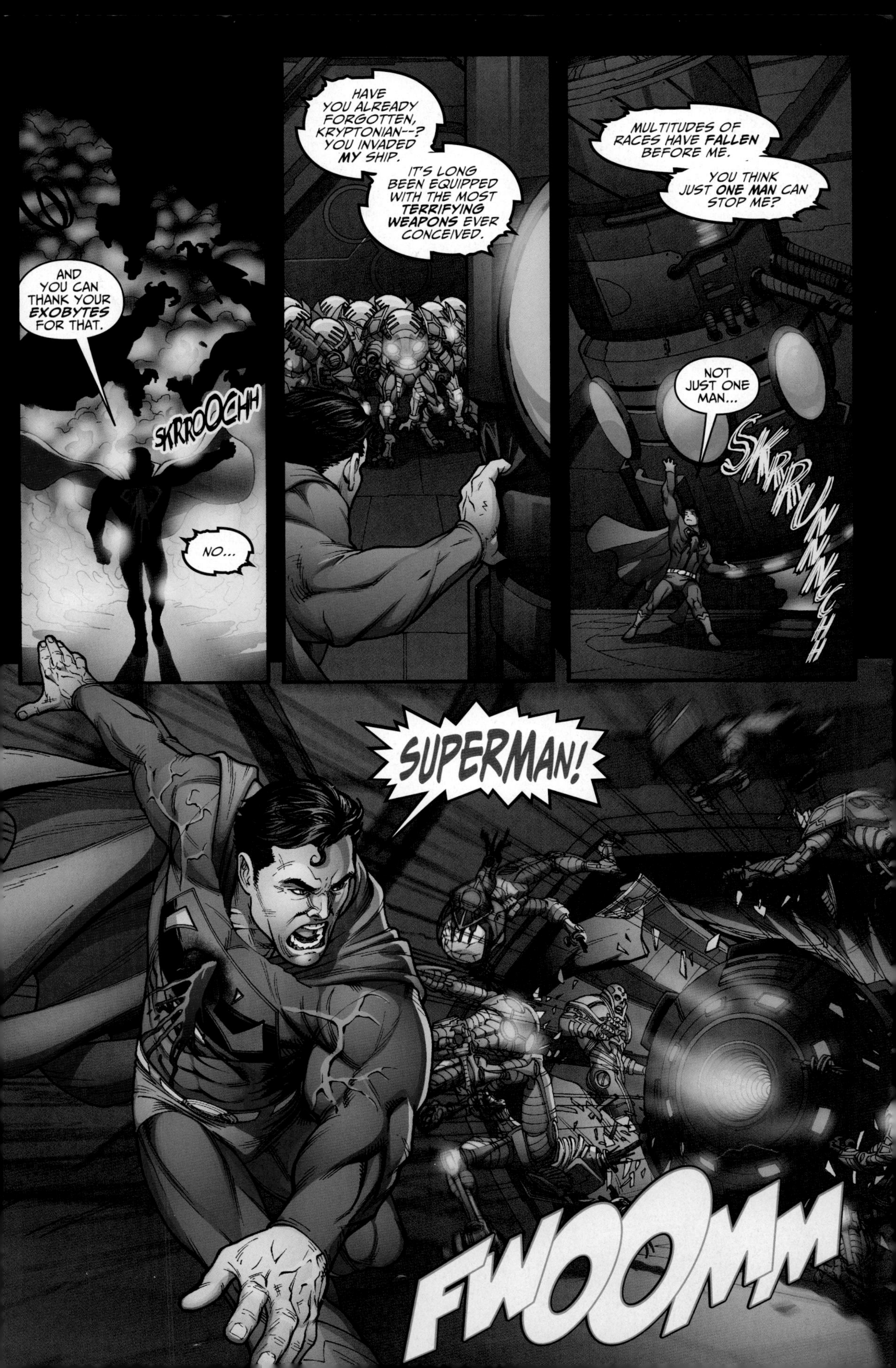

AND YOU CAN THANK YOUR EXOBYTES FOR THAT.
SKRROOCHH
NO...
HAVE YOU ALREADY FORGOTTEN, KRYPTONIAN--? YOU INVADED MY SHIP.
IT'S LONG BEEN EQUIPPED WITH THE MOST TERRIFYING WEAPONS EVER CONCEIVED.
MULTITUDES OF RACES HAVE FALLEN BEFORE ME.
YOU THINK JUST ONE MAN CAN STOP ME?
NOT JUST ONE MAN...
SKRRUNNCHH
SUPERMAN!
FWOOMM

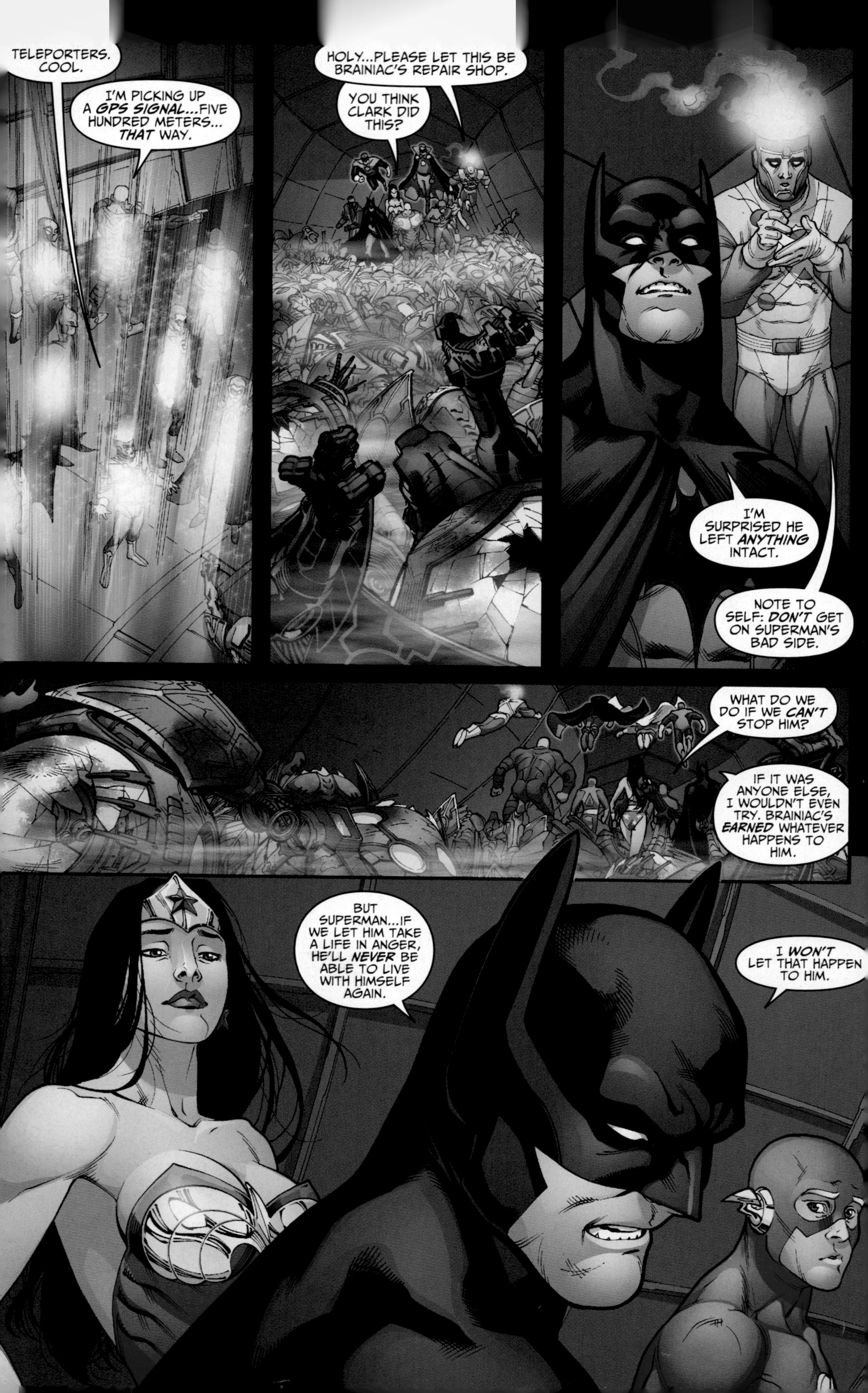
TELEPORTERS. COOL.
I'M PICKING UP A GPS SIGNAL...FIVE HUNDRED METERS... THAT WAY.
HOLY...PLEASE LET THIS BE BRAINIAC'S REPAIR SHOP.
YOU THINK CLARK DID THIS?
I'M SURPRISED HE LEFT ANYTHING INTACT.
NOTE TO SELF: DON'T GET ON SUPERMAN'S BAD SIDE.
WHAT DO WE DO IF WE CAN'T STOP HIM?
IF IT WAS ANYONE ELSE, I WOULDN'T EVEN TRY. BRAINIAC'S EARNED WHATEVER HAPPENS TO HIM.
BUT SUPERMAN...IF WE LET HIM TAKE A LIFE IN ANGER, HE'LL NEVER BE ABLE TO LIVE WITH HIMSELF AGAIN.
I WON'T LET THAT HAPPEN TO HIM.

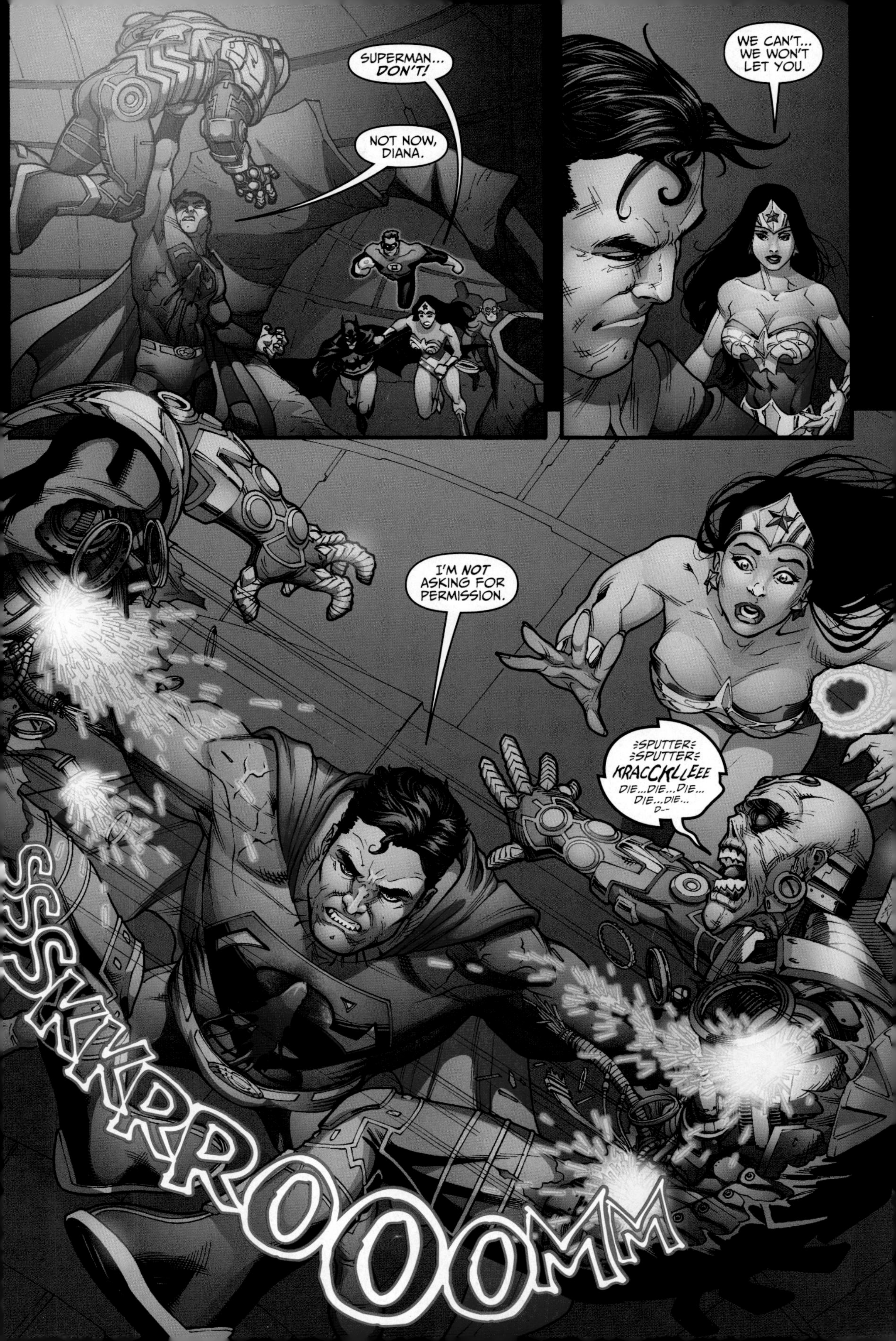
SUPERMAN... DON'T!
NOT NOW, DIANA.
WE CAN'T... WE WON'T LET YOU.
I'M NOT ASKING FOR PERMISSION.
SPUTTER SPUTTER KRACCKLLEEE
DIE...DIE...DIE... DIE...DIE... D--
SSKKRROOOMM

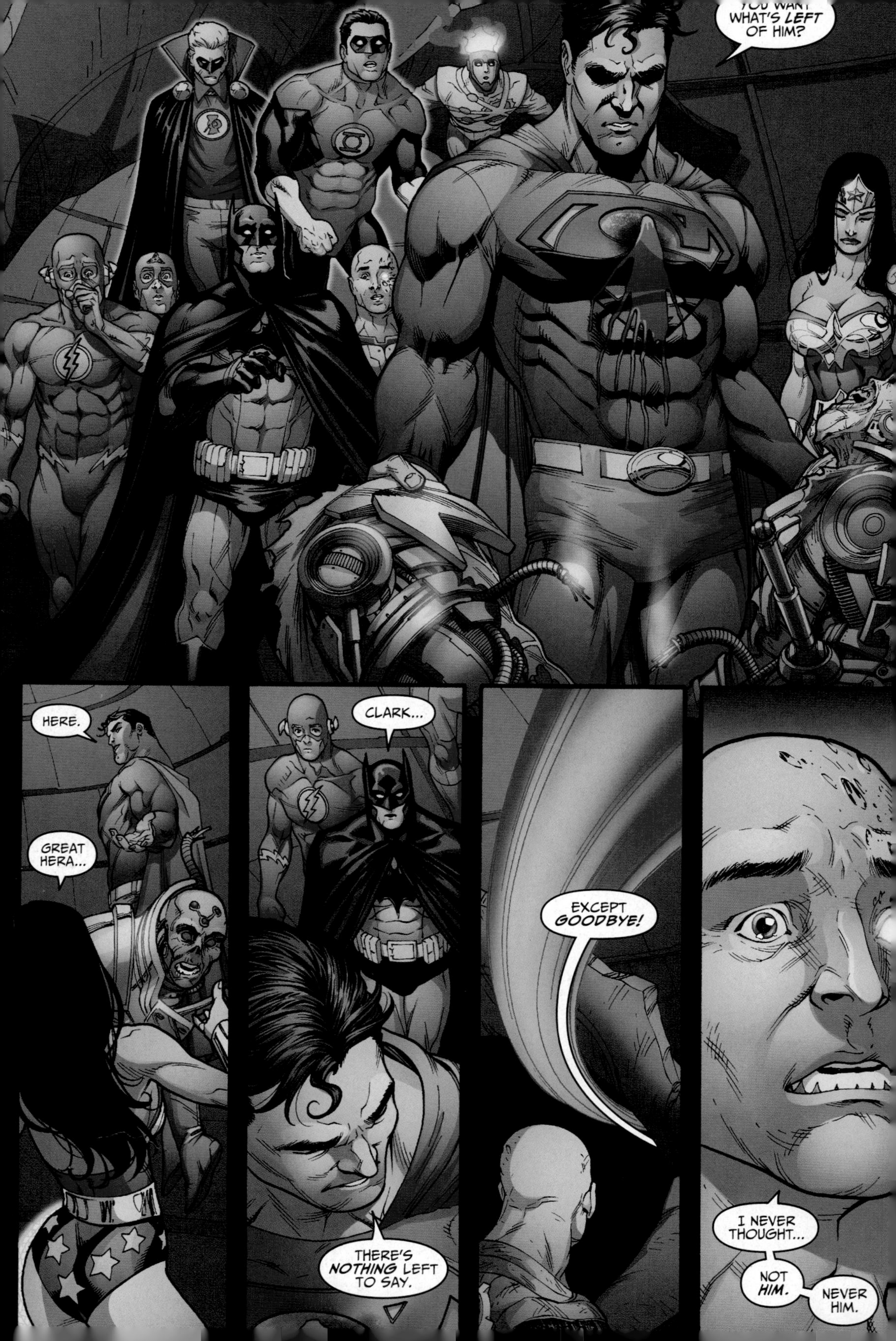

YOU WANT WHAT'S *LEFT* OF HIM?
HERE.
GREAT HERA...
CLARK...
THERE'S *NOTHING* LEFT TO SAY.
EXCEPT *GOODBYE!*
I NEVER THOUGHT...
NOT *HIM.*
NEVER HIM.

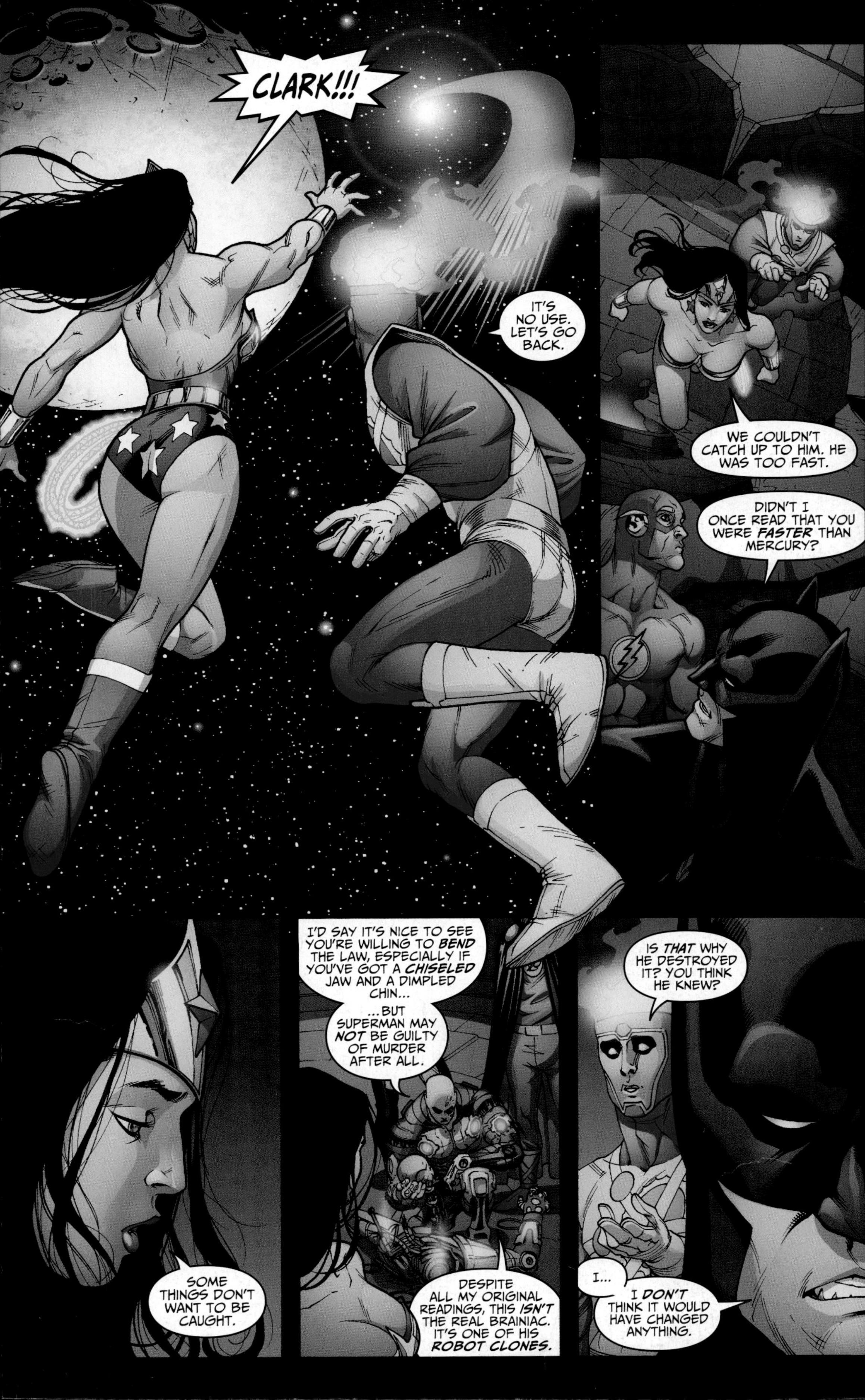
CLARK!!!
IT'S NO USE. LET'S GO BACK.
WE COULDN'T CATCH UP TO HIM. HE WAS TOO FAST.
DIDN'T I ONCE READ THAT YOU WERE FASTER THAN MERCURY?
SOME THINGS DON'T WANT TO BE CAUGHT.
I'D SAY IT'S NICE TO SEE YOU'RE WILLING TO BEND THE LAW, ESPECIALLY IF YOU'VE GOT A CHISELED JAW AND A DIMPLED CHIN...
...BUT SUPERMAN MAY NOT BE GUILTY OF MURDER AFTER ALL.
DESPITE ALL MY ORIGINAL READINGS, THIS ISN'T THE REAL BRAINIAC. IT'S ONE OF HIS ROBOT CLONES.
IS THAT WHY HE DESTROYED IT? YOU THINK HE KNEW?
I...
I DON'T THINK IT WOULD HAVE CHANGED ANYTHING.

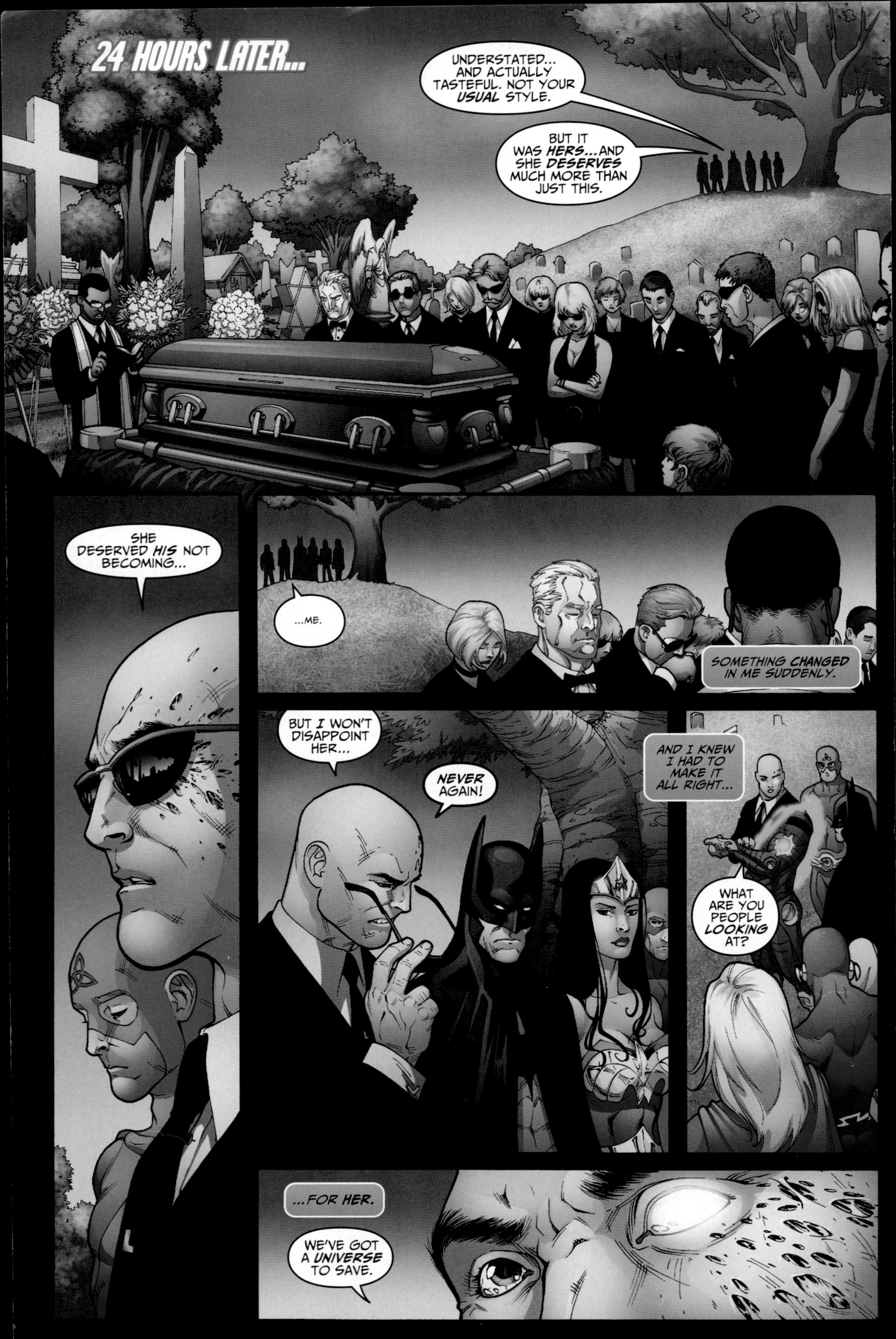
24 HOURS LATER...
UNDERSTATED... AND ACTUALLY TASTEFUL. NOT YOUR USUAL STYLE.
BUT IT WAS HERS...AND SHE DESERVES MUCH MORE THAN JUST THIS.
SHE DESERVED HIS NOT BECOMING...
...ME.
SOMETHING CHANGED IN ME SUDDENLY.
BUT I WON'T DISAPPOINT HER...
NEVER AGAIN!
AND I KNEW I HAD TO MAKE IT ALL RIGHT...
WHAT ARE YOU PEOPLE LOOKING AT?
...FOR HER.
WE'VE GOT A UNIVERSE TO SAVE.

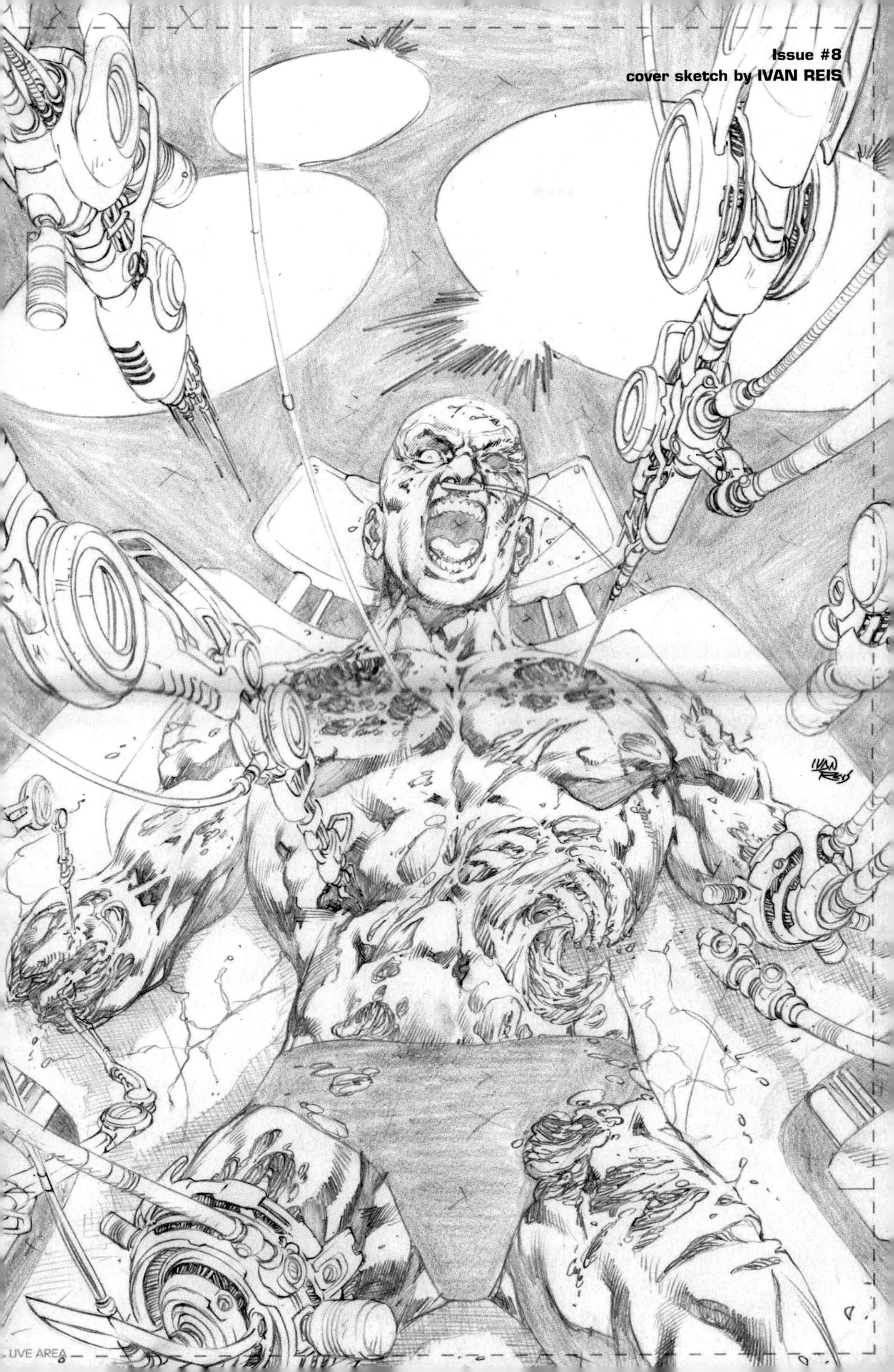
IVAN REIS
LIVE AREA

Issue #8
cover sketch by IVAN REIS

Issue #9
cover sketch by IVAN REIS

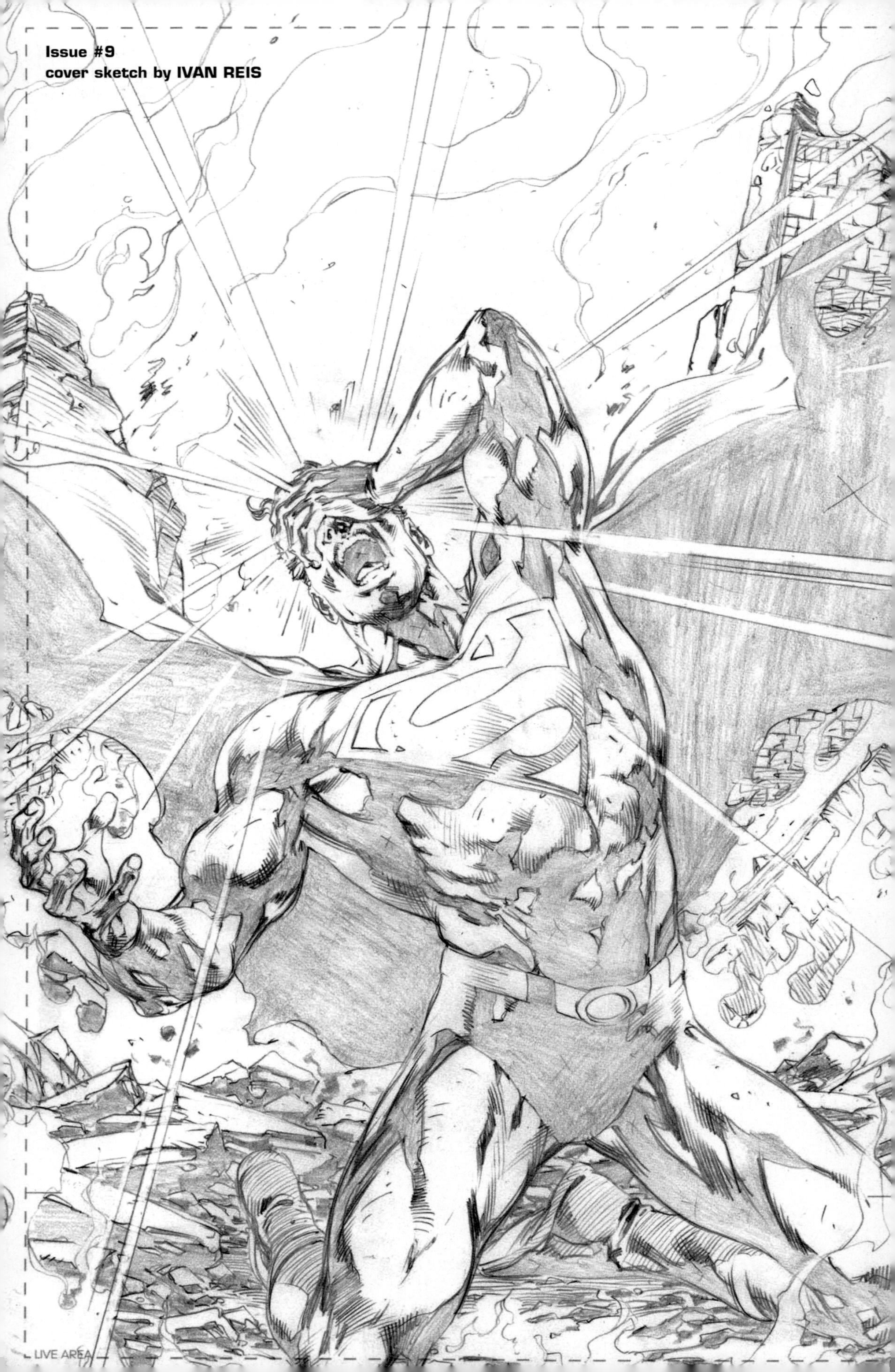
LIVE AREA

Issue #10
cover sketches
by ED BENES

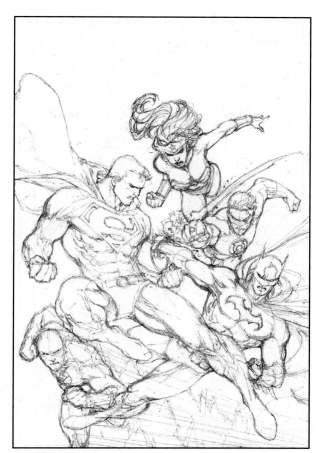

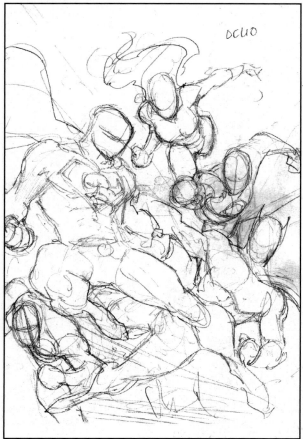

Issue #11
cover sketches
by ED BENES

DCUO

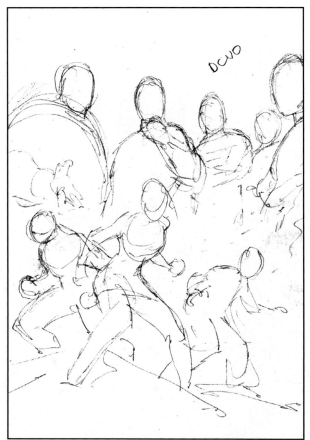

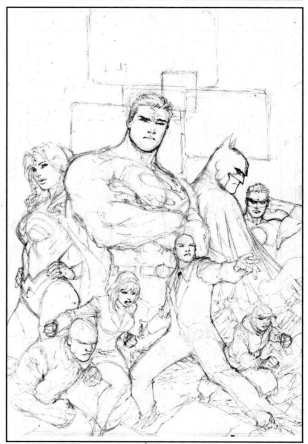

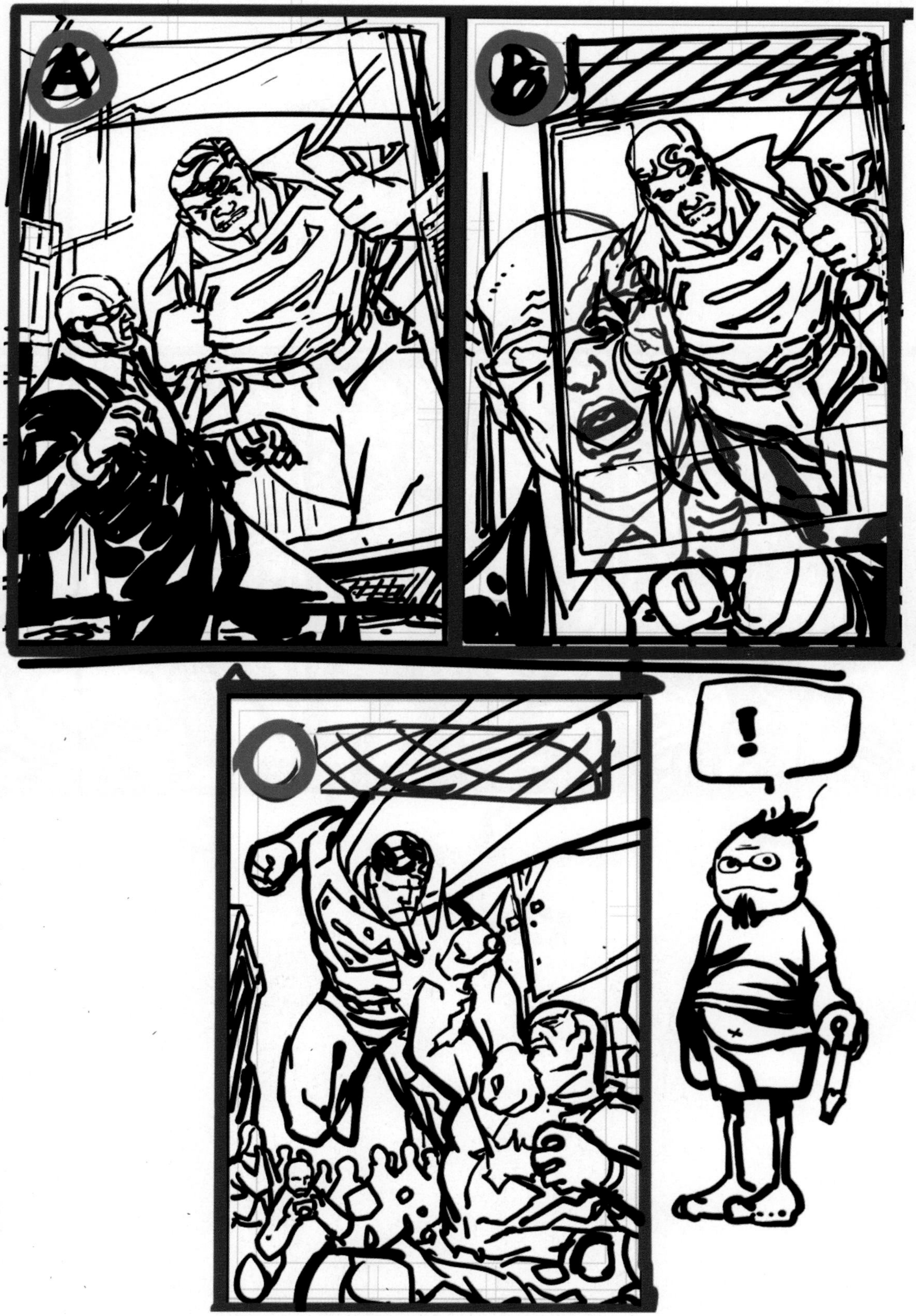
A
B
!

Issue #12
cover sketches by HOWARD PORTER

Issue #13
cover sketches by HOWARD PORTER

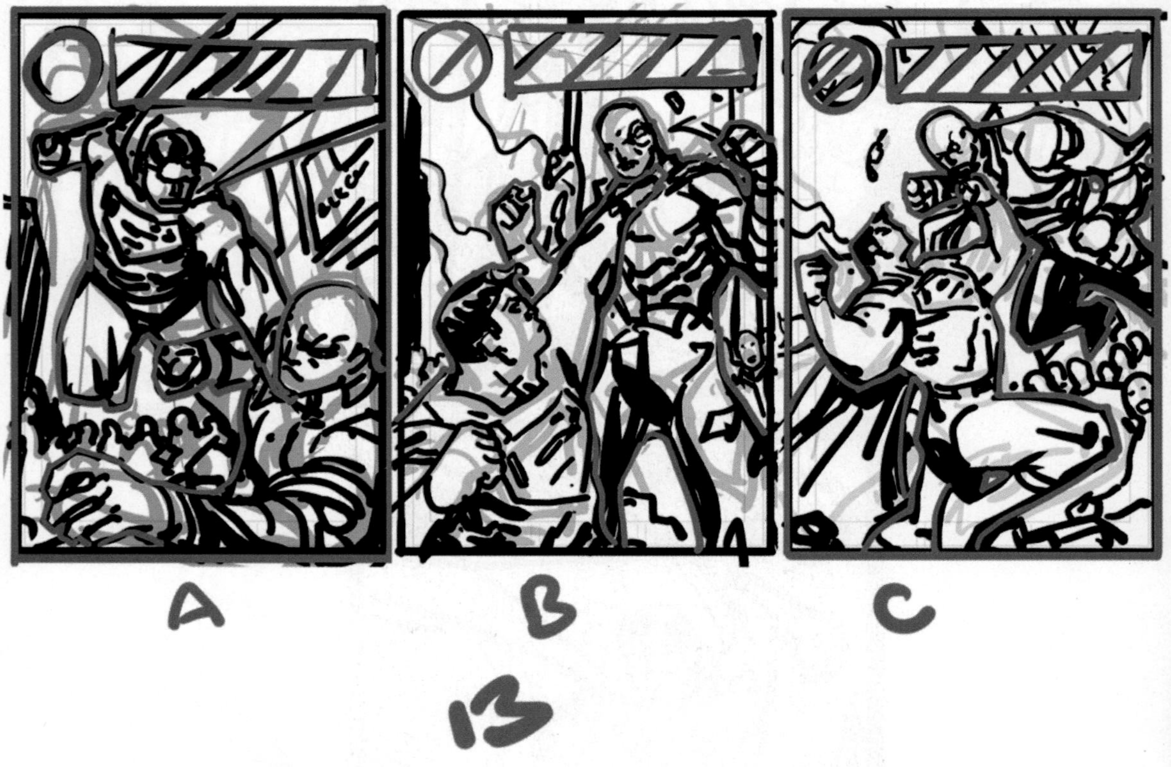
A
B
C
13

Issue #14
cover sketches
by IVAN REIS

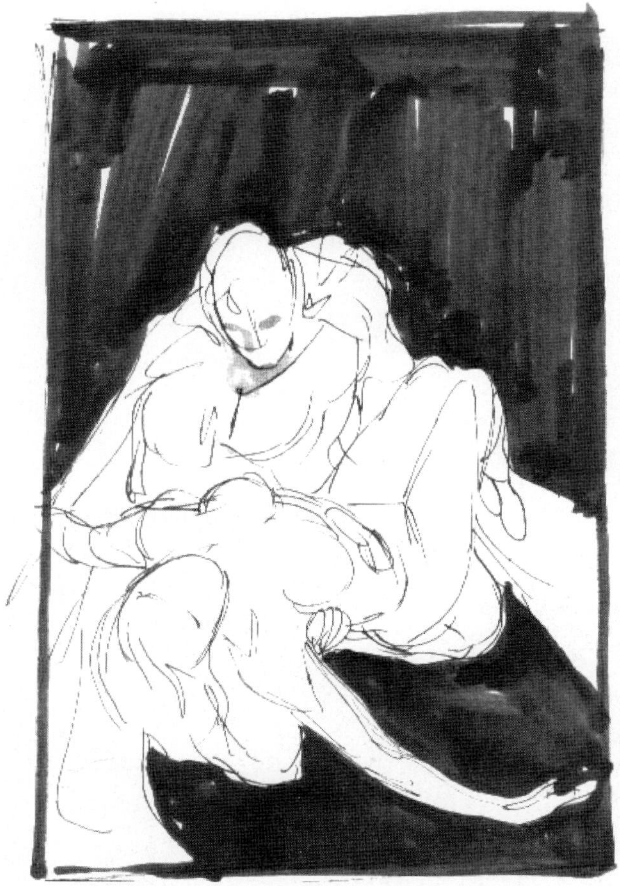

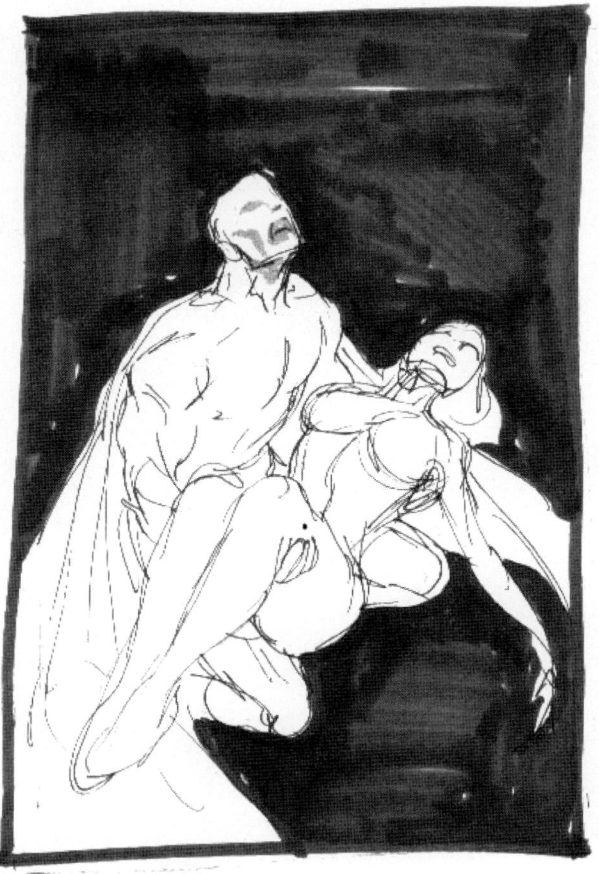

Issue #15
cover sketches by
MIKE S. MILLER

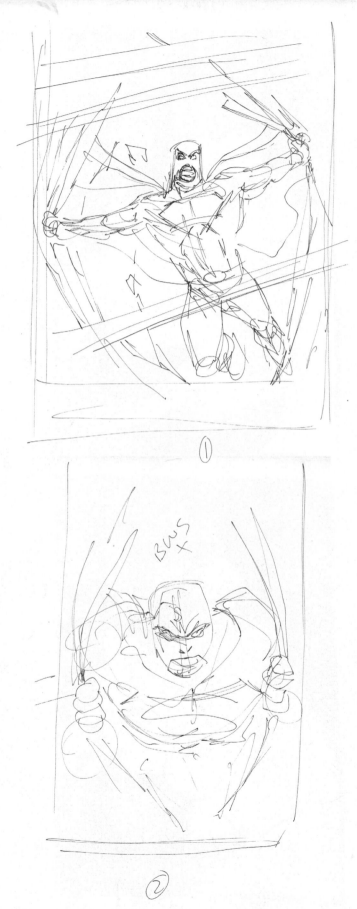

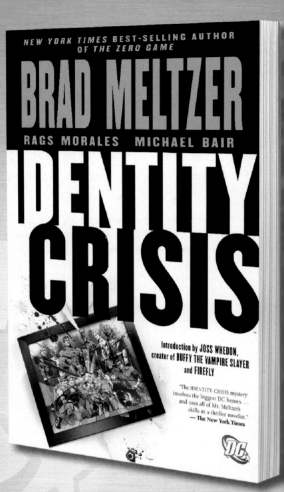

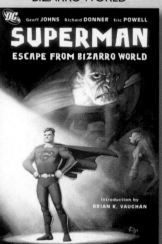

FROM THE WRITER OF
GREEN LANTERN *AND* INFINITE CRISIS

GEOFF JOHNS
IVAN REIS

BLACKEST NIGHT
"The talk of the comic book world." —USA WEEKEND
GEOFF JOHNS
IVAN REIS
OCLAIR ALBERT
JOE PRADO

BLACKEST NIGHT:
GREEN LANTERN

BLACKEST NIGHT
GEOFF JOHNS
DOUG MAHNKE
GREEN LANTERN

with
GEOFF JOHNS
DOUG MAHNKE

BLACKEST NIGHT:
GREEN LANTERN CORPS

BLACKEST NIGHT
PETER J. TOMASI
PATRICK GLEASON
GREEN LANTERN CORPS

with
PETER J. TOMASI
PATRICK GLEASON

READ THE COMPLETE EPIC IN THESE GRAPHIC NOVELS

BLACKEST NIGHT:
BLACK LANTERN CORPS
VOL. 1

BLACKEST NIGHT
BLACK LANTERN CORPS

with
JAMES ROBINSON,
J.T. KRUL, ARDIAN SYAF,
& EDDY BARROWS

BLACKEST NIGHT:
BLACK LANTERN CORPS
VOL. 2

BLACKEST NIGHT
BLACK LANTERN CORPS
VOLUME TWO

with
GEOFF JOHNS, JAMES ROBINSON,
GREG RUCKA, SCOTT KOLINS,
EDDY BARROWS & NICOLA SCOTT

BLACKEST NIGHT:
RISE OF THE
BLACK LANTERNS

BLACKEST NIGHT
RISE OF THE BLACK LANTERNS

with
GEOFF JOHNS, PETER TOMASI,
JAMES ROBINSON
& OTHERS

BLACKEST NIGHT:
TALES OF THE CORPS

BLACKEST NIGHT
TALES OF THE CORPS

with
GEOFF JOHNS,
PETER TOMASI
& OTHERS

SEARCH THE GRAPHIC NOVELS SECTION OF
DCCOMICS.COM
FOR ART AND INFORMATION ON ALL OF OUR BOOKS!

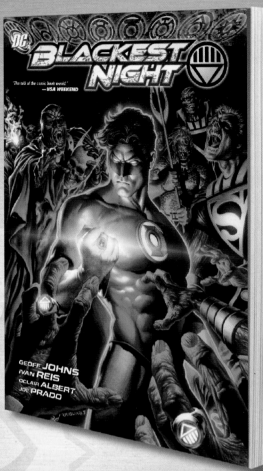